Semantics and Syntax in Lexical Functional Grammar

The Resource Logic Approach

edited by Mary Dalrymple

A Bradford Book

The MIT Press
Cambridge, Massachusetts
London, England

This book was set in Palatino by the editor and was printed and bound in the United States of America.

Library of Congress Cataloging-in-Publication Data

Semantics and syntax in lexical functional grammar: the resource logic approach / edited by Mary Dalrymple.
    p.   cm.—(Language, speech, and communication)
"A Bradford book."
Includes bibliographical references and indexes.
ISBN 0-262-04171-5 (hc: alk. paper)
    1. Lexical-functional grammar. 2. Semantics. 3. Grammar, Comparative and general—Syntax. I. Dalrymple, Mary. II. Series.
P158.25.S46   1999
415—dc21   98-40622
                                                                 CIP

Contents

Preface

The work presented here had its beginnings in 1990, in a series of discussions on semantic composition and representation involving John Lamping, Vijay Saraswat, and me. After a brief flurry of false starts, dead ends, and detours, the framework presented in this work emerged, and we have been pleased and gratified at the interest it has generated. This volume, sprung from a seed planted by Jim Blevins in an e-mail message more than a year ago, contains many of the results stemming from nearly a decade of research and collaboration involving, besides the contributors to this book, Joan Bresnan, Anette Frank, Kris Halvorsen, Angie Hinrichs, Ron Kaplan, Stefan Kaufmann, Jonas Kuhn, John Maxwell, Hadar Shemtov, and Annie Zaenen. Some of the papers here are reprints or reworkings of previously published work; others were written especially for this volume.

Many people were generous with their time and expertise in helping with reviews and comments on the papers collected here. Besides John Fry, Mark Johnson, Andy Kehler, Dick Oehrle, and Vijay Saraswat, who did double duty as reviewers as well as contributors to the volume, I thank David Beaver, Gosse Bouma, Wojciech Buszkowski, Bob Carpenter, Jan van Eijck, Jonathan Ginzburg, Ron Kaplan, Esther König, Chris Manning, Glyn Morrill, Reinhard Muskens, Johan van Benthem, and Jürgen Wedekind for their help. I am especially grateful to John Fry for reviewing and editorial assistance going far beyond the call of duty.

I have always felt incredibly lucky to have begun this work with John Lamping and Vijay Saraswat, and even luckier that our collaboration has endured over the years. No one could hope for better colleagues or more knowledgable, creative, and congenial research partners than John and Vijay. I have enjoyed our lengthy partnership more than I can say, and I look forward with anticipation to many more years of fruitful work together.

I am grateful to Ron Kaplan, Jeanette Figueroa, Kris Halvorsen, and the members of the Natural Language Theory and Technology group at Xerox Palo Alto Research Center for a warm, supportive, and endlessly stimulating and challenging work environment. I thank Amy Brand, Deborah Cantor-Adams, Yasuyo Iguchi, and the rest of the staff at MIT Press for greatly easing the stresses and clearing up the confusions of editing this book. And, finally and always, my gratitude and love to Ken and David Kahn for keeping the home fires burning.

Contributors

Richard Crouch is a lecturer in the Department of Computer Science at the University of Nottingham, UK. His current interests lie in under-specification and the syntax-semantics interface.

Mary Dalrymple is a researcher in the Natural Language Theory and Technology group at Xerox Palo Alto Research Center and a Consulting Associate Professor in the Department of Linguistics at Stanford University. Her recent work focuses on the syntax-semantics interface.

John Fry is a Ph.D. candidate in Linguistics at Stanford University. His work is mainly in the area of computational approaches to natural language semantics.

Vineet Gupta is a researcher in the Intelligent Systems Group at the NASA Ames Research Center. His primary interest is modeling and reasoning about physical systems, but he is also interested in the use of logic in natural language analysis.

Mark Johnson is an Associate Professor in the Department of Cognitive and Linguistic Sciences at Brown University. His research focuses on computational models of natural language understanding.

Andrew Kehler is currently a Senior Computer Scientist in the Artificial Intelligence Center at SRI International. His research in linguistics has centered on discourse processing, addressing problems in ellipsis, anaphora, and coherence resolution.

John Lamping is a researcher in the Embedded Computation group at Xerox Palo Alto Research Center. He has worked on various computer science problems with a common theme of designing formal systems that align well with a problem domain.

Dick Oehrle is currently Professor in the Department of Linguistics at the University of Arizona. His principal current interest is in the application of logical methods to linguistic analysis.

Fernando Pereira heads the Machine Learning and Information Retrieval Research department at AT&T Laboratories. His current research focuses on combining symbolic and probabilistic models in natural-language processing and speech recognition.

Vijay Saraswat is a researcher at AT&T Laboratories, and is developing the framework of *mass computing*, in support of network or online communities (groups of people from all over the world who spend time together online, talking, working, learning, playing, socializing, browsing, shopping...). The framework seeks to develop a "New Net" sharing with the current Web the fundamental idea of "equal opportunity authoring", but built around the notion of people, places, and persistent objects with interactive behavior, rather than around dead HTML documents.

Josef van Genabith is a lecturer in the Computer Applications department at Dublin City University. His recent work is mainly on the syntax-semantics interface and underspecification.

Semantics and Syntax in
Lexical Functional Grammar

1

Overview and Introduction

Mary Dalrymple, John Lamping, Fernando Pereira, and Vijay Saraswat

A natural language utterance is rich in structures of different kinds: sounds form recurring patterns and morphemes, words form phrases, grammatical functions emerge from morphological and phrasal structure, and patterns of phrases evoke a complex meaning. These structures are distinct but related; each structure contributes to and constrains the structure of other kinds of information. Linear precedence and phrasal organization are related both to the morphological structure of words and to the functional organization of sentences. And the functional structure of a sentence—relations like *subject-of, object-of, modifier-of,* and so on—is crucial to determining what the sentence means.

Isolating and defining these structures and the relations between them is a central task of linguistics. It is important for the representations of each kind of linguistic structure to be appropriate, so that our study of linguistic structure and organization is not impeded by a poor choice of representation that leads us astray.

Lexical Functional Grammar recognizes two different kinds of syntactic structures: the outer, visible hierarchical organization of words into phrases, and the inner, more abstract hierarchical organization of grammatical functions into complex functional structures. Languages vary greatly in the phrasal organization they allow, and in the order and means by which grammatical functions are realized. Word order

Portions of this chapter originally appeared in "Quantifiers, anaphora, and intensionality," by Mary Dalrymple, John Lamping, Fernando Pereira, and Vijay Saraswat, *Journal of Logic, Language, and Information* 6(3), pages 219–273, July 1997.

may be more or less constrained, or almost completely free. In contrast, the more abstract functional organization of languages varies comparatively little: languages with widely divergent phrasal organization nevertheless exhibit subject, object, and modifier properties that have been well-studied by traditional grammarians for centuries.

Various proposals have been made for representing these different kinds of syntactic structure. In the earliest work in generative grammar, Chomsky (1955) proposed to classify strings of words into phrases by the use of a phrase-structure tree. This successfully captures the intuition that sentences are hierarchically organized into phrases and that phrases are linearly ordered. This proposal has been almost universally followed.

However, it is not so clear that phrase structure trees are an appropriate representation for other kinds of linguistic information. In representing functional syntactic information, we find that a hierarchical organization is appropriate, but that the additional imposition of linear order does not make sense. Functional syntactic organization is very different from phrasal structure, and the intuitions and generalizations that work well in thinking about phrase structure break down when we try to use the same representations for this very different kind of information. Instead, with Kaplan and Bresnan (1982), we believe that an attribute-value structure, the *functional structure* or *f-structure* of Lexical Functional Grammar (LFG), is right for representing functional syntactic organization. F-structures provide a uniform representation of syntactic information that abstracts away from details of phrase structure and linear order that vary between languages.

As Halvorsen (1988) and Reyle (1988) note, however, the flatter, unordered functional structure of LFG does not fit well with traditional views of semantic compositionality, which are oriented to the ordered structure of phrasal syntactic organization. In considering how to characterize how meanings of natural language utterances are put together, then, we are led to a more flexible approach, which does not enforce a rigid order of compositionality. Approaches to semantic interpretation that encode semantic representations in attribute-value structures (Pollard and Sag 1987; Fenstad et al. 1987; Pollard and Sag 1994) offer such a relaxation of compositionality, but are unable to represent basic constraints on variable binding and scope (Pereira 1990).

The approach presented in this volume, in which linear logic is used to specify the relation between f-structures and their meanings, provides just what is required in a calculus of semantic composition for LFG. It can directly represent the constraints on the creation and use of semantic units in sentence interpretation, including those pertaining to variable binding and scope, without forcing a particular hierarchical order of composition beyond what is required by the properties of particular lexical entries. Of course, although the present research was motivated specifically by the semantic interpretation problem in LFG, its results would seem to be applicable to other grammatical frameworks that assume a representation of functional syntactic structure and in which functional syntactic relations like *subject-of* can be exploited for semantic interpretation.

This chapter provides an overview of LFG and linear logic, an introduction to the framework we assume, and a guide to the contents of this book.

1   The Linguistic Framework: Lexical Functional Grammar

1.1   Syntactic assumptions

LFG assumes two syntactic levels of representation. Constituent structure (*c-structure*) encodes phrasal dominance and precedence relations, and is represented as a phrase structure tree. Functional structure (*f-structure*) encodes syntactic predicate-argument structure, and is represented as an attribute-value matrix. The c-structure and f-structure for sentence (1) are given in (2):

(1)   Sam greeted Terry.

(2)   C-structure: F-structure:

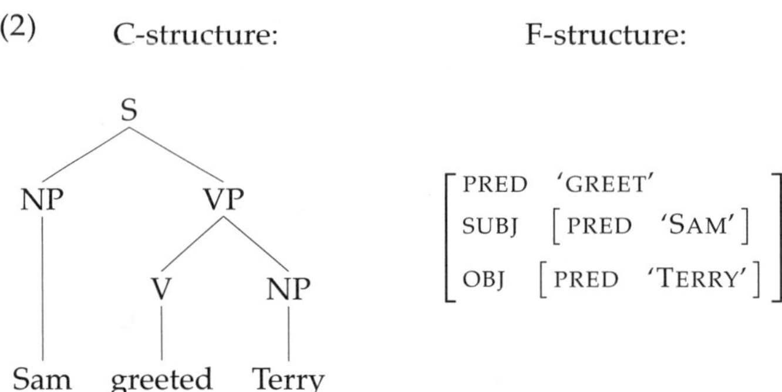

As illustrated, an f-structure consists of a collection of attributes, such as PRED, SUBJ, and OBJ, whose values can, in turn, be other f-structures.

The relationship between c-structure trees and the corresponding f-structures is given by a *functional projection* function ϕ from c-structure nodes to f-structures. More generally, LFG analyses involve several levels of linguistic representation called *projections*, related by means of *projection functions* (Kaplan 1987; Halvorsen and Kaplan 1988). For instance, phonological, morphological, or discourse structure might be represented by a phonological, morphological, or discourse projection, related to other projections by means of functional specifications.

The following annotated phrase-structure rule is used in the analysis of sentence (1):

(3) S $\longrightarrow$ NP   VP
                ($\uparrow$ SUBJ) = $\downarrow$ $\uparrow$ = $\downarrow$

The annotations on the rule indicate that the f-structure for the S (the metavariable $\uparrow$ in the annotation on the NP node) has a SUBJ attribute whose value is the f-structure for the NP daughter (the metavariable $\downarrow$ in the annotation on the NP node), and that the S node corresponds to an f-structure which is the same as the f-structure for the VP daughter. More generally, in each rule or lexical entry constraint, the $\uparrow$ metavariable refers to the ϕ-image of the mother c-structure node, and the $\downarrow$ metavariable refers to the ϕ-image of the node labeled by the constraint (Kaplan and Bresnan 1982, page 183).

When the phrase-structure rule for S is used in the analysis of a particular sentence, the metavariables $\uparrow$ and $\downarrow$ are instantiated to particular f-structures placed in correspondence with nodes of the c-structure. We refer to actual f-structures by giving them names such as f, g, and h. The instantiated phrase structure rule is given in (4), together with the minimal c-structure and f-structure that this rule describes; other annotated phrase structure rules or lexical entries may also contribute additional information about the f-structure, so that when the sentence as a whole is considered, a more complicated f-structure is described. The ϕ correspondence between c-structure nodes and f-structures is indicated by arrows leading from nodes in the c-structure tree to f-structures:

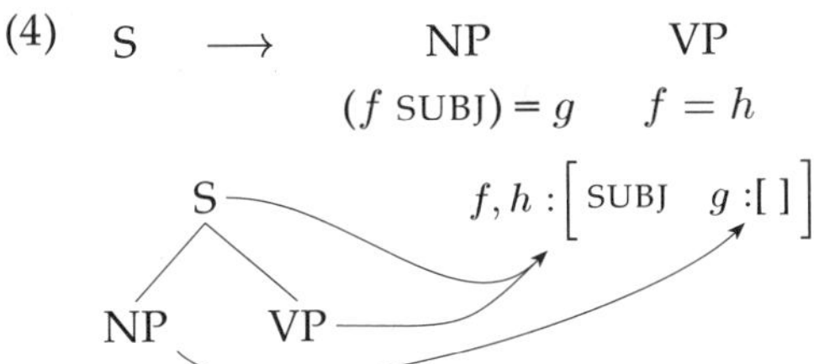

(4) S $\longrightarrow$ NP   VP

                (f SUBJ) $= g$ $f = h$

This diagram should be understood as follows: there are three c-structure nodes, S, NP, and VP, where S is the mother of NP and VP. The ϕ correspondence maps S and VP to the f-structure $\begin{bmatrix} \text{SUBJ} & [\,] \end{bmatrix}$ and NP to the f-structure [ ]. f and h name the f-structure $\begin{bmatrix} \text{SUBJ} & [\,] \end{bmatrix}$, and g names [ ].

Lexical entries also use the metavariables $\uparrow$ and $\downarrow$ to encode information about the f-structures of the preterminal nodes that immediately dominate them. A partial lexical entry for the word *Sam* is:

(5) Sam   NP ($\uparrow$ PRED) $=$ 'SAM'

The constraint ($\uparrow$ PRED) $=$ 'SAM' states that the preterminal node immediately dominating the terminal symbol *Sam* has an f-structure whose value for the attribute PRED is 'SAM'. Since our concern here is semantic assembly and not detailed syntactic analysis, we provide only the most minimal f-structural representations, leaving aside all details of syntactic specification; in this example, for instance, person, number, and other syntactic features of *Sam* have been omitted.

For a particular instance of use of the word *Sam*, the following c-structure and f-structure configuration results:

(6) $(g \text{ PRED}) = \text{'SAM'}$

$$\text{NP} \qquad g : \begin{bmatrix} \text{PRED} & \text{'SAM'} \end{bmatrix}$$
$$\text{Sam}$$

Note that the metavariable ↑ in the lexical entry of *Sam* ranging over f-structures for the nonterminal node dominating *Sam* has been instantiated to the particular f-structure g for its use in this case.

Other lexical entries similarly specify features of the f-structure of the immediately dominating preterminal node. The following is a list of the phrase structure rules and lexical entries used in the analysis of example (1):[1]

(7) S ⟶ NP   VP
         (↑ SUBJ) = ↓   ↑ = ↓

    VP ⟶ V   NP
          ↑ = ↓   (↑ OBJ) = ↓

(8) Sam   NP (↑ PRED) = 'SAM'

    greeted V   (↑ PRED) = 'GREET'

    Terry   NP (↑ PRED) = 'TERRY'

Given these rules and lexical items, we produce the following constituent structure tree, annotated with as yet uninstantiated constraints on the f-structures that correspond to each node:

---

[1] Those familiar with other analyses within the LFG framework will notice that we have not included a list of grammatical functions subcategorized for by the verb *greet*; this is because we assume a different treatment of the LFG requirements of completeness and coherence. We return to this point in Section 2.2 below.

(9)

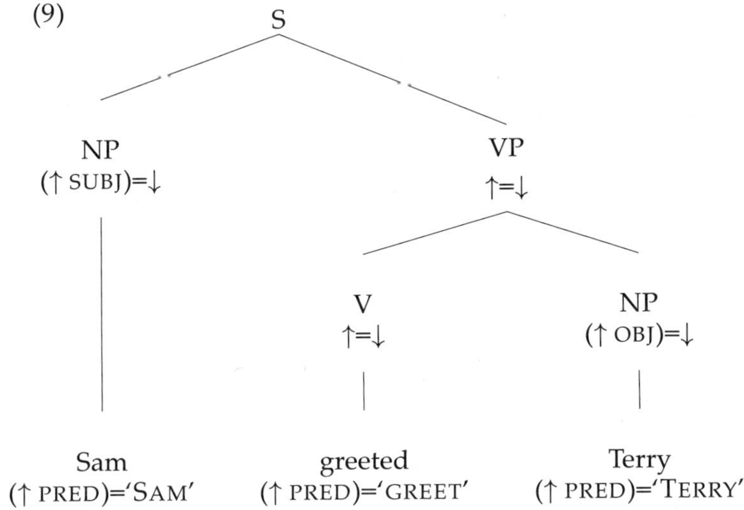

The metavariables ↑ and ↓ in each rule or lexical entry refer to particular f-structures which stand in the ϕ correspondence to the relevant nodes of the c-structure tree. We replace the metavariables by the names of the actual f-structures that are relevant in this instance:

(10)

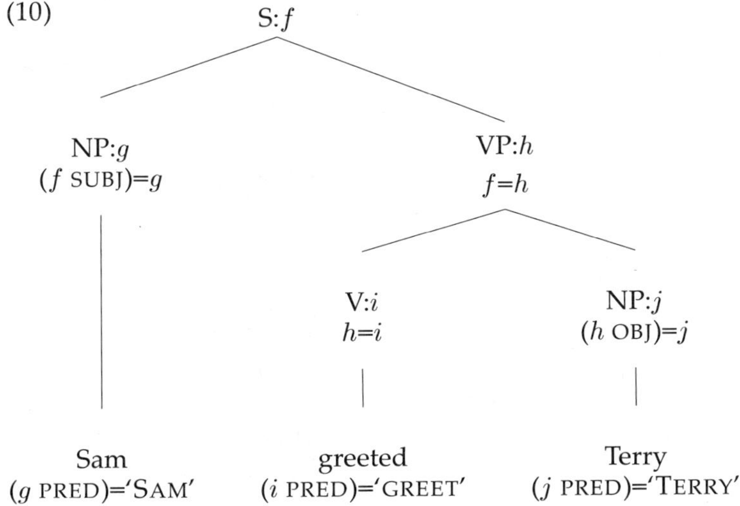

These instantiated constraints require the c-structure for this sentence to be related to the following f-structure:

(11)

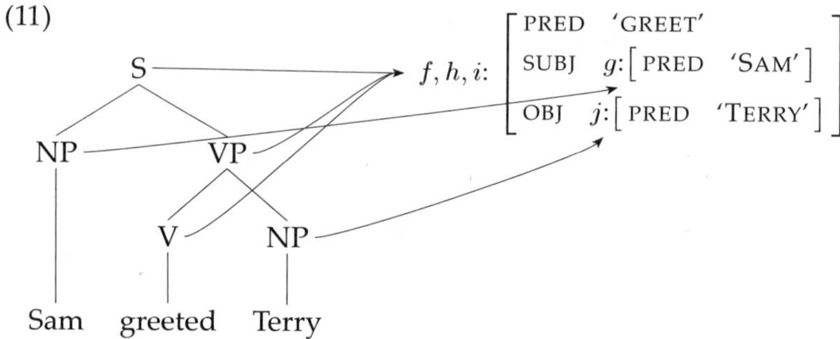

For a more complete explication of the syntactic assumptions of LFG, see Bresnan (1982), Levin et al. (1983), Dalrymple, Kaplan, Maxwell, and Zaenen (1995), and the references cited there.

1.2   Rules for semantic assembly

A distinguishing feature of our work (and of other work within the LFG framework) is that semantic composition does not take phrasal dominance and precedence relations as the main input. Instead, we follow other work in LFG (Kaplan and Bresnan 1982; Halvorsen 1983; Fenstad et al. 1987; Halvorsen and Kaplan 1988, and many others) in assuming that the functional syntactic information encoded by f-structures plays the largest role in determining semantic composition. That is, we hold that meaning composition is mainly determined by syntactic relations such as *subject-of, object-of, modifier-of,* and so on. Those relations are realized by different c-structure forms in different languages, but are represented directly and uniformly in the f-structure.

There are, of course, cases in which information not represented at f-structure, such as intonation or linear order, contributes to and constrains semantic interpretation. We do not require all of the information relevant to semantic composition to be stated in functional syntactic terms; other structures and other kinds of information may also be relevant in guiding the assembly of meanings. In the following and elsewhere in this book, however, we rely on f-structure as the principal determinant of meaning composition.

Our goal is to enable deductions of the following general form, given a syntactic analysis of a sentence such as *Sam greeted Terry*:

$$
\begin{array}{ll}
(f \text{ SUBJ})_\sigma \rightsquigarrow Sam & \text{(The subject means } Sam.) \\
(f \text{ OBJ})_\sigma \rightsquigarrow Terry & \text{(The object means } Terry.) \\
\forall X, Y. \ (f \text{ SUBJ})_\sigma \rightsquigarrow X & \text{(If the subject means } X \\
\quad \otimes (f \text{ OBJ})_\sigma \rightsquigarrow Y & \qquad \text{and the object means } Y, \\
\underline{\quad \multimap f_\sigma \rightsquigarrow greet(X, Y)} & \qquad \text{then the sentence means } greet(X, Y).)
\end{array}
$$

$$
f_\sigma \rightsquigarrow greet(Sam, Terry) \qquad \text{(The sentence means } greet(Sam, Terry).)
$$

In the remainder of this section, we explain the reasoning used in such deductions and the source of their premises.

In LFG, functional syntactic predicate-argument structure is projected from lexical entries. Therefore, its effect on semantic composition is for the most part determined by lexical entries, not by phrase-structure rules. In particular, the two phrase-structure rules given above for S and VP need not encode semantic information, but only specify how grammatical functions such as SUBJ are expressed in English.

Of course, there is no requirement that meanings must be contributed only by lexical entries and not by particular syntactic constructions. In some cases, a syntactic construction may make a direct semantic contribution, as when properties of the construction as a whole and not just of its lexical elements are responsible for the interpretation of the construction. Such cases include, for instance, relative clauses with no complementizer, such as *the man Sam met*, where none of the lexical items in the construction is responsible for the interpretation of *Sam met* as a relative clause modifier of *man*. In this work, we will not provide specific discussion of construction-specific interpretation rules. However, their inclusion in the theory is straightforward; just as phrase structure rules are annotated with constraints on the f-structures they correspond to, they can also be annotated with information about the semantic contributions they make.

How can we express the meanings contributed by lexical entries and meaningful syntactic constructions, and how can we constrain how they are combined? We propose to use a scaffolding of *semantic struc-*

tures corresponding to functional structures, together with a set of instructions on how to put meanings together based on their functional relations. Semantic structures provide anchors for the meaning contributions involved in the meaning assembly process. Meaning assembly uses a set of instructions expressed in a particular logical language—the 'glue language'—for combining meaning contributions associated with semantic projections in particular ways. In the same way as the functional projection function ϕ associates f-structures to c-structures as described above, we use a *semantic or σ projection function σ* to associate f-structures to semantic or σ structures.

For the purposes of this book, it is not necessary to specify the exact nature of semantic structures. We require only that, like f-structures, semantic structures may have several attributes associated with them. A semantic structure attribute takes as its value a semantic structure. Semantic structures may contain other, undetermined information: for instance, information about selectional restrictions. In this volume, when semantic structures are presented, some of that information may be elided. Therefore the reader should not infer that two semantic structures which are depicted with identical attributes and values are identical.

In referring to semantic structures, the expression $\uparrow_\sigma$ represents the semantic structure that results from applying the projection function σ to the f-structure denoted by $\uparrow$. We refer to this structure as the *semantic or σ-projection* of $\uparrow$ (when we wish to emphasize its relation to the f-structure $\uparrow$) or equivalently as the semantic or σ-structure $\uparrow_\sigma$. For particular f-structures, we use the name g_σ to refer to the semantic projection of the f-structure g:

(12)

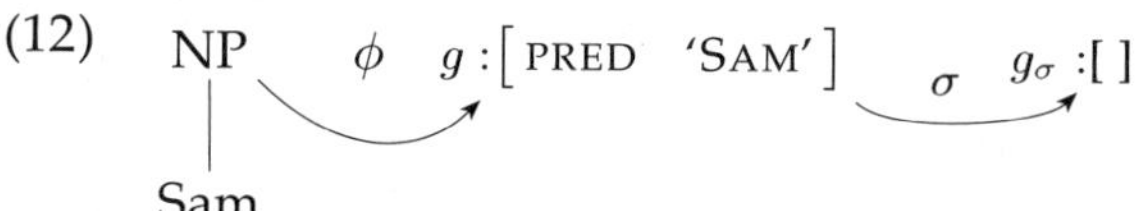

Above, we use the notation $g_\sigma : [\,]$ to indicate a semantic structure, the interpretation of the term g_σ, which has no depicted attributes.

1.3 Association between semantic structures and meanings

The most important property of semantic structures is that they may be put in correspondence with meanings. In the following, we make the simplifying assumption that a name like *Sam* refers directly to the individual named Sam, and so our aim is to associate the semantic structure of the word *Sam* with the constant meaning *Sam*.

The lexical entry for *Sam* given in (13) extends (8) with a constraint on semantic structure:

(13)   Sam   NP $(\uparrow \mathrm{PRED}) = \text{'SAM'}$
$\uparrow_\sigma \rightsquigarrow Sam$

The additional constraint

$$\uparrow_\sigma \rightsquigarrow Sam$$

is what we call the *meaning constructor* of the entry. As above, for a particular use of *Sam*, the metavariable $\uparrow$ is replaced by a particular f-structure g, with semantic projection g_σ:

(14) $(g\ \mathrm{PRED}) = \text{'SAM'}$

$g_\sigma \rightsquigarrow Sam$

$$\text{NP} \qquad g : \big[\, \mathrm{PRED} \quad \text{'SAM'} \,\big] \qquad g_\sigma : [\,] \rightsquigarrow Sam$$
$$|$$
$$\text{Sam}$$

More generally, the association between a semantic structure g_σ and a meaning P is represented by the atomic formula $g_\sigma \rightsquigarrow P$, where $\rightsquigarrow$ is an otherwise uninterpreted binary predicate symbol. In fact, we use not one but a family of relations $\rightsquigarrow_\tau$ indexed by the semantic type of the intended second argument, although for simplicity we omit the type subscript whenever it is determinable from context.

We can now explain the meaning constructor in (13). If a particular occurrence of *Sam* in a sentence is associated with f-structure g, the syntactic constraint in the lexical entry for *Sam* is instantiated as:

$$(g\ \mathrm{PRED}) = \text{'SAM'}$$

and the semantic constraint is instantiated as:

$$g_\sigma \rightsquigarrow Sam$$

representing the association between g_σ and the constant *Sam* representing its meaning.[2] We will sometimes say informally that g means P, or P is g's meaning, without referring to the role of the semantic structure g_σ in $g_\sigma \rightsquigarrow P$.

In general, however, f-structures and their semantic projections must be distinguished, because there is not always a one-to-one correspondence between f-structures and semantic structures. In some cases, the semantic structure may have more internal structure relevant to semantic composition than the f-structure it corresponds to. For example, in Dalrymple, Lamping, Pereira, and Saraswat's analysis of quantification, presented in Chapter 2, the semantic structure for a quantified noun phrase has subsidiary semantic structures representing the restriction of the quantifier and the variable bound in the restriction.

1.4   Logical representation of semantic composition

We now turn to an examination of the lexical entry for a transitive verb like *greeted*. In this case, the meaning constructor is more complex, as it relates the meanings of the subject and object of a clause to the clause's meaning:

(15)   greeted   V $(\uparrow \text{PRED}) = \text{'GREET'}$
$$\forall X, Y. (\uparrow \text{SUBJ})_\sigma \rightsquigarrow X \otimes (\uparrow \text{OBJ})_\sigma \rightsquigarrow Y$$
$$\multimap \uparrow_\sigma \rightsquigarrow greet(X, Y)$$

The meaning constructor is the linear-logic formula:

$$\forall X, Y. (\uparrow \text{SUBJ})_\sigma \rightsquigarrow X \otimes (\uparrow \text{OBJ})_\sigma \rightsquigarrow Y \multimap \uparrow_\sigma \rightsquigarrow greet(X, Y)$$

in which the linear-logic connectives of multiplicative conjunction $\otimes$ and linear implication $\multimap$ are used to specify how the meaning of a

---

[2]In Chapter 5, Kehler, Dalrymple, Lamping, and Saraswat propose a slightly different approach, in which the 'means' operator $\rightsquigarrow$ relates *occurrences* of f-structures to meanings, rather than relating f-structures to meanings. For most of the papers in this book, this distinction is not relevant, since the only cases that are considered are ones in which each f-structure occurs exactly once.

clause headed by the verb is composed from the meanings of the arguments of the verb. The fragment of linear logic that we use arises from transferring to linear logic the ideas underlying the concurrent constraint programming scheme of Saraswat (1989). We describe this fragment incrementally as we discuss examples, and more fully in Section 2 of this chapter. For the moment, we can think of the linear connectives $\otimes$ and $\multimap$ as playing the same role as the analogous classical connectives conjunction $\wedge$ and implication $\rightarrow$, but we will soon see that the specific properties of the linear connectives are essential to guarantee that lexical entries bring into the interpretation process all and only the information provided by the corresponding words.

The meaning constructor for *greeted* asserts that if the subject (SUBJ) of a clause with main verb *greeted* means X and its object (OBJ) means Y, then the whole clause means $greet(X, Y)$.[3] Most of our meaning constructors have this implicational form, with universally-quantified variables like X and Y standing for the meaning fragments that will be assembled by the constructor, the antecedent of the implication specifying the values for those variables and the consequent of the implication specifying the output of the constructor.

A particular use of *greeted* produces the following c-structure, f-structure, semantic structure, and meaning constructor:

(16)

$$V \qquad f : \begin{bmatrix} \text{PRED} & \text{'GREET'} \\ \text{SUBJ} & [\,] \\ \text{OBJ} & [\,] \end{bmatrix} \qquad f_\sigma : [\,]$$

greeted

$$\forall X, Y.\ (f\ \text{SUBJ})_\sigma \rightsquigarrow X \otimes (f\ \text{OBJ})_\sigma \rightsquigarrow Y \multimap f_\sigma \rightsquigarrow greet(X, Y)$$

---

[3] In fact, we believe that the correct treatment of the relation between a verb and its arguments requires the use of *mapping principles* specifying the relation between the array of semantic arguments required by a verb and their possible syntactic realizations (Bresnan and Kanerva 1989; Alsina 1993; Butt 1996). A verb like *greeted*, for example, might specify that one of its arguments is an agent and the other is a theme. Mapping principles then specify that agents can be realized as subjects and themes as objects. Here and elsewhere in this volume we make the simplifying assumption (valid for English) that the arguments of verbs have already been linked to syntactic functions and that this linking is represented in the lexicon. See Butt et al. (1997) for a proposal to incorporate a theory of linking between thematic roles and grammatical functions into the overall approach pursued in this volume.

The instantiated meaning constructor asserts that

- if f's subject (f SUBJ) has meaning X

- and ($\otimes$) f's object (f OBJ) has meaning Y

- then ($\multimap$) f has meaning $greet(X, Y)$.

It is not an accident that the form of the meaning constructor for *greeted* is analogous to the type $(e \times e) \rightarrow t$ which, in its curried form $e \rightarrow e \rightarrow t$, is the standard type for a transitive verb in a compositional semantics setting (Gamut 1991). In general, the propositional structure of the meaning constructors of lexical entries parallels the types assigned to the meanings of the same words in compositional analyses. This is further discussed by Dalrymple, Gupta, Lamping, and Saraswat in Chapter 7. A crucial difference, suggested by the difference between $(e \times e) \rightarrow t$ and $e \rightarrow e \rightarrow t$, is that our formulation does not rely on argument order to identify the different inputs of a meaning constructor, allowing for a more flexible connection between syntactic structure and semantic interpretation.

As mentioned above, in most cases, phrase-structure rules make no semantic contributions of their own. Thus, all the semantic information for a sentence like *Sam greeted Terry* is provided by the lexical entries for *Sam*, *greeted*, and *Terry*:

(17) Sam   NP   ($\uparrow$ PRED) = 'SAM'
$\uparrow_\sigma \rightsquigarrow Sam$

greeted   V   ($\uparrow$ PRED) = 'GREET'
$\forall X, Y. (\uparrow \text{SUBJ})_\sigma \rightsquigarrow X \otimes (\uparrow \text{OBJ})_\sigma \rightsquigarrow Y$
$\multimap \uparrow_\sigma \rightsquigarrow greet(X, Y)$

Terry   NP   ($\uparrow$ PRED) = 'TERRY'
$\uparrow_\sigma \rightsquigarrow Terry$

In summary, the semantic contribution of each lexical entry is a linear-logic formula, its meaning constructor, that specifies the 'assembly instructions' for combining the meaning contributions of the syntactic arguments of the lexical entry to obtain the meaning contribution of the whole entry. Thus, linear logic serves as a *glue language* to specify how to assemble or glue together the meaning contributions of the parts of a syntactic structure to produce the meaning contribution of the whole structure.

2   Linear Logic as Linguistic "Glue"

We use logical deduction to assign meanings to sentences, starting from information about their functional structure and about the semantic contributions of their lexical items. Traditional compositional approaches use function application to assemble meanings, relying on the ordering in a binary-branching phrase-structure tree to specify how to apply functors to arguments. In contrast, our logic-based approach allows the premises carrying semantic information to commute while keeping their connection to the functional structure, and is thus more compatible with the flat and relatively free-form organization of functional structure.

An important motivation for using *linear* logic is that it allows us to directly capture the generalization that lexical items and phrases each contribute exactly once to the meaning of a sentence. As noted by Klein and Sag (1985, page 172):

> Translation rules in Montague semantics have the property that the translation of each component of a complex expression occurs exactly once in the translation of the whole.... That is to say, we do not want the set S [of semantic representations of a phrase] to contain *all* meaningful expressions of IL which can be built up from the elements of S, but only those which use each element exactly once.

In our terms, the semantic contributions of the constituents of a sentence are not context-independent assertions that may be used or not in the derivation of the meaning of the sentence depending on the course of the derivation. Instead, the semantic contributions are *occurrences* of information which are generated and used exactly once. For example, the formula $g_\sigma \rightsquigarrow Sam$ provides one occurrence of the meaning *Sam* associated with the semantic projection g_σ. That meaning must be consumed exactly once in the derivation of a meaning for the entire utterance.

It is this 'resource-sensitivity' of natural language semantics—an expression is used exactly once in a semantic derivation—that linear logic can model. The basic insight underlying linear logic is that logical formulas are *resources* that are produced and consumed in the deduction process. This gives rise to a resource-sensitive notion of implication, the *linear implication* '$\multimap$': the formula $A \multimap B$ can be thought of as an action that can *consume* (one copy of) A to produce (one copy of) B. Thus, the formula $A \otimes (A \multimap B)$ linearly entails B. It does not entail $A \otimes B$ (because the deduction consumes A), and it does not entail $(A \multimap B) \otimes B$ (because the linear implication is also consumed in doing the deduction).

This resource-sensitivity not only disallows arbitrary duplication of formulas, but also disallows arbitrary deletion of formulas. Thus the linear multiplicative conjunction $\otimes$ is sensitive to the multiplicity of formulas: $A \otimes A$ is not equivalent to A (the former has two copies of the formula A). For example, the formula $A \otimes A \otimes (A \multimap B)$ linearly entails $A \otimes B$ (there is still one A left over) but does not entail B (there must still be one A present). In this way, linear logic checks that a formula is used once and only once in a deduction, enforcing the requirement that each component of an utterance contributes exactly once to the assembly of the utterance's meaning.

2.1   Deductive assembly of meanings

As we have seen, lexical entries supply their contributions to meaning in the form of linear-logic formulas, the meaning constructors. We will now show how sentence meanings are derived from those constructors by linear-logic deduction. The full set of proof rules for the linear-logic fragment we use is given in Figure 1.5, page 27. For readability, however, we often present derivations informally.

As a first example, consider the lexical entries in (17) and the f-structures f, g and h in:

$$(18) \quad f: \begin{bmatrix} \text{PRED} & \text{'GREET'} \\ \text{SUBJ} & g: \begin{bmatrix} \text{PRED} & \text{'SAM'} \end{bmatrix} \\ \text{OBJ} & h: \begin{bmatrix} \text{PRED} & \text{'TERRY'} \end{bmatrix} \end{bmatrix}$$

Instantiating the lexical entries for *Sam*, *Terry*, and *greeted* appropriately, we obtain the following meaning constructors, abbreviated as **sam**, **terry**, and **greet**:

$$\begin{aligned} \textbf{sam:} & \quad g_\sigma \rightsquigarrow Sam \\ \textbf{terry:} & \quad h_\sigma \rightsquigarrow Terry \\ \textbf{greet:} & \quad \forall X, Y.\, g_\sigma \rightsquigarrow X \otimes h_\sigma \rightsquigarrow Y \multimap f_\sigma \rightsquigarrow greet(X, Y) \end{aligned}$$

These formulas show how the generic semantic contributions in the lexical entries are instantiated to reflect their participation in this particular f-structure. Since the entry *Sam* gives rise to f-structure g, the meaning constructor for *Sam* provides a meaning for g_σ. Similarly, the meaning constructor for *Terry* provides a meaning for h_σ. In the case of the verb *greeted*, the meaning constructor is a glue language formula consisting of instructions on how to assemble the meaning of a sentence with main verb *greeted*. The verb *greeted* requires two pieces of information, the meanings of its subject and object, in no particular order, to produce a meaning for the clause. As instantiated, the f-structures corresponding to the subject and object of the verb are g and h, respectively, and f is the f-structure for the entire clause. Thus, the instantiated entry for *greeted* shows how to combine meanings for g (its subject) and h (its object) to generate a meaning for f (the entire clause).

From these premises, a meaning for the sentence can be derived:

$$(19) \quad f_\sigma \rightsquigarrow greet(Sam, Terry)$$

There are several ways in which the proof can be presented, which we show in Figures 1.1–1.3 for completeness. In all of the proof presentations, $\vdash$ stands for the linear-logic derivability relation. While we show complete, formal proofs here, less formal and more readable proofs are used wherever possible in the rest of the volume.

Figure 1.1 presents a full sequent-style proof of the conclusion in (19) from the premises **sam**, **terry**, and **greet**. This proof does not make use of the *Cut rule*, a rule which allows a proof to make use of intermediate lemmas not present in the premises or the conclusion; see Figure 1.5, page 27, for a statement of Cut. The fragment of linear logic that we use as our glue language, like linear logic more generally, has the property that whenever some conclusion is provable from a set of premises by the use of Cut, it is also provable without using Cut (Cut elimination: Prawitz 1965; Girard 1989; Troelstra 1992). In the derivation of the meaning of *Sam greeted Terry*, the proof that does not use Cut is actually considerably simpler than the proof with Cut.

Proofs can also be shown as *proof nets*, a graphical format that makes explicit how the antecedents of implications are satisfied without specifying a particular order in which the proof steps are taken. Thus, a proof net represents a family of proofs that are the same except for the order of steps. A proof net for the derivation of the meaning of *Sam greeted Terry* is provided in Figure 1.2. In Chapter 3, Fry provides more discussion of proof nets in meaning assembly.

It is also possible to present an alternative proof from these premises which makes use of the Cut rule; such a proof is displayed in Figure 1.3. For easier reading, we define the auxiliary formula **sam-greet** as follows:

$$\textbf{sam-greet:}\quad \forall Y.\ h_\sigma \rightsquigarrow Y \multimap f_\sigma \rightsquigarrow greet(Sam, Y)$$

In fact, we can summarize the proof in Figure 1.3 as the following three steps:

$$
\begin{array}{clll}
(20) & \textbf{sam} \otimes \textbf{terry} \otimes \textbf{greet} & \text{(Premises)} \\
\vdash & \textbf{sam-greet} \otimes \textbf{terry} & X \mapsto Sam \\
\vdash & f_\sigma \rightsquigarrow greet(Sam, Terry) & Y \mapsto Terry
\end{array}
$$

Each step in the deduction is annotated with the variable substitutions (universal instantiations) required to derive it from the preceding one: $A \mapsto M$ indicates that the variable A is instantiated to M. In the following and elsewhere in this volume, we often present proofs in this convenient form, since this shorter form illustrates the derivation succinctly and transparently.

$$\dfrac{\dfrac{g_\sigma \leadsto Sam \vdash g_\sigma \leadsto Sam \qquad h_\sigma \leadsto Terry \vdash h_\sigma \leadsto Terry}{g_\sigma \leadsto Sam, h_\sigma \leadsto Terry \vdash g_\sigma \leadsto Sam \otimes h_\sigma \leadsto Terry \qquad f_\sigma \leadsto greet(Sam, Terry) \vdash f_\sigma \leadsto greet(Sam, Terry)}}{\dfrac{g_\sigma \leadsto Sam, h_\sigma \leadsto Terry, g_\sigma \leadsto Sam \otimes h_\sigma \leadsto Terry \multimap f_\sigma \leadsto greet(Sam, Terry) \vdash f_\sigma \leadsto greet(Sam, Terry)}{\dfrac{g_\sigma \leadsto Sam, h_\sigma \leadsto Terry, \forall Y.\, g_\sigma \leadsto Sam \otimes h_\sigma \leadsto Y \multimap f_\sigma \leadsto greet(Sam, Y) \vdash f_\sigma \leadsto greet(Sam, Terry)}{g_\sigma \leadsto Sam, h_\sigma \leadsto Terry, \forall X, Y.\, g_\sigma \leadsto X \otimes h_\sigma \leadsto Y \multimap f_\sigma \leadsto greet(X, Y) \vdash f_\sigma \leadsto greet(Sam, Terry)}}}$$

Figure 1.1: Sequent proof of *Sam greeted Terry.*

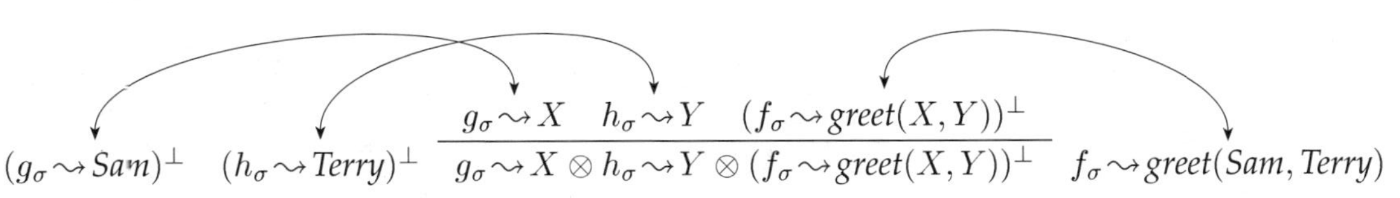

Figure 1.2: Proof net for *Sam greeted Terry.*

$$\dfrac{\dfrac{\dfrac{\dfrac{\dfrac{\dfrac{h_\sigma \leadsto U \vdash h_\sigma \leadsto U \qquad \mathbf{sam} \vdash g_\sigma \leadsto Sam}{h_\sigma \leadsto U, \mathbf{sam} \vdash g_\sigma \leadsto Sam \otimes h_\sigma \leadsto U} \qquad f_\sigma \leadsto greet(Sam, U) \vdash f_\sigma \leadsto greet(Sam, U)}{h_\sigma \leadsto U, \mathbf{sam}, g_\sigma \leadsto Sam \otimes h_\sigma \leadsto U \multimap f_\sigma \leadsto greet(Sam, U) \vdash f_\sigma \leadsto greet(Sam, U)}}{\mathbf{sam}, g_\sigma \leadsto Sam \otimes h_\sigma \leadsto U \multimap f_\sigma \leadsto greet(Sam, U) \vdash h_\sigma \leadsto U \multimap f_\sigma \leadsto greet(Sam, U)}}{\mathbf{sam}, \forall Y.\, g_\sigma \leadsto Sam \otimes h_\sigma \leadsto Y \multimap f_\sigma \leadsto greet(Sam, Y) \vdash h_\sigma \leadsto U \multimap f_\sigma \leadsto greet(Sam, U)}}{\mathbf{sam}, \forall Y.\, g_\sigma \leadsto Sam \otimes h_\sigma \leadsto Y \multimap f_\sigma \leadsto greet(Sam, Y) \vdash \forall Y.\, h_\sigma \leadsto Y \multimap f_\sigma \leadsto greet(Sam, Y)}}{\mathbf{sam}, \mathbf{greet} \vdash \mathbf{sam\text{-}greet}}$$

$$\dfrac{\mathbf{sam}, \mathbf{greet} \vdash \mathbf{sam\text{-}greet} \qquad \dfrac{\dfrac{\mathbf{terry} \vdash h_\sigma \leadsto Terry \quad f_\sigma \leadsto greet(Sam, Terry) \vdash f_\sigma \leadsto greet(Sam, Terry)}{\mathbf{terry}, h_\sigma \leadsto Terry \multimap f_\sigma \leadsto greet(Sam, Terry) \vdash f_\sigma \leadsto greet(Sam, Terry)}}{\mathbf{sam\text{-}greet}, \mathbf{terry} \vdash f_\sigma \leadsto greet(Sam, Terry)}}{\mathbf{sam}, \mathbf{terry}, \mathbf{greet} \vdash f_\sigma \leadsto greet(Sam, Terry)}$$

Figure 1.3: Proof of *Sam greeted Terry* using the Cut rule.

Besides the proof summarized in (20), an alternate proof leading to the same conclusion and using the Cut rule is also possible, which we show here in our summarized format. If we define the formula **greeted-terry** as:

$$\textbf{greeted-terry}: \quad \forall X.\ g_\sigma \rightsquigarrow X \multimap f_\sigma \rightsquigarrow greet(X, Terry)$$

Then the alternative derivation using Cut is:

$$
\begin{array}{lll}
(21) & \textbf{sam} \otimes \textbf{terry} \otimes \textbf{greet} & \text{(Premises)} \\
\vdash & \textbf{sam} \otimes \textbf{greeted-terry} & Y \mapsto Terry \\
\vdash & f_\sigma \rightsquigarrow greet(Sam, Terry) & X \mapsto Sam
\end{array}
$$

While the order of composition is different in this derivation, the result is the same. That is because the use of propositions to satisfy antecedents of implications is the same as in the previous derivation. The two simplified derivations have the same proof net, shown in Figure 1.2.

In summary, the deduction of the meaning of a sentence begins with a set of meaning constructors relating the semantic projections of specific f-structures in the LFG analysis to representations of their meanings. From these glue language formulas, the interpretation process attempts to deduce an atomic formula relating the semantic projection of the whole sentence to a representation of the sentence's meaning. Alternative derivations with different basic structure may yield different such conclusions, corresponding to ambiguities of semantic interpretation.

2.2   The syntax-semantics interface

Earlier LFG proposals assume that the locus of the relation between syntax and semantics is the value of the PRED attribute, termed a 'semantic form'. Kaplan and Bresnan (1982) assume PRED values for verbs of the following form:

$$
(22) \quad \text{'greet}< (\uparrow \text{SUBJ}), (\uparrow \text{OBJ}) >'
$$
$$
\phantom{(22)\quad \text{'greet}<}\ \text{agent} \quad \text{theme}
$$

According to Kaplan and Bresnan (1982), these semantic forms can be regarded as encoding four types of information:

1. Specification of the semantic relation

2. Mapping of grammatical functions to semantic roles

3. Subcategorization information (the *governed grammatical functions*, or arguments syntactically required by the predicate)

4. Instantiation to indicate semantic distinctness (predicate uniqueness)

Encoding these kinds of information by means of a single formal device permits the syntactically relevant aspects of meaning to be confined to a single place in the f-structure without making a commitment to a particular means by which meanings are represented or composed.

Kaplan (personal communication) observes that the effect of our approach is to flesh out and elaborate the treatment of these different kinds of information. The semantic relation is specified by the meaning constructors: a verb like 'greet', for example, specifies that its meaning is $greet(X, Y)$ when given arguments X and Y. The mapping of grammatical functions to semantic roles, involving the specification of syntactic subcategorization information for a predicate, is given by a set of *mapping principles* specifying permissible relations between semantic roles and grammatical functions (see Butt et al. 1997). And the resource-sensitivity of our glue language, linear logic, ensures predicate uniqueness: only one semantic contribution is made and consumed for each syntactic argument.

Further, our use of linear logic as a glue language permits a concise restatement of the constraints of functional *completeness* and *coherence* (Dalrymple et al. 1993). Kaplan and Bresnan (1982, pages 211–212) define completeness and coherence in the following way:

> An f-structure is *locally complete* if and only if it contains all the governable grammatical functions that its predicate governs. An f-structure is *complete* if and only if all its subsidiary f-structures are locally complete. An f-structure is *locally coherent* if and only if all the governable grammatical functions that it contains are governed by a local predicate. An f-structure is *coherent* if and only if all its subsidiary f-structures are locally coherent.

Informally, an incomplete f-structure is missing some of the arguments it needs:

(23)   *John devoured. [incomplete]

An incoherent f-structure contains some extra unneeded arguments:

(24)   *John arrived Sam the sink. [incoherent]

A feature structure f of an utterance is associated with the ($\otimes$) conjunction ϕ of all the formulas associated with the lexical items in the utterance. The conjunction is said to be *semantically complete and coherent* if and only if

$$Th \vdash \phi \multimap f_\sigma \rightsquigarrow P \text{ (for some term } P)$$

where *Th* is the background theory of general linguistic principles. Each P is a valid meaning for the sentence. This guarantees that the entries are used exactly once in building up the denotation of the utterance: no requirements may be left unfulfilled, and no meaning contribution may remain unused.[4]

2.3   Modification

Another pleasant consequence of the use of linear logic is that it allows for an intuitive treatment of modification (Dalrymple et al. 1993; Dalrymple, Lamping, Pereira, and Saraswat 1995), where the role of a modifier (such as an adverb or adjective) is to consume an unmodified meaning and produce a modified meaning. This is accomplished without requiring the introduction of otherwise unmotivated syntactic constituents with which to associate the unmodified and modified meanings.

---

[4]This approach provides a logical account of subcategorization requirements for semantically contentful arguments of a predicate. However, there is still a question of how this treatment should be generalized for arguments of predicates that make no semantic contribution, such as the pleonastic subject *It* in a sentence such as *It is raining*, or the subject of a raising verb like *seems*. Two possibilities exist. First, such arguments might make a semantic contribution which does not play a role in the final meaning; instead, the predicate checks for and then discards the semantic contribution of its argument. However, this possibility goes against the view presented in Chapter 7, on which meaning terms play no role in affecting or limiting glue-language deductions. Second, such arguments may be assumed not to make a semantic contribution, and their presence is controlled solely by syntactic requirements, so that completeness and coherence remain as syntactic as well as semantic requirements. This approach is explored in the logical approach to the architecture of LFG presented by Saraswat in Chapter 8.

Consider the following sentence, containing the sentential modifier *obviously*, and its f-structure:

(25)   Sam obviously greeted Terry.

(26)
$$f:\begin{bmatrix} \text{PRED} & \text{`GREET'} \\ \text{SUBJ} & [\text{PRED} \quad \text{`SAM'}] \\ \text{OBJ} & [\text{PRED} \quad \text{`TERRY'}] \\ \text{MODS} & \{[\text{PRED} \quad \text{`OBVIOUSLY'}]\} \end{bmatrix}$$

We assume that the meaning of the sentence can be represented by the following formula:

(27) $obviously(greet(Sam, Terry))$

Here, we take advantage of the fact that linear logic supports a coherent notion of *consumption* and *production* of meanings. We propose that modifiers such as *obviously* make a contribution like the following:

$$\textbf{obviously}: (\forall P.\ f_\sigma \rightsquigarrow P \ \multimap \ f_\sigma \rightsquigarrow obviously(P))$$

That is, a modifier functions to *consume* the unmodified meaning of the phrase it modifies and *produce* a new, modified meaning; note that the meaning of the modified structure f_σ in the meaning constructor contributed by *obviously* appears on *both* sides of $\multimap$.

In presenting the deduction of the meaning of *Sam obviously greeted Terry*, we begin with the meaning derived above for *Sam greeted Terry* and the meaning constructor for the adverb *obviously*:

$$f_\sigma \rightsquigarrow greet(Sam, Terry) \otimes \textbf{obviously}$$
$$\vdash \quad f_\sigma \rightsquigarrow obviously(greet(Sam, Terry)) \qquad P \mapsto greet(Sam, Terry)$$

The linear implication introduced by *obviously* consumes the previous value for f_σ and produces the new and final value. By using linear logic, each step of the derivation keeps track of what resources have been consumed by linear implications. The value for f_σ is a meaning for this sentence only if there is no other information left. Thus, the derivation could not stop at the next to last step, because the linear implication introduced by 'obviously' was still left. The final step provides the only complete and coherent meaning derivable for the utterance.

2.4   Background on linear logic

Linear logic was first introduced by Girard (1987), and has since aroused much interest among logicians and computer scientists as well as linguists. Categorial grammarians have found particular interest in linear logic, since the Lambek calculus, introduced in 1958 by Joachim Lambek as a system for syntactic analysis, is a fragment of noncommutative multiplicative linear logic (Lambek 1958).

Linear logic grew out of a shift in logical perspective which can be described in very simple proof-theoretic terms: essentially, the structural rules in Gentzen-style proof systems for classical and intuitionistic logic are examined carefully, and the rules for weakening and contraction are dropped. This means that in an inference it is not possible to copy or discard arbitrary formulas. From this, a system of *resource-sensitive logic* emerges in which the multiplicity of formulas is important: logical formulas can now be regarded as *dynamic resources* that may be consumed or produced in a derivation.

In this setting, two distinct notions of conjunction emerge, the multiplicative (tensor, $\otimes$) and the additive ('with', &), corresponding to two distinct but hitherto conflated notions of conjunction. The multiplicative conjunction or tensor corresponds to the notion of simultaneously possessing two resources *both* of which can be consumed in an interaction, while the additive conjunction corresponds to possessing the potential to use *either* of two resources. As the usual adjunct of the multiplicative (tensor) conjunction, the notion of *linear implication* $\multimap$ arises, which captures the notion of 'consumption' of resources. Thus, from $p \otimes q \otimes (p \multimap r)$ one can derive $q \otimes r$, but not $p \otimes q \otimes r$ (the single occurrence of p is "used up" in discharging the antecedent of $p \multimap r$). Interestingly, classical and intuitionistic logic can be encoded in linear logic by using the "of course" connective '!'. Formulas marked with '!' can be weakened and contracted arbitrarily. For more background on linear logic, Troelstra (1993) and Scedrov (1993) give tutorial introductions, and Saraswat and Lincoln (1992) provide an explicit formulation for the higher-order version of the linear concurrent constraint programming scheme.

The glue language we will explore in this volume is a fragment of higher-order linear logic, the *tensor fragment*, that is closed under

$$
\begin{array}{rll}
G & ::= & S\leadsto_\tau M \quad \text{(Basic assertion)} \\
  & | & G\otimes G \quad \text{(Multiplicative conjunction)} \\
  & | & G\multimap G \quad \text{(Linear implication)} \\
  & | & \Pi\lambda X.\,G \quad \text{(Quantification over meaning terms)} \\
  & | & \Pi\lambda H.\,G \quad \text{(Quantification over } \sigma\text{-terms)}
\end{array}
$$

Figure 1.4: Glue language formulas

conjunction, universal quantification, and implication: see Figure 1.4. Expressions in glue language contain three kinds of terms: meaning terms, f-structures, and semantic or σ-structures. Glue-language formulas are built up using linear connectives from atomic formulas of the form $S\leadsto_\tau M$, which indicate that the meaning associated with σ-structure S is denoted by term M of type τ. As noted in Section 1.3, we often omit the type subscript τ when it can be determined from context. We usually write $\Pi\lambda X.\,G$ as $\forall X.\,G$, and similarly for $\Pi\lambda H.\,G$.

3   Meaning Language

We have noted that meaning constructors contain terms of the following form:

(28) $g_\sigma \leadsto P$

where g_σ is a semantic structure, P is a meaning, and $\leadsto$ is a binary relation between semantic structures and meanings. Our use of linear logic as a glue language does not dictate the choice of language for expressing natural language meanings, although certain analyses may impose requirements on that choice. For instance, the analysis of quantification presented in Chapter 2 imposes one requirement on the choice of meaning language: it must allow for the creation of abstractions and their application to arguments. Within such limits, the choice of meaning language depends entirely on the chosen theory of natural language semantics.[5]

---

[5]A similar separation between meaning language and semantic composition mechanisms has been used in natural-language understanding systems (Grosz et al. 1982; Johnson and Kay 1990).

Identity	$\overline{F \vdash F}$

Cut
$$\frac{\Gamma_1 \vdash F \qquad \Gamma_2, F \vdash D}{\Gamma_1, \Gamma_2 \vdash D}$$

Exchange
$$\frac{\Gamma_1, F, G, \Gamma_2 \vdash D}{\Gamma_1, G, F, \Gamma_2 \vdash D}$$

λ
$$\frac{\Gamma, F' \vdash D \qquad F \to_\lambda F'}{\Gamma, F \vdash D} \qquad \frac{\Gamma \vdash D \qquad D \to_\lambda D'}{\Gamma \vdash D'}$$

$\otimes$
$$\frac{\Gamma, F, G \vdash D}{\Gamma, (F \otimes G) \vdash D} \qquad \frac{\Gamma_1 \vdash F \qquad \Gamma_2 \vdash G}{\Gamma_1, \Gamma_2 \vdash (F \otimes G)}$$

$\multimap$
$$\frac{\Gamma_1 \vdash F \qquad \Gamma_2, G \vdash D}{\Gamma_1, \Gamma_2, (F \multimap G) \vdash D} \qquad \frac{\Gamma, F \vdash G}{\Gamma \vdash (F \multimap G)}$$

Π
$$\frac{\Gamma, Pt \vdash D}{\Gamma, \Pi P \vdash D} \qquad \frac{\Gamma \vdash Py}{\Gamma \vdash \Pi P}$$

The right Π rule only applies if y is not free in Γ, Σ, and any nonlogical theory axioms. We write $M \to_\lambda N$ to indicate that N can be obtained from M by one or more applications of α- or β- reduction, or by the application of the rule:

$$\check{}(\hat{}(Q)) \to Q$$

to a sub-term of M.

Some of the analyses in this volume rely on the ability to 'turn off' resource accounting by using the *of course* connective '!'. For those analyses, we would also need the following left rules for *of course*:

Weakening
$$\frac{\Gamma \vdash D}{\Gamma, !F \vdash D}$$

Contraction
$$\frac{\Gamma, !F, !F \vdash D}{\Gamma, !F \vdash D}$$

Dereliction
$$\frac{\Gamma, F \vdash D}{\Gamma, !F \vdash D}$$

Figure 1.5: Proof rules for intensional higher-order linear logic

$$
\begin{array}{lllll}
M & ::= & c & \text{(Constants} \\
& | & x & \text{(Lambda-variables)} \\
& | & \lambda x\, M & \text{(Abstraction)} \\
& | & M\, M & \text{(Application)} \\
& | & X & \text{(Glue-language variables)} \\
& | & {}^\wedge & \text{(``cap'' operator)} \\
& | & {}^\vee & \text{(``cup'' operator)}
\end{array}
$$

Figure 1.6: Syntax of meaning language of intensional logic

Many of the papers in this volume assume some version of Montague's intensional logic (Montague 1974) as meaning language. That is, terms on the right-hand side of the "means" relation $\rightsquigarrow$ are terms of intensional logic such as *Sam* or $greet(X,Y)$:

(29) $g_\sigma \rightsquigarrow Sam$

   $f_\sigma \rightsquigarrow greet(X,Y)$

The reader familiar with Montague may be surprised by the apparently purely extensional form of the meaning terms in these examples, in contrast with Montague's use of intensional expressions even in purely extensional cases to allow for uniform translation rules. The reasons for this divergence are detailed in Chapter 2, Section 4, where meaning terms such as $seek(Sam, {}^\wedge \lambda R.({}^\vee R)(Z))$ are also used.

The syntax of this meaning language is given in Figure 1.6. Terms are typed in the usual way; logical connectives such as *every* and *a* are represented by constants of appropriate type. The "up" operator is polymorphic, and of type $\alpha \rightarrow (s \rightarrow \alpha)$; similarly the "down" operator is of type $(s \rightarrow \alpha) \rightarrow \alpha$. For readability, we often "uncurry" $M N_1 \cdots N_m$ as $M(N_1, \ldots, N_m)$. Note that we allow variables in the glue language to range over meaning terms.

Of course, it is not necessary to represent meaning terms as terms of intensional logic; other means for representing meanings can also be used. To provide a concrete illustration of that possibility, we briefly sketch a derivation of the meaning of the sentence *Sam left* using

Lambda DRT (Kamp and Reyle 1993; Bos et al. 1994) as the meaning language. We assume the following lexical entries for *Sam* and *left*:[6]

(30) Sam   NP $(\uparrow \text{PRED}) = \text{`SAM'}$
$$\forall H, P.\ (\forall X.\ \uparrow_\sigma \rightsquigarrow X \multimap H \rightsquigarrow P(X))$$
$$\multimap H \rightsquigarrow [y \mid y = Sam] \otimes P(y)$$

left   V $(\uparrow \text{PRED}) = \text{`LEAVE'}$
$$\forall X.\ (\uparrow \text{SUBJ})_\sigma \rightsquigarrow X \multimap \uparrow_\sigma \rightsquigarrow [\ \mid leave(X)]$$

The f-structure for the sentence *Sam left* is:

$$(31) \quad f : \begin{bmatrix} \text{PRED} & \text{`LEAVE'} \\ \text{SUBJ} & g : [\text{PRED} \quad \text{`SAM'}] \end{bmatrix}$$

Instantiating the meaning constructors for *Sam* and *left* appropriately, we obtain the following premises:

sam: $\forall H, P.\ (\forall X.\ g_\sigma \rightsquigarrow X \multimap H \rightsquigarrow P(X))$
$$\multimap H \rightsquigarrow [y \mid y = Sam] \otimes P(y)$$
leave: $\forall X.\ g_\sigma \rightsquigarrow X \multimap f_\sigma \rightsquigarrow [\ \mid leave(X)]$

From these premises, we conclude:

$$f_\sigma \rightsquigarrow [y \mid y = Sam] \otimes [\ \mid leave(y)]$$

By the rules of Lambda DRT, this is equivalent to:

$$f_\sigma \rightsquigarrow [y \mid y = Sam, leave(y)]$$

or, in the more familiar box notation:

$$f_\sigma \rightsquigarrow \boxed{\begin{array}{l} y \\ y = Sam \\ leave(y) \end{array}}$$

This brief exposition illustrates that other languages for expressing meanings besides intensional logic can be incorporated into this approach. In Chapter 6, van Genabith and Crouch present a full exposition of the use of alternative meaning languages such as DRT in the current approach.

---

[6]Lambda DRT also uses the symbol $\otimes$ as a connective. To avoid confusion with the linear logic multiplicative conjunction $\otimes$, we have substituted the larger boldface symbol $\otimes$ for the Lambda DRT connective $\otimes$.

4   Contents of This Volume

In the foregoing, we have presented an introduction to the syntactic framework of LFG as well as a basic overview of the glue approach, This material provides an anchor and guidepost for the basic assumptions made in the other papers in the book.

The rest of the papers in this book fall into three groups. The first group, comprising Chapters 2–5, is oriented to the characterization and analysis of a range of linguistic phenomena with the tools and methods presented above. The second group, comprising Chapters 6–7, discusses the formal and computational properties of the current approach and related approaches to the syntax-semantics interface in LFG. The third group, comprising Chapters 8–10, presents reanalyses and recastings of the entire LFG framework, giving new views of syntactic as well as semantic representation and composition.

4.1   Linguistic analyses

The first group of papers builds on the introductory material presented in this chapter, going beyond the analysis of simple sentences to the treatment of a range of linguistic phenomena, including quantification, negative polarity items, anaphora, intensional verbs, ellipsis, and context management.

Chapter 2: Quantification, Anaphora, and Intensionality, by Mary Dalrymple, John Lamping, Fernando Pereira, and Vijay Saraswat, presents an in-depth examination of a glue analysis of one particular construct: quantified noun phrases like *someone* and *every man*. In particular, it shows how the analysis constrains scope possibilities in the presence of anaphoric relations involving quantifiers, and how it supports intensional verbs such as *seek*, which take a quantifier as an argument. The analysis of quantification presented in this chapter is assumed as a starting point by many of the other papers in the volume.

Chapter 3: Proof Nets and Negative Polarity Licensing, by John Fry, presents an analysis of negative polarity items and their licensers. The analysis relies on a remarkable property of linear logic: additional information, such as the information that a certain semantic operator can license negative polarity items, can serve to constrain the proof, so that only well-formed scopings—where the negative polarity item is within the scope of its licenser—are allowed. Tensor conjunction allows this additional licensing information to be provided in parallel with the licenser's semantic contribution. Fry's paper also explicates the use of proof nets, which permit efficient checking for correct proofs and are useful as a succinct visual demonstration of why a proof fails.

Chapter 4: Context Change, Underspecification and the Structure of Glue Language Derivations, by Richard Crouch and Josef van Genabith, uses the resource sensitivity of the meaning assembly language to provide an analysis of context management and contextual resolution. They propose to treat context update as a part of meaning assembly: the deduction of the meaning of a sentence involves not just the assembly of the sentential meaning but also the creation and update of associations between contextually-derived properties and referents accessible for anaphora resolution. This allows for a more general treatment of anaphora than the one presented in Chapter 2. Additionally, the paper proposes a means for specifying an ordering over nodes that represents and constrains the form and structure of the deduction. The resulting "audit trails" render explicit the choices that were made in the course of the derivation, and are used in a new treatment of ellipsis resolution.

Chapter 5: Resource Sharing in Glue Language Semantics, by Andrew Kehler, Mary Dalrymple, John Lamping, and Vijay Saraswat, addresses a basic tenet of the glue approach requiring that the semantic contributions of linguistic elements are used exactly once during the course of a meaning derivation. This tenet is challenged by the existence of syntactic constructions (including, but not limited to, coordination) in which certain linguistic elements contribute to multiple aspects of the interpretation. This paper shows that such constructions do not necessitate an abandonment of resource sensitivity, but instead lead to a more sophisticated view of the syntax-semantics interface, in which resources come not only from linguistic elements but also from aspects of their syntactic configuration.

4.2   Formal properties of the syntax-semantics interface

The second group of papers provides an overview and discussion of the formal and computational properties of the syntax-semantics interface in LFG, setting the glue approach in a larger context and exploring its formal properties more fully.

Chapter 6: Dynamic and Underspecified Semantics for LFG, by Josef van Genabith and Richard Crouch, provides a useful overview of approaches to the syntax-semantics interface in LFG and to recent developments in semantic representation. The paper presents three ways of providing dynamic, underspecified representations for LFG. First, a method is provided for mapping LFG f-structures directly to underspecified semantic representations such as Underspecified Discourse Representation Structures (Reyle 1993) and Quasi-Logical Forms (Alshawi and Crouch 1992). Second, a dynamic meaning language like Compositional Discourse Representation Theory (Muskens 1994) is used; in this setting, the premises for the deduction of a sentences meaning are seen as a type of underspecified meaning representation. Third, the approach outlined in Chapter 4 can be followed, in which the dynamic nature of the semantic representation comes not from the use of a particular dynamic meaning language, but from the process of semantic assembly itself.

Chapter 7: Relating Resource-based Semantics to Categorial Semantics, by Mary Dalrymple, Vineet Gupta, John Lamping, and Vijay Saraswat, shows that many analyses within the glue framework use a fragment of linear logic which is equivalent to typed linear lambda calculus, where the type reflects the syntactic role of a constituent in the sentence and the lambda term captures the meaning of the constituent. The meanings themselves play no role in constraining the process of composition; rather, the meaning is built up by performing function abstraction and application as dictated by the structure of the proof resulting from the type structure. This work builds a connection between the glue approach described in this volume and categorial approaches, which share this property.

4.3   Explicating and revising the overall architecture of LFG

The third group of papers reflects more generally on the architecture of the theory of Lexical Functional Grammar, rethinking and recasting the theory of syntactic composition and representation as well as semantics.

Chapter 8: LFG as Concurrent Constraint Programming, by Vijay Saraswat, sheds new light on the standard assumptions and overall architecture of LFG by restating the theory in constraint-based, declarative logical terms. Saraswat develops a linear concurrent constraint programming language for expressing LFG grammars, enabling them to be viewed as theories within the logic he presents. The paper gives new insight into the formal and computational nature of the various kinds of structures and constraints traditionally assumed by LFG grammarians.

Chapter 9: LFG as Labeled Deduction, by Dick Oehrle, casts LFG in the framework of Labeled Deduction, giving a new theory of syntactic and semantic representation and composition in LFG which is more closely related to categorial approaches. This theoretical move helps to clarify the relationship between LFG and other frameworks, especially with regard to type-theoretical analyses of quantification and scope. Like the proposal by Saraswat presented in Chapter 8, Oehrle's proposal makes LFG a deductive, logically based theory. Unlike Saraswat's proposals, however, Oehrle's proposals involve some changes and modifications to the standard architecture of LFG. In particular, existential and negative constraints are incompatible with the constructive character of labeled deductive systems. With further research and comparison between the standard version of the theory and Oehrle's new proposals, it may turn out that these changes are overly drastic, and that Oehrle's reanalysis of LFG does not have sufficient formal power to allow for a satisfactory reanalysis of all previous proposals made within standard LFG theory; on the other hand, the changes Oehrle proposes may turn out to be welcome simplifications if the range of describable phenomena remains unchanged in this new setting.

Chapter 10: Type-driven Semantic Interpretation and Feature Dependencies in R-LFG, by Mark Johnson, proposes the most radical recasting of the LFG framework, presenting a new theory, R-LFG, in which resource accounting is extended into the syntax. Syntactic features in R-LFG are treated as resources, and feature dependencies are formally modeled within a resource-based logical framework. Semantic composition proceeds in tandem with construction of the syntactic representation via the Curry-Howard correspondence. Like the Saraswat and Oehrle proposals, this paper offers a fresh perspective on the formal architecture of LFG, and opens up new ways of thinking about the relation between syntax and semantics. Further research will show whether this resource-based view of functional structure allows for a clean and intuitive recasting of previous LFG syntactic and semantic analyses in this new framework.

References

Alshawi, Hiyan and Richard Crouch. 1992. Monotonic semantic interpretation. In *Proceedings of the Thirtieth Annual Meeting of the ACL*, Newark, Delaware, pages 32–39. Association for Computational Linguistics.

Alsina, Alex. 1993. *Predicate Composition: A Theory of Syntactic Function Alternations*. PhD thesis, Stanford University.

Bos, Johan, Elsbeth Mastenbroek, Scott McGlashan, Sebastian Millies, and Manfred Pinkal. 1994. A compositional DRS-based formalism for NLP applications. In *Proceedings of the International Workshop on Computational Semantics*, Tilburg. Also published as *Verbmobil Report 59*, Universität des Saarlandes, Saarbrücken, Germany.

Bresnan, Joan, editor. 1982. *The Mental Representation of Grammatical Relations*. The MIT Press, Cambridge, MA.

Bresnan, Joan and Jonni M. Kanerva. 1989. Locative inversion in Chicheŵa: A case study of factorization in grammar. *Linguistic Inquiry*, 20(1):1–50. Also in Eric Wehrli and Tim Stowell, editors, *Syntax and Semantics 26: Syntax and the Lexicon*. New York: Academic Press. 1992.

Butt, Miriam. 1996. *The Structure of Complex Predicates in Urdu*. PhD thesis, Stanford University. *Dissertations in Linguistics* series, CSLI Publications, Stanford University. Revised and corrected version of 1993 Stanford University dissertation.

Butt, Miriam, Mary Dalrymple, and Anette Frank. 1997. The nature of argument structure. In Miriam Butt and Tracy Holloway King, editors, *On-line Proceedings of the LFG97 Conference*, 1997. http://www-csli.stanford.edu/publications/LFG2/butt-dalrymple-frank-lfg97.ps.

Chomsky, Noam.   1955.   *The Logical Structure of Linguistic Theory*. Mimeographed, MIT Library, Cambridge. Reprinted in 1975, Plenum, New York.

Dalrymple, Mary, John Lamping, and Vijay Saraswat. 1993. LFG semantics via constraints. In *Proceedings of the Sixth Meeting of the European ACL*, pages 97–105, University of Utrecht. European Chapter of the Association for Computational Linguistics.

Dalrymple, Mary, Ronald M. Kaplan, John T. Maxwell, III, and Annie Zaenen, editors. 1995. *Formal Issues in Lexical-Functional Grammar*. CSLI Publications, Stanford University.

Dalrymple, Mary, John Lamping, Fernando C. N. Pereira, and Vijay Saraswat. 1995. Linear logic for meaning assembly. In Suresh Manandhar, Gabriel Pereira Lopes, and Werner Nutt, editors, *Proceedings of Computational Logic for Natural Language Processing*, Edinburgh.

Fenstad, Jens Erik, Per-Kristian Halvorsen, Tore Langholm, and Johan van Benthem. 1987. *Situations, Language and Logic*. D. Reidel, Dordrecht.

Gamut, L. T. F. 1991. *Logic, Language, and Meaning*, volume 2: Intensional Logic and Logical Grammar. The University of Chicago Press, Chicago.

Girard, Jean-Yves. 1987. Linear logic. *Theoretical Computer Science*, 50:1–102.

Girard, Jean-Yves. 1989. *Proofs and Types*, volume 7 of *Cambridge Tracts in Theoretical Computer Science*. Cambridge University Press. Translated and with appendices by Y. Lafont and P. Taylor.

Grosz, Barbara, Norman Haas, Gary G. Hendrix, Jerry Hobbs, Paul Martin, Robert Moore, Jane Robinson, and Stan Rosenschein. November 1982. Dialogic: A core natural-language processing system. Technical Note 270, Artificial Intelligence Center, SRI International, Menlo Park, California.

Halvorsen, Per-Kristian. 1983. Semantics for Lexical-Functional Grammar. *Linguistic Inquiry*, 14(4):567–615.

Halvorsen, Per-Kristian. 1988. Situation Semantics and semantic interpretation in constraint-based grammars. In *Proceedings of the International Conference on Fifth Generation Computer Systems (FGCS-88)*, Tokyo, Japan, pages 471–478. Also published as CSLI Technical Report CSLI-TR-101, Stanford University, 1987. Reprinted in Mary Dalrymple, Ronald M. Kaplan, John Maxwell, and Annie Zaenen, editors, *Formal Issues in Lexical-Functional Grammar*, pages 293–309. CSLI Publications, Stanford University. 1995.

Halvorsen, Per-Kristian and Ronald M. Kaplan. 1988. Projections and semantic description in Lexical-Functional Grammar. In *Proceedings of the International Conference on Fifth Generation Computer Systems (FGCS-88)*, pages 1116–1122, Tokyo, Japan. Reprinted in Mary Dalrymple, Ronald M. Kaplan, John

Maxwell, and Annie Zaenen, editors, *Formal Issues in Lexical-Functional Grammar*, pages 279–292. CSLI Publications, Stanford University. 1995.

Johnson, Mark and Martin Kay. 1990. Semantic abstraction and anaphora. In Hans Karlgren, editor, *Proceedings of the 13th International Conference on Computational Linguistics (COLING-90)*, Helsinki, Finland, pages 17–27. Helsinki University.

Kamp, Hans and Uwe Reyle. 1993. *From Discourse to Logic: An Introduction to Modeltheoretic Semantics of Natural Language, Formal Logic and Discourse Representation Theory*. Kluwer Academic Publishers, Dordrecht.

Kaplan, Ronald M. and Joan Bresnan. 1982. Lexical-Functional Grammar: A formal system for grammatical representation. In Joan Bresnan, editor, *The Mental Representation of Grammatical Relations*, pages 173–281. The MIT Press, Cambridge, MA. Reprinted in Mary Dalrymple, Ronald M. Kaplan, John Maxwell, and Annie Zaenen, editors, *Formal Issues in Lexical-Functional Grammar*, pages 29–130. CSLI Publications, Stanford University. 1995.

Kaplan, Ronald M. 1987. Three seductions of computational psycholinguistics. In Peter Whitelock, Mary McGee Wood, Harold L. Somers, Rod Johnson, and Paul Bennett, editors, *Linguistic Theory and Computer Applications*, pages 149–188. Academic Press, London. Also: CCL/UMIST Report No. 86.2: Alvey/ICL Workshop on Linguistic Theory and Computer Applications: Transcripts of Presentations and Discussions. Center for Computational Linguistics, University of Manchester, Institute of Science and Technology, Manchester. Reprinted in Mary Dalrymple, Ronald M. Kaplan, John Maxwell, and Annie Zaenen, editors, *Formal Issues in Lexical-Functional Grammar*, pages 337–367. CSLI Publications, Stanford University. 1995.

Klein, Ewan and Ivan A. Sag. 1985. Type-driven translation. *Linguistics and Philosophy*, 8:163–201.

Lambek, Joachim. 1958. The mathematics of sentence structure. *American Mathematical Monthly*, 65:154–170.

Levin, Lori S., Malka Rappaport, and Annie Zaenen, editors. 1983. *Papers in Lexical-Functional Grammar*. Indiana University Linguistics Club, Bloomington, IN.

Montague, Richard. 1974. The proper treatment of quantification in ordinary English. In Richmond Thomason, editor, *Formal Philosophy*. Yale University Press, New Haven.

Muskens, Reinhard. 1994. Categorial grammar and Discourse Representation Theory. In *Proceedings of the 15th International Conference on Computational Linguistics (COLING '94)*, Kyoto, pages 508–514.

Pereira, Fernando C. N. 1990. Categorial semantics and scoping. *Computational Linguistics*, 16(1):1–10.

Pollard, Carl and Ivan A. Sag. 1987. *Information-Based Syntax and Semantics, Volume I.* CSLI Lecture Notes, number 13. CSLI Publications, Stanford University.

Pollard, Carl and Ivan A. Sag. 1994. *Head-Driven Phrase Structure Grammar.* The University of Chicago Press, Chicago.

Prawitz, Dag. 1965. *Natural Deduction: A Proof-Theoretical Study.* Almqvist and Wiksell, Uppsala, Sweden.

Reyle, Uwe. 1988. Compositional semantics for LFG. In Uwe Reyle and Christian Rohrer, editors, *Natural language parsing and linguistic theories.* D. Reidel, Dordrecht.

Reyle, Uwe. 1993. Dealing with ambiguities by underspecification: Construction, representation and deduction. *Journal of Semantics*, 10:123–179.

Saraswat, Vijay A. 1989. *Concurrent Constraint Programming Languages.* PhD thesis, Carnegie-Mellon University. Reprinted by MIT Press, Doctoral Dissertation Award and Logic Programming Series, 1993.

Saraswat, Vijay A. and Patrick Lincoln. 1992. Higher-order, linear concurrent constraint programming. Technical report, Xerox Palo Alto Research Center.

Scedrov, Andre. 1993. A brief guide to linear logic. In G. Rozenberg and A. Salomaa, editors, *Current Trends in Theoretical Computer Science.* World Scientific Publishing Co. Revised and expanded version of the article originally appearing in *Bulletin of the European Assoc. for Theoretical Computer Science* 41, 1990.

Troelstra, A. S. 1992. *Lectures on Linear Logic.* CSLI Lecture Notes, number 29. CSLI Publications, Stanford University.

Troelstra, A. S. 1993. A tutorial on linear logic. In Peter Schroeder-Heister and Kosta Došen, editors, *Studies in Logic and Computation 2*, pages 327–355. Oxford University Press, Oxford.

2

Quantification, Anaphora, and Intensionality

Mary Dalrymple, John Lamping, Fernando Pereira, and Vijay Saraswat

The use of linear logic (Girard 1987) to describe the semantic interpretation of LFG f-structures, introduced in Chapter 1, is extended in this chapter to account for important observed interactions between quantifier scope ambiguity, bound anaphora and intensionality. Our linear-logic formalization of the compositional properties of quantifying expressions in natural language obviates the need for special mechanisms, such as Cooper storage, in representing the scoping possibilities of quantifying expressions. Instead, the semantic contribution of a quantifier is recorded as a linear-logic formula whose use in a proof will establish the scope of the quantifier. Different proofs can lead to different scopes. In each complete proof, the properties of linear logic ensure that quantifiers are properly scoped.

The interactions between quantified NPs and intensional verbs such as *seek* are also accounted for in this deductive setting. A single specification in linear logic of the argument requirements of intensional verbs is sufficient to derive the correct reading predictions for intensional-verb clauses both with nonquantified and with quantified direct objects. In particular, both *de dicto* and *de re* readings are derived for quantified objects. The effects of type-raising or quantifying-in rules in other frameworks just follow here as linear-logic theorems.

While our approach resembles current categorial approaches in important ways (Moortgat 1988, 1996; Carpenter 1994; Morrill 1994) it differs from them in allowing the greater compositional flexibility of

An earlier version of this paper appeared in *Journal of Logic, Language, and Information* 6(3), pages 219–273, July 1997.

categorial semantics (van Benthem 1991) while maintaining a precise connection to syntax. As a result, we are able to provide derivations for certain readings of sentences with intensional verbs and complex direct objects whose derivation in purely categorial accounts of the syntax-semantics interface appears to require otherwise unnecessary semantic decompositions of lexical entries.

1   Introduction

In Chapter 1, we introduced our approach to semantic interpretation in LFG, in which linear logic is used to represent the connection between two dissimilar levels of linguistic representation: f-structures and their semantic interpretations. We have also shown elsewhere how the linear-logic formalization of the syntax-semantics interface for LFG provides simple and general analyses of modification, functional completeness and coherence, and complex predicate formation (Dalrymple, Lamping, and Saraswat 1993; Dalrymple, Hinrichs, Lamping, and Saraswat 1993). In the present paper, which consolidates and refines earlier studies (Dalrymple et al. 1994, 1995), the analysis is extended to the interpretation of quantified NPs. We present our analysis of the compositional properties of quantified NPs, and we show that the analysis accounts correctly for scope ambiguity and its interactions with bound anaphora. We also present an analysis of intensional verbs, which take quantified arguments, and show that our approach predicts the full range of acceptable readings without appealing to additional machinery.

2   Quantification

There have been a variety of proposals for semantic interpretation in LFG (Halvorsen 1983; Fenstad et al. 1987; Reyle 1988; Halvorsen and Kaplan 1988) that address the interpretation of quantified NPs. However, none of those proposals dealt in detail with the issues raised by interactions between scope and bound anaphora, or with the need for non-clausal quantification scopes arising from complex NPs and from intensional verbs with NP complements like *seek*. To address these problems, we formalize in linear logic the informal treatment of quantification and bound anaphora of Pereira (1990, 1991). As we present our analysis, we will explain how it extends and refines the previous proposals.

As outlined in Chapter 1 of this volume, we assume that the deduction of the meaning of a sentence proceeds from a set of premises in linear logic, called *meaning constructors*, introduced by the words of the sentence (and possibly by certain meaning-bearing phrasal constructions). For example, the meaning constructor provided in the lexical entry for a transitive verb such as *greet* looks for two meanings, the meaning of its subject and the meaning of its object, and consumes those meanings to produce a meaning for the sentence:

$$(1) \quad \forall X, Y. \, (\uparrow \text{SUBJ})_\sigma \rightsquigarrow X \otimes (\uparrow \text{OBJ})_\sigma \rightsquigarrow Y \multimap \uparrow_\sigma \rightsquigarrow greet(X, Y)$$

This meaning constructor asserts that if the subject (SUBJ) of a clause with main verb *greeted* means X and its object (OBJ) means Y, then the whole clause ($\uparrow$) means $greet(X, Y)$. As noted in Chapter 1, the form of this meaning constructor is mirrored in the standard type for transitive verbs: $(e \times e) \rightarrow t$.

2.1 Quantifier meanings

The basic idea for our analysis of quantified noun phrases can be seen as a logical counterpart at the glue level of the standard type assignment for generalized quantifiers (Barwise and Cooper 1981). The generalized quantifier meaning of a natural language determiner has type $(e \rightarrow t) \rightarrow (e \rightarrow t) \rightarrow t$, that is, the type of functions from two properties, the quantifier's restriction and scope, to propositions. At the semantic glue level, we can understand that type as follows. For any determiner, if for arbitrary x we can construct a meaning $R(x)$ for the quantifier's restriction, and again for arbitrary x we can construct a meaning $S(x)$ for the quantifier's scope, where R and S are suitable properties (functions from entities to propositions), then we can construct the meaning $Q(R, S)$ for the whole sentence containing the determiner, where Q is the meaning of the determiner.

The meaning contribution of a determiner like *every* is a linear-logic formula involving the relations between a set of semantic structures and the meanings they correspond to. By analogy with the standard generalized quantifier meaning for determiners, assume for the moment that we have determined the following semantic structures: *restr* for the restriction (a common noun phrase), *restr-arg* for its implicit argument, *scope* for the scope of quantification, and *scope-arg* for the grammatical function filled by the quantified NP. Then the foregoing analysis can be represented in linear logic by the following schematic formula:[1]

(2)   Schematic formula for generalized quantifiers:

$$\forall R, S.\ (\forall x.\ \textit{restr-arg} \leadsto_e x \multimap \textit{restr} \leadsto_t R(x))$$
$$\otimes\ (\forall x.\ \textit{scope-arg} \leadsto_e x \multimap \textit{scope} \leadsto_t S(x))$$
$$\multimap\ \textit{scope} \leadsto_t Q(R, S)$$

Given the equivalence between $A \otimes B \multimap C$ and $A \multimap (B \multimap C)$, the propositional part of (2) parallels the generalized quantifier type $(e{\rightarrow}t){\rightarrow}(e{\rightarrow}t){\rightarrow}t$.

In addition to providing a semantic type assignment for determiners, (2) uses glue language quantification to express how the meanings of the restriction and scope of quantification are determined and combined into the meaning of the quantified clause. The subformula

$$\forall x.\ \textit{restr-arg} \leadsto x \multimap \textit{restr} \leadsto R(x)$$

specifies that *restr* has meaning $R(x)$ if for arbitrary x *restr-arg* has meaning x, that is, it gives the dependency of the meaning of a common noun phrase on its implicit argument. Property R is the representation of that dependency as a function in the meaning language. Similarly, the subformula

$$\forall x.\ \textit{scope-arg} \leadsto x \multimap \textit{scope} \leadsto S(x)$$

---

[1] We use lower-case letters for *essentially universal* variables, that is, variables that stand for new local constants (eigenvariables) in a proof. We use capital letters for *essentially existential* variables, that is, Prolog-like variables that become instantiated to particular terms in a proof. In other words, essentially existential variables stand for specific but as yet unspecified terms, while essentially universal variables stand for arbitrary constants, that is, constants that could be replaced by *any* term while still maintaining the validity of the derivation. In the linear-logic fragment we use here, essentially existential variables arise from universal quantification with outermost scope, while essentially universal variables arise from universal quantification whose scope is a conjunct in the antecedent of an outermost implication.

specifies the dependency of the meaning $S(x)$ of a semantic structure *scope* on the meaning x of one of its arguments *scope-arg*. If both dependencies hold, then R and S are an appropriate restriction and scope for the determiner meaning Q.

Computationally, the nested universal quantifiers substitute unique new constants for the quantified variable x, and the nested implications try to prove their consequents with their antecedents added to the current set of assumptions. For the restriction (the case of the scope is similar), this will in particular involve solving an equation of the form $R(x) = t$, where $restr \leadsto t$ has been derived. The equation must be solved modulo α-, β- and η-conversion, and any solution R must not contain occurrences of x, since R's scope is wider than x's. Higher-order unification (Huet 1975) is a procedure suitable for solving such equations.[2]

2.2   Quantifier restrictions

We have seen that since the meaning of the restriction of a quantifier is a property (type $e{\rightarrow}t$), its meaning constructor has the form of an implication, just like a verb. In (2), the first line of the determiner's meaning constructor

$$(\forall x.\ restr\text{-}arg \leadsto x \multimap restr \leadsto R(x))$$

requires a meaning x for *restr-arg* to produce the meaning $R(x)$ for *restr*, defining the restriction R of the quantifier. We thus need to identify the semantic projections *restr-arg* and *restr*.

The f-structure of a quantified NP has the general form:

$$(3) \qquad f{:}\begin{bmatrix} \text{SPEC} & q \\ \text{PRED} & n \end{bmatrix}$$

where q is the determiner f-structure and n the noun f-structure. None of the f-structures f, q or n is a natural syntactic correlate of the argument or result of the quantifier restriction. This contrasts with the treat-

---

[2]While higher-order unification is in general undecidable, the unification problems involved here are of one of the forms $F(x) = t$ or $p(X) = t$ where t is a closed term, F and X essentially existential variables and x and p essentially universal variables. These cases fall within the $l\lambda$ fragment of Miller (1990), for which a decidable extension of first-order unification is sufficient.

ment of verbs, since the semantic contributions and argument dependencies of verbs are directly associated with appropriate syntactic units of the clauses they head. Therefore, we take the semantic projection f_σ of the quantified NP to have two attributes $(f_\sigma\ \text{VAR})$ and $(f_\sigma\ \text{RESTR})$:

$$(4)\quad \text{Det}\quad\quad f:\begin{bmatrix} \text{SPEC} & \text{'EVERY'} \end{bmatrix}\quad\quad f_\sigma:\begin{bmatrix} \text{VAR} & [\,] \\ \text{RESTR} & [\,] \end{bmatrix}$$

$$\text{every}$$

The value of VAR will play the role of *restr-arg*, supplying an entity-type variable, and the value of RESTR will play the role of *restr* in the meaning constructor of the determiner. For a preliminary version of the lexical entry for *every*, we replace the relevant portions of our canonical determiner entry appropriately:

(5) Preliminary lexical entry for *every*:

$$\text{every}\quad \text{Det}\quad (\uparrow\text{SPEC}) = \text{'EVERY'}$$
$$\forall R, S.\ (\forall x.\ (\uparrow_\sigma\ \text{VAR})\rightsquigarrow x \multimap (\uparrow_\sigma\ \text{RESTR})\rightsquigarrow R(x))$$
$$\otimes (\forall x.\ \text{scope-arg}\rightsquigarrow x \multimap \text{scope}\rightsquigarrow S(x))$$
$$\multimap\ \text{scope}\rightsquigarrow \text{every}(R, S)$$

The restriction property R should of course be derived from the semantic contribution of the nominal part of the noun phrase. Therefore, meaning constructors for nouns must connect appropriately to the VAR and RESTR components of the noun phrase's semantic projection, as we shall now see.

2.3 Noun meanings

We will use the following phrase structure rule for simple noun phrases:

$$(6)\quad \text{NP}\ \longrightarrow\quad \text{Det}\quad\quad \text{N}$$
$$\uparrow = \downarrow\quad\quad \uparrow = \downarrow$$

This rule states that the determiner Det and noun N contribute equally to the f-structure for the NP. Lexical specifications ensure that the noun contributes the PRED attribute and its value, and the determiner contributes the SPEC attribute and its value.

The c-structure, f-structure, and semantic structure for *every voter*, together with the functional relations between them, are:

(7)

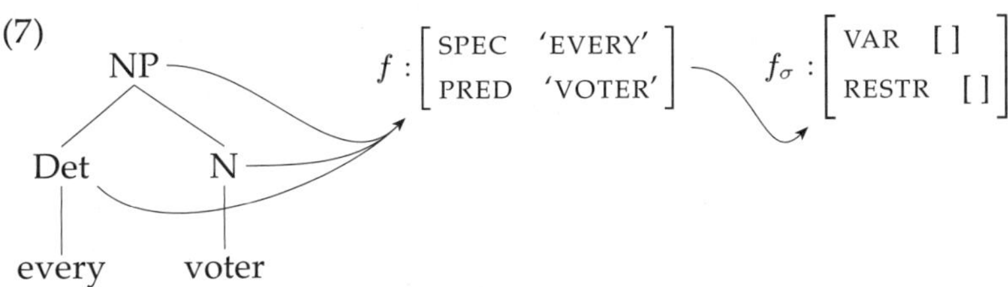

In rule (6), the meaning constructors of the noun *voter* and the determiner *every* make reference to the same semantic structure, and in particular to the same semantic projections VAR and RESTR. The noun will supply appropriate values for the VAR and RESTR attributes of the NP, and these will be consumed by the determiner's meaning constructor. Thus, the lexical entry for *voter* is:

(8)   voter   N $(\uparrow \text{PRED}) = \text{'VOTER'}$
$\forall X. (\uparrow_\sigma \text{VAR}) \rightsquigarrow X \multimap (\uparrow_\sigma \text{RESTR}) \rightsquigarrow voter(X)$

In general, the meaning constructor for a noun will have the form

$$\forall x. (\uparrow_\sigma \text{VAR}) \rightsquigarrow x \multimap (\uparrow_\sigma \text{RESTR}) \rightsquigarrow P(x)$$

where P is the meaning of the noun.[3] Given this entry and the one for *every* in (5), we obtain the following instantiated meaning constructors for (7):

every: $\forall R, S. (\forall x. (f_\sigma \text{VAR}) \rightsquigarrow x \multimap (f_\sigma \text{RESTR}) \rightsquigarrow R(x))$
$\otimes (\forall x. \textit{scope-arg} \rightsquigarrow x \multimap \textit{scope} \rightsquigarrow S(x))$
$\multimap \textit{scope} \rightsquigarrow every(R, S)$

voter: $\forall X. (f_\sigma \text{VAR}) \rightsquigarrow X \multimap (f_\sigma \text{RESTR}) \rightsquigarrow voter(X)$

---

[3]Of course, the derivation would be more complicated if the NP included adjective phrases or other noun modifiers; for the sake of brevity, we will not discuss the contribution of noun modifiers in this paper. Intuitively, the function of modifiers is to consume the meaning of the phrase they modify and produce a new, modified meaning of the same semantic shape, which can play the same semantic role as the unmodified phrase can play. Dalrymple, Lamping, and Saraswat (1993) provide a general discussion of modification in this framework.

Applying the variable substitutions $X \mapsto x, R \mapsto voter$ and modus ponens to those two premises, we obtain the meaning constructor for *every voter*:

(9)   **every-voter**: $\forall S.\ (\forall x.\ scope\text{-}arg \rightsquigarrow x \multimap scope \rightsquigarrow S(x))$
$\multimap scope \rightsquigarrow every(voter, S)$

In keeping with the parallel noted earlier between our meaning constructors and compositional types, the propositional part of this formula corresponds to the standard type for NP meanings, $(e \rightarrow t) \rightarrow t$.

To complete our analysis of the semantic contribution of determiners, we need to characterize how a quantified NP contributes to the meaning of sentences in which it appears, by specifying the semantic projections *scope-arg* and *scope* in quantified NP meaning constructors like (9).

2.4   Individual-type contribution

First, we require the meaning of the scope to depend on the meaning of (the position filled by) the quantified NP itself. Thus, *scope-arg* is the semantic projection for the quantified NP itself:

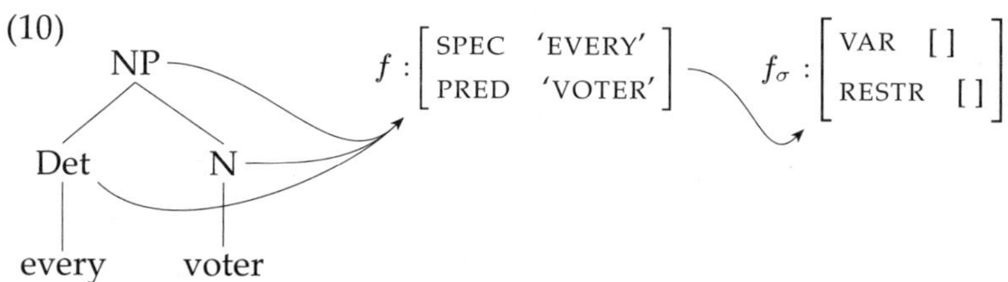

(10)

every-voter: $\forall S.\ (\forall x.\ f_\sigma \rightsquigarrow x \multimap scope \rightsquigarrow S(x)) \multimap scope \rightsquigarrow every(voter, S)$

Informally, the meaning constructor for *every voter* can be read as follows: if by giving the arbitrary meaning x of type e to f, the f-structure for *every voter*, we can derive the meaning $S(x)$ of type t for the scope of quantification *scope*, then S can be the property that the quantifier requires as its scope, yielding the meaning $every(voter, S)$ for *scope*. The quantified NP can thus be seen as providing two contributions to an interpretation: locally, a *referential import* x, which must be discharged when the scope of quantification is established; and globally, a *quantifi-*

cational import of type $(e{\to}t){\to}t$, which is applied to the meaning of the scope of quantification to obtain a quantified proposition.

Notice also that the assignment of a meaning to *scope* appears on both sides of the implication, and that in fact the meaning is not the same in the two instances. Linear logic allows for the *consumption* of the preliminary meaning in the antecedent of the implication, *producing* the final meaning for *scope* in the conclusion.

2.5   Scope of quantification

To complete our account of quantified NP interpretation, we need to explain how to select the possible scopes of quantification, for which we used the place-holder *scope* in (10).

As is well known, syntactic structure does not completely determine the scope of quantified NPs: in general, the interpretation of sentences with multiple quantified NPs may be ambiguous between different scopings. Therefore, any system for interpretation of quantified NPs must be able to generate those scoping alternatives. The specification of possible scopings involves three questions: (i) identifying possible scopes of quantification; (ii) determining global well-formedness constraints that restrict which quantifiers can take each possible scope; (iii) identifying additional linguistic constraints on scope. We will be concerned here mostly with questions (i) and (ii), although we will address a few remarks to question (iii) later in this section.

2.5.1   Possible scopes of quantification

Halvorsen (1983) and Reyle (1988) define possible scopes purely at the f-structure level, which requires scopes to be associated with specific f-structures. In fact, they further restrict scopes to the f-structures of clauses. However, in some cases those requirements are not met: in particular, cases in which the restriction of a quantifier forms the scope for another quantifier, although there is no corresponding syntactic unit at the f-structure level:

(11)   Every friend of a clergyman arrived.

One reading of this sentence is:

(12) $every(\lambda x.a(clergyman, \lambda y.friend\text{-}of(x, y)),$
               $\lambda x.arrived(x))$

An abbreviated f-structure for this sentence is:

(13)
$$
\begin{bmatrix}
\text{PRED} & \text{`ARRIVED'} \\
\text{SUBJ} & \begin{bmatrix}
\text{SPEC} & \text{`EVERY'} \\
\text{PRED} & \text{`FRIEND'} \\
\text{OBL}_{\text{OF}} & \begin{bmatrix}
\text{SPEC} & \text{`A'} \\
\text{PRED} & \text{`CLERGYMAN'}
\end{bmatrix}
\end{bmatrix}
\end{bmatrix}
$$

In this example, there is no f-structure that corresponds to the scope of *a clergyman*. It is thus necessary to assume a more finely structured representation to allow for all possible quantifier scopes.

Fenstad et al. (1987) sidestep this issue by specifying scope purely at the level of semantic representation. In their account, possible scopes of quantification are "abstracts" obtained from situation-theoretic fact schemas created during interpretation by abstracting over appropriate indeterminates. Additional restrictions may be imposed on possible scopes by the QMODE feature that gives instructions for the order in which the scopes of different quantifiers are computed, but Fenstad et al. do not specify precisely how QMODE itself is obtained.

Halvorsen and Kaplan (1988) provide the most detailed account of possible scopes in an LFG framework. They use *inside-out functional uncertainty* to choose nondeterministically among possible scope semantic structures for quantified noun phrases. Inside-out functional uncertainty allows for an f-structure or semantic structure to refer to larger structures that contain it. Halvorsen and Kaplan propose that the scope of a quantifier is determined by an expression involving inside-out functional uncertainty, anchored at the semantic structure for the quantifier, which chooses a containing semantic structure as the scope of the quantifier.

Halvorsen and Kaplan's approach, like ours, avoids the problems noted above with approaches that define quantifier scopes purely at the f-structure level. They also ensure correctly that the scope for a particular quantified NP contains the argument position filled by the NP. However, those results are obtained by stipulation: there is no connection between their constraints on scope and the composition principles for quantifier meanings. In contrast, our analysis satisfies the same constraint on scope simply as a consequence of the logical form of quantified NP meaning constructors. Recall the form of those constructors:

(14) **every-voter**: $\forall S.\ (\forall x.\ f_\sigma \leadsto x \multimap scope \leadsto S(x))$
$$\multimap scope \leadsto every(voter, S)$$

To prove $f_\sigma \leadsto x \multimap scope \leadsto S(x)$, $f_\sigma \leadsto x$ must be completely consumed in the production of $scope \leadsto S(x)$. Thus, no other reference to x will remain, and x can only occur in $scope \leadsto S(x)$. That is, the fact that the scope of a quantified NP includes the argument position filled by the NP is inherent in the form of the meaning contribution for the NP and requires no separate stipulation. This argument is presented more generally in Section 3.1.

2.5.2 Well-formedness constraints on scope

Pereira (1990, 1991) argues that previous accounts of the possible scopings of sentences with multiple quantified NPs, starting with Cooper storage, did not correctly capture the constraints on possible scopings arising from interactions between scope and bound anaphora. Those problems, which we will discuss in more detail later, typically manifest themselves at the semantic representation level as ill-formed representations in which occurrences of a variable (or indeterminate) are left outside the scope of their binding (or abstraction) operator. None of the previous proposals for semantic interpretation in LFG fully addresses this difficulty.

Fenstad et al. (1987) discuss both the interpretation of bound anaphora and of quantified NPs, but they do not analyze how their proposed representation of bound anaphora with multiple occurrences of a given indeterminate would interact with the inductive definition of quantifier interpretation and the scoping choices allowed in the QMODE feature. Their inductive definition assumes that the indeterminate IND.*i* associated with a quantified noun phrase does not occur outside the scope of quantification, but that cannot be guaranteed in the presence of bound anaphora without further constraints on QMODE. They do refer to the work of Gawron and Peters (1990) for a more detailed situation-theoretic account of bound anaphora. However, Gawron and Peters do not solve the problem in general, but only in the case of interactions between generalized quantifiers and (unscoped) singular terms.

The other proposals (Halvorsen 1983; Reyle 1988; Halvorsen and Kaplan 1988) do not consider bound anaphora, and none of their analyses address the problem under discussion.

Our approach, on the other hand, guarantees the well-formedness of interpretations (see Section 3) as a by-product of the shape of the semantic contributions for quantified NPs and pronouns. No separate well-formedness constraint is needed.

2.5.3   Linguistic constraints on scope

It has been argued that syntax can constrain the choice of possible scopes, if scope islands can be induced by particular syntactic configurations. Those putative constraints have also been used indirectly to block some of the ill-formed interpretations just discussed. For example, Rodman (1976) argues, based on examples such as (15), that relative clauses are always scope islands—that is, that quantifiers inside a relative clause may not scope outside that relative clause:

(15)   *Guinevere has a bone that is in every corner of the house.

According to an argument such as Rodman's, possible values for *scope* are constrained in syntactic terms: only values for *scope* that are inside the relative clause can be chosen. It would be possible to ensure a constraint such as this in a manner similar to the one presented by Halvorsen and Kaplan (1988): only semantic structures or their substructures that correspond to relative-clause-internal f-structures would be possible scopes. To state the constraint another way, a relative clause boundary could not be crossed between a quantifier and its *scope* structure. This kind of constraint is easily stated by means of inside-out functional uncertainty together with *off-path constraints*.[4]

However, a number of counterexamples have been presented to the argument that relative clauses are scope islands. For instance, Cooper (1979) gives this example, attributing it to Stanley Peters:

(16)   The man who builds each television set also repairs it.

---

[4]See Dalrymple (1993) for definition and discussion of off-path constraints and functional uncertainty.

In fact, while syntactic effects may play a significant role in scope preferences, most claims of scope islands are defeasible given appropriate choices of lexical items and context. Therefore, we will not place syntactic restrictions on the possible scopes a quantifier can take, but instead we will take as possible quantifier scopes all semantic projections for which a meaning of proposition type can be derived.

2.5.4 Determining scope

Assuming that any semantic structure of the proper semantic type is a possible scope for a quantifier, the meaning constructor for an NP should quantify universally over possible scopes, as follows:

(17) **every-voter**:

$$\forall H, S.\ (\forall x.\ f_\sigma \rightsquigarrow x \multimap H \rightsquigarrow S(x))\ \multimap H \rightsquigarrow every(voter, S)$$

We are led, then, to the following general meaning constructor for a determiner with meaning Q:

(18)   Meaning constructor for determiners:

$$\forall H, R, S.$$

$(\forall x.\ (\uparrow_\sigma \text{ VAR}) \rightsquigarrow x$	$\begin{cases} \text{if, by assuming an arbitrary} \\ \text{meaning } x \text{ for } (\uparrow_\sigma \text{ VAR}), \end{cases}$
$\multimap (\uparrow_\sigma \text{ RESTR}) \rightsquigarrow R(x))$	$\begin{cases} \text{a meaning } R(x) \text{ for } (\uparrow_\sigma \\ \text{RESTR}) \text{ can be derived,} \end{cases}$
$\otimes (\forall x.\ \uparrow_\sigma \rightsquigarrow x$	$\begin{cases} \text{and, by assuming an arbitrary} \\ \text{meaning } x \text{ for } \uparrow, \end{cases}$
$\multimap H \rightsquigarrow_t S(x))$	$\begin{cases} \text{a meaning } S(x) \text{ for some} \\ \text{scope } H \text{ can be derived,} \end{cases}$
$\multimap H \rightsquigarrow_t Q(R, S)$	$\begin{cases} \text{then we can derive a possible} \\ \text{complete meaning for } H \end{cases}$

where H ranges over semantic structures associated with meanings of type t.

Thus, the meaning constructor of an occurrence of *every* in f-structure f is:

$$\forall H, R, S.\ (\forall x.\ (f_\sigma\ \text{VAR})\rightsquigarrow x \multimap (f_\sigma\ \text{RESTR})\rightsquigarrow R(x))$$
$$\otimes\ (\forall x.\ f_\sigma\rightsquigarrow x \multimap H\rightsquigarrow S(x))$$
$$\multimap\ H\rightsquigarrow every(R, S)$$

and the meaning constructor of *every voter* is:

$$\forall H, S.\ (\forall x.\ f_\sigma\rightsquigarrow x \multimap H\rightsquigarrow S(x))\ \multimap\ H\rightsquigarrow every(voter, S)$$

Note that the VAR and RESTR components of the semantic projection for a quantified NP in our analysis play a similar role to the $/\!/$ category constructor in PTQ (Montague 1974), that of distinguishing syntactic configurations with identical semantic types but different contributions to the interpretation. The two PTQ syntactic categories t/e for intransitive verb phrases and $t/\!/e$ for common noun phrases correspond to the single semantic type $e\rightarrow t$; similarly, the two conjuncts in the antecedent of (18) correspond to the same semantic type, encoded with a linear implication, but to two different syntactic contexts, one relating the predication of an NP to its implicit argument and one relating a clause to an embedded argument.

2.6   Simple example of quantification

Before we look at quantifier scope ambiguity and interactions between scope and bound anaphora, we demonstrate the basic operation of our proposed meaning constructor for quantified NPs with a singly quantified, unambiguous sentence:

(19)   Sam convinced every voter.

We assume the analysis of transitive verbs and of simple noun phrases like *Sam* that was presented in Chapter 1. To carry out the analysis, we need a lexical entry for *convinced*:

(20)   convinced   V $(\uparrow \text{PRED})=\,$'CONVINCE'
$$\forall X, Y.\ (\uparrow \text{SUBJ})_\sigma\rightsquigarrow X\otimes(\uparrow \text{OBJ})_\sigma\rightsquigarrow Y$$
$$\multimap\ \uparrow_\sigma\rightsquigarrow convince(X, Y)$$

According to the meaning constructor in this lexical entry, *convince* consumes the meaning X of its subject and the meaning Y of its object to produce the meaning $convince(X, Y)$ for the f-structure it heads. The f-structure for (19) is:

$$(21) \quad f{:} \begin{bmatrix} \text{PRED} & \text{'CONVINCE'} \\ \text{SUBJ} & g{:}\begin{bmatrix} \text{PRED} & \text{'SAM'} \end{bmatrix} \\ \text{OBJ} & h{:}\begin{bmatrix} \text{SPEC} & \text{'EVERY'} \\ \text{PRED} & \text{'VOTER'} \end{bmatrix} \end{bmatrix}$$

The premises for the derivation are appropriately instantiated meaning constructors for *Sam* and *convinced* together with the instantiated meaning constructor derived earlier for the quantified NP *every voter*:

sam: $\qquad g_\sigma \rightsquigarrow Sam$

convinced: $\quad \forall X, Y.\ g_\sigma \rightsquigarrow X \otimes h_\sigma \rightsquigarrow Y \multimap f_\sigma \rightsquigarrow convince(X, Y)$

every-voter: $\quad \forall H, S.\ (\forall x.\ h_\sigma \rightsquigarrow x \multimap H \rightsquigarrow_t S(x))$
$$\multimap H \rightsquigarrow_t every(voter, S)$$

From **sam** and **convinced**, we can deduce

sam-convinced: $\quad \forall Y.\ h_\sigma \rightsquigarrow Y \multimap f_\sigma \rightsquigarrow convince(Sam, Y)$

This has exactly the form required for the antecedent of **every-voter**, where H is f_σ and S is $\lambda z.convince(Sam, z)$, so we can now derive:

$$f_\sigma \rightsquigarrow every(voter, \lambda z.convince(Sam, z))$$

Keeping track of the consumption of formulas, we have:

	sam⊗**convinced**⊗**every-voter**	(Premises)
⊢	**sam-convinced**⊗**every-voter**	$X \mapsto Sam$
⊢	$f_\sigma \rightsquigarrow every(voter, \lambda z.convince(Sam, z))$	$H \mapsto f_\sigma, Y \mapsto x$
		$S \mapsto \lambda z.convince(Sam, z)$

No derivation of a different formula $f_\sigma \rightsquigarrow_t P$ is possible. The formula **sam-convinced** represents the semantics of the scope of the determiner *every*. The derivable formula

$$\forall Y.\ h_\sigma \rightsquigarrow_e Y \multimap h_\sigma \rightsquigarrow_e Y$$

could at first sight be considered another possible, but erroneous, scope. However, the type subscripting of the $\rightsquigarrow$ relation used in the determiner lexical entry requires the scope to represent a dependency of a proposition on an individual, while this formula represents the dependency of an individual on itself. Therefore, it does not provide a valid scope for the quantifier.

2.7 Quantifier scope ambiguities

When a sentence contains more than one quantifier, scope ambiguities are of course possible. In our system, those ambiguities will appear as alternative successful derivations. We will take as our example this sentence:[5]

(22)   Every candidate appointed a manager.

We need the following additional lexical entries:

(23)   *a* $(\uparrow \text{SPEC}) = \text{'A'}$
$$\forall H, R, S.\ (\forall x.\ (\uparrow_\sigma \text{VAR}) \rightsquigarrow x \multimap (\uparrow_\sigma \text{RESTR}) \rightsquigarrow R(x))$$
$$\otimes\ (\forall x.\ \uparrow_\sigma \rightsquigarrow x \multimap H \rightsquigarrow S(x))$$
$$\multimap\ H \rightsquigarrow a(R, S)$$

(24)   *candidate* $(\uparrow \text{PRED}) = \text{'CANDIDATE'}$
$$\forall X.\ (\uparrow_\sigma \text{VAR}) \rightsquigarrow X \multimap (\uparrow_\sigma \text{RESTR}) \rightsquigarrow candidate(X)$$

(25)   *manager* $(\uparrow \text{PRED}) = \text{'MANAGER'}$
$$\forall X.\ (\uparrow_\sigma \text{VAR}) \rightsquigarrow X \multimap (\uparrow_\sigma \text{RESTR}) \rightsquigarrow manager(X)$$

The f-structure for sentence (22) is:

(26)
$$f:\begin{bmatrix} \text{PRED} & \text{'APPOINT'} \\ \text{SUBJ} & g:\begin{bmatrix} \text{SPEC} & \text{'EVERY'} \\ \text{PRED} & \text{'CANDIDATE'} \end{bmatrix} \\ \text{OBJ} & h:\begin{bmatrix} \text{SPEC} & \text{'A'} \\ \text{PRED} & \text{'MANAGER'} \end{bmatrix} \end{bmatrix}$$

We can derive meaning constructors for *every candidate* and *a manager* in the way shown in Section 2.3. Further derivations proceed from those

---

[5]To allow for apparent scope ambiguities, we adopt a scoping analysis of indefinites, as proposed, for example, by Neale (1990).

contributions together with the contribution of *appointed*:

every-candidate: $\quad \forall G, R.\ (\forall x.\ g_\sigma \rightsquigarrow x \multimap G \rightsquigarrow R(x))$
$$\multimap G \rightsquigarrow every(candidate, R)$$

a-manager: $\quad \forall H, S.\ (\forall y.\ h_\sigma \rightsquigarrow y \multimap H \rightsquigarrow S(y))$
$$\multimap H \rightsquigarrow a(manager, S)$$

appointed: $\quad \forall X, Y.\ g_\sigma \rightsquigarrow X \otimes h_\sigma \rightsquigarrow Y \multimap f_\sigma \rightsquigarrow appoint(X, Y)$

So far, we have not made any commitment about the scopes of the quantifiers; the scope semantic structure and scope meaning variables in **every-candidate** and **a-manager** have not been instantiated.

Scope ambiguities are manifested in two different ways in our system: through the choice of different semantic structures G and H, corresponding to different scopes for the quantified NPs, or through different relative orders of application for quantifiers that scope at the same point. For this example, the second case is relevant, and we must now make a choice to proceed. The two possible choices correspond to two equivalent rewritings of **appointed**:

appointed$_1$: $\quad \forall X.\ g_\sigma \rightsquigarrow X \multimap (\forall Y.\ h_\sigma \rightsquigarrow Y \multimap f_\sigma \rightsquigarrow appoint(X, Y))$
appointed$_2$: $\quad \forall Y.\ h_\sigma \rightsquigarrow Y \multimap (\forall X.\ g_\sigma \rightsquigarrow X \multimap f_\sigma \rightsquigarrow appoint(X, Y))$

These two equivalent forms correspond to the two possible ways of "currying" a two-argument function $f : \alpha \times \beta \rightarrow \gamma$ as a one-argument function:

$$\lambda u.\lambda v.f(u, v) : \alpha \rightarrow (\beta \rightarrow \gamma)$$

$$\lambda v.\lambda u.f(u, v) : \beta \rightarrow (\alpha \rightarrow \gamma)$$

We select *a manager* to take narrower scope by using the variable instantiations

$$H \mapsto f_\sigma, Y \mapsto y, S \mapsto \lambda v.appoint(X, v)$$

and transitivity of implication to combine **appointed**$_1$ with **a-manager** into:

appointed-a-manager:
$$\forall X.\ g_\sigma \rightsquigarrow X \multimap f_\sigma \rightsquigarrow_t a(manager, \lambda v.appoint(X, v))$$

This is now in a form suitable to satisfy the antecedent of **every-candidate**. We thus have the derivation

$$\textbf{every-candidate} \otimes \textbf{appointed}_1 \otimes \textbf{a-manager}$$
$$\vdash \quad \textbf{every-candidate} \otimes \textbf{appointed-a-manager}$$
$$\vdash \quad f_\sigma \leadsto_t every(candidate, \lambda u.a(manager, \lambda v.appoint(u, v)))$$

of the $\forall\exists$ reading of (22), where the last step uses the substitutions

$$G \mapsto f_\sigma, X \mapsto x, R \mapsto \lambda u.a(manager, \lambda v.appoint(u, v))$$

Alternatively, we could have chosen *every candidate* to take narrow scope, by combining **appointed**$_2$ with **every-candidate** to produce:

$$\textbf{every-candidate-appointed:}$$
$$\forall Y.\, h_\sigma \leadsto Y \multimap f_\sigma \leadsto_t every(candidate, \lambda u.appoint(u, Y))$$

with the variable substitutions

$$G \mapsto f_\sigma, X \mapsto x, R \mapsto \lambda u.appoint(u, Y)$$

This gives the derivation

$$\textbf{every-candidate} \otimes \textbf{appointed}_2 \otimes \textbf{a-manager}$$
$$\vdash \quad \textbf{every-candidate-appointed} \otimes \textbf{a-manager}$$
$$\vdash \quad f_\sigma \leadsto_t a(manager, \lambda v.every(candidate, \lambda u.appoint(u, v)))$$

for the $\exists\forall$ reading, where the last step uses the substitutions

$$H \mapsto f_\sigma, Y \mapsto y, S \mapsto \lambda v.every(candidate, \lambda u.appoint(u, v))$$

These are the only two possible outcomes of the derivation of a meaning for (22), as required.

2.8   Constraints on quantifier scoping

Sentence (27) contains two quantifiers and therefore might be expected to show a two-way ambiguity analogous to the one described in the previous section:

(27)   Every candidate dismissed a rumor about himself.

However, no such ambiguity is found, since the reflexive pronoun *himself* corefers with the subject *every candidate*. Only one reading is available, in which *a rumor about himself* takes narrow scope. Intuitively, this NP may not take wider scope than the quantifier *every candidate*, on which its restriction depends.

As we will soon see, the lack of a wide scope *a* reading follows without further stipulation from the form of meaning constructors for quantified NPs and pronouns. In Pereira's earlier work on deductive interpretation (Pereira 1990, 1991), the same result was achieved through constraints on the relative scopes of glue-level universal quantifiers representing the dependencies between meanings of clauses and the meanings of their arguments. Here, although universal quantifiers are used to support the extraction of properties representing the meanings of the restriction and scope (the variables R and S in the meaning constructors for determiners), the blocking of the unwanted reading follows from the propositional structure of the glue formulas, specifically the nested linear implications. This is more satisfactory, since it does not reduce the problem of proper quantifier scoping in the object language to the same problem in the metalanguage.

The f-structure for example (27) is:

$$(28) \quad f: \begin{bmatrix} \text{PRED} & \text{`DISMISSED'} \\ \text{SUBJ} & g: \begin{bmatrix} \text{SPEC} & \text{`EVERY'} \\ \text{PRED} & \text{`CANDIDATE'} \end{bmatrix} \\ \text{OBJ} & h: \begin{bmatrix} \text{SPEC} & \text{`A'} \\ \text{PRED} & \text{`RUMOR'} \\ \text{OBL}_{\text{ABOUT}} & i: [\text{PRED} \quad \text{`PRO'}] \end{bmatrix} \end{bmatrix}$$

We assume that *rumor* is a relational noun taking as its oblique argument a phrase with prepositional marker *about*, as indicated in the f-structure by the attribute $\text{OBL}_{\text{ABOUT}}$.

The meaning constructor for a relational noun has, as expected, the same propositional form as the binary relation type $e \times e \rightarrow t$: one argument represents the rumor itself, and the other represents what the rumor is about. The lexical entry for *rumor* is:

(29) rumor   N $(\uparrow \text{PRED}) = \text{'RUMOR'}$
$$\forall Z, X.\ (\uparrow_\sigma \text{VAR}) \rightsquigarrow Z \otimes (\uparrow \text{OBL}_{\text{ABOUT}})_\sigma \rightsquigarrow X$$
$$\multimap (\uparrow_\sigma \text{RESTR}) \rightsquigarrow \textit{rumor-about}(Z, X)$$

Given the f-structure in (28), the meaning constructor for *rumor* is:

(30) **rumor:** $\forall Z, X.\ (h_\sigma \text{VAR}) \rightsquigarrow Z \otimes i_\sigma \rightsquigarrow X$
$$\multimap (h_\sigma \text{RESTR}) \rightsquigarrow \textit{rumor-about}(Z, X)$$

2.8.1   Relationship between pronoun and antecedent

We now turn to a discussion of the syntactic and semantic contributions of the pronoun *himself*. Dalrymple (1993) provides a detailed discussion of the syntax of anaphoric binding in an LFG framework. We will not recapitulate that discussion in full; here we will provide only a sketch of the necessary background assumptions about the relation between a pronoun and its antecedent, and concentrate more fully on the semantic contribution of pronouns.

We assume that potential antecedents for pronouns like *himself*, *him*, and *his* are provided by a component incorporating discourse-relevant notions of salience, topichood, and focus. Different pronouns may place different syntactic requirements on where their antecedent can appear, and so at the f-structure level, the syntactic relation between the pronoun and its potential antecedent is checked for well-formedness. For example, the reflexive pronoun *himself* requires an antecedent that is relatively local, so that *Sam* is a syntactically acceptable antecedent for *himself* in (31a) but not in (31b):

(31) a. Sam_i saw himself_i in the mirror.

    b.   *Sam_i said that Terry saw himself_i in the mirror.

Conversely, the pronominal *him* does not permit a local antecedent, but allows a nonlocal one:

(32) a.   *Sam_i saw him_i in the mirror.

    b. Sam_i said that Terry saw him_i in the mirror.

Syntactic constraints on coreference relations also rule out examples such as:

(33)   *He$_i$ saw every man$_i$.

Coreference between nonpronouns such as *every man* and pronouns such as *he* is forbidden if the pronoun *f-commands* the nonpronoun.[6] In sum, an antecedent for a pronoun must not only be acceptable in terms of discourse structure, topicality, and salience, but must also conform to f-structural syntactic constraints on the pronoun-antecedent relation.

In the following, we assume that pronominal antecedents have been determined with respect to constraints on the structure of the discourse and coreference relations, and that the antecedent-pronoun relation obeys the syntactic constraints imposed by the particular pronoun used. That analysis is expressed in LFG by means of a variety of devices, including in particular inside-out functional uncertainty (Halvorsen and Kaplan 1988; Dalrymple 1993). Since we are not concerned with the details of that analysis here, we will assume that its results have been recorded explicitly in the semantic structure as follows: if the noun phrase with f-structure f is the licensed antecedent of the pronoun with f-structure g, then $(g_\sigma \text{ ANT}) = f_\sigma$. In case of anaphoric binding ambiguity, we assume that each consistent assignment of antecedent relations yields an alternative input to the semantic interpretation process, from which possible alternative semantic derivations are generated.

Our task, then, is to map the antecedent relations expressed in the semantic structure to constraints between meaning contributions in the glue language. The present analysis applies only to intrasentential anaphora, although at the end of this section we will suggest ways in which it might be modified to handle intersentential anaphora too.

2.8.2   Meaning constructors for pronouns

The meaning constructor for the reflexive pronoun *himself* or any other pronoun simply copies the meaning of the pronoun's antecedent as the meaning of the pronoun. This is accomplished in linear logic by a formula that consumes the meaning assignment for the antecedent and

---

[6]Bresnan (1982) defines f-command as a relation between f-structures analogous to the c-command relation that holds between nodes of a c-structure tree: for any functions GF1, GF2 in an f-structure, GF1 f-commands GF2 iff GF1 does not contain GF2 and every f-structure that contains GF1 contains GF2. See Dalrymple (1993) for further discussion.

simultaneously outputs the just-consumed assignment and an assignment of the consumed meaning to the pronoun's own semantic projection:

(34)   himself   N $(\uparrow \text{PRED}) = {}$'PRO'

$$\forall X. (\uparrow_\sigma \text{ANT}) \rightsquigarrow X \multimap ((\uparrow_\sigma \text{ANT}) \rightsquigarrow X \otimes \uparrow_\sigma \rightsquigarrow X)$$

We will begin by illustrating the derivation of the meaning of *a rumor about himself*, assuming that the antecedent of *himself* is *every candidate*. We also assume that in this case *about* makes no contribution to the meaning of the sentence, serving only to mark the prepositional case required for the argument of *rumor*. Therefore, we begin from the following premises:

a:$\qquad \forall H, R, S. (\forall x. (h_\sigma \text{VAR}) \rightsquigarrow x \multimap (h_\sigma \text{RESTR}) \rightsquigarrow R(x))$

$\qquad\qquad \otimes (\forall x. h_\sigma \rightsquigarrow x \multimap H \rightsquigarrow S(x))$

$\qquad\qquad \multimap H \rightsquigarrow a(R, S)$

rumor:$\qquad \forall Z, X. (h_\sigma \text{VAR}) \rightsquigarrow Z \otimes i_\sigma \rightsquigarrow X$

$\qquad\qquad \multimap (h_\sigma \text{RESTR}) \rightsquigarrow \textit{rumor-about}(Z, X)$

himself:$\qquad \forall X. g_\sigma \rightsquigarrow X \multimap g_\sigma \rightsquigarrow X \otimes i_\sigma \rightsquigarrow X$

First, we rewrite **rumor** into the equivalent form

rumor′:

$\forall X. i_\sigma \rightsquigarrow X \multimap$

$\qquad (\forall Z. (h_\sigma \text{VAR}) \rightsquigarrow Z \multimap (h_\sigma \text{RESTR}) \rightsquigarrow \textit{rumor-about}(Z, X))$

Noticing that the antecedent of **rumor′** now exactly matches the second conjunct in the consequent of **himself**, we can combine these two premises to yield:

rumor-about-himself:

$\forall X. g_\sigma \rightsquigarrow X \multimap$

$\qquad g_\sigma \rightsquigarrow X \otimes$

$\qquad (\forall Z. (h_\sigma \text{VAR}) \rightsquigarrow Z \multimap (h_\sigma \text{RESTR}) \rightsquigarrow \textit{rumor-about}(Z, X))$

In turn, the second conjunct in the consequent of **rumor-about-himself** matches the first conjunct in the antecedent of **a**, allowing us to derive

a-rumor-about-himself:
$$\forall X.\; g_\sigma \rightsquigarrow X \multimap$$
$$g_\sigma \rightsquigarrow X \otimes (\forall H, S.\; (\forall x.\; h_\sigma \rightsquigarrow x \multimap H \rightsquigarrow S(x)) \multimap$$
$$H \rightsquigarrow a(\lambda z.rumor\text{-}about(z, X), S))$$

with variable instantiations:

$$Z \mapsto x, R \mapsto \lambda x.rumor\text{-}about(z, X)$$

At this point the other formulas available are:

every-candidate:
$$\forall H, S.\; (\forall x.\; g_\sigma \rightsquigarrow x \multimap H \rightsquigarrow S(x))$$
$$\multimap H \rightsquigarrow every(candidate, S)$$

dismissed:
$$\forall Z, Y.\; g_\sigma \rightsquigarrow Z \otimes h_\sigma \rightsquigarrow Y \multimap f_\sigma \rightsquigarrow dismiss(Z, Y)$$

How can we proceed from here? The antecedent implication of **every-candidate** has an atomic conclusion and hence cannot be satisfied by **a-rumor-about-himself**, which has a conjunctive conclusion. Therefore, the only possible move is to combine **dismissed** and **a-rumor-about-himself**. We do this by first putting **dismissed** in the equivalent form

dismissed': $\forall Z.\; g_\sigma \rightsquigarrow Z \multimap (\forall Y.\; h_\sigma \rightsquigarrow Y \multimap f_\sigma \rightsquigarrow dismiss(Z, Y))$

We now can combine **dismissed'** with the first conjunct in the consequent of **a-rumor-about-himself**, substituting X for Z, to derive

dismissed-a-rumor-about-himself:
$$\forall X.\; g_\sigma \rightsquigarrow X \multimap$$
$$(\forall Y.\; h_\sigma \rightsquigarrow Y \multimap f_\sigma \rightsquigarrow dismiss(X, Y)) \otimes$$
$$(\forall H, S.\; (\forall x.\; h_\sigma \rightsquigarrow x \multimap H \rightsquigarrow S)$$
$$\multimap H \rightsquigarrow a(\lambda z.rumor\text{-}about(z, X), S))$$

Applying the substitutions

$$Y \mapsto x, H \mapsto f_\sigma, S \mapsto \lambda z.dismiss(X, z)$$

and modus ponens with the two conjuncts in the consequent as premises, we obtain

dismissed-a-rumor-about-himself$'$:

$$\forall X.\ g_\sigma \rightsquigarrow X \multimap f_\sigma \rightsquigarrow_t a(\lambda z.rumor\text{-}about(z, X), \lambda z.dismiss(X, z))$$

Finally, this formula can be combined with **every-candidate** to give the meaning of the whole sentence:

$$f_\sigma \rightsquigarrow_t every(candidate, \lambda w.a(\lambda z.rumor\text{-}about(z, w), \lambda z.dismiss(w, z)))$$

As we will show in the next section, this is the only derivable scoping; that is, our analysis blocks those putative scopings in which variables occur outside the scope of their binders.

Our pronoun meaning constructor assumes that the antecedent meaning assignment is available as a resource to be copied and duplicated when the pronoun is interpreted. However, that assumption seems difficult to maintain for intersentential anaphora. If we accept even a mild form of incremental interpretation requiring that the meanings of whole sentences be computed independently of the sentences that follow them in the discourse, the semantic resources internal to the sentence containing the antecedent will have been consumed in the derivation of a meaning for that sentence before the sentence containing the pronominal reference is interpreted. Thus the input required by the pronoun meaning constructor would not be available.

A possible solution for the problem is to change the semantic constructors of potential antecedents and of pronouns so that the copying associated with coreference is specified by the antecedent rather than by the pronoun. That is, an antecedent supplies a "reusable" resource that pronouns consume as necessary, similarly to how discourse markers in DRT are available for reference by referring expressions. We can accomplish this in our framework with the "!" (*of course*) connective of linear logic, which marks a formula as usable any number of times in a derivation (See the proof rules for ! in Chapter 1, Figure 1.5). The meaning constructors for NPs would be changed to supply a reusable referential resource. For instance, the meaning constructor for the proper noun *Sam* would be:

$$\uparrow_\sigma \rightsquigarrow Sam \otimes\ !(\uparrow_\sigma \rightsquigarrow Sam)$$

and the constructor for the quantified NP *every candidate* would be:

$$\forall H, S.\ (\forall x.\ \uparrow_\sigma \rightsquigarrow x\ \otimes\ !(\uparrow_\sigma \rightsquigarrow x)\ \multimap\ H \rightsquigarrow S(x))\ \multimap$$
$$H \rightsquigarrow every(candidate, S)$$

The new constructor for the proper noun supplies as many copies of $\uparrow_\sigma \rightsquigarrow Sam$ as required by the derivation. In a similar way, the quantified NP constructor makes available as many copies of $\uparrow_\sigma \rightsquigarrow x$ as necessary to derive $H \rightsquigarrow S(x)$. However, none of those copies can "leak out" from the inner implication because the proof rule for linear implication (given as right $\multimap$ in the proof rules in Chapter 1, Figure 1.5) requires that all of the antecedent of the implication be consumed in the proof of the consequent. In particular, any remaining copies of $!(\uparrow_\sigma \rightsquigarrow x)$ would have to be mopped up by the ! weakening rule for the derivation to go through. Thus the inner implication establishes the scope for the referential resource supplied by the quantified NP.

To complete the alternative analysis, we need the constructor for pronouns, which now is simply:

$$\forall X.\ (\uparrow_\sigma\ \text{ANT}) \rightsquigarrow X\ \multimap\ \uparrow_\sigma \rightsquigarrow X$$

For a simple example of how the alternative constructors would be used, consider the discourse

(35)   Sam won. He appointed Terry.

with sentence f-structures

(36)
$$f: \begin{bmatrix} \text{PRED} & \text{'WIN'} \\ \text{SUBJ} & g: \begin{bmatrix} \text{PRED} & \text{'SAM'} \end{bmatrix} \end{bmatrix} \quad h: \begin{bmatrix} \text{PRED} & \text{'APPOINT'} \\ \text{SUBJ} & i: \begin{bmatrix} \text{PRED} & \text{'PRO'} \end{bmatrix} \\ \text{OBJ} & j: \begin{bmatrix} \text{PRED} & \text{'TERRY'} \end{bmatrix} \end{bmatrix}$$

and antecedent relation $(i_\sigma\ \text{ANT}) = g_\sigma$. These f-structures provide the following semantic contributions:

sam':	$g_\sigma \rightsquigarrow Sam\ \otimes\ !(g_\sigma \rightsquigarrow Sam)$
won:	$\forall X.\ g_\sigma \rightsquigarrow X\ \multimap\ f_\sigma \rightsquigarrow win(X)$
he':	$\forall X.\ g_\sigma \rightsquigarrow X\ \multimap\ i_\sigma \rightsquigarrow X$
terry':	$j_\sigma \rightsquigarrow Terry\ \otimes\ !(j_\sigma \rightsquigarrow Terry)$
appointed:	$\forall X, Y.\ i_\sigma \rightsquigarrow X \otimes j_\sigma \rightsquigarrow Y\ \multimap\ f_\sigma \rightsquigarrow appoint(X, Y)$

Following earlier derivations, from **sam$'$** and **won** we can obtain

$$\textbf{sam-won}' : f_\sigma \rightsquigarrow win(Sam) \otimes \,!(g_\sigma \rightsquigarrow Sam)$$

Thus **sam-won$'$** provides both the completed meaning for the first sentence and the reusable referential resource for *Sam* that pronouns may refer to. From **sam-won$'$**, the dereliction proof rule for ! allows us to conclude:

$$f_\sigma \rightsquigarrow win(Sam) \otimes g_\sigma \rightsquigarrow Sam$$

which can then be combined with **he$'$** to yield:

$$\textbf{sam-won-he}: f_\sigma \rightsquigarrow win(Sam) \otimes i_\sigma \rightsquigarrow Sam$$

The weakening proof rule for ! allows us to delete a reusable resource and thus derive from **terry$'$**:

$$\textbf{terry}: j_\sigma \rightsquigarrow Terry$$

From this, **sam-won-he** and **appointed** we can finally derive by already familiar means the interpretation for the whole discourse:

$$f_\sigma \rightsquigarrow win(Sam) \otimes$$
$$g_\sigma \rightsquigarrow appoint(Sam, Terry)$$

As seen from the example, this alternative analysis of anaphoric binding captures basic aspects of intersentential anaphora. However, there are questions as to whether it will interact correctly with earlier work on the interpretation of modification and complex predicates (Dalrymple, Lamping, and Saraswat 1993; Dalrymple, Hinrichs, Lamping, and Saraswat 1993). Specifically, the alternative approach requires that any potential antecedent provide an explicit reusable referential resource for binding coreferential expressions. However, if antecedents can be modified, the reusable resource may not reflect all the effects of modification.

The problem may be circumvented by basing the reusable resource on a bound variable (as it is in quantified NPs) which is restricted as appropriate by the (potentially modified) antecedent. In this case, such scopes must be managed across sentence boundaries in a way reminiscent of the scope extrusion effects of dynamic predicate logic (Groenendijk and Stokhof 1991). Such an approach is developed in detail by Crouch and van Genabith in Chapter 4 of this volume, and as they show, their proposal can profitably be integrated with the approach to quantifiers presented here. In the following discussion, for simplicity, we will continue to use our original analysis of the semantic contributions of antecedents and pronouns.

3   Adequacy

Although there is no independent rigorous characterization of possible scopes, we can justify two important properties that seem to be required in any formal account of semantic compositionality. First, we show that our analysis automatically enforces the "free-variable constraint" of Pereira (1990): the scopes of quantified NPs are constrained to respect anaphoric dependencies among them. That is the property illustrated in the preceding section. Second, we show that the meaning terms derived in our analysis are built exclusively from meaning terms in the lexical entries, and cannot contain arbitrary extraneous material.

A further question that deserves investigation is the computational complexity of our interpretation method. While it is possible to encode $\mathcal{NP}$-hard problems in even the propositional fragment of multiplicative linear logic (Kanovich 1992), the formulas we work with here have a restricted form, so the sources of intractability for the fragment may not always be manifest in semantic interpretation. Nevertheless, we should appreciate that a sentence with n quantified NPs may have on the order of $n!$ interpretations, so a reasonable analysis must consider not the cost of generating all interpretations but rather the cost per interpretation. Furthermore, scoping constraints may block candidate derivations as we showed earlier. Thus, the number of actual derivations may be much smaller than the naïvely possible scopings. Clearly, further analysis is required.

3.1   The Free-Variable Constraint

Anaphoric dependencies on a quantified NP meaning

$$\forall G, R. \ (\forall x. \ f_\sigma \rightsquigarrow x \ \multimap \ G \rightsquigarrow R(x)) \ \multimap \ G \rightsquigarrow q(R)$$

are expressed through a derivation using (a copy of) $f_\sigma \leadsto x$. Scope determination for the quantified NP must involve the following (schematic) sequent derivation:

$$\vdots$$

$$\frac{\Gamma', f_\sigma \leadsto x \vdash G \leadsto R(x)}{\Gamma' \vdash f_\sigma \leadsto x \multimap G \leadsto R(x)}$$

$$\vdots \qquad\qquad\qquad \vdots$$

$$\frac{\Gamma \vdash f_\sigma \leadsto x \multimap G \leadsto R(x) \qquad \Delta, G \leadsto q(R) \vdash A}{\Gamma, \Delta, (f_\sigma \leadsto x \multimap G \leadsto R(x)) \multimap G \leadsto q(R) \vdash A}$$

where Γ results from Γ' by the application of some left rules. Any formulas on the left side of the final sequent that depend on $f_\sigma \leadsto x$ must then be in Γ to have access to $f_\sigma \leadsto x$, and all their results must be consumed in the production of $G \leadsto R(x)$. In particular, any quantified NP meaning that depends on $f_\sigma \leadsto x$ must be scoped on the left subderivation, and the corresponding meaning term will be a subterm of R, that is, the dependent NP meaning must be outscoped by the NP meaning it depends on.

3.2   Non-generativeness of meanings

Using a sound logical foundation ensures that we cannot generate propositions that are ill-formed from the point of view of the logic. But there can be dubious results that are well-formed. Consider, in particular, the logically well formed assertion $\forall X.\ f_\sigma \leadsto X$, which says, roughly, "$f_\sigma$ can mean anything". From this we could infer any meaning for f_σ, a most undesirable situation.

We do not, in fact, generate such results. Our inferences never "make up" arbitrary meanings for semantic structures. As the example illustrates, this requires more than using a sound logic. It is also necessary to restrict the starting premises so that they do not lead to a problematic conclusion.

Our premises conform to such a standard. Informally, we never use premises such as

$$\forall X.\ f_\sigma \leadsto X$$

$$\forall X.\ f_\sigma \leadsto see(Sam, X)$$

$$\forall Y. \ \forall X. \ g_\sigma \rightsquigarrow Y \multimap f_\sigma \rightsquigarrow see(Y, X)$$

which can introduce an arbitrary term into the meaning. When our premises use quantification, it is always in a situation such as

$$\forall Y. \ \forall X. \ g_\sigma \rightsquigarrow Y \multimap h_\sigma \rightsquigarrow X \multimap f_\sigma \rightsquigarrow see(Y, X)$$

where if a quantified variable occurs in a position where a meaning is produced, it also occurs in a position where a meaning is consumed.

Informally, this means that the universally quantified variable is being used as a function parameter: determined by the antecedent of an implication and used in the consequent. This ensures that the only instantiations of quantified variables that can contribute to the ultimate production of a meaning will be ones that match the (presumably acceptable) meanings that are consumed.

To precisely describe the condition, including handling nested implications, we turn to a formal definition. Our strategy is to identify a syntactic property of the formulas used in glue derivations, which we call "okayness". This property excludes the kind of problematic formulas above, and is preserved across deductions in linear logic. In Chapter 7, Dalrymple, Gupta, Lamping, and Saraswat present a further development of this intuition.

The definition has two parts. We first define the notion of a free variable being used like a function parameter, and then we define an expression to be okay if all universally quantified variables are used like function parameters.

To define the notion of a free variable being used like a function parameter, we define, via structural induction, a function v from a linear-logic formula and a variable to a truth value.

$$v(P \otimes Q, V) = v(P, V) \wedge v(Q, V)$$
$$v(P \multimap Q, V) = v(P, V) \rightarrow v(Q, V)$$
$$v(\forall X. \ P, V) = \begin{cases} true & \text{if } X = V \\ v(P, V) & \text{otherwise} \end{cases}$$
$$v(a, V) = \begin{cases} true & \text{if } V \notin var(a) \\ false & \text{otherwise} \end{cases}$$

We say that a formula M is functional in a variable X if $v(M, X) = true$. For instance, note that $f_\sigma \rightsquigarrow X$ is not functional in X.

A formula is okay if it is functional for each bound variable that occurs in it. Formally:

$$o(P \otimes Q) = o(P) \wedge o(Q)$$
$$o(P \multimap Q) = o(P) \wedge o(Q)$$
$$o(\forall X.\ P) = v(P, X) \wedge o(P)$$
$$o(a) = true$$

Theorem 1 *Let $D_1, \ldots, D_n \vdash D$ be a valid linear logic sequent in our fragment, such that each of $D_1, \ldots, D_n$ is okay. Then D is okay.*

Proof sketch: The proof is by structural induction on the proof of $D_1, \ldots, D_n \vdash D$. The induction hypothesis is the stronger statement that if $D_1, \ldots, D_n \vdash D$ is a valid linear logic sequent such that each of $D_1, \ldots, D_n$ is okay then D is okay and is functional in X whenever each of $D_1, \ldots, D_n$ is functional in X.

By examination, each of the formulas used in this paper is okay. Therefore we get:

Corollary 2 *It is not the case that meanings of the form $\forall X.\ f_\sigma \rightsquigarrow t$, with t in normal form, and X free in t, can be derived from the premises provided by the lexical entries of this paper.*

Similar reasoning applies to constants. In general, the only constants appearing in $f_\sigma \rightsquigarrow t$, whether individual constants or relations, will be those that appear in the premises. The meaning is entirely assembled out of the premises; no part is made up.

4   Intensional Verbs

Following Montague (1974), the meaning of an intensional verb like *seek* takes an NP meaning intension as direct-object argument. Montague's method for assembling meanings by function application forces the meanings of all expressions of a given syntactic category to be raised to their lowest common semantic type. In particular, every transitive verb meaning, whether intensional or not, must take a quantified NP meaning intension as direct-object argument. In contrast, our approach (like that of Partee and Rooth (1983)) allows the semantic contributions

of verbs to be of as low a type as possible. Nonetheless, the uniformity of the translation process is preserved because any required type
changes are derivable within the glue language, along lines similar to
type change in the undirected Lambek calculus (van Benthem 1988).

We will not represent intensional types explicitly at the glue level, in
contrast to categorial treatments of intensionality such as the one proposed by Morrill (1990, 1994). Instead, meaning constructors will correspond to the appropriate extensional types. The Montagovian intension
and extension operators ˆ and ˘ will appear only in meaning terms, that
is, as the second argument of the meaning relation $\rightsquigarrow$. Thus, while
the meaning of *seek* has type $e\rightarrow(s\rightarrow((e\rightarrow t)\rightarrow t))\rightarrow t$, the corresponding
meaning constructor in (38) parallels the type $e\rightarrow((e\rightarrow t)\rightarrow t)\rightarrow t$.

Our implicit treatment of intensional types imposes certain constraints on the use of functional abstraction and application in meaning terms, since β-reduction is only valid over *intensionally closed* terms,
that is, if the free occurrences of the bound variable do not occur in
intensional contexts (Gamut 1991, page 131). As we will see, that constraint is verified by all the semantic terms in our meaning constructors.
Thus, in carrying out proofs we will be justified in solving for free variables in meaning terms modulo the ˘ˆ-elimination schema ˘(ˆP) $= P$
and α-, β- and η-conversion.

Generalized quantifier meanings in Montague grammar are rela-
tions between properties, with type $(s\rightarrow e\rightarrow t)\rightarrow(s\rightarrow e\rightarrow t)\rightarrow t$. While we
maintain the propositional form of glue-level formulas corresponding
to the extensional generalized quantifier meanings discussed earlier,
the semantic terms in meaning constructors for determiners must be
adapted to match the new intensionalized generalized quantifier type:

$$\forall H, R, S.\ (\forall x.\ (\uparrow_\sigma \text{ VAR})\rightsquigarrow x\ \multimap\ (\uparrow_\sigma \text{ RESTR})\rightsquigarrow(\check{R})(x))$$
$$\otimes\ (\forall x.\ \uparrow_\sigma\rightsquigarrow x\ \multimap\ H\rightsquigarrow(\check{S})(x))$$
$$\multimap\ H\rightsquigarrow a(R, S)$$

Therefore, the meaning of a sentence such as (27) will now be written:

$$every(\hat{}candidate, \hat{}\lambda w.a(\hat{}\lambda z.rumor\text{-}about(z, w), \hat{}\lambda z.dismiss(w, z)))$$

The type-changing potential of the linear-logic formulation allows us
to give an intensional verb a single meaning constructor, and yet have

the expected *de re* / *de dicto* ambiguities follow without further stipulation. For example, we will see that for sentence

(37)   Sam seeks a unicorn.

we can derive the two readings:

$$de\ dicto\ \text{reading:}\quad seek(Sam, {}^{\wedge}\lambda Q.a({}^{\wedge}unicorn, Q))$$

$$de\ re\ \text{reading:}\quad a({}^{\wedge}unicorn, {}^{\wedge}\lambda u.seek(Sam, {}^{\wedge}\lambda Q.({}^{\vee}Q)(u)))$$

Given the foregoing analysis, the lexical entry for *seek* is:

(38)   seek

$$(\uparrow \text{PRED}) = \text{'SEEK'}$$
$$\forall Z, Y.\quad (\uparrow \text{SUBJ})_\sigma \rightsquigarrow Z$$
$$\otimes(\forall s, p.\ (\forall X.\ (\uparrow \text{OBJ})_\sigma \rightsquigarrow X \multimap s \rightsquigarrow ({}^{\vee}p)(X))$$
$$\multimap s \rightsquigarrow Y(p))$$
$$\multimap \uparrow_\sigma \rightsquigarrow seek(Z, {}^{\wedge}Y)$$

which can be paraphrased as follows:

$$\forall Z, Y.\ (\uparrow \text{SUBJ})_\sigma \rightsquigarrow Z \otimes$$

$\left\{\begin{array}{l}\text{The verb } \textit{seek} \text{ requires a} \\ \text{meaning } Z \text{ for its subject and}\end{array}\right.$

$$(\forall s, p.$$
$$(\forall X.\ (\uparrow \text{OBJ})_\sigma \rightsquigarrow X$$
$$\multimap s \rightsquigarrow ({}^{\vee}p)(X))$$
$$\multimap s \rightsquigarrow Y(p))$$

$\left\{\begin{array}{l}\text{a meaning } {}^{\wedge}Y \text{ for its object,} \\ \text{where } Y \text{ is an NP mean-} \\ \text{ing applied to the mean-} \\ \text{ing } p \text{ of an arbitrarily-chosen} \\ \text{``scope'' } s,\end{array}\right.$ (∗)

$$\multimap \uparrow_\sigma \rightsquigarrow seek(Z, {}^{\wedge}Y)$$

$\left\{\begin{array}{l}\text{to produce the clause mean-} \\ \text{ing } seek(Z, {}^{\wedge}Y).\end{array}\right.$

Rather than looking for a meaning of type e for its object, the requirement expressed by the subformula labeled (∗) describes meaning constructors of quantified NPs. Such a meaning constructor takes as input the meaning constructor for a scope, which by itself maps an arbitrary meaning X to the meaning $({}^{\vee}p)(X)$ for an arbitrary scope s. From that input, the quantified NP meaning constructor will produce a final quantified meaning M for s. That meaning is required to satisfy the equation $M = Y(p)$, and thus ${}^{\wedge}Y$ is the property of properties (predicate intensions) that *seek* requires as second argument. The argument p

of Y in the equation will be an intension because of the new determiner meaning constructor, so the β-conversion involved in equating M and $Y(p)$ is allowed.

The f-structure for (37) is:

$$
(39) \qquad f: \begin{bmatrix} \text{PRED} & \text{`SEEK'} \\ \text{SUBJ} & g{:}\begin{bmatrix} \text{PRED} & \text{`SAM'} \end{bmatrix} \\ \text{OBJ} & h{:}\begin{bmatrix} \text{SPEC} & \text{`A'} \\ \text{PRED} & \text{`UNICORN'} \end{bmatrix} \end{bmatrix}
$$

The meaning constructors associated with this f-structure are:

seeks: $\qquad \forall Z, Y.\ g_\sigma \rightsquigarrow Z$
$$\otimes (\forall s, p.\ (\forall X.\ h_\sigma \rightsquigarrow X \multimap s \rightsquigarrow (\check{p})(X)) \multimap s \rightsquigarrow Y(p))$$
$$\multimap f_\sigma \rightsquigarrow seek(Z, \hat{\ }Y)$$

sam: $\qquad g_\sigma \rightsquigarrow Sam$

a-unicorn: $\quad \forall H, S.\ (\forall x.\ h_\sigma \rightsquigarrow x \multimap H \rightsquigarrow (\check{\ }S)(x)) \multimap H \rightsquigarrow a(\hat{\ }unicorn, S)$

These are the lexical premises for deriving the meaning of sentence (37). From **sam** and **seeks** and the instantiation $Z \mapsto Sam$ we can conclude by modus ponens:

sam-seeks: $\quad \forall Y.\ (\forall s, p.\ (\forall X.\ h_\sigma \rightsquigarrow X \multimap s \rightsquigarrow (\check{p})(X)) \multimap s \rightsquigarrow Y(p))$
$$\multimap f_\sigma \rightsquigarrow seek(Sam, \hat{\ }Y)$$

Different derivations starting from the premises **sam-seeks** and **a-unicorn** will yield the alternative readings of *Sam seeks a unicorn*, as we shall now see.

4.1   De dicto reading

The formula **a-unicorn** is exactly what is required by the antecedent of **sam-seeks** provided that the following substitutions are performed:

$$H \mapsto s$$
$$S \mapsto p$$
$$X \mapsto x$$
$$Y \mapsto \lambda P.a(\hat{\ }unicorn, P)$$

$$\frac{\dfrac{h_\sigma \rightsquigarrow Al \vdash h_\sigma \rightsquigarrow Al \qquad s \rightsquigarrow (\check{}P)(Al) \vdash s \rightsquigarrow (\check{}P)(Al)}{h_\sigma \rightsquigarrow Al,\, h_\sigma \rightsquigarrow Al \multimap s \rightsquigarrow (\check{}P)(Al) \vdash s \rightsquigarrow (\check{}P)(Al)}}{\dfrac{h_\sigma \rightsquigarrow Al,\, (\forall x.\, h_\sigma \rightsquigarrow x \multimap s \rightsquigarrow (\check{}P)(x)) \vdash s \rightsquigarrow (\check{}P)(Al)}{\dfrac{h_\sigma \rightsquigarrow Al \vdash (\forall x.\, h_\sigma \rightsquigarrow x \multimap s \rightsquigarrow (\check{}P)(x)) \multimap s \rightsquigarrow (\check{}P)(Al)}{h_\sigma \rightsquigarrow Al \vdash \forall P.\, (\forall x.\, h_\sigma \rightsquigarrow x \multimap s \rightsquigarrow (\check{}P)(x)) \multimap s \rightsquigarrow (\check{}P)(Al)}}}$$

Figure 2.1: Proof that **al** can function as a quantifier

We can thus conclude the desired *de dicto* reading:

$$f_\sigma \rightsquigarrow seek(Sam, \hat{}\lambda P.a(\hat{}unicorn, P)))$$

To show how the premises also support a *de re* reading, we consider first the simpler case of nonquantified direct objects.

4.2 Nonquantified objects

The meaning constructor for *seek* also allows for nonquantified objects as arguments, without needing a special type-raising rule. Consider the f-structure for the sentence *Sam seeks Al*:

$$(40) \qquad f: \begin{bmatrix} \text{PRED} & \text{`SEEK'} \\ \text{SUBJ} & g: \begin{bmatrix} \text{PRED} & \text{`SAM'} \end{bmatrix} \\ \text{OBJ} & h: \begin{bmatrix} \text{PRED} & \text{`AL'} \end{bmatrix} \end{bmatrix}$$

The lexical entry for *Al* is analogous to the one for *Sam*. We begin with the premises **sam-seeks** and **al**:

sam-seeks: $\forall Y.\, (\forall s, p.\, (\forall X.\, h_\sigma \rightsquigarrow X \multimap s \rightsquigarrow (\check{}p)(X)) \multimap s \rightsquigarrow Y(p))$
$\multimap f_\sigma \rightsquigarrow seek(Sam, \hat{}Y)$

al: $h_\sigma \rightsquigarrow Al$

For the derivation to proceed, **al** must supply the NP meaning constructor that **sam-seeks** requires. This is possible because **al** can map a proof π of the meaning for s from the meaning for h into a meaning for s, simply by supplying $h_\sigma \rightsquigarrow Al$ to π. Formally, from **al** we can prove (Figure 2.1):

$$(41) \quad \forall P.\, (\forall x.\, h_\sigma \rightsquigarrow x \multimap s \rightsquigarrow (\check{}P)(x)) \multimap s \rightsquigarrow (\check{}P)(Al)$$

This corresponds to the Montagovian type-raising of a proper name meaning to an NP meaning, and also to the undirected Lambek calculus derivation of the sequent $e \Rightarrow (e{\rightarrow}t){\rightarrow}t$.

Formula (41) with the substitutions

$$P \mapsto p, Y \mapsto \lambda P.(\check{}P)(Al)$$

can then be used to satisfy the antecedent of **sam-seeks** to yield the desired result:

$$f_\sigma \rightsquigarrow seek(Sam, \hat{}\lambda P.(\check{}P)(Al))$$

It is worth contrasting the foregoing derivation with treatments of the same phenomenon in a λ-calculus setting. The function $\lambda x.\lambda P.(\check{}P)(x)$ raises a term like Al to the quantified NP form $\lambda P.(\check{}P)(Al)$, so it is easy to modify Al to make it suitable for **seek**. Because a λ-term must specify exactly how functions and arguments combine, the conversion must be explicitly applied somewhere, either in a meaning postulate or in an alternate definition for *seek*. Thus, it is impossible to write a function term that is indifferent with respect to whether its argument is Al or $\lambda P.(\check{}P)(Al)$.

In our deductive framework, on the other hand, the exact way in which different propositions can interact is not prescribed, although it is constrained by their logical structure. Thus $h_\sigma \rightsquigarrow Al$ can function as any logical consequence of itself, in particular as:

$$\forall S, P. \ (\forall x. \ h_\sigma \rightsquigarrow x \multimap S \rightsquigarrow (\check{}P)(x)) \multimap S \rightsquigarrow (\check{}P)(Al)$$

This flexibility, which is also found in syntactic-semantic analyses based on the Lambek calculus and its variants (Moortgat 1988, 1992; van Benthem 1991), seems to align well with some of the type flexibility in natural language.

4.3   Type-raising and quantifying in

The derivation in Figure 2.1 can be generalized as shown in Figure 2.2 to prove the general type-raising theorem:

(42) $\forall I, Z. \ I \rightsquigarrow Z \multimap$
    $(\forall S, P. \ (\forall x. \ I \rightsquigarrow x \multimap S \rightsquigarrow (\check{}P)(x)) \multimap S \rightsquigarrow (\check{}P)(Z))$

$$\frac{\dfrac{I \rightsquigarrow Z \vdash I \rightsquigarrow Z \qquad S \rightsquigarrow (\check{}P)(Z) \vdash S \rightsquigarrow (\check{}P)(Z)}{\dfrac{I \rightsquigarrow Z, I \rightsquigarrow Z \multimap S \rightsquigarrow (\check{}P)(Z) \vdash S \rightsquigarrow (\check{}P)(Z)}{\dfrac{I \rightsquigarrow Z, (\forall x.\ I \rightsquigarrow x \multimap S \rightsquigarrow (\check{}P)(x)) \vdash S \rightsquigarrow (\check{}P)(Z)}{\dfrac{I \rightsquigarrow Z \vdash (\forall x.\ I \rightsquigarrow x \multimap S \rightsquigarrow (\check{}P)(x)) \multimap S \rightsquigarrow (\check{}P)(Z)}{\dfrac{I \rightsquigarrow Z \vdash \forall S, P.\ (\forall x.\ I \rightsquigarrow x \multimap S \rightsquigarrow (\check{}P)(x)) \multimap S \rightsquigarrow (\check{}P)(Z)}{\dfrac{\vdash I \rightsquigarrow Z \multimap \forall S, P.\ (\forall x.\ I \rightsquigarrow x \multimap S \rightsquigarrow (\check{}P)(x)) \multimap S \rightsquigarrow (\check{}P)(Z)}{\vdash \forall I, Z.\ I \rightsquigarrow Z \multimap \forall S, P.\ (\forall x.\ I \rightsquigarrow x \multimap S \rightsquigarrow (\check{}P)(x)) \multimap S \rightsquigarrow (\check{}P)(Z)}}}}}}$$

Figure 2.2: General Type-Raising Theorem

This theorem can be used to raise meanings of e type to $(e{\rightarrow}t){\rightarrow}t$ type, or, dually, to quantify into verb argument positions. For example, with the variable instantiations

$$I \mapsto h_\sigma$$
$$X \mapsto x$$
$$P \mapsto p$$
$$S \mapsto s$$
$$Y \mapsto \lambda R.(\check{}R)(Z)$$

we can use transitivity of implication to combine (42) with **sam-seeks** to derive:

sam-seeks$'$: $\forall Z.\ h_\sigma \rightsquigarrow Z \multimap f_\sigma \rightsquigarrow seek(Sam, \hat{}\lambda R.(\check{}R)(Z))$

This formula can then be combined with arguments of type e to produce a meaning for f_σ. For instance, it will take the non-type-raised $h_\sigma \rightsquigarrow Al$ to yield the same result

$$f_\sigma \rightsquigarrow seek(Sam, \hat{}\lambda R.(\check{}R)(Al))$$

as the combination of **sam-seeks** with the type-raised version of **al**. In fact, **sam-seeks$'$** corresponds to type $e{\rightarrow}t$, and can thus be used as the scope of a quantifier, which would then quantify into the intensional direct object argument of *seek*. As we will presently see, that is exactly what is needed to derive *de re* readings.

4.4   De re reading

We have just seen how theorem (42) provides a general mechanism for quantifying into intensional argument positions. In particular, it allowed the derivation of **sam-seeks$'$** from **sam-seeks**. Now, given the premises

sam-seeks$'$: $\forall Z.\, h_\sigma \rightsquigarrow Z \multimap f_\sigma \rightsquigarrow seek(Sam, {}^\wedge\lambda R.({}^\vee R)(Z))$

a-unicorn: $\forall H, S.\ (\forall x.\, h_\sigma \rightsquigarrow x \multimap H \rightsquigarrow ({}^\vee S)(x)) \multimap H \rightsquigarrow a({}^\wedge unicorn, S)$

and the variable substitutions

$$Z \mapsto x$$
$$H \mapsto f_\sigma$$
$$S \mapsto {}^\wedge\lambda z.seek(Sam, {}^\wedge\lambda R.({}^\vee R)(z))$$

we can apply modus ponens to derive the *de re* reading of *Sam seeks a unicorn*:

$$f_\sigma \rightsquigarrow a({}^\wedge unicorn, {}^\wedge\lambda z.seek(Sam, {}^\wedge\lambda R.({}^\vee R)(z)))$$

5   Comparison with Categorial Syntactic Approaches

The use of formal deduction in semantic interpretation is implicit in deductive systems for categorial syntax (Lambek 1958), and has been made explicit through applications of the Curry-Howard parallelism between proofs and terms in more recent work on categorial semantics (van Benthem 1988, 1991), labeled deductive systems (Moortgat 1992), flexible categorial systems (Hendriks 1993) and multimodal type-logical grammar (Morrill 1994; Moortgat 1995).

There are close connections between our approach and various systems of categorial syntax and semantics. Those systems (Moortgat 1988; Hepple 1990; Morrill 1990) were developed as calculi of syntactic/semantic types, with propositional formulas representing syntactic categories or semantic types. Indeed, the Lambek calculus (Lambek 1958), introduced as a logic of syntactic combination, turns out to be a fragment of noncommutative multiplicative linear logic. Given the types for the lexical items in a sentence as assumptions, the sentence is syntactically well-formed in the Lambek calculus if the type of the sentence can be derived from the assumptions arranged as an ordered list. Furthermore, the Curry-Howard isomorphism between proofs and terms (Howard 1980) allows the extraction of a term representing the meaning of the sentence from the proof that the sentence is well-formed (van Benthem 1986). If permutation is added to Lambek's system, its left- and right-implication connectives ($\backslash$ and $/$) collapse into a single implication connective with behavior identical to $\multimap$. This undirected version of the Lambek calculus was developed by van Benthem (1988, 1991) to account for the semantic combination possibilities of phrase meanings. This and other related commutative calculi provide an analysis of the possibilities of meaning combination independently of the syntactic realizations of those meanings, but do not offer a mechanism for relating semantic combination possibilities to the corresponding syntactic combination possibilities.

Our system follows categorial semantics in using the "propositional skeleton" of glue formulas to encode the types of phrase meanings and thus their composition potential. In addition, however, first-order quantification over semantic projections maintains the connection between those types and the corresponding syntactic objects, while quantification over semantic terms is used to build the meanings of those syntactic objects. This tripartite organization reflects the three linked systems of representation that participate in semantic interpretation: syntactic structure, semantic types and semantic interpretations themselves. In this way, we can take advantage of the principled description of potential meaning combinations arising from categorial semantics without losing track of the constraints imposed by syntax on the possible combinations of those meanings. As we discuss later in this section, there are significant parallels between our tripartite system and the string-based multidimensional system of Oehrle (1994, 1995).

Multimodal and labeled deductive systems (Moortgat 1992; Morrill 1994) have been proposed as refinements of the Lambek systems that are able to represent synchronized derivations involving multiple levels of representation: for instance, a level of head-dependent representations and a level of syntactic functor-argument representations. However, these systems cannot represent directly the connections between flat syntactic representation in terms of grammatical functions, such as the f-structure of LFG, and a function-argument semantic representation. The problem is that they cannot express at the type level the link between particular syntactic structures (f-structures in our case) and particular contributions to meaning. The extraction of meanings from derivations following the Curry-Howard isomorphism that is standard in categorial systems demands that the order of syntactic combination coincide with the order of semantic combination so that functor-argument relations at the syntactic and semantic level are properly aligned. To maintain the synchronization between syntactic and semantic application while supporting a range of structural variation, for instance scoping ambiguities, those systems must rely on carefully-chosen connectives to keep track of the structural transformations between syntactic and semantic levels at each point in a derivation, while in our approach the connection between syntax and semantics is carried by the bindings of glue-language variables.

Nevertheless, there are strong similarities between the analysis of quantification that we present and analyses of the same phenomena discussed by Morrill (1994) and Carpenter (1994). Following Moortgat (1996), they add to an appropriate version of the Lambek calculus (Lambek 1958) the *scope* connective ↑, subject to the following proof rules:

$$\frac{\Gamma[v : A] \Rightarrow u : B \qquad \Delta[t(\lambda v.u) : B] \Rightarrow C}{\Delta[\Gamma[t : A \uparrow B]] \Rightarrow C} \quad [\text{QL}]$$

$$\frac{\Gamma \Rightarrow u : A}{\Gamma \Rightarrow \lambda v.v(u) : A \uparrow B} \quad [\text{QR}]$$

In terms of the scope connective, a quantified NP is given the category N ↑ S, which semantically corresponds to the type $(e{\to}t){\to}t$ and agrees with the propositional structure of our linear formulas for quantified NPs. A phrase of category N ↑ S is an infix functor that binds a variable of type e, the type of individual NPs N, within a scope of type t, the type of sentences S. An intensional verb like *seek* has, then, category (N \ S)/(N ↑ S), with corresponding type $((e{\to}t){\to}t){\to}e{\to}t$.[7] Thus the intensional verb will take as direct object a quantified NP, as required.

---

[7] These category and type assignments are an oversimplification since intensional verbs like *seek* require a direct object of type $s{\to}((e{\to}t){\to}t)$, but for the present discussion the simpler category and type are sufficient. Morrill (1994) provides a full treatment.

A problem arises, however, with sentences such as

(43)   Sam seeks a conversation with every unicorn.

This sentence has five possible interpretations:

(44)   a.   *seek(Sam,^λP.every(^unicorn,^λu.a(^λz.conv-with(z, u), P)))*

     b.   *seek(Sam,^λP.a(^λz.every(^unicorn,^λu.conv-with(z, u)), P))*

     c.   *every(^unicorn,^λu.seek(Sam,^λP.a(^λz.conv-with(z, u), P)))*

     d.   *every(^unicorn,^λu.a(^λz.conv-with(z, u),*
                       ^λz.seek(Sam,^λP.(˘P)(z)))))

     e.   *a(^λz.every(^unicorn,^λu.conv-with(z, u)),*
       ^λz.seek(Sam,^λP.(˘P)(z)))

Both our approach and the categorial analysis using the scope connective have no problem in deriving interpretations (44b), (44c), (44d) and (44e). In those cases, the scope of *every unicorn* is an appropriate term of type $e{\rightarrow}t$. However, the situation is different for interpretation (44a), in which both the conversations and the unicorn are *de dicto*, but the conversations sought may be different for different unicorns sought. As we will show below, this interpretation can be easily derived within our framework. However, a similar derivation requires a different view of the categorial scoping connective and changes in the lexical entry for *seek*.

The difficulty for most categorial accounts is that the category N ↑ S represents a phrase that plays the role of a category N phrase where it appears, but takes an S (dependent on the N) as its scope. In the derivation of (44a), however, the scope of *every unicorn* is *a conversation with*, which is not of category S. Semantically, *a conversation with* is represented by:

(45) $\lambda P.{}^{\wedge}\lambda u.a({}^{\wedge}\lambda z.conv\text{-}with(z, u), P) : (s{\rightarrow}e{\rightarrow}t){\rightarrow}(s{\rightarrow}e{\rightarrow}t)$

The *undirected* Lambek calculus (van Benthem 1991) allows us to compose (45) with the interpretation of *every unicorn*:

(46) $\lambda Q.every({}^{\wedge}unicorn, Q) : (s{\rightarrow}e{\rightarrow}t){\rightarrow}t$

to yield:

(47) $\lambda P.every(\hat{}unicorn, \hat{}\lambda u.a(\hat{}\lambda z.conv\text{-}with(z, u), P)) : (s{\rightarrow}e{\rightarrow}t){\rightarrow}t$

As we will see below, our linear logic formulation also allows that derivation step.

In contrast, as Moortgat (1996) points out, the categorial rule [QR] is not powerful enough to raise N ↑ S to take as scope any functor whose result is a S. In particular, the sequent

(48)   N ↑ S $\Rightarrow$ N ↑ (N ↑ S)

is not derivable, whereas the corresponding "semantic" sequent (up to permutation)

(49) $q : (e{\rightarrow}t){\rightarrow}t \Rightarrow$
$\qquad \lambda R.\lambda P.q(\lambda x.R(P)(x)) : ((e{\rightarrow}t){\rightarrow}(e{\rightarrow}t)){\rightarrow}(e{\rightarrow}t){\rightarrow}t$

is derivable in the undirected Lambek calculus. Sequent (49) will in particular raise (46) to a function that, applied to (45), produces (47), as required.

Furthermore, the solution proposed by Morrill (1994) to make the scope calculus complete is to restrict the intended interpretation of ↑ so that (48) is not valid. Thus, *contra* Carpenter (1994), Morrill's logically more satisfying account of ↑ is not a step towards making reading (44a) available. The only apparent solution to this problem within Morrill's analysis is to assume a lexical decomposition of *seek* into *try to find*, with appropriate type assignments. With that decomposition, there will be a constituent of type S to serve as scope for *a conversation with*, and a reading parallel to (44a) will become available. Indeed, Morrill (1994) gives examples of semantic derivations for quantified *try to find* sentences and the corresponding *de re/de dicto* alternations.

The decomposition of *seek* into *try to find*, although otherwise unmotivated, may be satisfactory for some examples; however, there are many examples (such as the following examples from *The New York Times*) for which decomposition of *seek* into *try to find* does not work well:

(50)   a.   Smith said Friday that he would return to the State Legislature in April to seek a change in the statute to make faith healing more easily defended.

b. Unless the FDIC does more, Rangel said, he will seek congressional hearings examining the decision to close the bank.

c. Goodstein is seeking a five-year contract.

It might be argued that *seek* is in fact semantically ambiguous, with alternative decompositions *try to find* and *try to obtain*, but this only adds to the stipulations that the decomposition analysis must make. We also agree with Montague (1974, page 267) that a lexical decomposition approach does not successfully carry over to other verbs with similar intensional properties such as *fear*, *imagine*, or *conceive*, or to intensional prepositions such as *about*.

Moortgat (1997) appeals to a carefully designed multimodal system to solve the incompleteness problem of the scoping calculus, which turns out to help solve the problem under discussion.[8] It would take us too far afield to present his modal analysis of scoping constructs in detail here. However, the basic idea is to represent a scoping construct as a modal formula, whose modalities interact with other connectives to define the possible structural positions within a scope in which the scoping construct may occur, and which are abstracted over when the construct takes its scope. In a derivation of this kind, the path to the abstracted position is first marked as the abstract is being built, and then the marks are used to move the lexical scoping construct to its *in situ* position, in a process reminiscent of transformational treatments of scoping, except that instead of coindexing, explicitly marked paths are used. The one additional stipulation required to make a derivation of (44a) go through in Moortgat's system is to give *seek* category

(51) *seek* : $(N \setminus S)/(S/(N \setminus S))$.

It is easy to see that the sequents

(52) a. $A \uparrow B \Rightarrow B/(A \setminus B)$

b. $A \uparrow B \Rightarrow (B/A) \setminus B$

follow from [QL] (which still holds in Moortgat's system) and the residuation laws for $/$ and $\setminus$. Crucially, the Geach-style type-raising law

---

[8] Michael Moortgat, personal communication

(53) $N \uparrow S \Rightarrow N \uparrow (S/(N \setminus S))$

also holds in Moortgat's system. In particular, if we set $A = N, B = S/(N \setminus S)$ in (52b), we can give "every unicorn" the category $((S/(N \setminus S))/N) \setminus (S/(N \setminus S))$. On the other hand, (52a) allows us to give category $(S/(N \setminus S))/N$ to "a conversation with." Thus "every unicorn" can take as (left) argument—and thus outscope—"a conversation with," yielding the category $S/(N \setminus S)$, which is an appropriate direct object for *seek* under (51). Note, however, that this approach still differs significantly from ours: first, this treatment of quantification relies on an explicit encoding of possible binding paths in a purpose-built logic; second, the lexical entry for *seek* only represents indirectly the requirement that the direct object be a quantified noun phrase.

We now give the derivation of the interpretation (44a) in our framework. The f-structure for (43) is:

(54)
$$f: \begin{bmatrix} \text{PRED} & \text{`SEEK'} \\ \text{SUBJ} & g{:}\begin{bmatrix} \text{PRED} & \text{`SAM'} \end{bmatrix} \\ \text{OBJ} & h{:}\begin{bmatrix} \text{SPEC} & \text{`A'} \\ \text{PRED} & \text{`CONVERSATION'} \\ \text{OBL}_{\text{WITH}} & i{:}\begin{bmatrix} \text{SPEC} & \text{`EVERY'} \\ \text{PRED} & \text{`UNICORN'} \end{bmatrix} \end{bmatrix} \end{bmatrix}$$

The two formulas **sam-seeks** and **every-unicorn** can be derived as described before:

sam-seeks: $\forall Y. \, (\forall s, p. \, (\forall X. \, h_\sigma \rightsquigarrow X \multimap s \rightsquigarrow (\check{p})(X)) \multimap s \rightsquigarrow Y(p))$
                  $\multimap f_\sigma \rightsquigarrow seek(Sam, \hat{Y})$

every-unicorn: $\forall G, S. \, (\forall x. \, i_\sigma \rightsquigarrow x \multimap G \rightsquigarrow (\check{S})(x))$
                  $\multimap G \rightsquigarrow every(\hat{unicorn}, S)$

The remaining lexical premises for (54) are:

a: $\forall H, R, T. \, ((\forall x. \, (h_\sigma \text{VAR}) \rightsquigarrow x \multimap (h_\sigma \text{RESTR}) \rightsquigarrow (\check{R})(x))$
                $\otimes (\forall x. \, h_\sigma \rightsquigarrow x \multimap H \rightsquigarrow (\check{T})(x)))$
                $\multimap H \rightsquigarrow a(R, T)$

conv-with: $\forall Z, X. \, (h_\sigma \text{VAR}) \rightsquigarrow Z \otimes i_\sigma \rightsquigarrow X$
                $\multimap (h_\sigma \text{RESTR}) \rightsquigarrow conv\text{-}with(Z, X)$

From these premises we immediately derive

$$\forall X, H, T.\ i_\sigma \rightsquigarrow X \otimes (\forall x.\ h_\sigma \rightsquigarrow x \multimap H \rightsquigarrow (\check{}T)(x))$$
$$\multimap H \rightsquigarrow a(\hat{}\lambda z.conv\text{-}with(z, X), T)$$

which can be rewritten as:

(55) $\forall H, T.\ (\forall x.\ h_\sigma \rightsquigarrow x \multimap H \rightsquigarrow (\check{}T)(x)) \multimap$
$$\forall X.\ (i_\sigma \rightsquigarrow X \multimap H \rightsquigarrow a(\hat{}\lambda z.conv\text{-}with(z, X), T))$$

If we apply the substitutions

$$X \mapsto x, G \mapsto H, S \mapsto \hat{}\lambda u.a(\hat{}\lambda z.conv\text{-}with(u, v), T),$$

formula (55) can be combined with **every-unicorn** to yield the required
quantifier-type formula:

(56) $\forall H, T.\ (\forall x.\ h_\sigma \rightsquigarrow x \multimap H \rightsquigarrow (\check{}T)(x)) \multimap$
$$H \rightsquigarrow every(\hat{}unicorn, \hat{}\lambda u.a(\hat{}\lambda z.conv\text{-}with(z, u), T))$$

Using substitutions

$$\begin{aligned} H &\mapsto s \\ T &\mapsto p \\ Y &\mapsto \lambda R.every(\hat{}unicorn, \hat{}\lambda u.a(\hat{}\lambda z.conv\text{-}with(z, u), R)) \end{aligned}$$

and modus ponens, we then combine (56) with **sam-seeks** to obtain the
desired final result:

$$f_\sigma \rightsquigarrow seek(Sam, \hat{}\lambda R.every(\hat{}unicorn, \hat{}\lambda u.a(\hat{}\lambda z.conv\text{-}with(z, u), R)))$$

Thus, we see that our more flexible connection between syntax and semantics permits the full range of type flexibility provided by categorial
semantics without losing the rigorous connection to syntax. In contrast,
current categorial accounts of the syntax-semantics interface do not appear to offer the needed flexibility when syntactic and semantic composition are more indirectly connected, as in the present case.

Oehrle (1994, 1995) independently proposed a multidimensional categorial system that explicitly expresses the connection between (categorial) syntactic analyses, semantic types and the corresponding meaning terms. He uses the undirected Lambek calculus LP for his type

system, but ensures that semantic composition and syntactic structure agree by labeling each syntactic type with a string term that specifies the surface-combination order of the constituents whose semantic combination mode is expressed by the type. Each type is also labeled with a meaning term specifying the corresponding contribution to meaning. These *labeled types* are thus triples of a string function S (expressed as a λ term over constant strings and string concatenation), a type τ and a meaning term M (expressed as a λ term over lexical constants), written $S : \tau \rightsquigarrow M$. There is a rough correspondence between Oehrle's labeled types and our meaning contributions: the labeled type

$$\lambda s_1. \ldots . \lambda s_k.S : \tau_1 \rightarrow \cdots \rightarrow \tau_k \rightarrow \tau \rightsquigarrow \lambda x_1. \ldots . \lambda x_k.M$$

is analogous to our glue formula

$$f_{\sigma 1} \rightsquigarrow x_1 \otimes \cdots \otimes f_{\sigma k} \rightsquigarrow x_k \multimap f_\sigma \rightsquigarrow M$$

where the syntactic role of s_i in S corresponds to the role of $f_{\sigma i}$ in f_σ. The connection is even more explicit in Oehrle's *indexed term* version of his system, in which the connection between levels of representation encoded by parallel λ-abstraction in labeled types is instead performed by coindexing between string terms, types and semantic terms. Oehrle's proof rules for labeled types extend the rules for LP (which are a particular case of the proof rules for linear logic we use) with computations on labels that maintain the desired correspondence between syntactic terms, types and meaning terms. Scope ambiguities arise in his system from alternative decompositions of a string into a string function applied to a string argument and corresponding use of proof rules in different orders.

There are, however, significant differences between Oehrle's system and ours. Most obviously, the relationship between f-structures and c-structures in LFG is more flexible than the relationships between strings and their substrings expressible in Oehrle's system, and thus allows our system to isolate semantic composition from the vagaries of surface constituent structure.

More generally, it is not clear how to extend a categorial system with an analysis of pronominal reference that interacts with quantification in the ways predicted by our model. Oehrle's multimodal account of binding (Oehrle 1997) brings the ideas of dynamic interpretation into a categorial setting. However, his analysis does not specifically address bound anaphora and does not appear to constrain possible semantic derivations. Instead, as is usual with dynamic interpretation approaches, the meaning produced by a derivation is a relation between assignments of referential indices to domain entities. In such an account, the scopings blocked in our approach are still available, but their conflict with anaphoric binding is absent because the conflicting antecedents are hidden by the manipulations of assignments carried out inside the meanings of expressions. In other words, some of the computations and constraints that we place in the glue-language derivations are pushed into the denotational domain in dynamic interpretation. Jäger (1997) proposes a different categorial analysis specifically directed at bound anaphora, but it remains to be seen whether it will interact with quantification in the expected ways.

6   Conclusion

Our approach exploits the f-structure of LFG for syntactic information needed to guide semantic composition, and also exploits the resource-sensitive properties of linear logic to express the semantic composition requirements of natural language. The use of linear logic as the glue language in a deductive semantic framework allows a natural treatment of quantification which automatically gives the right results for quantified NPs, their scopes and bound anaphora, and allows for a clean and natural treatment of verbs and their arguments.

Indeed, the same basic facts are also accounted for in other recent treatments of compositionality, in particular categorial analyses with discontinuous constituency connectives (Moortgat 1996, 1997). These results suggest the advantages of a generalized form of compositionality in which the meaning constructors of phrases are represented by logical formulas rather than by functional abstractions as in traditional compositionality. The fixed application order and fixed type requirements of λ terms are just too restrictive when it comes to encoding the freer order of information presentation in natural language.

Our treatment is thus closely related to systems of syntactic and semantic type assignment based on the Lambek calculus and its variants. However, we differ from those categorial approaches in providing an explicit link between functional structures and semantic derivations that does not depend on linear order and constituency in syntax to keep track of predicate-argument relations. Thus we avoid the need to force syntax and semantics into an uncomfortably tight categorial embrace.

Acknowledgments

Portions of this work were originally presented at the Second CSLI Workshop on Logic, Language, and Computation, Stanford University, published as Dalrymple et al. (1995), and at the Conference on Information-Oriented Approaches to Logic, Language and Computation, held at Saint Mary's College, Moraga, California, published as Dalrymple et al. (1994). We are grateful to the audiences at these venues for helpful comments. We would particularly like to thank Johan van Benthem, Bob Carpenter, Max Copperman, Marc Dymetman, Jan van Eijck, John Fry, Kris Halvorsen, Angie Hinrichs, David Israel, Mark Johnson, Ron Kaplan, Andy Kehler, Chris Manning, John Maxwell, Michael Moortgat, Glyn Morrill, Dick Oehrle, John Nerbonne, Stanley Peters, Manfred Pinkal, Henriëtte de Swart and an anonymous reviewer for the Second CSLI Workshop on Logic, Language, and Computation for comments and discussion, and John Fry for a careful review of the manuscript. They are not responsible for any remaining errors, and we doubt that they will endorse all our analyses and conclusions, but we are sure that the end result is much improved for their help.

References

Barwise, Jon and Robin Cooper. 1981. Generalized quantifiers and natural language. *Linguistics and Philosophy*, 4:159–219.

Bresnan, Joan. 1982. Control and complementation. *Linguistic Inquiry*, 13:343–434. Reprinted in Joan Bresnan, editor, *The Mental Representation of Grammatical Relations*, pages 282–390. The MIT Press, Cambridge, MA.

Carpenter, Bob. 1994. Quantification and scoping: a deductive account. In Raul Aranovich, William Byrne, Susanne Preuss, and Martha Senturia, editors, *Proceedings of the 13th West Coast Conference on Formal Linguistics*. San Diego. CSLI Publications, Stanford University.

Cooper, Robin. 1979. Variable binding and relative clauses. In F. Guenther and S. J. Schmidt, editors, *Formal Semantics and Pragmatics for Natural Languages*. D. Reidel, Dordrecht.

Dalrymple, Mary. 1993. *The Syntax of Anaphoric Binding*. CSLI Lecture Notes, number 36. CSLI Publications, Stanford University.

Dalrymple, Mary, John Lamping, and Vijay Saraswat. 1993. LFG semantics via constraints. In *Proceedings of the Sixth Meeting of the European ACL*, University of Utrecht, pages 97–105. European Chapter of the Association for Computational Linguistics.

Dalrymple, Mary, Angie Hinrichs, John Lamping, and Vijay Saraswat. 1993. The resource logic of complex predicate interpretation. In Keh-jiann Chen and Chu-Ren Huang, editors, *Proceedings of the 1993 Republic of China Computational Linguistics Conference (ROCLING)*, Hsitou National Park, Taiwan. Computational Linguistics Society of Republic of China. Also published as Xerox Technical Report ISTL-NLTT-1993-08-03.

Dalrymple, Mary, John Lamping, Fernando C. N. Pereira, and Vijay Saraswat. 1994. Intensional verbs without type-raising or lexical ambiguity. In Jerry Seligman and Dag Westerståhl, editors, *Logic, Language and Computation*. CSLI Publications, Stanford University, pages 167–182. Also in *Proceedings of the Conference on Information-Oriented Approaches to Logic, Language and Computation/Fourth Conference on Situation Theory and its Applications*, Saint Mary's College of California, Moraga, California. June 1994.

Dalrymple, Mary, John Lamping, Fernando C. N. Pereira, and Vijay Saraswat. 1995. A deductive account of quantification in LFG. In Makoto Kanazawa, Christopher J. Piñón, and Henriëtte de Swart, editors, *Quantifiers, Deduction, and Context*. CSLI Publications, Stanford University.

Fenstad, Jens Erik, Per-Kristian Halvorsen, Tore Langholm, and Johan van Benthem. 1987. *Situations, Language and Logic*. D. Reidel, Dordrecht.

Gamut, L. T. F. 1991. *Logic, Language, and Meaning*, volume 2: Intensional Logic and Logical Grammar. The University of Chicago Press, Chicago.

Gawron, Jean Mark and Stanley Peters. 1990. *Anaphora and quantification in Situation Semantics*. CSLI Lecture Notes, number 19. CSLI Publications, Stanford University.

Girard, Jean-Yves. 1987. Linear logic. *Theoretical Computer Science*, 50:1–102.

Groenendijk, Jeroen and Martin Stokhof. 1991. Dynamic predicate logic. *Linguistics and Philosophy*, 14(1):39–100.

Halvorsen, Per-Kristian. 1983. Semantics for Lexical-Functional Grammar. *Linguistic Inquiry*, 14(4):567–615.

Halvorsen, Per-Kristian and Ronald M. Kaplan. November 1988. Projections and semantic description in Lexical-Functional Grammar. In *Proceedings of the International Conference on Fifth Generation Computer Systems (FGCS-88)*, Tokyo, Japan, pages 1116–1122. Reprinted in Mary Dalrymple, Ronald M. Kaplan, John Maxwell, and Annie Zaenen, editors, *Formal Issues in Lexical-Functional Grammar*, pages 279–292. CSLI Publications, Stanford University. 1995.

Hendriks, Herman. 1993. *Studied Flexibility: Categories and Types in Syntax and Semantics*. ILLC dissertation series 1993-5, University of Amsterdam, Amsterdam.

Hepple, Mark. 1990. *The Grammar and Processing of Order and Dependency: a Categorial Approach*. PhD thesis, University of Edinburgh.

Howard, W.A. 1980. The formulae-as-types notion of construction. In J.P. Seldin and J.R. Hindley, editors, *To H.B. Curry: Essays on Combinatory Logic, Lambda Calculus and Formalism*, pages 479–490. Academic Press, London, England.

Huet, Gérard. 1975. A unification algorithm for typed $\overline{\lambda}$-calculus. *Theoretical Computer Science*, 1:27–57.

Jäger, Gerhard. 1997. Anaphora and ellipsis in type-logical grammar. In P. Dekker, M. Stokhof, and Y. Vanema, editors, *Proceedings of the 11th Amsterdam Colloquium*, pages 175–180. ILLC, University of Amsterdam.

Kanovich, Max I. 1992. Horn programming in linear logic is NP-complete. In *Seventh Annual IEEE Symposium on Logic in Computer Science*, Santa Cruz, pages 200–210. IEEE Computer Society Press, Los Alamitos, CA.

Lambek, Joachim. 1958. The mathematics of sentence structure. *American Mathematical Monthly*, 65:154–170.

Miller, Dale A. 1990. A logic programming language with lambda abstraction, function variables and simple unification. In Peter Schroeder-Heister, editor, *Extensions of Logic Programming, Lecture Notes in Artificial Intelligence*. Springer-Verlag.

Montague, Richard. 1974. The proper treatment of quantification in ordinary English. In Richmond Thomason, editor, *Formal Philosophy*. Yale University Press, New Haven.

Moortgat, Michael. 1988. *Categorial Investigations: Logical and Linguistic Aspects of the Lambek Calculus*. PhD thesis, University of Amsterdam, Amsterdam.

Moortgat, Michael. 1992. Labelled deductive systems for categorial theorem proving. In P. Dekker and M. Stokhof, editors, *Proceedings of the Eighth Amsterdam Colloquium*, pages 403–423, Institute for Logic, Language and Computation, Amsterdam.

Moortgat, Michael. 1995. Multimodal linguistic inference. *Bulletin of the Interest Group in Pure and Applied Logics*, 3(2,3):371–401.

Moortgat, Michael. 1996. Generalized quantifiers and discontinuous type constructors. In Harry Bunt and Arthur van Horck, editors, *Discontinuous Constituency*, pages 181–207. Mouton de Gruyter, Berlin.

Moortgat, Michael. 1997. In situ binding: a modal analysis. In P. Dekker and M. Stokhof, editors, *Proceedings of the 10th Amsterdam Colloquium*, pages 539–549. ILLC, University of Amsterdam.

Morrill, Glyn V. 1990. Intensionality and boundedness. *Linguistics and Philosophy*, 13(6):699–726.

Morrill, Glyn V. 1994. *Type Logical Grammar: Categorial Logic of Signs*. Kluwer Academic Publishers, Dordrecht.

Neale, Stephen. 1990. *Descriptions*. The MIT Press, Cambridge, MA.

Oehrle, Richard T. 1994. Term-labeled categorial type systems. *Linguistics and Philosophy*, 17(6):633–678.

Oehrle, Richard T. 1995. Some 3-dimensional systems of labelled deduction. *Bulletin of the Interest Group in Pure and Applied Logics*, 3(2,3):429–448.

Oehrle, Richard T. 1997. Binding as deduction. In Geert-Jan Kruijff, Glyn V. Morrill, and Richard T. Oehrle, editors, *Formal Grammar 1997: Linguistic Aspects of Logical and Computational Perspectives on Language*, pages 40–54, Aix en Provence. European Summer School in Logic, Language and Information.

Partee, Barbara and Mats Rooth. 1983. Generalized conjunction and type ambiguity. In Rainer Bauerle, Christoph Schwarze, and Arnim von Stechow, editors, *Meaning, Use, and Interpretation of Language*, pages 361–383. De Gruyter, Berlin.

Pereira, Fernando C. N. 1990. Categorial semantics and scoping. *Computational Linguistics*, 16(1):1–10.

Pereira, Fernando C. N. 1991. Semantic interpretation as higher-order deduction. In Jan van Eijck, editor, *Logics in AI: European Workshop JELIA'90*, pages 78–96. Springer-Verlag, Amsterdam.

Reyle, Uwe. 1988. Compositional semantics for LFG. In Uwe Reyle and Christian Rohrer, editors, *Natural Language Parsing and Linguistic Theories*. D. Reidel, Dordrecht.

Rodman, Robert. 1976. Scope phenomena, "movement transformations", and relative clauses. In Barbara Partee, editor, *Montague Grammar*, pages 165–176. Academic Press, New York.

van Benthem, Johan. 1986. Categorial grammar and lambda calculus. In D. Skordev, editor, *Mathematical Logic and its Application*, pages 39–60. Plenum Press, New York.

van Benthem, Johan. 1988. The Lambek calculus. In Richard T. Oehrle, Emmon Bach, and Deirdre Wheeler, editors, *Categorial Grammars and Natural Language Structures*, pages 35–68. D. Reidel, Dordrecht.

van Benthem, Johan. 1991. *Language in Action: Categories, Lambdas and Dynamic Logic*. North-Holland, Amsterdam. Republished, with addenda and supplemental bibliography, in 1995 by North-Holland and MIT Press.

3

Proof Nets and Negative Polarity Licensing

John Fry

1   Introduction

In addition to its role in assembling semantic scope readings, the linear logic glue language approach developed in this volume can also be harnessed to *constrain* the combinatorics of scope readings at the syntax-semantics interface in a variety of interesting ways. For example, Chapter 2 shows how properties of the glue language prevent certain scopings which are ill-formed due to their interaction with bound anaphora. In this paper I propose a glue language implementation of another constraint, this one observed by Ladusaw (1979), that negative polarity items (NPIs) like *ever* and *any* are licensed within the semantic scope of a negative or monotonically decreasing context, as in e.g. *Nobody ever left*.

The technical presentation here differs from the other contributions in this volume in that I carry out derivations using proof nets (Girard 1987) rather than Gentzen-style deductions. The proof net diagrams for individual sentences serve to demonstrate visually how certain unwanted readings are blocked and how correct readings are proved. The proof-checking algorithm used here is due to Gallier (1992).

This paper is an expanded version of material that appeared previously in Fry (1997a) and Fry (1997b).

2   Review of Quantification

Recall that in the account of quantification presented in Chapter 2, a quantified NP like *every boy* is assigned the following structures:

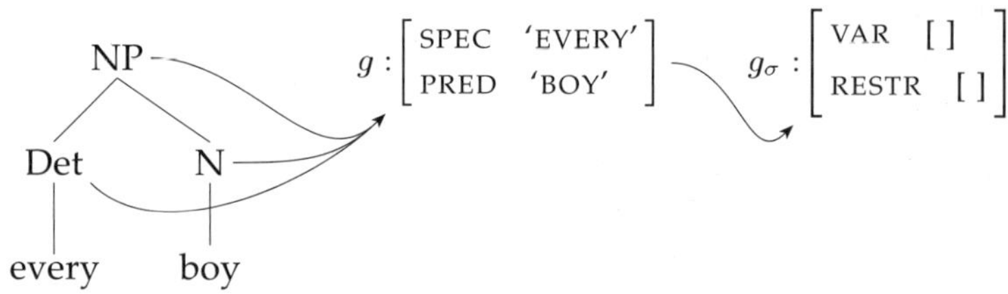

The individual words *every* and *boy* come with *meaning constructors* specified in the lexicon. The full meaning constructor for the determiner *every* after it has been instantiated with the f-structure label g is shown in (1).

$$(1) \quad \textbf{every:} \quad \forall H, R, S.\ (\forall x.\ (g_\sigma\ \text{VAR})\leadsto_e x \multimap (g_\sigma\ \text{RESTR})\leadsto_t R(x))$$
$$\otimes\ (\forall y.\ g_\sigma\leadsto_e y \multimap H\leadsto_t S(y))$$
$$\multimap H\leadsto_t every(R, S)$$

In a typical proof, the meaning constructor for a noun will supply appropriate values for the VAR and RESTR attributes of the NP, and these resources will be consumed by the determiner's meaning constructor. In this example, the noun is *boy* and its meaning constructor is (2).

$$(2) \quad \textbf{boy:} \quad \forall X.\ (g_\sigma\ \text{VAR})\leadsto_e X \multimap (g_\sigma\ \text{RESTR})\leadsto_t boy(X)$$

Together, the meaning constructors (1) and (2) act as premises for the deduction of *every boy*. Specifically, applying the variable substitutions $X \mapsto x$ and $R \mapsto boy$ followed by modus ponens on (1) and (2) yields formula (3).

$$(3) \quad \textbf{every-boy:} \quad \forall H, S.\ (\forall y.\ g_\sigma\leadsto_e y \multimap H\leadsto_t S(y))$$
$$\multimap H\leadsto_t every(boy, S)$$

Recall how this quantified NP contributes to the meaning of a sentence in which it appears, for example (4):

(4)   Every boy left.

$$f: \begin{bmatrix} \text{PRED} & \text{`LEAVE'} \\ \text{SUBJ} & g: \begin{bmatrix} \text{SPEC} & \text{`EVERY'} \\ \text{PRED} & \text{`BOY'} \end{bmatrix} \end{bmatrix}$$

First, we add the meaning constructor for the intransitive verb *left* (after it has been instantiated with the values in (4)), shown in (5).

(5)   **left:** $\forall Y.\ g_\sigma \leadsto_e Y \multimap f_\sigma \leadsto_t leave(Y)$

To derive a meaning for (4), we apply the substitutions $H \mapsto f_\sigma$, $Y \mapsto y$ and $S \mapsto \lambda y.leave(y)$ and apply modus ponens to (3) and (5). This produces what is in this simple case the only possible reading:

(6)   **every-boy-left:** $f_\sigma \leadsto_t every(boy, \lambda y.leave(y))$.

2.1   Scope ambiguities

In the case of a sentence with more than one quantifier, its multiple scope readings emerge with each unique derivation. Consider the sentence

(7)   Every boy saw a girl.

$$f: \begin{bmatrix} \text{PRED} & \text{`SEE'} \\ \text{SUBJ} & g: \begin{bmatrix} \text{SPEC} & \text{`EVERY'} \\ \text{PRED} & \text{`BOY'} \end{bmatrix} \\ \text{OBJ} & h: \begin{bmatrix} \text{SPEC} & \text{`A'} \\ \text{PRED} & \text{`GIRL'} \end{bmatrix} \end{bmatrix}$$

In this case the new premise **a-girl** is made available:

a-girl: $\forall H, S.\ (\forall z.\ h_\sigma \leadsto_e z \multimap H \leadsto_t S(z)) \multimap H \leadsto_t a(girl, S)$

The two possible readings depend on the relative order of application of the generalized quantifiers **a-girl** and **every-boy**. If **every-boy** is applied to the predicate before **a-girl**, we obtain the wide-scope $\forall\exists$ reading

$$f_\sigma \leadsto_t every(boy, \lambda u.a(girl, \lambda v.see(u, v))).$$

Otherwise the narrow-scope $\exists\forall$ reading is produced:

$$f_\sigma \leadsto_t a(girl, \lambda v.every(boy, \lambda u.see(u, v))).$$

3   Meaning Deduction via Proof Nets

In this section I will use proof nets to derive reading (6) from Section 2 in a more formal manner. A *proof net* (Girard 1987) is an undirected, connected graph whose node labels are propositions. A theorem of multiplicative linear logic corresponds to only one proof net; thus the manipulation of proof nets can be more efficient than sequent deduction, in which the same theorem might have different proofs corresponding to different orderings of the inference steps. A further advantage of proof nets for our purposes is that an invalid meaning deduction, e.g. one corresponding to some spurious scope reading of a particular sentence, can be illustrated by exhibiting its defective graph which demonstrates visually why no proof exists for it.[1]

The remainder of this section explains how to construct a proof net from a set of premises, and then demonstrates the $O(n^2)$ algorithm of Gallier (1992) which checks whether a given proof net is valid, i.e. corresponds to a proof. This process, together with the application of higher-order unification to the meaning terms, is used to derive the final meaning or meanings for a sentence. The process consists of four steps: (1) rewrite the premises in a normalized form, (2) assemble the premises into a graph, (3) connect together the positive ("producer") and negative ("consumer") meaning terms, unifying them in the process, and (4) apply a recursive decomposition algorithm to the resulting graph which tests whether or not it encodes a proof.

3.1   Step 1: Set up the sequent

Proof net diagrams for even simple sentences can grow rather large. To produce more compact diagrams, I will eliminate universal quantifiers from the expressions and just assume that free (upper-case) variables are universally quantified. For the example at hand, I further abbreviate $(g_\sigma$ VAR) as v and $(g_\sigma$ RESTR) as r. The three premises from the

---

[1] Proof net techniques have become popular within the categorial grammar community recently—see e.g. Morrill (1996) and Lecomte and Retoré (1995).

example in Section 2 now take the form

$$\textbf{every:} \quad (v \leadsto_e x \multimap r \leadsto_t R(x)) \otimes (g_\sigma \leadsto_e y \multimap H \leadsto_t S(y))$$
$$\multimap H \leadsto_t every(R, S)$$

$$\textbf{boy:} \quad v \leadsto_e X \multimap r \leadsto_t boy(X)$$

$$\textbf{left:} \quad g_\sigma \leadsto_e Y \multimap f_\sigma \leadsto_t leave(Y)$$

The goal of the deduction is to derive, from the above premises, a meaning M for the f-structure f of the entire sentence—in other words, a proof of the form

$$\textbf{every} \otimes \textbf{boy} \otimes \textbf{left} \vdash f_\sigma \leadsto_t M.$$

Glue language semantics has so far been restricted to the *multiplicative* fragment of linear logic, which uses only the multiplicative conjunction operator $\otimes$ (*tensor*) and the linear implication operator $\multimap$. The same fragment is obtained by replacing $\multimap$ with the operators $\sharp$ and $\perp$, where $\sharp$ (*par*) is the multiplicative or operator and $\perp$ is linear negation and $(A \multimap B) \equiv (A^\perp \sharp B)$. Using the version without $\multimap$, we normalize two-sided sequents of the form $A_1, \ldots, A_m \vdash B_1, \ldots, B_n$ into right-sided sequents of the form $\vdash A_1^\perp, \ldots, A_m^\perp, B_1, \ldots, B_n$. (In sequent representations of this style, the comma represents $\otimes$ on the left side of the sequent and $\sharp$ on the right side.) In our new format, then, the proof takes the form

$$\vdash \textbf{every}^\perp, \textbf{boy}^\perp, \textbf{left}^\perp, f_\sigma \leadsto_t M.$$

The proof net further requires that sequents be in negation normal form, in which negation is applied only to atomic terms. Moving the negations inward (the usual double-negation and de Morgan properties hold), and displaying the full premises, we obtain the normalized sequent

$$\vdash \quad ((v \leadsto_e x)^\perp \sharp r \leadsto_t R(x)) \otimes ((g_\sigma \leadsto_e y)^\perp \sharp H \leadsto_t S(y))$$
$$\otimes (H \leadsto_t every(R, S))^\perp,$$
$$v \leadsto_e X \otimes (r \leadsto_t boy(X))^\perp,$$
$$g_\sigma \leadsto_e Y \otimes (f_\sigma \leadsto_t leave(Y))^\perp,$$
$$f_\sigma \leadsto_t M.$$

Note that noncompound terms are referred to as 'literal' or 'atomic' terms because they are atomic from the point of view of the glue language, even though these terms are in fact of the form $S \leadsto_\tau M$, where

S is an expression over LFG structures and M is a type-τ expression in the meaning language.

3.2   Step 2: Create the graph

The next step is to create a graph whose nodes consist of all the terms which occur in the sequent. That is, a node is created for each literal C and for each negated literal $C^{\perp}$; a node is created for each compound term $A \otimes B$ or $A \,\natural\, B$; and nodes are also created for its subterms A and B. Once created, the nodes are connected as follows. For each node of the form $A \,\natural\, B$, we draw a soft edge in the form of a horizontal dashed line connecting it to nodes A and B. For each node of the form $A \otimes B$, we draw a hard edge (solid line) connecting it to nodes A and B. In the example at hand, the graph is made up of the following subgraphs:

every **subgraph:**

$$\dfrac{(v \leadsto_e x)^{\perp} \quad r \leadsto_t R(x) \qquad \dfrac{(g_\sigma \leadsto_e y)^{\perp} \quad H \leadsto_t S(y)}{((g_\sigma \leadsto_e y)^{\perp} \,\natural\, H \leadsto_t S(y))} \quad (H \leadsto_t every(R,S))^{\perp}}{\dfrac{((v \leadsto_e x)^{\perp} \,\natural\, r \leadsto_t R(x)) \qquad ((g_\sigma \leadsto_e y)^{\perp} \,\natural\, H \leadsto_t S(y)) \otimes (H \leadsto_t every(R,S))^{\perp}}{((v \leadsto_e x)^{\perp} \,\natural\, r \leadsto_t R(x)) \otimes ((g_\sigma \leadsto_e y)^{\perp} \,\natural\, H \leadsto_t S(y)) \otimes (H \leadsto_t every(R,S))^{\perp}}}$$

boy subgraph: $\dfrac{v \leadsto_e X \quad (r \leadsto_t boy(X))^{\perp}}{v \leadsto_e X \otimes (r \leadsto_t boy(X))^{\perp}}$

left subgraph: $\dfrac{g_\sigma \leadsto_e Y \quad (f_\sigma \leadsto_t leave(Y))^{\perp}}{g_\sigma \leadsto_e Y \otimes (f_\sigma \leadsto_t leave(Y))^{\perp}}$

conclusion subgraph: $f_\sigma \leadsto_t M$

3.3   Step 3: Connect the literals

The final step in assembling a proof net is to connect together the literal nodes at the top of each subgraph. It is at this stage that higher-order unification is applied to the variables in order to assign them the values they will assume in the final meaning. This is also the point at which the process can become exponential, since every valid way of connecting the literals and instantiating their variables corresponds to a different reading for the sentence. For example, a sentence containing n generalized quantifiers has, at least in principle, $n!$ possible scope readings and therefore $n!$ unique proof nets.

Step 3 proceeds as follows. For each literal, we draw an arc connecting it to a matching literal of opposite sign. In other words, each literal A is connected to a literal $B^{\perp}$ where A unifies with B. Every literal in the graph must be connected in this way. If for some literal A there exists no matching literal B of opposite sign then the graph does not encode a proof and the algorithm fails. Such a case might correspond to a failure of unification or type mismatch in the meaning language, or else a violation of resource accounting in the linear logic, as displayed e.g. by the invalid formula

$$(a \multimap b) \otimes (a \multimap c) \vdash a \multimap (b \otimes c).$$

(one sees immediately that such a formula is invalid simply by its odd number of a's).

For the example at hand, there is exactly one way to connect the literals and hence at most one reading for the sentence. The final proof net is shown in Figure 3.1.

3.4   Step 4: Test the graph for validity

The final step is to apply Gallier's (1992) algorithm to the connected graph in order to check that it corresponds to a proof. This algorithm consists essentially of recursively decomposing the graph from the bottom up and checking for cycles. Here I present the algorithm informally; for proofs of its correctness and $O(n^2)$ time complexity see Gallier (1992).

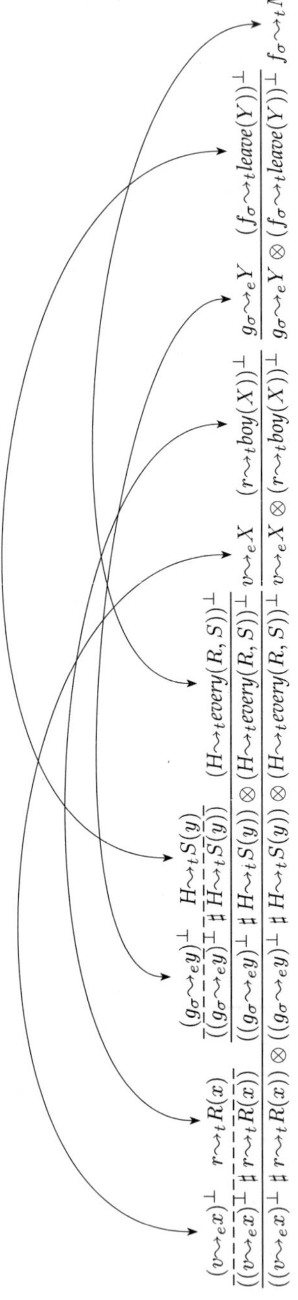

Figure 3.1: Proof net for *Every boy left*.

Base case: If the graph consists of a single link between literals A and $A^\perp$, the algorithm succeeds and the graph corresponds to a proof.

Recursive case 1: We begin the decomposition by deleting the bottom-level par nodes. If there is some terminal node $A \mathbin{\sharp} B$ connected to higher nodes A and B, then we delete $A \mathbin{\sharp} B$. This of course removes the dashed edge from $A \mathbin{\sharp} B$ to A and to B, but does not remove nodes A and B. We then run the algorithm on the resulting smaller (possibly unconnected) graph.

Recursive case 2: Otherwise, if no terminal par node is available, we find a terminal tensor node to delete. This case is more complicated because not every way of deleting a tensor node necessarily leads to success, even for a valid proof net. We therefore choose nondeterministically some terminal tensor node $A \otimes B$. If deleting that node results in a single, connected (i.e. cyclic) graph, then that node was not a valid splitting tensor and we must choose a different one instead, or else halt with failure if none is available. Otherwise, deleting $A \otimes B$ leaves nodes A and B belonging to two unconnected graphs $G1$ and $G2$. We then run the algorithm on $G1$ and $G2$.

The case where all terminal tensors lead to cyclic graphs corresponds to a formula in which the linear logic resources are potentially available and yet no proof exists.

The above procedure, together with the unifications from Step 3, verifies the proof net. For example, when applied to the net in Figure 3.1, the algorithm succeeds and establishes the proof of $f_\sigma \leadsto_t every(boy, \lambda y.leave(y))$. The higher-order variables in Figure 3.1 are shown uninstantiated in order to save space in the diagram; however, by this stage they would already be bound as follows: $X \mapsto x$, $R \mapsto boy$, $H \mapsto f_\sigma$, $S \mapsto \lambda y.leave(y)$, $M \mapsto every(boy, \lambda y.leave(y))$.

In later sections I will give more examples of deductions using proof nets. First, though, let us turn our attention to negative polarity licensing.

4 Negative Polarity Licensing

Ladusaw (1979) established what is now a well-known generalization in semantics, namely that negative polarity lexical items (NPIs) are licensed within the semantic scope of downward-entailing operators. Examples of NPIs are found across several categories, including adverbs (*ever, yet, anymore, at all, even*), determiners (*any*), and certain idiomatic expressions (*give a damn, lift a finger*). As illustrated in sentence pairs (8)-(10), NPIs cannot appear felicitously in a sentence without being licensed by some sort of negative or decreasing context.

(8)   No boy has ever been to Moscow.
      *A boy has ever been to Moscow.

(9)   Neither Sue nor Bill lifted a finger to help.
      *Sue lifted a finger to help.

(10) Kim rarely had any fun.
      *Kim had any fun.

NPI licensers include certain adverbs (*rarely, hardly*) and certain affective predicates (*be amazed that, too* [ADJ] *to*). NPIs are also licensed by 'monotone decreasing' quantifiers, which are built from determiners like *no, not all, at most four, less than half*, and *neither ... nor ....* A determiner Q is monotone decreasing if it validates inferences from bigger toward smaller sets—i.e., iff $Q(A, B) \models Q(A, B \cap C)$. Examples of such decreasing entailments are given in (11) and (12).

(11) no boy came home $\models$ no boy came home late

(12) neither Sue nor Bill sang $\models$ neither Sue nor Bill sang *Fidelio*

The negative or decreasing context created by a licenser can apparently license more than one NPI within its scope. For example, we can add an additional NPI to each example in (8)-(10), producing the felicitous sentences in (13)-(15).

(13) No boy has ever been to Moscow even once.

(14)   Neither Sue nor Bill ever lifted a finger to help.

(15)   Kim rarely had any fun at all.

Although NPIs require a negative or decreasing licenser, the converse is not the case. That is, licensers are just as free as non-licensers to occur in sentences which contain no NPIs. This is demonstrated by the grammaticality of (16)-(18).

(16)   No boy went to Moscow.
       A boy went to Moscow.

(17)   Neither Sue nor Bill helped us.
       Sue helped us.

(18)   Kim rarely had fun.
       Kim had fun.

5   A Glue Language Treatment of NPI Licensing

This section gives a glue language implementation of NPI licensing, using a simple modification of the relevant meaning constructors specified in the lexicon.

5.1   Meaning constructors for NPIs

There is a resource-based interpretation of the NPI phenomenon described in the previous section. The negative or decreasing licensing operator must make available a resource, call it ℓ, which will license the NPIs, if any, within its scope. If no such resource is made available then the NPIs are unlicensed.

How can NPIs be made to require the ℓ resource? The way one implements such a requirement in linear logic is to put the required resource on the left side of the implication operator $-\circ$. This is precisely the approach taken here. However, since the NPI is just 'borrowing' the license, not consuming it (after all, more than one NPI may be licensed, as in examples (13)-(15)), we also add the resource to the right hand side of the implication. That is, for a meaning constructor of the form $A \multimap B$ (which consumes an "old" meaning A in order to produce a "new" meaning B), we construct a corresponding NPI meaning constructor of the form

$$(A \otimes \ell) \multimap (B \otimes \ell).$$

For example, the meaning constructor proposed in Dalrymple et al. (1993) for the sentential modifier *obviously* is

(19)   **obviously**: $\forall P.\ f_\sigma \rightsquigarrow_t P \multimap f_\sigma \rightsquigarrow_t obviously(P).$

Under this analysis of sentential modification, NPI adverbs such as *yet* or *ever* would take the same form as (19), but with the licensing apparatus added:

$\quad\quad$ **ever**: $\forall P.\ (f_\sigma \rightsquigarrow_t P \otimes \ell) \multimap (f_\sigma \rightsquigarrow_t ever(P) \otimes \ell).$

This technique can be applied to the other categories of NPI as well. In the case of determiners, we assign them meaning constructors from the same template as *every* ((1), repeated here as (20)).

(20)   **every**: $\forall H, R, S.\ (\forall x.\ (g_\sigma\ \text{VAR}) \rightsquigarrow_e x \multimap (g_\sigma\ \text{RESTR}) \rightsquigarrow_t R(x))$
$\quad\quad\quad\quad\quad \otimes\ (\forall y.\ g_\sigma \rightsquigarrow_e y \multimap H \rightsquigarrow_t S(y))$
$\quad\quad\quad\quad\quad \multimap H \rightsquigarrow_t every(R, S)$

For the NPI determiner *any*[2] the licensing apparatus is added to the template in (20) to produce the meaning constructor in (21).[3]

(21)   **any**: $\forall H, R, S.\ (\forall x.\ (g_\sigma\ \text{VAR}) \rightsquigarrow_e x \multimap (g_\sigma\ \text{RESTR}) \rightsquigarrow_t R(x))$
$\quad\quad\quad\quad\quad \otimes\ (\forall y.\ g_\sigma \rightsquigarrow_e y \multimap H \rightsquigarrow_t S(y) \otimes \ell)$
$\quad\quad\quad\quad\quad \multimap (H \rightsquigarrow_t any(R, S) \otimes \ell)$

The function of the $\ell \multimap \ell$ pattern inside an NPI is to consume the resource ℓ and then produce it again. However, for this to happen,

---

[2] *Any* also has another, so-called "free choice" interpretation (as in, e.g., *Any pen will do*) (Ladusaw 1979; Kadmon and Landman 1993), which I ignore here.

[3] Note that we have kept the left-side licensing resource ℓ *inside* the scope constructor of *any*, attached to $S(y)$. Although this particular placement is not necessary for ensuring that *any* gets licensed, it is necessary for ensuring that other NPIs can be licensed <u>after</u> *any*. Such a case is found in, e.g., *No girl gave any present to any boy*.

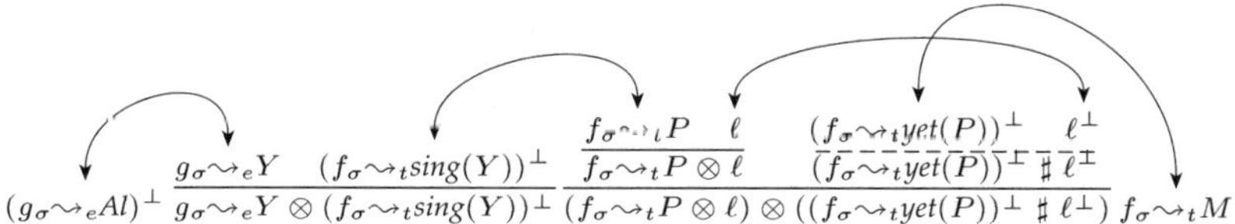

Figure 3.2: Invalid proof net of *Al sang yet*.

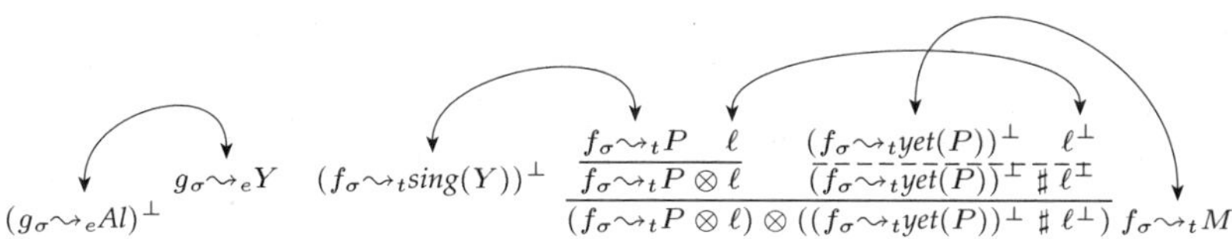

Figure 3.3: Point of failure. Bottom tensor node cannot be deleted.

the resource ℓ will have to be generated by some licenser whose scope includes the NPI, as shown below. If no outside ℓ resource is made available, then the extraneous, unconsumed ℓ material in the NPI guarantees that no proof will be generated. In proof net terms, the output ℓ cannot feed back into the input ℓ without producing a cycle.

Let us now see how the derivation is blocked for a sentence containing an unlicensed NPI such as (22).

(22)   *Al sang yet.

$$f: \begin{bmatrix} \text{PRED} & \text{'SING'} \\ \text{SUBJ} & g:\begin{bmatrix} \text{PRED} & \text{'AL'} \end{bmatrix} \\ \text{MODS} & \{\begin{bmatrix} \text{PRED} & \text{'YET'} \end{bmatrix}\} \end{bmatrix}$$

The relevant meaning constructors are

al: $g_\sigma \leadsto_e Al$

sang: $g_\sigma \leadsto_e Y \multimap f_\sigma \leadsto_t sing(Y)$

yet: $(f_\sigma \leadsto_t P \otimes \ell) \multimap (f_\sigma \leadsto_t yet(P) \otimes \ell)$

The proof net for (22), shown in Figure 3.2, is spurious and does not encode a proof. The reason is shown in Figure 3.3. At this point in the algorithm, we have deleted the leftmost terminal tensor node. However, the only remaining terminal tensor node cannot be deleted, since doing so would leave a single connected subgraph; the cycle is in the edge from ℓ to $\ell^{\perp}$. At this point the algorithm fails and no meaning is derived.

5.2   Meaning constructors for NPI licensers

It is clear from the proposal so far that lexical items like *no* and *rarely* which license NPIs will need to produce a ℓ resource within their scope which can then be consumed by the NPI. However, that is not enough; a licenser can still occur inside a sentence without an NPI, as in e.g. *No one left*. The resource accounting of linear logic requires that we 'clean up' by consuming any excess ℓ resources in order for the meaning deduction to go through.

Fortunately, we can solve this problem within the licenser's meaning constructor itself. For a lexical category whose meaning constructor is of the form $A \multimap B$, we assign to the NPI licensers of that category the meaning constructor

$$(\ell \multimap (A \otimes \ell)) \multimap B.$$

By its logical structure, being embedded inside another implication, the inner implication here serves to introduce 'hypothetical' material. All of the NPI licensing occurs within the hypothetical (left) side of the outermost implication. Since the ℓ resource is made available to the NPI only within this hypothetical, it is guaranteed that the NPI is assembled within, and therefore falls under, the scope of the licenser. Furthermore, the formula is 'self cleaning', in that the ℓ resource, even if not used by an NPI, does not survive the hypothetical and so cannot affect the meaning of the licenser in some other way. That is, the licensing constructor $(\ell \multimap (A \otimes \ell)) \multimap B$ can derive all of the same meanings as the nonlicensing version $A \multimap B$.

Fact $(\ell \multimap (A \otimes \ell)) \multimap B \vdash A \multimap B$

Proof We construct the proof net of the equivalent right-sided sequent

$$\vdash (\ell^{\perp} \,\sharp\, (A \otimes \ell)) \otimes B^{\perp}, A^{\perp}, B$$

and then test that it is valid.

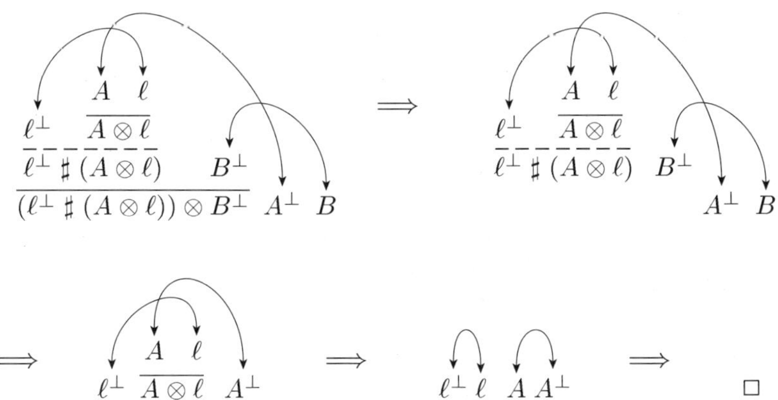

This self-cleaning property means that a licensing resource is exactly that—a license. Within its scope, it is available to be used once, several times (in a "chain" of NPIs which pass it along), or not at all, as required.[4]

A simple example is provided by the NPI-licensing adverb *rarely*. We modify the sentential adverb template in (19) to create a meaning constructor for *rarely* which licenses an NPI within the sentence it modifies.

$$\textbf{rarely}: \quad \forall P.\ (\ell \multimap (f_\sigma \leadsto_t P \otimes \ell)) \multimap f_\sigma \leadsto_t rarely(P)$$

The case of the monotonic decreasing determiners such as *no* and *few* is slightly more complex but follows the same pattern. A preliminary meaning constructor for *no* is given in (23).

$$(23) \quad \textbf{no}: \quad \forall H, R, S.\ (\forall x.\ (g_\sigma\ \text{VAR}) \leadsto_e x \multimap (g_\sigma\ \text{RESTR}) \leadsto_t R(x))$$
$$\otimes\ (\forall y.\ (g_\sigma \leadsto_e y \otimes \ell) \multimap (H \leadsto_t S(y) \otimes \ell))$$
$$\multimap H \leadsto_t no(R, S)$$

I will demonstrate (23) in two sentences, one without and another with an NPI. The first example is (24).

---

[4]Note that this multiple-use effect can be achieved more directly using the exponential operator; however this unnecessary step would take us outside of the multiplicative fragment and preclude the proof net techniques described earlier.

(24)   No boy went.

$$f: \begin{bmatrix} \text{PRED} & \text{`GO'} \\ \text{SUBJ} & g: \begin{bmatrix} \text{SPEC} & \text{`NO'} \\ \text{PRED} & \text{`BOY'} \end{bmatrix} \end{bmatrix}$$

The premises are:

no: $(v \leadsto_e x \multimap r \leadsto_t R(x)) \otimes ((g_\sigma \leadsto_e y \otimes \ell) \multimap (H \leadsto_t S(y) \otimes \ell))$
$\multimap H \leadsto_t no(R, S)$

boy: $v \leadsto_e X \multimap r \leadsto_t boy(X)$

went: $g_\sigma \leadsto_e Y \multimap f_\sigma \leadsto_t go(Y)$

The proof net is shown in Figure 3.4. Note that the ℓ and $\ell^\perp$ literals are within subgraphs that are connected by a soft (par) edge. Since terminal par nodes can be deleted freely, it should be clear that the cyclicity problem of Figure 3.3 does not apply here and that the ℓ resources are properly disposed of.

Finally, I will derive a meaning for (25), in which the determiners *no* and *any* play the role of licenser and NPI, respectively.

(25)   No boy saw any girl.

$$f: \begin{bmatrix} \text{PRED} & \text{`SEE'} \\ \text{SUBJ} & g: \begin{bmatrix} \text{SPEC} & \text{`NO'} \\ \text{PRED} & \text{`BOY'} \end{bmatrix} \\ \text{OBJ} & h: \begin{bmatrix} \text{SPEC} & \text{`ANY'} \\ \text{PRED} & \text{`GIRL'} \end{bmatrix} \end{bmatrix}$$

Normally, a sentence with two quantifiers would generate two different scope readings—in this case, (26) and (27).

(26) $f_\sigma \leadsto_t no(boy, \lambda x.any(girl, \lambda y.see(x, y)))$

(27) $f_\sigma \leadsto_t any(girl, \lambda y.no(boy, \lambda x.see(x, y)))$

However, Ladusaw's generalization is that negative polarity items are licensed *within the scope* of their licensers. In fact, Ladusaw (1979, pages 96-101) gives several arguments why *any* cannot take wide scope in such a case. The goal is therefore to derive only (26) and block (27).

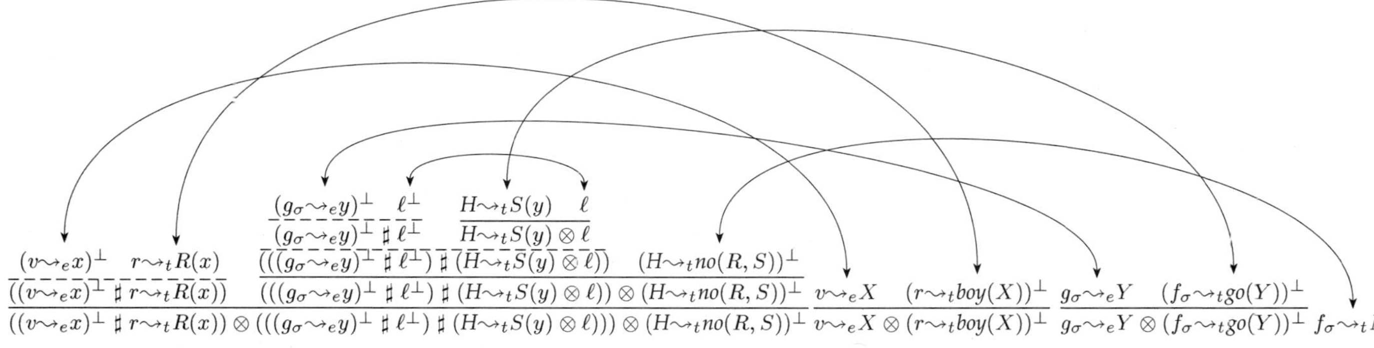

Figure 3.4: Proof net for *No boy went.*

To save space in the proof net, I will pre-compose the meaning constructors of the determiners (**no, any**) and the nouns (**boy, girl**) into single generalized quantifiers (**no-boy, any-girl**), so that only the scopes need to be solved. The premises, then, are:

no-boy: $\quad ((g_\sigma \leadsto_e x \otimes \ell) \multimap (H \leadsto_t S(x) \otimes \ell)) \multimap H \leadsto_t no(boy, S)$

saw: $\quad (g_\sigma \leadsto_e X \otimes h_\sigma \leadsto_e Y) \multimap f_\sigma \leadsto_t see(X, Y)$

any-girl: $\quad (h_\sigma \leadsto_e y \multimap I \leadsto_t T(y) \otimes \ell) \multimap (I \leadsto_t any(girl, T) \otimes \ell)$

The proof net for reading (26) is shown in Figure 3.5.[5] As required, the net in Figure 3.5, corresponding to wide scope for *no*, is valid. The first step in the proof of Figure 3.5 is to delete the only available splitting tensor, which is boxed in the figure.

A second way of linking the positive and negative literals in Figure 3.5 produces a net which corresponds to (27), the spurious reading in which *any* has wide scope. In that graph, however, all three of the available terminal tensor nodes produce a single, connected (cyclic) graph if deleted, so decomposition cannot even begin and the algorithm fails. Once again, it is the licensing resources which are enforcing the desired constraint.

6   Leftward Licensing

So far I have restricted discussion of decreasingness to the "right-decreasing" entailment pattern. However, leftward polarity licensing is also captured under this analysis. A determiner Q is monotonic *left decreasing* if it validates inferences of the form

$$Q(A, B) \models Q(A \cap C, B).$$

In other words, the restriction, rather than the scope, is the decreasing set. Examples of such left-decreasing entailments are given in (28) and (29).

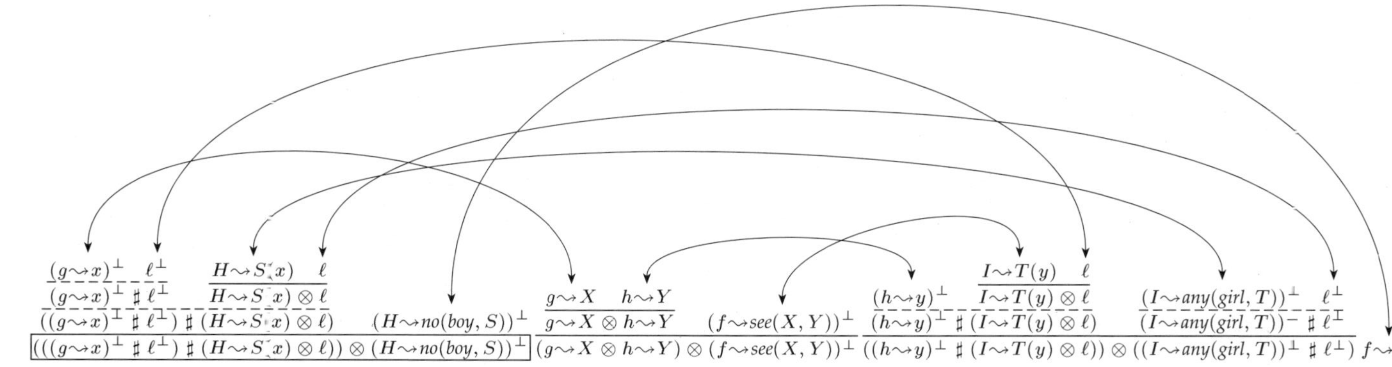

Figure 3.5: Valid proof net for *No boy saw any girl* where *no* has wide scope (reading (26)). The initial splitting tensor is shown boxed (bottom left).

(28)   every boy left $\models$ every boy I admire left

(29)   no boy came home $\models$ no good boy came home

This shows that the determiners *every* and *no* are both left-decreasing, though recall *every* is not right-decreasing. The complete meaning constructors, then, for *every* and *no* can be given as follows.

$$\textbf{every:} \quad \forall H, R, S. \ (\forall x. \ ((g_\sigma \ \text{VAR}) \leadsto_e x \otimes \ell) \multimap ((g_\sigma \ \text{RESTR}) \leadsto_t R(x) \otimes \ell))$$
$$\otimes (\forall y. \ g_\sigma \leadsto_e y \multimap H \leadsto_t S(y))$$
$$\multimap H \leadsto_t every(R, S)$$

$$\textbf{no:} \quad \forall H, R, S. \ (\forall x. \ ((g_\sigma \ \text{VAR}) \leadsto_e x \otimes \ell) \multimap ((g_\sigma \ \text{RESTR}) \leadsto_t R(x) \otimes \ell))$$
$$\otimes (\forall y. \ (g_\sigma \leadsto_e y \otimes \ell) \multimap (H \leadsto_t S(y) \otimes \ell))$$
$$\multimap H \leadsto_t no(R, S)$$

In the case of *every*, the ℓ resource is only made available within the embedded implication that comprises the restriction, so only NPIs within the restriction will be licensed. *No*, on the other hand, licenses within the restrictor, within the scope, or within both, if necessary. Thus the meaning constructors above account for all of the data in (30) and (31).

(30)   Every boy had fun.
       Every boy who ever had the measles had fun.
       *Every boy had any fun.
       *Every boy who ever had the measles had any fun.

(31)   No boy had fun.
       No boy who ever had the measles had fun.
       No boy had any fun.
       No boy who ever had the measles had any fun.

7   Categorial Grammar Approaches

The ℓ atom used here is somewhat analogous to the (negative) lexical 'monotonicity markers' proposed by Sánchez-Valencia (1991, 1995) and Dowty (1994) for categorial grammar. In these approaches, categories of the form A/B are marked with monotonicity properties, i.e. as A^+/B^+, A^+/B^-, A^-/B^+, or A^-/B^-, and similarly for left-leaning categories of the form $A\backslash B$. Then monotonicity constraints can be enforced using category assignments like the following from Dowty (1994):

$$\mathbf{no}: \quad \left\{ \begin{array}{l} (S^+/VP^-)/CN^- \\ (S^-/VP^+)/CN^+ \end{array} \right\}$$

$$\mathbf{any}: \quad (S^-/VP^-)/CN^-$$

$$\mathbf{ever}: \quad VP^-/VP^-$$

Sánchez-Valencia and Dowty, however, are less concerned with the distribution of NPIs than they are with using monotonicity properties to characterize valid inference patterns, an issue which I have ignored here. Hence their work emphasizes *logical* polarity, where an odd number of negative marks indicates negative polarity, and an even number of negatives cancel each other to produce positive polarity. For example, the category of **no** above "flips" the polarity of its argument. By contrast, the system proposed here, like Ladusaw's (1979) original proposal, is "intuitionistic" (Dowty 1994, pages 134-137): since multiple negative contexts do not cancel each other out, I allow doubly-licensed NPIs, as in *Nobody rarely sees anyone*. To handle such cases, while at the same time accounting for monotonic inference properties, Dowty (1994) proposes a double-marking framework whereby categories like A^-_-/B^+_- are marked for both logical polarity and syntactic polarity.

8   Problem: Not Restrictive Enough

The constraint enforced by the licensing system described in this paper produces two desirable effects. First, for grammatical sentences like (25), the constraint blocks unwanted scope readings such as (27), repeated here as (32).

(32) $*any(girl, \lambda y.no(boy, \lambda x.see(x, y)))$

Secondly, this constraint allows us reject bad sentences such as those in (33) for which no readings can be derived.

(33)   *Al sang yet.
       *Kim had any fun.
       *Most boys ever left.

Let us refer to these two accomplishments as *constraining* (scope readings) and *rejecting* (sentences), respectively. Unfortunately, the approach presented above is not quite restrictive enough at either task.

8.1   More constraining needed

One problem is that this system still overgenerates licensing possibilities. For example, since *surprised* and the negative morpheme *–n't* are both licensers, an NPI like *lift a finger* could get licensed either as shown in (34) or (35):

(34)   I'd be surprised if John didn't$_\ell$ lift a finger$_\ell$ to help.

(35)   I'd be surprised$_\ell$ if John didn't lift a finger$_\ell$ to help.

The licensing in (35) is made possible by the self-cleaning property of the licenser *–n't*, i.e. the same property that permits a sentence with no NPIs like *John didn't help*. However, it seems to me that only (34) represents a legitimate licensing in this case.

This state of affairs might lead one to propose a constraint limiting licensing to the licenser with narrowest possible scope. Indeed, explicit negations (i.e. "n-words") seem to behave in this way.[6] However, there seem to be exceptions among less overt licensers. For example, (36) has two licensers, *–n't* and *refuse*.

(36)   Doctors shouldn't be allowed to refuse to treat anybody.

In this case, both the narrow and wide licensing possibilities seem to be available. In reading (37), the negation *n't* licenses the NPI *anybody*.

(37) $\neg_\ell$ allowed: doctor(x), anybody(y)$_\ell$: x refuses to treat y.

The second, less plausible reading in (38) is actually the narrower one where *refuse* scopes over and licenses *anybody*.

---

[6] I'm grateful to Bill Ladusaw (p.c.) for the observations in this paragraph.

(38) $\neg$ allowed: doctor(x): x refuses$_\ell$ to treat anybody$_\ell$.

Assuming then that explicitly negative "n-word" licensers like *no* always take the narrowest licensing scope, we can characterize such licensers as *strong*,in contrast to *weak* licensers such as *refuse* and *few*. The weak licensers, in other words, have the option of passing up the opportunity to license an NPI, allowing it to be licensed by a strong licenser in a higher clause; the strong licensers, on the other hand, have no such option.

As a consequence, sentence (39) has only one reading, given in (40):

(39)   Few people think no doctor treated anyone.

(40)   few people think: no$_\ell$ doctors(x), anybody(y)$_\ell$, x treats y

In sentence (41), on the other hand, the weak licenser *few* can optionally pass up the licensing of *anybody*, producing the two readings (42) and (43).

(41)   Nobody thinks few doctors treated anyone.

(42)   nobody thinks: few$_\ell$ doctors(x), anybody(y)$_\ell$, x treats y

(43)   nobody$_\ell$ thinks: anybody(y)$_\ell$, few doctors(x), x treats y

In fact, in Fry (1997b) I describe a modification to the NPI licensing scheme which handles the weak/strong distinction described above by ensuring that strong licensers can never pass up their licensing to some outer licenser. However, the modification is rather ungainly, involving new variables and new ℓ resources. If an even more intricate taxonomy of NPIs and their licensers is used, such as the one in Zwarts (1997), then even more maneuvering would probably be required to handle the licensing complexities.

8.2   More rejection needed

The system presented above is also not restrictive enough at the rejection task. Since it assumes that scope-taking is basically unconstrained (except for the licensing constraint itself), this approach will accept bad sentences like (44)-(46), because the indicated (properly licensed) readings can be derived.

(44)   *Any girl saw no boy.
$no(boy, \lambda y.any(girl, \lambda x.see(x, y)))$

(45)   *Any boy rarely left.
$rarely(any(boy, \lambda x.leave(x)))$

(46)   *Anyone didn't leave.
$not(any(person, \lambda x.leave(x)))$

The unconstrained scope-taking in the above examples is of course unrealistic. For example, monotone decreasing objects are known to not take wide scope (Szabolcsi 1997) as I have allowed in (44).

In any case, the policy of accepting a sentence whenever any legitimate reading can be derived is too liberal. Rather the requirement for acceptance must be the ability to derive the reading whose scope order corresponds to the linear order of the scope-taking elements in the sentence. In other words, although Ladusaw's licensing constraint is expressed in terms of semantic scope, the felicitous use of NPIs in an English sentence s does not depend on any possible scope reading for s but rather on the decreasing context established by the reading whose scope order follows the order of the words in s.

This situation echoes a recurring theme in the literature on the distribution of negative polarity items: that the phenomenon apparently cannot be characterized exclusively within syntax nor semantics, but rather seems to be situated at the interface between the two. The approach given earlier is a constraint on *semantic* assembly that is not sufficient to account for all the surface string facts.

9   Conclusion

In this chapter I first showed how linear logic proof nets can be used for efficient meaning deductions within the glue language semantics framework. I then presented a glue language treatment of negative polarity licensing based on the addition of explicit licenses (ℓ's) to the relevant meaning constructors within the lexicon. This system ensures that NPIs are licensed within the semantic scope of their licensers in both left- and right-decreasing contexts. The ℓ-marking approach has the advantage of being a simple and local way to enforce scope constraints during meaning assembly without introducing global rules, and presumably this technique can be used for any type of scope constraint that can be expressed in terms of licensers and licensees. Finally, however, I showed that the system as presented is too rough-grained to be able to account for all the facts about NPI distribution in English.

Acknowledgments

I'm grateful to Mary Dalrymple, John Lamping, and Stanley Peters for helpful discussions of this material, and also to Vineet Gupta, Martin Kay, Bill Ladusaw, Fernando Pereira, Vijay Saraswat, Henriëtte de Swart, and the reviewers and audiences of LLC6, LFG-97 and ACL-97 for helpful comments. Naturally mistakes and views are my own.

References

Dalrymple, Mary, John Lamping, and Vijay Saraswat. 1993. LFG semantics via constraints. In *Proceedings of the Sixth Meeting of the European ACL*, University of Utrecht, pages 97–105. European Chapter of the Association for Computational Linguistics.

Dowty, David. 1994. The role of negative polarity and concord marking in natural language reasoning. In Mandy Harvey and Lynn Santelmann, editors, *Proceedings of SALT IV*, pages 114–144, Cornell University, Ithaca, NY.

Fry, John. 1997a. Negative polarity licensing at the syntax-semantics interface. In *Proceedings of the Thirty-Fifth Annual Meeting of the ACL and Eighth Conference of the EACL*, Madrid, pages 144–150. Association for Computational Linguistics.

Fry, John. 1997b. Polarity sensitivity and scope in "glue language" semantics. In Miriam Butt and Tracy Holloway King, editors, *Proceedings of the LFG-97 Conference*, University of California-San Diego. CSLI Publications, Stanford University.

Gallier, Jean. 1992. Constructive logics. Part II: Linear logic and proof nets. MS, Department of Computer and Information Science, University of Pennsylvania.

Girard, Jean-Yves. 1987. Linear logic. *Theoretical Computer Science*, 50:1–102.

Kadmon, Nirit and Fred Landman. 1993. Any. *Linguistics and Philosophy 16*, pages 353–422.

Ladusaw, William A. 1979. *Polarity Sensitivity as Inherent Scope Relations*. PhD thesis, University of Texas, Austin. Reprinted in Jorge Hankamer, editor, *Outstanding Dissertations in Linguistics*. Garland, 1980.

Lecomte, Alain and Christian Retoré. 1995. Pomset logic as an alternative categorial grammar. In Glyn V. Morrill and Richard T. Oehrle, editors, *Formal Grammar*, 1995. Proceedings of the Conference of the European Summer School in Logic, Language, and Information, Barcelona, 1995.

Morrill, Glyn V. 1996. Memoisation of categorial proof nets: parallelism in categorial processing. In V. Michele Abrusci and Claudia Casadio, editors, *Proceedings, Roma Workshop on Proofs and Linguistic Categories*, Rome.

Sánchez-Valencia, Victor. 1991. *Studies on natural logic and categorial grammar*. PhD thesis, University of Amsterdam.

Sánchez-Valencia, Victor. 1995. Parsing-driven inference: natural logic. *Linguistic Analysis*, 25(3-4):258–285.

Szabolcsi, Anna. 1997. *Ways of Scope Taking*. Kluwer Academic Publishers, Dordrecht.

Zwarts, Franz. 1997. Three types of polarity. In Fritz Hamm and Erhard Hinrichs, editors, *Plurality and Quantification*. D. Reidel, Dordrecht.

4

Context Change, Underspecification, and the Structure of Glue Language Derivations

Richard Crouch and Josef van Genabith

1 Introduction

The interpretation of a natural language utterance typically both depends on its context of utterance, and has the effect of updating that context. This context-sensitivity raises two issues. First, how does one model context update? Second, in the absence of context many sentences appear ambiguous; computationally it is desirable to produce some form of initial underspecified semantic representation that can be progressively refined in the light of contextual factors.

This paper is a preliminary exploration of how context update and underspecification, which both have context-dependency as a common cause, can be approached from a common perspective. Our starting point will be the glue language approach to semantics, mapped out in a series of papers by Mary Dalrymple and colleagues and presented in Chapter 1 and elsewhere in this book, which uses a fragment of linear logic as a meta-level glue for deductively piecing together the (object-level) meanings assigned to various words in a syntactically analysed sentence. Under this approach, semantic derivations correspond to logical derivations, or proofs, in linear logic.

There are two reasons for taking the glue language approach as a starting point. First, the resource sensitivity of linear logic makes it a good tool for modelling various forms of update. It is therefore natural to wonder whether linear logic can be deployed to model context update in natural language.

Second, in the case of quantifier scope ambiguities, different derivations from the same set of glue language premises can generate alternative scope readings for a sentence, as described in Chapter 2. The premises thus define a set of derivations of all possible (scoped) meanings for the sentence. The addition of further constraints carving out subsets of these derivations would furnish an underspecified representation of scope. More generally, stating constraints on the structure of glue language derivations would offer a promising approach to (under)specifying a variety of semantic and contextual phenomena.

Before spelling out a glue language treatment of context update and underspecification in more detail, let us address these initial motivations in more detail.

1.1   Context and semantic interpretation

The observation that the interpretation of a sentence's meaning both depends on and updates context shows that context and semantic interpretation must somehow interact. But it says little about the form this interaction takes. One can look at semantic interpretation as a two stage process:

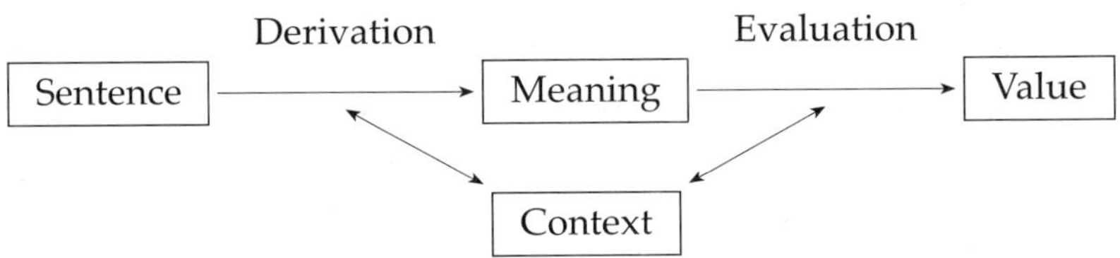

First there is a *derivation* of a meaning from a (syntactically analysed) sentence. This meaning is then *evaluated* against a model to obtain some kind of semantic value associated with the sentence, e.g. truth or falsity. Context can potentially play a role either in the derivation of a meaning from a sentence, or in the evaluation of a meaning against a model.

The prevailing view on context update, as exemplified by the use of dynamic logics such as Dynamic Predicate Logic (Groenendijk and Stokhof 1991), locates the effects of context dependency on the side of semantic evaluation. Meanings are treated as update functions on contexts, and evaluation consists of applying a meaning to a context to furnish an updated context. The derivation of a meaning from a sentence on the other hand tends to be strictly compositional and independent of context.

The arguably prevailing view on underspecification, e.g. Nerbonne (1991); Alshawi and Crouch (1992); Reyle (1993); Muskens (1995); Poesio (1994); Bos et al. (1996); Pinkal (1996), is somewhat different. In various guises, it holds that underspecified semantic representations are essentially sets of constraints defining a range of possible semantic derivations. Contextual resolution amounts to the addition of further constraints, further restricting the range of permissible derivations. Thus underspecification tends towards locating context dependency in the derivation of meanings from sentences.

One way of motivating this approach to underspecification is as follows. Assume a weak notion of compositionality; namely, that the meaning of a sentence is derived from (a) the meanings of its words, and (b) the way in which those meanings are combined. However, because of context-dependency, the syntactic structure of a sentence and lexical semantics are not always sufficient to fully determine either the meanings of some words or constituents (e.g., pronouns), or the way in which those meanings are combined (e.g., scope ambiguities). Context is required to fill in the gaps, and underspecified semantic representations show where these gaps are and how they are filled.

All of this points to a tension between prevailing treatments of context update and semantic underspecification. Treatments of update, via various forms of dynamic semantics, locate the effects of context in the evaluation rather than the derivation of meanings. But treatments of underspecification locate the effects of context in the derivation of meanings rather than their evaluation. This tension is not irreconcilable; context could well affect both derivation and evaluation, and accounts such as Underspecified Discourse Representation Theory (Reyle 1993) indicate how this could be so. But it would be interesting to see whether an approach locating context-dependency in just one place is tenable.

1.2   Context and glue

The approach to update and underspecification sketched here attempts to locate all context-dependency, and in particular context update, in the derivation of meanings from sentences.[1] The basis of this treatment is that the glue language approach uses a fragment of linear logic to carry out semantic derivation, and that the resource sensitivity of linear logic makes it well suited to modelling update.

1.2.1   Glue and update

The basic glue language approach relies on assigning object level meaning expressions to syntactic constituents (more strictly, to nodes in semantic projections of f-structures). This assignment is achieved by means of the uninterpreted relation symbol $\leadsto$: thus $\sigma \leadsto \phi$, where σ is a constant referring to a particular syntactic constituent and ϕ is an expression in the meaning language, can be read as saying that constituent σ is assigned the meaning ϕ.

Meaning assignments to constituents can be updated. Suppose for example that a sentential constituent s is assigned a certain meaning

$$s \leadsto sleep(john)$$

before the effects of a sentential adverbial are taken into account. And suppose that the adverbial gives rise to the following meaning constructor:

$$\forall \phi.\ s \leadsto \phi \multimap s \leadsto probably(\phi)$$

This can be combined with the initial assignment to s (via *modus ponens*) to produce an updated assignment

$$s \leadsto probably(sleep(john))$$

The use of linear implication ensures that this really is an update, since the following pattern of inference is *not* valid:

$$A,\ A \multimap B \nvdash A \otimes B$$

In   concluding B (e.g. $s \leadsto probably(sleep(john))$)   from A (e.g. $s \leadsto sleep(john)$) and $A \multimap B$, both the premises A and $A \multimap B$

---

[1]The glue language approach is not committed to this position; see van Genabith and Crouch (1997) and Chapter 6 of this volume for an illustration of how the glue approach can be used in conjunction with a dynamic meaning language, where context update does take place as part of semantic evaluation.

are consumed. This means that the premise A is no longer available to be conjoined with the conclusion B. That is, we cannot draw the (contradictory) conclusion that

$$s \leadsto probably(sleep(john)) \otimes s \leadsto sleep(john)$$

since the initial assignment to s is consumed. This should be contrasted to the valid pattern of inference in classical logic, $A,\ A \to B \vdash A \land B$, which would allow the original and revised assignments to co-exist.

To model context update, we will introduce a second uninterpreted binary relation symbol $\hookrightarrow$, similar to the meaning assignment predicate $\leadsto$. The context assignment predicate, $\hookrightarrow$, will associate constituents with meaning level expressions representing contextually derived properties. We will use these contextually derived properties to implement a (rudimentary) E-type analysis of pronouns. The basic idea is that glue language derivations will build up a meaning assignment for the sentence plus a collection of context assignments for its various sub-constituents. These contextual assignments may be used in the construction of the meanings assigned to pronouns, and typically the contextual assignments will be updated as a result of doing this. Contextual assignments derived from the interpretation of one sentence may also be passed on as additional contextual premises to subsequent sentences.

For example, a glue language derivation for a sentence like *"A man walked"* might yield a conclusion

$$s \leadsto a(man, walk) \otimes subj \hookrightarrow \lambda x.man(x) \land walk(x)$$

which consists of a meaning assignment to the sentence s plus a contextual assignment to the subject *subj*. This context assignment can then be used as a premise for constructing the meaning of the pronoun in a subsequent sentence *"He whistled"*. Here, the meaning of the pronoun is constructed by selecting some antecedent like *subj*, and using the property contextually assigned to it as the restriction for the pronominal quantifier (see Section 3).

This approach to context update differs from that familiar from dynamic logics in that it is the derivation of the meaning that updates context, and not the meaning thus derived. Thus it permits a treatment of context dynamics while keeping to an ordinary, static, meaning language. This has the advantage, compared to approaches using dynamic logics, of furnishing meaning representations for which standard and well understood proof theories are defined.

No great originality is claimed for the observation that dynamic meanings and context update are independent notions. In some respects classical DRT (Kamp 1981) also shares the property of locating context update in the construction of semantic representations. And Jaap van der Does has presented a categorial treatment of E-type anaphora bearing some parallels to the approach to be sketched here (van der Does 1996). But the use of linear logic to give an explicit modelling of the mechanics of context update is, as far as we know, novel.

1.2.2   Glue and underspecification

Once context assignments are added to the glue language approach, glue derivations aim to establish conclusions of the form

$$\Gamma, \Delta_1 \vdash s \leadsto \phi \otimes \Delta_2$$

where Γ is a set of lexical premises, Δ_1 is an initial set of context assignments, $s \leadsto \phi$ is a single meaning assignment to the sentence, and Δ_2 is an enlarged and updated set of context assignments.

From a given set of lexical and contextual premises, Γ and Δ_1, a number of alternative derivations of different sentential meanings are often possible. For example, different ways of combining lexical premises can give rise to different scopings. Selection of different contextual premises can give rise to alternative readings for pronouns; for example in *"John saw Bill. He said hello."* the two readings for the pronoun *he* arise from building its meaning either from the property assigned to the noun phrase *John* or from the property assigned to *Bill*.

Recalling the notion of weak compositionality, where the meaning of a sentence depends on the meanings of its words and the way these are combined, but where syntactic structure and lexical semantics may not fully specify either, we can draw the following parallel. Glue language derivations are precisely derivations of meanings. The contribution of lexical semantics and syntactic structure are jointly represented by the lexical premises to a glue language derivation. As the glue treatment of scope ambiguities indicates, these premises alone do not fully determine the range of possible derivations. Different ways of combining meanings are possible, which corresponds to differing orders of inference steps in the glue language derivations. Furthermore, the range of contextually dependent meanings open to words such as pronouns corresponds to differing choices of contextual premise used at various points in a glue language derivation. That is:

	Semantic Composition	Glue Derivation
Pronouns	Meaning of word	Choice of premise
Scope	Mode of combination	Order of derivation

This parallel is not sufficient to establish sets of lexical and contextual glue language premises as fully fledged underspecified semantic representations. They are a way of representing the set of all possible valid semantic derivations. What is required is the ability to represent explicitly additional constraints dictating premise choice and derivation order, in order to whittle away at the range of permissible derivations. Constraints for scope relations and anaphoric co-indexing, and which constrain the range of glue language derivations in the appropriate way, are presented below. The explicit representation of such constraints also turns out to have application to the analysis of ellipsis.

1.3 Outline of paper

Section 2 reviews the treatment of quantifier scope ambiguities presented in Chapter 2. It then introduces an ordering over syntactic constituents (nodes in semantic projections of f-structures) that can be used to partially specify scope relations. The node-ordering reflects certain properties in the structure of (normalized) glue language derivations. By demanding that a derivation from a given set of lexical premises additionally satisfies these structural properties, we can enforce or prohibit certain scope relations. The node-ordering thus acts as a way of specifying quantifier scopes, and can be shown to bear a close relation to label orderings in UDRS (Reyle 1993) and index orderings in QLF (Alshawi and Crouch 1992) playing the same role.

Section 3 introduces the context assignment symbol, $\hookrightarrow$. This is used to build up E-type properties (Cooper 1979; Lappin and Francez 1994;

van der Does 1996) associated with noun phrases in a sentence. These contextually assigned properties are used to construct the meanings of pronouns and other anaphors. The resource sensitivity of linear logic, in particular linear implication, allows these contextual assignments to be built and updated in the course of a glue language derivation. The interactions of context assignments with scope are addressed at some length in Section 4.

Section 5 brings together the issues of context update and underspecification by proposing the construction of audit trails. In addition to building meaning and context assignments, glue language derivations are modified to also explicitly construct a conjunction of constraints which have the effect of recording how the derivation is structured. Section 6 makes use of this audit trail to briefly describe a substitutional treatment of ellipsis, covered in greater depth in Crouch (1998). Section 7 concludes.

2 Specifying Scope

This section briefly reviews the glue language treatment of scope ambiguity presented in Chapter 2, and proceeds to show how scope can be partially specified via constraints on the structure of normalized glue language derivations.

2.1 Generating scope ambiguities

The sentence

(1)   Every candidate appointed a manager.

is scopally ambiguous, depending on whether the subject noun phrase takes wide or narrow scope with respect to the object. This ambiguity is accounted for by the analysis of quantifier scope presented by Dalrymple, Lamping, Pereira, and Saraswat in Chapter 2. They assume the following meaning constructors for the sentence (pre-combining the constructors for the determiners and their restrictions, and giving the nodes in the semantic projections more mnemonic names):

(2)   **appoint** $\vdash$
$\forall X, Y.\ (subj \leadsto X \otimes obj \leadsto Y) \multimap s \leadsto appoint(X, Y)$

(3)   **every-candidate** $\vdash$

   $\forall Scope, S.\ (\forall x.\ subj \leadsto x \multimap Scope \leadsto S(x))$

   $\multimap Scope \leadsto every(candidate, S)$

(4)   **a-manager** $\vdash$

   $\forall Scope, S.\ (\forall x.\ obj \leadsto x \multimap Scope \leadsto S(x))$

   $\multimap Scope \leadsto a(manager, S)$

From the premises, we need to derive a conclusion consisting of a single meaning assignment to the sentence (s) constituent, i.e.,

(5)   **appoint, every-candidate, a-manager** $\vdash s \leadsto \phi$

In line with the ambiguity of the sentence, there are two derivations that conclude with distinct sentential meaning assignments.

One derivation gives the subject wide scope. It starts by rewriting the constructor for **appoint** into an equivalent form:

(6)   **appoint1** $\vdash$

   $\forall X.\ subj \leadsto X \multimap (\forall Y.\ obj \leadsto Y \multimap s \leadsto appoint(X, Y))$

Under suitable instantiation of universally quantified variables

$$Scope \mapsto s, \quad S \mapsto \lambda y.\ appoint(X, y)$$

the consequent implication of **appoint1** matches the antecedent implication of **a-manager**. Through modus ponens, the constructors **appoint1** and **a-manager** can be combined to give

(7)   **appoint, a-manager** $\vdash$

   $\forall X.\ subj \leadsto X \multimap s \leadsto a(manager,\ \lambda y.\ appoint(X, y))$

Under suitable instantiation, this matches the antecedent implication of **every-candidate**, so that through modus ponens we have

(8)   **appoint, a-manager, every-candidate** $\vdash$

   $s \leadsto every(candidate,\ \lambda x.\ a(manager,\ \lambda y.\ appoint(x, y)))$

The conclusion is a single meaning assignment to s derived from all the premises, and constitutes one possible reading for the sentence.

The second derivation starts by instead rewriting **appoint** to another equivalent form

(9)   **appoint2** $\vdash$
$$\forall Y.\; obj \rightsquigarrow X \;\multimap\; (\forall X.\; subj \rightsquigarrow X \;\multimap\; s \rightsquigarrow appoint(X, Y))$$

Under suitable instantiations, the consequent implication of **appoint2** matches the antecedent implication of **every-candidate**, and they can be combined to give

(10)   **appoint, every-candidate** $\vdash$
$$\forall Y.\; obj \rightsquigarrow Y \;\multimap\; s \rightsquigarrow every(candidate,\; \lambda x.\; appoint(x, Y))$$

This in turn matches the antecedent implication of **a-manager**, so that

(11)   **appoint, a-manager, every-candidate** $\vdash$
$$s \rightsquigarrow a(manager,\; \lambda y.\; every(candidate,\; \lambda x.\; appoint(x, y)))$$

And this is the second scoping, obtained by an alternative derivation from the same premises.

No other derivations with different conclusions (in the form of a single meaning assignment to s) are possible (see Chapter 2 for discussion of this point).

2.2   Node orderings

The conjunction of premises plus the constraint that the conclusion be a single meaning assignment to the sentence can be viewed as a form of completely underspecified representation of the sentence's scope. However, completely underspecified representations are of little use. What we need is a way of progressively imposing further constraints that will eventually pick out one meaning assignment or the other.

To a first approximation, the difference between the two derivations above lies in the different order in which the premises are combined. Unfortunately a simple ordering over premise usage in the derivations is insufficient for constraining scope. However, a more detailed inspection of the derivations reveals a structural property that does directly reflect scope.

If we look at a sequent style derivation tree, the leaves of the tree will all be instances of axiom schema, in this case

$$\underline{app \vdash app} \qquad \underline{man \vdash man} \qquad \underline{cand \vdash cand}$$

where "app", "man" and "cand" abbreviate the meaning constructors for **appoint, a-manager** and **every-candidate** shown above.[2] The root of the tree will be a sequent

$$\overline{\text{app, man, cand} \vdash s \leadsto \phi}$$

Taking the leaves of the tree together, there will be meaning assignments for the nodes s, *subj* and *obj* on both the left- and right-hand sides of the turnstiles. But by the time we reach the conclusion at the root of the tree, all meaning assignments to nodes except s will have been moved so that they only occur on the left-hand side of the turnstile. At some point in going from the leaves to the root of the derivation tree, each node will have all of its meaning assignments moved out of the right-hand sides of the sequents. The relative order in which the *subj* and *obj* nodes are moved out of the right-hand sides reflects the scoping of the quantifiers associated with the two nodes.

2.2.1 Illustrations

In the next subsection we will properly establish the connection between the node ordering and scope. For now, we will merely illustrate it in action, and give some intuitive justification of why it works.

A schematic derivation tree giving the subject noun phrase wide scope in sentence (1) is shown below:

$$\cfrac{\cfrac{\text{app} \vdash \text{app} \qquad\qquad\qquad \text{man} \vdash \text{man}}{\text{app, man} \vdash \forall X.subj \leadsto X \ \multimap\ s \leadsto a(manager, \ldots X \ldots)} 1 \qquad \text{cand} \vdash \text{cand}}{\text{app,man,cand} \vdash s \leadsto every(candidate, \lambda x.a(manager, \ldots))} 2$$

Below point [1] in the derivation tree, no meaning assignments for the node *obj* occur anywhere on the right-hand sides of sequents in the tree. Below point [2], which is itself below point [1], there are no occurrences of meaning assignments to *subj* on the right-hand sides of sequents. The derivation tree gives rise to a node-ordering

$$s \succ subj \succ obj$$

---

[2]Thus app $\vdash$ app abbreviates $\forall X, Y. \ (subj \leadsto X \otimes obj \leadsto Y) \ \multimap\ s \leadsto appoint(X,Y) \ \vdash \ \forall X, Y. \ (subj \leadsto X \otimes obj \leadsto Y) \ \multimap\ s \leadsto appoint(X,Y).$

which states that assignments to *obj* are moved out of the right-hand sides of sequents before assignments to *subj*, which in turn are moved before assignments to *s*.

A schematic derivation tree giving the object wide scope is

$$
\frac{
\dfrac{app \vdash app \qquad\qquad\qquad\qquad\qquad cand \vdash cand}
{app, man \vdash \forall Y.obj \rightsquigarrow Y \;\multimap\; s \rightsquigarrow every(candidate, \ldots Y \ldots) \qquad man \vdash man}
}{app, man, cand \vdash s \rightsquigarrow a(manager, \lambda y.every(candidate, \ldots))}
$$

This derivation tree gives rise to the node ordering

$$
s \succ obj \succ subj
$$

The reason that node ordering reflects scope is as follows. The lexical premises to a glue language derivation contain various 'channel terms' (Dalrymple, Hinrichs, Lamping, and Saraswat 1993) of the form *Node* $\rightsquigarrow$ *Meaning*. Usually, there will be several different channel terms for each node. Some of these channel terms will act as consumers of the node's meaning (generally, a channel term is a consumer if it occurs in the antecedent of a linear implication). Other channel terms will act as producers of meanings for the node (if they occur in the consequent of an implication). A successful glue language derivation is one that matches all producer terms with consumer terms, with the exception of a final unmatched producer for the meaning of the sentence as a whole.

Putting this another way, ignore scope for the moment, and suppose we have a node n with immediate subconstituents a, b and c. Then a producer term for n will be built by consuming producer terms for a, b and c. That is we will have an implication of the form

$$
\forall M_a, M_b, M_c.
$$
$$
(a \rightsquigarrow M_a \otimes b \rightsquigarrow M_b \otimes c \rightsquigarrow M_c) \multimap n \rightsquigarrow f(M_a, M_b, M_c)
$$

If we can match the consumer terms in the antecedent with producer terms for a, b and c, then we can consume the subconstituent producer terms to build a producer on n, $n \rightsquigarrow f(M_a, M_b, M_c)$. This producer term for n may then be matched and consumed by a consumer term for n associated with its superordinate constituent. That is, we use up the meaning assignment for subconstituents to build the meaning assignment for a constituent.

We can say that a node is *active* at some point in a derivation if at that point there are still unmatched producer terms for the node. When all the producers are matched with consumers, the node becomes inactive: essentially the node has made all of its contribution to the meaning of the sentence, and plays no further role in the derivation. The node ordering we have been using states the relative order in which nodes become inactive in the derivation.

In terms of the sequent-style derivations we have been using, a node becoming inactive corresponds to it being completely moved out of the right-hand sides of sequents (and never subsequently being reactivated and reappearing on the right[3]). This can be informally justified by looking at the inference rule for modus ponens (the rule used to match producers with consumers). Each application of the rule will move a consumer and a producer term out of the right-hand side

$$\multimap E \frac{\Gamma \vdash A \multimap B \qquad \Delta \vdash A}{\Gamma, \Delta \vdash B}$$

Assuming that the two occurrences of A above the line are matching a consumer and a producer term for some node, note that below the line they no longer occur on the right of the sequent. Of course, if there is more than one consumer-producer pair for a given node, this rule will have to be applied repeatedly. The node will only become inactive once the final pair is moved across the turnstile by modus ponens.

Turning back to scope, in their discussion of soundness and completeness presented in Chapter 2, Dalrymple, Lamping, Pereira, and Saraswat note that the form of the antecedent implication in the meaning constructor for noun phrases enforces a certain constraint. Namely, that when the NP is scoped, only its immediate scope is allowed to depend on the meaning of the NP. That is, there must be no further unmatched consumers and producers on the NP. In other words, the point in the derivation at which the NP is scoped must constitute the final match of a consumer-producer pair for the NP. Which means that scoping the NP makes the NP node inactive. Thus the relative order

---

[3]To avoid spurious reactivation of a node, we assume normalized derivations throughout. This matter is taken up below.

in which NP nodes become inactive in a derivation corresponds to the relative order in which the NPs are scoped.

The relation between node orders and disactivation orders explains a superficial oddity in the node orders. When two NPs are subject to the node ordering $np_1 \succ np_2$, this means that NP_1 has wide scope over NP_2. We might therefore expect that when an NP has immediate scope over some scope node s, the ordering should be $np \succ s$. But in fact, the reverse is the correct order, $s \succ np$. This is because when the NP is scoped over s, the NP node becomes inactive, but the s node is still an active producer of meanings.

However, the ordering $np \succ scp$ does still mean that the NP has wide scope over some scope node scp. It is just that scp cannot be the immediate scope of NP. Thus, in a sentence like

(12)   Every candidate for a job failed.

there are two potential scope nodes for the NP *a job*:[4] either the prepositional phrase (whose node we shall name pp), or the sentence (node s). For the reading

$$s \leadsto every(\lambda x.candidate(x) \wedge a(job, \lambda y.for(x, y)), \ \lambda x.fail(x))$$

where *a job* (node j) takes scope over the PP, but within the restriction of the subject NP, the node ordering is

$$s \succ subj \succ pp \succ j$$

2.3   Formal properties of node orders

To show that node orderings really do what we claim above, we need a more precise formulation of glue language derivations, and to establish certain properties of the ordering.

2.3.1   Derivations and node orders

Assume sequent style natural deduction rules for the linear logic glue language (derived from Troelstra (1992)):

---

[4]A preliminary version of this material presented in Crouch and van Genabith (1996) presents the analysis of this sentence in more detail. Space prevents repetition of it here.

$$\otimes I \frac{\Gamma \vdash A \qquad \Delta \vdash B}{\Gamma, \Delta \vdash A \otimes B} \qquad\qquad \otimes E \frac{\Gamma \vdash A \otimes B \qquad \Delta, A, B \vdash C}{\Gamma, \Delta \vdash C}$$

$$\multimap I \frac{\Gamma, A \vdash B}{\Gamma \vdash A \multimap B} \qquad\qquad \multimap E \frac{\Gamma \vdash A \multimap B \qquad \Delta \vdash A}{\Gamma, \Delta \vdash B}$$

$$\forall I \frac{\Gamma \vdash A[x/y]}{\Gamma \vdash \forall x\, A} \qquad\qquad \forall E \frac{\Gamma \vdash \forall x\, A}{\Gamma \vdash A[x/t]}$$

$$\lambda_1 \frac{\Gamma \vdash A' \qquad A' \rightarrow_\lambda A}{\Gamma \vdash A} \qquad\qquad \lambda_2 \frac{\Gamma \vdash A \qquad A' \rightarrow_\lambda A}{\Gamma \vdash A'}$$

$$Axiom \frac{}{A \vdash A}$$

where $\rightarrow_\lambda$ indicates λ-reducibility. The standard side condition applies to universal introduction: y does not occur free in Γ.

A derivation is a tree-like structure of sequents, whose leaves are instances of the axiom sequent $A \vdash A$. (In glue language derivations, there will be one leaf for each lexical premise.) Each sequent in the tree must be derivable from those immediately preceding it via one of the above rules of inference. Represent derivations $\mathcal{D}$ as triples $\langle S, >_S, \$ \rangle$ where S is the set of points in the tree, $>_S$ is a transitive, asymmetric ordering over them, and $\$$ is a function mapping the points onto their corresponding sequents.

Sequents within a glue language derivation will contain literals (channel terms) of the form $Node \rightsquigarrow Meaning$, where $Node$ is a constant referring to some node in the semantic projection. A channel/node is *active* at a certain point s in a derivation if a literal referring to that channel occurs both on the left and the right hand side of s's sequent:

Definition 1 (Active Channel/Node)   *A channel c is active at point s in a derivation iff*

a) $\$(s) = \Gamma \vdash \phi$,

b) A literal of the form $c \rightsquigarrow M_1$ is a subexpression of Γ, and

c) A (possibly different) literal of the form $c \rightsquigarrow M_2$ is a subexpression of ϕ

Given the ordering $>_S$ over points in a derivation, and the definition of an active channel / node, we can now define an ordering over nodes

Definition 2 ($A \succ B$)   *A node A remains active in a derivation $\mathcal{D}$ after a node B, $A \succ B$, iff*

a) There is some point s in $\mathcal{D}$ at which A is active,

b) For all points $s' >_S s$, B is not active at s', and

c) There is some point s'' s.t. $s >_S s''$ at which B is active.

2.3.2   Properties of the ordering

We need to show that (i) only scoping an NP moves all the remaining NPs' channel terms to the left hand side of the sequent, and (ii) no subsequent derivation steps can move a channel term back to the right hand side. For (ii) we confine our attention to normalized derivations (in the proof theoretic sense), since a detour—an introduction step immediately followed by an elimination step—can always vacuously reintroduce and then eliminate a channel term.

Point (i) follows from the fact that there must be no outstanding dependencies on an NP when it is scoped (as noted in Chapter 2 in the discussion of completeness) and inspection of the canonical form of the final $\multimap$ -elimination step involved in scoping:

$$\frac{\Gamma_1 \vdash (\forall x.np \rightsquigarrow x \multimap scp \rightsquigarrow S(x)) \multimap scp \rightsquigarrow Q(S) \qquad \Gamma_2 \vdash \forall x.np \rightsquigarrow x \multimap scp \rightsquigarrow S(x)}{\Gamma_1, \Gamma_2 \vdash scp \rightsquigarrow Q(S)}$$

Given that (a) a single determiner premise introduces a producer on the NP channel, (b) a single premise (usually corresponding to the lexical head of the constituent subcategorizing for the NP) introduces a consumer on the NP channel, and (c) any other premises dependent on the NP meaning (e.g. anaphors) are both consumers and producers (i.e., have NP channel terms in both the antecedent and consequent of an implication), it follows that only scoping moves all channel terms for an NP to the left-hand side of a sequent.

For point (ii) note that only three rules can add channel terms to the right hand side of a sequent: the axiom $A \vdash A$, $\multimap$-introduction, and $\forall$-elimination (universal instantiation). All the other rules either leave things unchanged, or move channel terms from the right hand to the left hand sides of sequents.

If $A \vdash A$ is used to reintroduce an NP channel term, there needs to be some active consumer on that channel still present. Otherwise it will not be possible to eliminate the channel term again, as demanded by the final conclusion of the derivation, which must be a single channel term for the sentence. But when the NP is scoped there must be no outstanding consumers.

Universal instantiation can reintroduce an NP channel by instantiating a variable introduced by one of the premises. The only variables of the right type to be instantiated to a node in a semantic projection are the '*Scope*' variables. But these should only be instantiated to nodes that could serve as scopes for quantifiers.

With $\multimap$-introduction we can undo the effects of the $\multimap$-elimination in the final step of scoping. But as there are no other outstanding consumers on the NP node, we can only eliminate the NP channel term by repeating the $\multimap$-elimination, introducing a detour in the derivation.

It is at this last point to do with $\multimap$-introduction that the restriction to normalized derivations is important. The following is a valid final part of a (schematic) glue language derivation for *Every candidate appointed a manager*:

$$\cfrac{\cfrac{\text{app, cand, man} \vdash s \rightsquigarrow a(\ldots every(\ldots))}{\text{app, man} \vdash \text{cand} \multimap s \rightsquigarrow a(\ldots every(\ldots))} \multimap I \qquad \text{cand} \vdash \text{cand}}{\text{app, cand, man} \vdash s \rightsquigarrow a(\ldots every(\ldots))} \multimap E$$

This gives a narrow scope reading to the subject, but where the subject node is the last one (apart from s) to be finally moved to the left. This would indicate a $s \succ subj \succ obj$ node order. However, although valid, the derivation is not in normal form. It contains a detour that spuriously re-introduces a channel term for *subj* on the right hand side via $\multimap$ -I, only to immediately move it back again in the next step. The restriction to normal form derivations prohibits this, without reducing the range of conclusions that can be derived.

From the foregoing we can conclude that in normalized glue language derivations it is only scoping that moves NP channel terms irrevocably to the left hand side of sequents. So node orderings really do constrain NP scope. By supplementing glue language premises with sets of node orderings to further constrain the range of possible derivations we have a mechanism for underspecifying scope. (Note, we assume that the scope orderings are provided by some independent scope resolution mechanism.)

Given the mappings between f-structure, QLF and UDRS presented in Chapter 6 of this volume, it is also straightforward to translate the glue language node orderings into UDRS label orderings or QLF index orderings, which are also used to constrain scope.

3   Introducing Context Update

We will now introduce a second uninterpreted binary predicate symbol, $\hookrightarrow$, to represent context assignments to nodes. The behaviour of $\hookrightarrow$ is analogous to the meaning assignment predicate, $\rightsquigarrow$. Nodes in semantic projections are assigned both a meaning and a contextual contribution, both of which are expressions in the object-level meaning language. The meanings and/or contextual contributions of some nodes may depend on the meanings and/or contextual contributions of other nodes; and the meaning/context constructors may also update these assignments by means of the linear implication, $\multimap$.

The main difference brought about by introducing context assignments in addition to meaning assignments is in the desired result of glue language derivations. Previously, we needed to establish conclusions of the form

$$\Gamma \vdash s \rightsquigarrow M$$

where Γ was the entire set of lexical premises, and a single meaning assignment occurred on the right hand side. Now, however, the desired result is:

$$\Gamma, \Delta \vdash s \rightsquigarrow M \otimes \delta_0 \otimes \ldots \otimes \delta_i$$

Here, Γ is a set of lexical premises as before. Δ is a set of context assignments (derived from interpreting previous sentences), and $\delta_0 \ldots \delta_i$ is a set of possibly updated context assignments.

An important feature of context assignments that needs to be captured is that, unlike meaning assignments, they do not need to be used exactly once. They may not be used at all (e.g., an NP that is never referred back to by an anaphor), or they may be used repeatedly. However, when contextual contributions are used repeatedly, each re-use is liable to update the contextual contribution made. It is for this reason that it is inappropriate to make use of linear logic's 'of course' modality, !, to allow zero or repeated use of context assignments. Use of the modality would undo the effects of any update. Instead we modify the form of the desired result of glue language derivations to allow any number of context assignments to occur on the right hand side of the turnstile. These output context assignments may either be passed on directly from the input assignments in Δ, or may be updated versions of assignments in Δ, or context assignments to entirely new constituents. The output assignments $\delta_0, \ldots, \delta_i$ will form the input assignments Δ for the next sentence to be interpreted.

3.1 A simplified illustration

The use of context assignments can be illustrated in an (over-) simplified form by looking at the mini-discourse

(13)   *A man walked. He whistled.*

for which we will give a (simplified) E-type analysis of the pronoun.[5]

Taking the first sentence, *"A man walked"*, we assume the following lexical constructors

---

[5]For a fuller justification of E-type analyses, see Lappin and Francez (1994) and van der Does (1996).

(14)   **a**:
$\forall Scope, R, S.$
$$((\forall x.subj1.var \leadsto x \multimap subj1.rstr \leadsto R(x))$$
$$\otimes$$
$$(\forall x.subj1 \leadsto x \multimap Scope \leadsto S(x)))$$
$$\multimap$$
$$(Scope \leadsto a(R,S) \quad \otimes$$
$$subj1 \hookrightarrow \lambda y.R(y) \wedge S(y))$$

(15)   **man**:
$$\forall X. subj1.var \leadsto X \multimap subj1.rstr \leadsto man(X)$$

(16)   **walked**:
$$\forall X. subj1 \leadsto X \multimap s1 \leadsto walk(X)$$

Starting with a null context, we can combine these constructors to show that

(17)   **a, man, walked** $\vdash$
$$s1 \leadsto a(man, walk)$$
$$\otimes$$
$$subj1 \hookrightarrow \lambda y.man(y) \wedge walk(y)$$

In other words, as well as building the meaning of the s node, we have also constructed a contextual assignment for the subject noun phrase, $subj1$, which associates it with the property of being a man that walked.

For the second sentence, *"He whistled"*, we have the constructors

(18)   **he**:
$\forall Scope, \ Ante, P, S.$
$$(Ante \hookrightarrow P$$
$$\otimes$$
$$(\forall x.subj2 \leadsto x \multimap Scope \leadsto S(x)))$$
$$\multimap$$
$$(Scope \leadsto exists(P,S)$$
$$\otimes subj2 \hookrightarrow \lambda y.P(y) \wedge S(y))$$

(19)   **whistled**:
$$\forall X. subj2 \leadsto X \multimap s2 \leadsto whistle(X)$$

The meaning constructor for **he** contains an additional antecedent conjunct that quantifies over a contextual assignment to some chosen antecedent node, $Ante \hookrightarrow P$. The consequent scopes the pronoun by existentially quantifying the property P over the chosen scope. In addition, it sets up a contextual assignment for the pronoun, and updates the contextual assignment to the antecedent by removing it altogether.

Assuming that we instantiate the variable $Ante$ to $subj1$ and P to the property assigned to $subj1$, namely $\lambda y.man(y) \wedge walk(y)$, then these constructors can be put together, along with the context assignment for the first sentence to show that

(20) **he, whistled,** $subj1 \hookrightarrow \lambda y.man(y) \wedge walk(y), \vdash$
$\quad\quad s2 \rightsquigarrow exists(\lambda x.man(x) \wedge walk(x), \ \lambda x.whistle(x))$
$\quad\quad\quad\quad \otimes subj2 \hookrightarrow \lambda y.man(y) \wedge walk(y) \wedge whistle(y)$

Two comments. First, the meaning derived for the second sentence entails that derived for the first sentence, and is truth-conditionally equivalent to a Dynamic Predicate Logic (Groenendijk and Stokhof 1991) style meaning for the entire discourse,

$$\exists x.(man(x) \wedge walk(x)) \wedge whistle(x)$$

However, in the glue language case the dynamics resides in the composition of the meaning rather than in the meaning itself.

Second, we have adopted an extreme form of update to the antecedent contextual assignment: we have deleted it. This means that subsequent anaphoric references to the man that walked and whistled may only be brought about by picking up the context assignment to $subj2$. The node $subj1$ is no longer available for anaphoric reference. Alternatives to this are possible. For example, the consequent of the pronominal meaning constructor could also set up a revised context assignment for $subj1$, e.g.,

(21) **he**$'$:

$\forall Scope,\ Ante, P, S.$

$\quad(Ante \hookrightarrow P$

$\qquad\otimes$

$\quad(\forall x.subj2 \rightsquigarrow x \multimap Scope \rightsquigarrow S(x)))$

$\qquad\multimap$

$\quad(Scope \rightsquigarrow exists(P, S)$

$\qquad\otimes\ subj2 \hookrightarrow \lambda y.P(y) \wedge S(y)$

$\qquad\otimes\ Ante \hookrightarrow \lambda y.P(y) \wedge S(y))$

But for anaphors of strict identity there is no need to do this. We can generate all the meanings we want by preserving just one of the assignments to identical properties. More complex phenomena, however, would dictate a less extreme form of update.

4   Context Assignments, Scope, and Bound Variables

The example in the last section was simplified in order to introduce the idea of context update with minimal clutter. Interactions between context assignments and quantifier scope introduce some extra complexities, to which we now turn.

First, we will illustrate how context assignments can be built up for simple sentences like

(22)   Every candidate appointed a manager.

containing a transitive verb and two quantified NPs. Then, we show how the context assignments can deal with the bound variable anaphor in the sentence

(23)   Every candidate appointed himself.

Appendix A illustrates some more complex examples, namely

(24)   Every candidate appointed a manager. They paid them.

which involve multiple intra-sentential, quantificational anaphors; and donkey anaphora as manifested in the sentence

(25)   Every candidate with a manager paid him.

As before, the treatments provide an E-type analysis of anaphora. We do not pretend to have a fully worked out glue language account of anaphora, dealing with such things as strong and weak readings of pronouns or the intricacies of plural anaphora. Our aim is only to lay some of the groundwork for a fuller treatment and exhibit the potential of a glue language approach.

This section descends into the low-level details of how linear logic can be used for context management. Readers not interested in this may gain an impression of what is involved by reading Section 4.1, and then skipping to Section 4.4. Readers concerned by the apparent complexity of the derivations to follow should also refer to Section 4.4.

4.1   Every candidate appointed a manager

To see how context assignments need to be revised to handle scope and transitive verbs, reconsider the sentence *"Every candidate appointed a manager"*. Our aim is to allow two derivations, corresponding to the different scopings of the subject and object noun phrases, that lead to the conclusions

Wide scope subject   :

$$s \rightsquigarrow every(candidate, \lambda x.a(manager, \lambda y.appoint(x, y)))$$
$$\otimes\ subj \hookrightarrow \lambda x.candidate(x) \wedge a(manager, \lambda y.appoint(x, y))$$
$$\otimes\ \forall P.\ subj \hookrightarrow P \multimap$$
$$subj \hookrightarrow P \otimes obj \hookrightarrow \lambda y.manager(y) \wedge \exists x.\ P(x) \wedge appoint(x, y)$$

Wide scope object   :

$$s \rightsquigarrow a(manager, \lambda y.every(candidate, \lambda v.appoint(x, y)))$$
$$\otimes\ obj \hookrightarrow \lambda y.manager(x) \wedge every(candidate, \lambda x.appoint(x, y))$$
$$\otimes\ \forall P.\ obj \hookrightarrow P \multimap$$
$$obj \hookrightarrow P \otimes subj \hookrightarrow \lambda x.candidate(x) \wedge \exists y.\ P(y) \wedge appoint(x, y)$$

In both cases, the context assignment to the narrow scope NP is dependent on the contextual assignment to the wide scope NP. Thus, for the wide scope subject reading, the property associated with the narrow scope *a manager* is the property of being a manager such that some individual that satisfies the property associated with the subject appointed the manager.

4.1.1   Two problems

There are two main problems confronting the task of achieving conclusions like this.

Passing contexts around.   The first problem arises from the need to build up a collection of context assignments in addition to a single meaning assignment for the sentence. In building a meaning assignment for any constituent, a collection of context assignments for the constituent and its subconstituents will be built up alongside it.

Recall that meaning constructors for NPs have the general form

$$(\forall x.np \rightsquigarrow x \multimap Scp \rightsquigarrow S(x)) \multimap Scp \rightsquigarrow Quant(S)$$

But because derivations build meaning assignments conjoined with collections of context assignments, we will need to match the antecedent of this implication with something of the form

$$\forall x.np \rightsquigarrow x \multimap (Scp \rightsquigarrow S(x) \otimes \gamma)$$

where γ represents the additional context assignments. The presence of γ blocks the match.

What we would like is a pattern of inference that allows

$(A \multimap B) \multimap C$
$A \multimap (B \otimes \gamma)$
Therefore $C \otimes \gamma$

so that the additional context assignments γ (a) do not block the match and (b) can be passed up (unchanged) when the NP is scoped. Unfortunately this pattern of inference is invalid in linear logic.

We can get round this by going higher-order. The following is valid

$\forall \Delta. (A \multimap (B \otimes \Delta)) \multimap (C \otimes \Delta),$
$A \multimap (B \otimes \gamma),$
Therefore $C \otimes \gamma$

where the higher-order variable Δ ranges over additional contextual assignments like γ. (As noted in Section 4.4, this move to higher-order quantification is relatively benign.) We therefore modify NP meaning constructors to include additional higher-order quantification over glue language propositions corresponding to collections of context assignments. In rough outline:

$$\forall \Delta. \ (\forall x.np \rightsquigarrow x \multimap (Scp \rightsquigarrow S(x) \otimes \Delta))$$
$$\multimap (Scope \rightsquigarrow Quant(S) \otimes (\Delta \otimes np \hookrightarrow \ldots))$$

The consequent of the implication passes up the original context assignments in Δ, and adds a new one for the NP just scoped.

Inside-out scoping.   The second problem is that scoping has to work 'inside-out' on contextual assignments. For the wide scope subject reading of *every candidate appointed a manager*, the property associated with the object is conditional on the wider scope subject:

$$\forall P.subj \hookrightarrow P \ \multimap \ obj \hookrightarrow [\lambda y.manager(y) \wedge \exists x. \ P(x) \wedge appoint(x,y)]$$

> the property of being a manager y such that some x sat-
> isfying the property P assigned to the subject appointed
> y[6]

In the meaning assignment the subject quantifier gets wide scope over the object. But in the contextual assignment above, the subject property P occurs within the scope of the abstraction $(\lambda y. \ldots)$ forming the object assignment.

To account for this we need additional context assignments to scope nodes, e.g. an initial assignment for the s node dependent on the contextual assignments P and Q to the (subcategorized) *subj* and *obj* nodes:

$$\forall P, Q.(subj \hookrightarrow P \otimes obj \hookrightarrow Q) \ \circ$$
$$s \hookrightarrow \exists x, y. \ P(x) \wedge Q(y) \wedge appoint(x,y)$$

---

[6]In fact we also need to recreate the subject assignment as follows

$$\forall P.subj \hookrightarrow P \ \multimap \ subj \hookrightarrow P \otimes obj \hookrightarrow [\lambda y.manager(y) \wedge \exists x. \ P(x) \wedge appoint(x,y)]$$

but we ignore this complication for the moment.

When an NP is given scope over a node, we need to update both the meaning and context assignments for the scope node. The meaning assignment is updated in the familiar way by giving the NP's quantifier scope over it. To see how the context assignment is updated, suppose the object is given narrow scope with respect to the subject. We first convert the context assignment for s to the equivalent form:

$$\forall P.subj \hookrightarrow P \multimap$$
$$(\forall Q.obj \hookrightarrow Q \multimap s \hookrightarrow \exists x, y.\ P(x) \wedge Q(y) \wedge appoint(x, y))$$

Looking at just the contextual part of constructor for the object, this now must take (approximately) the form

$$\forall S.\ (\forall q.obj \hookrightarrow q \multimap s \hookrightarrow S(q)) \multimap$$
$$(s \hookrightarrow a(manager, \lambda y.S(\lambda u.u = y))$$
$$\otimes\ obj \hookrightarrow \lambda y.manager(y) \wedge S(\lambda u.u = y))$$

Essentially, this takes the property q associated with the object NP and replaces it by a (bound) variable property $\lambda u.u = y$. The free variable y gets bound by the (contextual) quantifier associated with the NP.

Combining the two (and instantiating $Q \mapsto q$) we get

$$\forall P.subj \hookrightarrow P \multimap$$
$$(s \hookrightarrow a(manager, \lambda u.\exists x, y.u = y \wedge P(x) \wedge appoint(x, y))$$
$$\otimes\ obj \hookrightarrow \lambda u.manager(u) \wedge \exists x, y.u = y \wedge P(x) \wedge appoint(x, y))$$

Simplifying equalities, this is equivalent to

$$\forall P.subj \hookrightarrow P \multimap$$
$$(s \hookrightarrow a(manager, \lambda y.\exists x.\ P(x) \wedge appoint(x, y))$$
$$\otimes\ obj \hookrightarrow \lambda y.manager(y) \wedge \exists x.\ P(x) \wedge appoint(x, y))$$

That is, after scoping we have an updated contextual assignment to s, dependent only on the contextual assignment to the unscoped *subj* node, but no longer dependent on the assignment to the *obj* node. We also have a new context assignment to the *obj* node.[7]

---

[7] When we come to scoping the *subj* node, the context assignment to *obj* will need to be passed up by the higher-order trick noted earlier.

4.1.2 Meaning constructors

The initial lexical premises for the sentence *every candidate appointed a manager* are (with determiners and nouns pre-combined):

(26) **appoint** $\vdash$

$\forall X, P.\ subj \leadsto X \multimap (subj \leadsto X \otimes\ !(subj \hookrightarrow P))$

$\otimes$

$\forall Y, Q.\ obj \leadsto Y \multimap (obj \leadsto Y \otimes\ !(obj \hookrightarrow Q))$

$\otimes$

$\forall X, Y.\ (subj \leadsto X \otimes obj \leadsto Y) \multimap$

$\qquad (s \leadsto appoint(X, Y)$

$\qquad\qquad \otimes\ \forall P, Q.\ (subj \hookrightarrow P \otimes obj \hookrightarrow Q) \multimap$

$\qquad\qquad\qquad s \hookrightarrow \exists x, y. P(x) \wedge Q(y) \wedge appoint(x, y)))$

(27) **every candidate** $\vdash$

$\forall Scope, S, S', \Delta, \Gamma.$

$\quad [\forall x, p.\ subj \leadsto x \multimap$

$\qquad (subj \hookrightarrow p \otimes Scope \leadsto S(x, p)$

$\qquad\quad \otimes\ \forall p'. subj \hookrightarrow p' \multimap (\Gamma \multimap (Scope \hookrightarrow S'(p', p) \otimes \Delta(p', p))))]$

$\quad \multimap$

$\quad [Scope \leadsto every(candidate,\ \lambda x. S(x, \lambda u. u = x))$

$\qquad \otimes\ [\Gamma \multimap$

$\qquad\quad (Scope \hookrightarrow every(candidate,\ \lambda x. S'(\lambda u. u = x, \lambda u. u = x))$

$\qquad\qquad \otimes\ subj \hookrightarrow \lambda x. (candidate(x) \wedge S'(\lambda u. u = x, \lambda u. u = x))$

$\qquad\qquad \otimes\ \forall p'.\ subj \hookrightarrow p' \multimap (subj \hookrightarrow p' \otimes \Delta(p', p')))]]$

(28) **a manager** $\vdash$

$\forall Scope, S, S', \Delta, \Gamma.$

$\quad [\forall y, q.\ obj \leadsto y \multimap$

$\qquad (obj \hookrightarrow q \otimes Scope \leadsto S(y, q)$

$\qquad\quad \otimes\ \forall q'. obj \hookrightarrow q' \multimap (\Gamma \multimap (Scope \hookrightarrow S'(q', q) \otimes \Delta(q', q))))]$

$\quad \multimap$

$\quad [Scope \leadsto a(manager,\ \lambda y. S(y, \lambda u. u = y))$

$\qquad \otimes\ [\Gamma \multimap$

$\qquad\quad (Scope \hookrightarrow a(manager,\ \lambda y. S'(\lambda u. u = y, \lambda u. u = y))$

$\qquad\qquad \otimes\ obj \hookrightarrow \lambda y. (manager(y) \wedge S'(\lambda u. u = y, \lambda u. u = y))$

$\qquad\qquad \otimes\ \forall q'.\ obj \hookrightarrow q' \multimap (obj \hookrightarrow q' \otimes \Delta(q', q')))]]$

These are doubtless in need of further explanation.

First, let us make the overall structure of these meaning constructors clearer. Meaning constructors for potential scope nodes, like **appoint**, consist of a number of separate conjuncts. For each subcategorized NP, there is a conjunct setting up an initial context assignment. The remaining conjunct takes the form:

$$Unscoped\text{-}NP\text{-}meaning\text{-}assignments \multimap$$
$$(Scope\text{-}meaning\text{-}assignment$$
$$\otimes \,[Unscoped\text{-}NP\text{-}context\text{-}assignments \multimap$$
$$(Scope\text{-}context\text{-}assignment$$
$$\otimes \, Subconstituent\text{-}context\text{-}assignments)])$$

In the case of **appoint**, however, there are no further subconstituent context assignments, so that this conjunct corresponds to $\top$, which may be removed (or added) at will. Meaning constructors for noun phrases have the outline structure:

$$(initial\text{-}NP\text{-}meaning\text{-}assignment \multimap$$
$$(initial\text{-}NP\text{-}context\text{-}assignment$$
$$\otimes \, Scope\text{-}meaning$$
$$\otimes \, [NP\text{-}context\text{-}assignment \multimap$$
$$(Unscoped\text{-}NP\text{-}context\text{-}assignments \; \Gamma \multimap$$
$$(Scope\text{-}context\text{-}assignment$$
$$\otimes \, Subconstituent\text{-}context\text{-}assignments \; \Delta))]))$$
$$\multimap$$
$$Updated\text{-}Scope\text{-}meaning$$
$$\otimes \, Unscoped\text{-}NP\text{-}context\text{-}assignments \; \Gamma \multimap$$
$$(Updated\text{-}Scope\text{-}context\text{-}assignment$$
$$\otimes \, Updated\text{-}np\text{-}context\text{-}assignment$$
$$\otimes \, Subconstituent\text{-}context\text{-}assignments \; \Delta)$$

Turning to specifics, the constructor for **appoint** comprises three conjuncts. The first is

$$\forall X, P. \; subj \rightsquigarrow X \multimap (subj \rightsquigarrow X \otimes \,!(subj \hookrightarrow P))$$

The motivation for this conjunct, and the parallel one for the object NP, arises mainly from the need to deal with bound variable anaphora, especially where several anaphors may be bound to the same variable. It allows whatever context assignment P that *subj* receives before scoping to be used repeatedly. In more detail, it says: suppose you can assume that $subj \rightsquigarrow X$ for some X, i.e., that the subject has not yet been scoped and so there is still an active meaning producer for the *subj* node. Then you can reconstruct the meaning, and furthermore whatever property P is contextually assigned to *subj*, the assignment $subj \hookrightarrow P$ can be repeated zero, one or more times.[8]

The third conjunct of **appoint** makes a meaning and a context assignment to s dependent on the meanings assigned to *subj* and *obj*. The meaning assignment is constructed in the familiar way. The context assignment only holds when neither the *subj* nor the *obj* have been scoped, since it is also dependent on *subj* and *obj* meaning assignments. If neither have been scoped, then a context assignment to s is set up dependent on the contextual assignments, P and Q to the subject and object.

$$\forall P, Q. \, (subj \hookrightarrow P \otimes obj \hookrightarrow Q) \multimap$$
$$s \hookrightarrow \exists x, y. P(x) \wedge Q(y) \wedge appoint(x, y)$$

Scoping one of the NPs will have the effect of (i) removing the dependency on the NP's context assignment, and (ii) updating the embedded assignment to s, in the way sketched on p. 142.

The meaning constructor for **every candidate** (and for **a manager**) has an outermost quantification over the variables $Scope, S, S', \Delta$ and Γ. The variables $Scope$ and S range over potential scope nodes and the meanings initially assigned to them. S' ranges over the expressions initially serving as a contextual assignment to the scope node. The variables Δ and Γ both range over glue language propositions corresponding to collections of contextual assignments. Δ ranges over the context assignments that have been built up for subconstituents of the scope node. Γ ranges over assignments to the unscoped NPs on which Δ and the assignment to $Scope$ still depend.

The antecedent implication of the constructor

---

[8]Note that this does not allow you to have multiple assignments of *different* contextual properties to *subj*. By leaving the universal quantifier over P outside the scope of the ! modality, we are saying that you can take any one property P and repeat *subj* assignments to that property. If the universal had been within the scope of !, we would instead have been saying that you can repeatedly (i) select any property and then (ii) make a *subj* assignment out of it.

$$\forall x, p.\ subj \rightsquigarrow x \multimap$$
$$(subj \hookrightarrow p \otimes Scope \rightsquigarrow S(x,p) \otimes$$
$$\forall p'.\ subj \hookrightarrow p' \multimap (\Gamma \multimap (Scope \hookrightarrow S'(p',p) \otimes \Delta(p',p))))$$

can be understood as follows. Assuming any arbitrary meaning x for the subject and any arbitrary property p, you can conclude that

(a)   The subject receives an initial contextual assignment to the property p (typically p will be the 'bound variable' property, $\lambda u.u = x$, but we do not build this assumption in);

(b)   The scope node has a meaning $S(x,p)$, dependent on the meaning of the subject, and possibly also on its initial contextual assignment (in case it contains any (bound variable) anaphors referring to the subject);

(c)   The contextual assignment to the scope node, $S'(p',p)$ is conditional on (i) any contextual assignment p' that *subj* subsequently receives, (ii) context assignments to other as yet unscoped NPs, as given by Γ, and (iii) possibly also on the initial context assignment p to *subj* (again, in case it contains any bound variable anaphors). Furthermore, any other context assignments contained in Δ may also depend on these three things.

This explanation raises three further questions. First, what is the significance of using lower case variables, p and p'? Second, why is reference made to two different assignments, p and p', to *subj*? Third, why do we allow any arbitrary initial context assignment to *subj* when in fact it should be quite tightly constrained by the meaning x assigned to *subj*?

The use of lower case variables follows the notational convention adopted in Chapter 2. That is, they stand for 'essentially universal' variables that stand for new local constants in a proof. Upper case variables stand for 'essentially existential' variables, which act like Prolog variables and become instantiated to particular terms derived elsewhere in a proof. That is, upper case variables stand for specific but as yet unspecified terms, whereas lower case variables stand for arbitrary constants that could validly be replaced by any term.

The reference to two different properties p and p' assigned to *subj* stems from the fact the subject receives an initial assignment p before it is scoped, and an updated one after it is scoped. The variable p' stands for any assignment that *subj* gets, either before or after scoping. The variable p stands only for the assignment received prior to scoping.

Given the assumption that the subject means x, it might seem safer to conclude that its initial contextually assigned property is $\lambda u.u = x$, i.e. the property of being identical to x. Yet we seem to be allowing it to be assigned any arbitrary property p. The reason that this is safe is that all we are interested in is recording the *dependency* of other meanings and context assignments on the initial assignment to *subj*. And for this, we do not require any knowledge about the actual value of the initial assignment. Moreover, it is important *not* to instantiate p to any more specific value, such as $\lambda u.u = x$. By keeping p as a variable bound within the scope of quantifiers binding S, S' and Δ, expressions such as $S(x, p)$ are guaranteed to make whatever value we choose for S to abstract over all occurrences of the variable p, and hence record *all* the dependencies on this assignment.[9]

Turning now to the consequent of the main implication in **every-candidate**, this can be understood as follows. Suppose you can show the antecedent implication to hold. Then you can conclude

$$[Scope \rightsquigarrow every(candidate,\ \lambda x.S(x, \lambda u.u = x))$$
$$\otimes\ [\Gamma \multimap$$
$$(Scope \hookrightarrow every(candidate,\ \lambda x.S'(\lambda u.u = x, \lambda u.u = x))$$
$$\otimes\ subj \hookrightarrow \lambda x.candidate(x) \wedge S'(\lambda u.u = x, \lambda u.u = x)$$
$$\otimes\ \forall p'.\ subj \hookrightarrow p' \multimap (subj \hookrightarrow p' \otimes \Delta(p', p')))]]$$

That is:

(a)   The meaning of the scope node is updated, replacing any occurrences of the initial assignment p to *subj* by the bound variable property $\lambda u.u = x$;

(b)   The scope's context assignment is no longer conditional on the assignment p' to *subj*, but only on the other unscoped assign-

---

[9]The same line of reasoning is used by Dalrymple, Lamping, Pereira, and Saraswat in Chapter 2 to show that their treatment of scoping is sound in that all meaning level variables are properly bound.

ments in Γ. However, the scope's assignment is updated to (i) give a subject quantifier scope over it and (ii) replace any occurrences within it of properties assigned to *subj* by the bound variable property $\lambda u.u = x$;

(c)   A new contextual assignment to *subj* is created;

(d)   The dependence of all the other contextual assignments in Δ on the (new) assignment to *subj* (plus all the other assignments in Γ) is reiterated.

An important point to note here is that at no stage do we *instantiate* the initial (and antecedent) contextual assignment p to the subject to a more specific value. This is because, depending on where the initial assignment occurs, it needs to be 'instantiated' to different values. Within the updated scope and *subj* assignments, where there is some binder of the subject's meaning variable x, we need to replace p by a bound variable property, $\lambda u.u = x$. But within the other context assignment in Δ, where there is no binder for x, we need to replace p by p'—the variable standing for the assignment *subj* gets after scoping. Instantiation of p would not permit it to take on different values in different places. Instead, we rely on abstracting p out over S, S' and Δ, and then applying the abstracts to different arguments.

These modifications to the meaning constructor for **every-candidate** aside, note that it has the same basic implicational form as the original presented in Chapter 2, given in (3).

In addition to the meaning constructors, derivations also rely on the standard rules of inference (Troelstra 1992):

$$\top I\frac{}{\vdash\top} \qquad\qquad \top E\frac{\Gamma\vdash\top \qquad \Delta\vdash A}{\Gamma,\Delta\vdash A}$$

where $\top$ is the identity proposition for multiplicative conjunction (approximately: an infinitely reusable or discardable, vacuously true proposition). With this premise, the following patterns of inference are valid:

$$\frac{A}{A \otimes \top} \qquad\qquad \frac{A \otimes \top}{A}$$

$$\frac{A}{\top \multimap A} \qquad\qquad \frac{\top \multimap A}{A}$$

This is used to allow us to represent empty sets of context assignments (i.e. possible values of Γ and Δ) as $\top$.

4.1.3 Derivation

We now present a derivation from the premises above, where the subject receives wide scope. The first thing we need to do is rearrange the meaning constructor for **appoint** so that it matches the antecedent implication of the **a-manager** constructor. Observe the following valid pattern of inference:

$A \multimap (A \otimes B)$

$A \multimap C$

Therefore: $A \multimap (C \otimes B)$

This can be used to combine the second and third conjuncts of the **appoint** constructor to place a contextual assignment to *obj* within the consequent of the third conjunct:

(29) **appoint** $\vdash$

$\forall X, P.\ subj \rightsquigarrow X \multimap (subj \rightsquigarrow X \otimes\ !(subj \hookrightarrow P))$

$\otimes$

$\forall X.\ subj \rightsquigarrow X$

$\multimap (\forall Y, Q.\ obj \rightsquigarrow Y$

$\multimap (!(obj \hookrightarrow Q) \otimes s \rightsquigarrow appoint(X, Y)$

$\otimes\ \forall P', Q'.\ (subj \hookrightarrow P' \otimes obj \hookrightarrow Q')$

$\multimap s \hookrightarrow \exists x, y.\ P'(x) \wedge Q'(y) \wedge appoint(x, y)))$

From this, one can derive (by dropping the !, temporarily instantiating P' to an arbitrary constant p' and further rearrangement):

(30)   **appoint** $\vdash$

$$\forall X, P.\; subj \rightsquigarrow X \multimap (subj \rightsquigarrow X \otimes\; !(subj \hookrightarrow P))$$

$$\otimes$$

$$\forall X.\; subj \rightsquigarrow X$$
$$\multimap (\forall Y, Q.\; obj \rightsquigarrow Y$$
$$\multimap (obj \hookrightarrow Q \otimes s \rightsquigarrow appoint(X, Y)$$
$$\otimes \forall Q'.\; obj \hookrightarrow Q' \multimap$$
$$(subj \hookrightarrow p'$$
$$\multimap s \hookrightarrow \exists x, y.\; p'(x) \wedge Q'(y) \wedge appoint(x, y))))$$

This now matches the antecedent implication of **a-manager** under the variable instantiations

$$Scope \mapsto s; \quad \Delta \mapsto \lambda_{-,-}.\; \top; \quad \Gamma \mapsto subj \hookrightarrow p'; \quad Q \mapsto q;$$
$$Q' \mapsto q';$$
$$S \mapsto \lambda y, \_.\; appoint(X, y)$$
$$S' \mapsto \lambda Q', \_.\; \exists x, y.p'(x) \wedge Q'(y) \wedge appoint(x, y);$$

(where $\_$ is used to indicate vacuously abstracted variables). Hence we get from the consequent of the implication

(31)   **appoint, a manager** $\vdash$

$$\forall X, P.\; subj \rightsquigarrow X \multimap (subj \rightsquigarrow X \otimes\; !(subj \hookrightarrow P))$$

$$\otimes$$

$$\forall X.\; subj \rightsquigarrow X \multimap$$
$$(s \rightsquigarrow a(manager,\; \lambda y.appoint(X, y))$$
$$\otimes subj \hookrightarrow p' \multimap$$
$$[s \hookrightarrow a(manager,\; \lambda y.\exists x', y'.\; p'(x') \wedge y = y' \wedge appoint(x', y'))$$
$$\otimes obj \hookrightarrow \lambda y.manager(y) \wedge \exists x', y'.\; p'(x') \wedge y = y' \wedge appoint(x', y')$$
$$\otimes \forall q.obj \hookrightarrow q \multimap (obj \hookrightarrow q \otimes \top)])$$

Requantifying the variable p', simplifying equalities[10], and removing a trivially true conjunct, we get

---

[10]Strictly, simplification of equalities in meaning expressions does not take place during glue language derivations. But it aids readability.

(32)   **appoint, a manager** $\vdash$

$\forall X, P.\; subj \rightsquigarrow X \multimap (subj \rightsquigarrow X \otimes\; !(subj \hookrightarrow P))$

$\otimes$

$\forall X.\; subj \rightsquigarrow X \multimap$

$\quad (s \rightsquigarrow a(manager,\; \lambda y.appoint(X, y))$

$\quad\quad \otimes\, \forall P'.\; subj \hookrightarrow P' \multimap$

$\quad\quad\quad [s \hookrightarrow a(manager,\; \lambda y.\exists x.\; P'(x) \wedge appoint(x, y))$

$\quad\quad\quad\quad \otimes\, obj \hookrightarrow \lambda y.manager(y) \wedge \exists x.\; P'(x) \wedge appoint(x, y)])$

We can now rearrange this by combining the two top level conjuncts
in the same way as before, to produce something that will match the
antecedent implication of **every candidate**:

(33)   **appoint, a manager** $\vdash$

$\forall X, P.\; subj \rightsquigarrow X \multimap$

$\quad (!(subj \hookrightarrow P)$

$\quad\quad \otimes\, s \rightsquigarrow a(manager,\; \lambda y.appoint(X, y))$

$\quad\quad \otimes\, \forall P'.\; subj \hookrightarrow P' \multimap$

$\quad\quad\quad [s \hookrightarrow a(manager,\; \lambda y.\exists x.P'(x) \wedge appoint(x, y))$

$\quad\quad\quad\quad \otimes\, obj \hookrightarrow \lambda y.manager(y) \wedge \exists x.P'(x) \wedge appoint(x, y)])$

Dropping the !, this matches **every candidate** under the variable instantiations

$Scope \mapsto s;\quad \Gamma \mapsto \top;\quad P \mapsto p;\quad P' \mapsto p';$

$S \mapsto \lambda x, \_.\; a(manager, \lambda y.\; appoint(x, y));$

$S' \mapsto \lambda P', \_.\; a(manager, \lambda y.\exists x.P'(x) \wedge appoint(x, y));$

$\Delta \mapsto \lambda P', \_.\; obj \hookrightarrow \lambda y.manager(y) \wedge \exists x.P'(x) \wedge appoint(x, y)$

Hence we get

(34)   **every candidate, appointed, a manager** $\vdash$

$s \rightsquigarrow every(candidate,\; \lambda x.a(manager, \lambda y.appoint(x, y)))$

$\otimes$

$\top \multimap$

$\quad (s \hookrightarrow every(candidate, \lambda x.a(manager, \lambda y.\exists x'.x' = x \wedge appoint(x', y)))$

$\quad\quad \otimes\, subj \hookrightarrow \lambda x.candidate(x) \wedge a(manager, \lambda y.\exists x'.x' = x \wedge appoint(x', y))$

$\quad\quad \otimes\, \forall p.\; subj \hookrightarrow p \multimap$

$\quad\quad\quad subj \hookrightarrow p \otimes obj \hookrightarrow \lambda y.manager(y) \wedge \exists x.p(x) \wedge appoint(x, y)$

Simplifying equalities and dropping $\top$ we finally get:

(35) **every candidate, appointed, a manager** $\vdash$

$s \leadsto every(candidate, \lambda x.a(manager, \lambda y.appoint(x,y)))$

$\otimes$

$s \hookrightarrow every(candidate, \; \lambda x.a(manager, \lambda y.appoint(x,y)))$

$\otimes \; subj \hookrightarrow \lambda x.candidate(x) \wedge a(manager, \lambda y. \wedge appoint(x,y))$

$\otimes \; \forall p. \; subj \hookrightarrow p \multimap$

$\qquad subj \hookrightarrow p \otimes obj \hookrightarrow \lambda y.manager(y) \wedge \exists x.p(x) \wedge appoint(x,y)$

The derivation where the object noun phrase receives wide scope is analogous to the one just given, except that the context assignment to the subject NP in **appoint** is absorbed first.

4.2   Every candidate appointed himself

Having shown how quantified noun phrases introduce contextual assignments, we now turn to the question of how pronouns quantify over these contextually assigned properties, in this case to give bound variable readings.

We will assume the following meaning constructor for the (reflexive, singular) pronoun *himself*. For the sake of presentation, we are glossing over differences between reflexive and non-reflexive pronouns:[11]

---

[11] To be more specific, we are assuming that the difference between reflexive and non-reflexive pronouns is primarily a syntactic constraint on where antecedents may be picked up from. Apart from this, the actual meanings are the same. The current example is used merely to illustrate the simplest possible form of bound variable anaphora. We have also simplified the meaning constructor for the pronoun in some minor respects. The constructors for the pronouns **them** and **they** given in appendix A.1 provide full and correct examples of pronoun meaning constructors. But the details added there do not affect the derivation in this section.

(36) **himself**:

$$\forall Scope, S, S', \Gamma, \Delta, Ante, A.$$
$$[Ante \hookrightarrow A$$
$$\otimes \forall y, q.\ obj \rightsquigarrow y \multimap$$
$$(obj \hookrightarrow q$$
$$\otimes Scope \rightsquigarrow S(y, q)$$
$$\otimes \forall q'.obj \hookrightarrow q' \multimap (\Gamma \multimap (Scope \hookrightarrow S'(q', q) \otimes \Delta(q', q))))]$$
$$\multimap$$
$$[Scope \rightsquigarrow exists(A,\ \lambda y.\ S(y, \lambda u.u = y))$$
$$\otimes \Gamma \multimap$$
$$(Scope \hookrightarrow exists(A,\ \lambda y.\ S'(\lambda u.u = y, \lambda u.u = y))$$
$$\otimes obj \hookrightarrow \lambda y.\ A(y) \wedge S'(\lambda u.u = y, \lambda u.u = y)$$
$$\otimes \forall q'.\ obj \hookrightarrow q' \multimap (obj \hookrightarrow q' \otimes \Delta(q', q')))]$$

This is basically the same as the constructor for any quantified NP. The differences are

- An extra conjunct, $Ante \hookrightarrow A$ in the antecedent of the main implication to pick up the pronoun antecedent *Ante* and its contextual property A.

- The pronoun acts as an existential quantifier (since it is a singular pronoun) whose restriction is given by the antecedent property A.

The other constructors for **appoint** and **every candidate** are as before, i.e., (26, 27).

The derivation proceeds by first rearranging **appoint** as in (29) so that **himself** can be given scope over it. This matches the inner implication of **himself** under the variable instantiations

$$Scope \mapsto s;\quad \Gamma \mapsto subj \hookrightarrow p';\quad \Delta \mapsto \lambda_{-,\,-}.\ \top;$$
$$Q \mapsto q;\quad Q' \mapsto q';$$
$$S \mapsto \lambda y,\_.\ s \rightsquigarrow appoint(X, y);$$
$$S \mapsto \lambda Q',\_.\ s \hookrightarrow \exists x, y.\ p'(x) \wedge Q'(y) \wedge appoint(x, y)$$

Further instantiating *Ante* to the antecedent node of the pronoun, namely *subj*, we get

(37) **appoint, himself** $\vdash$

$\forall X, P.\ subj \rightsquigarrow X \multimap (subj \rightsquigarrow X \otimes\ !(subj \hookrightarrow P))$

$\otimes$

$\forall X.\ subj \rightsquigarrow X \multimap$

$\quad \forall A.\ subj \hookrightarrow A \multimap$

$\qquad (s \rightsquigarrow exists(A,\ \lambda y.appoint(X, y))$

$\qquad \otimes\ \forall P'.\ subj \hookrightarrow P' \multimap$

$\qquad\quad [s \hookrightarrow exists(A, \lambda y.\exists x', y'.P'(x') \wedge y = y' \wedge appoint(x', y'))$

$\qquad\qquad \otimes\ obj \hookrightarrow \lambda y.A(y) \wedge \exists x', y'.P'(x') \wedge y = y' \wedge appoint(x', y')])$

Merging the two top-level conjuncts (and simplifying equalities) we get

(38) **appoint, himself** $\vdash$

$\forall X, P.\ subj \rightsquigarrow X \multimap$

$\quad (!(subj \hookrightarrow P) \otimes$

$\quad \forall A.\ subj \hookrightarrow A \multimap$

$\qquad (s \rightsquigarrow exists(A,\ \lambda y.appoint(X, y))$

$\qquad \otimes\ \forall P'.\ subj \hookrightarrow P' \multimap$

$\qquad\quad [s \hookrightarrow exists(A,\ \lambda y.\exists x'.P'(x') \wedge appoint(x', y'))$

$\qquad\qquad \otimes\ obj \hookrightarrow \lambda y.A(y) \wedge \exists x'.P'(x') \wedge appoint(x', y)])$

We then produce two copies of the assignment, $subj \hookrightarrow P \otimes subj \hookrightarrow P$, in place of the $!(subj \hookrightarrow P)$ conjunct, and also instantiate A to P:

(39) **appoint, himself** $\vdash$

$\forall X, P.\ subj \rightsquigarrow X \multimap$

$\quad (subj \hookrightarrow P \otimes subj \hookrightarrow P \otimes$

$\quad subj \hookrightarrow P \multimap$

$\qquad (s \rightsquigarrow exists(P,\ \lambda y.appoint(X, y))$

$\qquad \otimes\ \forall P'.\ subj \hookrightarrow P' \multimap$

$\qquad\quad [s \hookrightarrow exists(P,\ \lambda y.\exists x'.P'(x') \wedge appoint(x', y))$

$\qquad\qquad \otimes\ obj \hookrightarrow \lambda y.P(y) \wedge \exists x'.P'(x') \wedge appoint(x', y))])$

From which, by modus ponens we get

(40)   **appoint, himself** $\vdash$
$\quad \forall X, P. \; subj \leadsto X \multimap$
$\qquad (subj \hookrightarrow P$
$\qquad \quad \otimes \; s \leadsto exists(P, \; \lambda y.appoint(X, y)) \otimes$
$\qquad \quad \forall P'. \; subj \hookrightarrow P' \multimap$
$\qquad \qquad [s \hookrightarrow exists(P, \; \lambda y.\exists x'.P'(x') \wedge appoint(x', y'))$
$\qquad \qquad \quad \otimes \; obj \hookrightarrow \lambda y.P(y) \wedge \exists x'.P'(x') \wedge y = y' \wedge appoint(x', y))])$

Note how, because of the pronoun, the context assignments depend on both the initial assignment P to *subj*, and on the general assignment P'.

This now matches the antecedent implication of **every candidate** under the variable instantiations

$\quad Scope \mapsto s; \quad \Gamma \mapsto \top;$
$\quad S \mapsto \lambda x, P. \; exists(P, \lambda y.appoint(x, y));$
$\quad S' \mapsto \lambda P', P. \; exists(P, \lambda y.\exists x'. \; P'(x') \wedge appoint(x', y));$
$\quad \Delta \mapsto \lambda P', P. \; obj \hookrightarrow \lambda y. \; P(y) \wedge \exists x'. \; P'(x') \wedge appoint(x', y)$

The two can then be combined to give

(41)   **every candidate, appointed, himself** $\vdash$

$\quad s \leadsto every(candidate, \; \lambda x.exists(\lambda y.y = x, \; \lambda y.appoint(x, y))) \otimes$
$\quad \top \multimap$
$\qquad s \hookrightarrow every(candidate, \lambda x.exists(\lambda y.y = x, \lambda y.\exists x'.x' = x \wedge appoint(x', y)))$
$\qquad \otimes \; subj \hookrightarrow \lambda x.candidate(x) \wedge exists(\lambda y.y = x, \lambda y.\exists x'.x' = x \wedge appoint(x', y))$
$\qquad \otimes \; \forall p. \; subj \hookrightarrow p \multimap$
$\qquad \qquad (subj \hookrightarrow p \otimes obj \hookrightarrow \lambda y. \; p(y) \wedge \exists x'.p(x') \wedge appoint(x', y))$

The points to note here are that

- By instantiating A to P we ensure that the antecedent property is identical to the contextual property assigned to *subj* before it is scoped.

- The property P is replaced by the bound variable property, $\lambda u.u = x$ in the updated context assignments to s and *subj*.

- Other instances of P that may occur in the remaining context assignments Δ are replaced by the universally bound variable p, and correspond to the assignment *subj* gets after it is scoped.

Dropping $\top$ and simplifying equalities, this gives

(42) **every candidate, appointed, himself** $\vdash$
$s \rightsquigarrow every(candidate, \ \lambda x.appoint(x, x)))$
$\otimes s \hookrightarrow every(candidate, \ \lambda x.appoint(x, x))$
$\otimes subj \hookrightarrow \lambda x. \ candidate(x) \wedge appoint(x, x))$
$\otimes \forall p. \ subj \hookrightarrow p \multimap$
$\qquad (subj \hookrightarrow p \otimes obj \hookrightarrow \lambda y. \ p(y) \wedge \exists x'.p(x') \wedge appoint(x', y))$

It is important to note that the reverse scoping, where the pronoun receives wide scope over its subject antecedent, is unavailable. To see this, consider the combination of the verb and subject:

(43) **every candidate, appoint** $\vdash$
$\forall Y, Q. \ obj \rightsquigarrow Y \multimap$
$\qquad (!(obj \hookrightarrow Q) \otimes s \rightsquigarrow every(candidate, \ \lambda x.appoint(x, Y))$
$\qquad \otimes \forall Q'. \ obj \hookrightarrow Q' \multimap$
$\qquad\qquad (s \hookrightarrow every(candidate, \lambda x.\exists y'.Q'(y') \wedge appoint(x, y'))$
$\qquad\qquad \otimes subj \hookrightarrow \lambda x.candidate(x) \wedge \exists y'.Q'(y') \wedge appoint(x, y')))$

Combining this with the pronoun meaning we get

(44) **every candidate, appoint, himself** $\vdash$
$\forall A. \ subj \hookrightarrow A \multimap$
$\quad [s \rightsquigarrow exists(A, \ \lambda y.every(candidate, \ \lambda x.appoint(x, y)))$
$\quad \otimes s \hookrightarrow exists(A, \ \lambda y.every(candidate, \ \lambda x.appoint(x, y)))$
$\quad \otimes obj \hookrightarrow \lambda y. \ A(y) \wedge every(candidate, \ \lambda x.appoint(x, y))$
$\quad \otimes \forall q.obj \hookrightarrow q \multimap$
$\qquad (obj \hookrightarrow q \otimes$
$\qquad subj \hookrightarrow \lambda x. \ candidate(x) \wedge \exists y. \ q(y) \wedge appoint(x, y))]$

The meaning assignment to s is dependent on an undischargeable context assignment A to the subject. Although a context assignment to the subject is created, it too is dependent on A. Thus we cannot establish a conclusion consisting of a single meaning assignment conjoined with a collection of context assignments.

More generally, our treatment prohibits any anaphor from receiving wide scope over its antecedent.

4.3   Other examples

An appendix to this paper gives derivations for two more complex cases

(45)   Every candidate appointed a manager. They paid them.

(46)   Every candidate with a manager paid him.

These serve to illustrate the potential coverage of a glue language approach to context update. In particular, for (45) we are able to derive a reading where each candidate pays (all) the manager(s) he appointed. For the donkey sentence (46) we derive a weak reading where every candidate with a manager pays at least one of his managers. A strong reading, where every candidate pays all of his managers, is derivable if we instead associate a universal quantifier with the singular pronoun *him*. However, choice of different pronominal quantifiers is beyond the scope of this paper.

4.4   Comments, completeness, and complexity

4.4.1   Completeness of scoping

At first sight it might seem that our treatment of context update undercuts the soundness and completeness of the treatment of scope in Chapter 2. Their proof of completeness relied on the linear form of the implication

$$\forall x.\ np \rightsquigarrow x \multimap Scope \rightsquigarrow S(x)$$

employed in scoping, which demanded that there be no further dependencies on the NP meaning other than that of the scope. But to pass context assignments around, the form of the implication instead becomes

$$\forall \Delta.(\forall x.\ np \rightsquigarrow x \multimap Scope \rightsquigarrow S(x) \otimes \Delta)$$

What guarantee is there that no additional dependencies on the NP meaning occur in Δ?

The guarantee lies in an implicit restriction we have been employing on the form of lexical meaning constructors. The collections of context assignments, which serve as possible instantiations of Δ, are carefully set up so that they contain no meaning assignments, only context assignments.

Although not strictly necessary, we could enforce this restriction even more strongly by imposing sortal restrictions on the higher order glue language variables, Γ and Δ. We can distinguish two sorts of glue language propositions: meanings and contexts. Meanings comprise any proposition that can be built up purely from meaning assignments and glue language connectives and quantifiers. Contexts comprise any proposition that can be built up purely from context assignments and glue language connectives and quantifiers. Imposing the restriction that Γ and Δ must be of sort context doubly guarantees completeness.

Soundness of scoping (all variables are bound) is preserved in exactly the same way as discussed in Chapter 2, and is extended to soundness of context assignments. Namely, essentially universal variables, corresponding to either meaning level variables or properties, all occur within the scope of quantifiers binding essentially existential variables.

4.4.2 Higher-order costs

Although a fragment of higher-order linear logic is employed in Chapter 2 and elsewhere in this volume, there is a sense in which the higher-order component was confined to the meaning level. That is, in practice higher-order glue language variables only ranged over higher order expressions in the meaning language. Our treatment of context update has made things more higher-order in that we now have variables ranging over glue language expressions.

Two observations may be made to diminish concerns about this. First, linear logic is well suited to higher-order quantification (this was one of the original motivations behind it). And, technically, everything still lies within the higher-order multiplicative fragment employed in Chapter 2.

Second, the form of higher-order unification used to instantiate higher order glue variables is decidable. All equations to be solved are either of the form $F(x) = t$ or $p(X) = t$, where t is a closed term, F and X are essentially existential variables, and x and p are essentially universal variables. As pointed out in Chapter 2, such cases fall within a decidable extension of first order unification.

4.4.3   Complexity of derivations

A natural reaction to all of the foregoing is to question the viability of any approach that commits itself to such daunting looking derivations for such simple sentences. There are a number of responses to this.

First, the number of steps in derivations tends to be low. The elaborate structure of the meaning constructors places fairly tight restrictions on how one meaning constructor can be matched up against another. Thus the apparent complexity of the derivations in terms of how much has to be written down after each step in fact means that the search space involved in looking for possible derivations is relatively small.

Second, some of the sequences of individual inference steps (e.g. for scoping a quantifier) are fairly regular and standardised, suggesting that in terms of automated theorem proving they could be assembled into higher level macros or proof tactics. Similarly with lexical meaning constructors: they consist of various combinations of standard chunks of glue. One can speculate as to whether these components could be viewed as implementations of the kinds of higher level semantic operators advocated by Johnson and Kay (1990).

Third, the use of linear logic forces one to look at update in very low-level terms. Other approaches to context dynamics may take notions such as updating the value of a register or variable as primitive, and not in need of further elaboration. But here, the details of this cannot be brushed under the carpet, and need to be made (painfully) explicit.

4.4.4   Final comments

This section (plus appendix) has indicated how a glue language approach to context update might deal with interactions between contexts, scope and bound variable anaphors. It has provided an E-type analysis of intra- and inter-sentential anaphora that is able to deal uniformly with bound variable and other anaphors of strict identity. However, it offers no more than a sketch of how this might be done. A fuller E-type analysis would need to tackle such things as collective and distributive readings of plural noun phrases and anaphors, the choice of strong or weak readings for donkey anaphors, and much else besides.

One of the advantages of the way that we have treated E-type contextual update is the smooth way in which it can be integrated with the underspecification of anaphoric relations, to which we now turn.

5   Audit Trails and Underspecification

So far we have shown in a glue language approach how (a) scope relations may be partially specified by node orderings, and (b) how the creation and update of E-type properties may be modelled. However, we have not as yet said anything about how the choice of pronoun antecedents may be partially specified. This turns out to be fairly simple to do, and also suggests a convenient way of representing node order scope constraints.

5.1   Audit markers for anaphoric co-indexing

The meaning constructor for a pronoun takes the outline form

$$(47) \quad \forall Scope, Meaning, Context, Ante, A.$$
$$[Ante \hookrightarrow A$$
$$\otimes$$
$$\forall x, p.\ pro \rightsquigarrow x \multimap$$
$$(pro \hookrightarrow p \otimes Scope \rightsquigarrow Meaning \otimes Context)]$$
$$\multimap$$
$$(Scope \rightsquigarrow Quant(A, Meaning) \otimes Updated(Context))$$

That is, the result of scoping the pronoun is an updated meaning assignment to *Scope* and an updated collection of context assignments.

Suppose that we were to add a third conjunct to this result: a term recording the antecedent selected for the pronoun through the instantiation of the variable *Ante*:

(48) $\forall Scope, Meaning, Context, Ante, A.$
  $[Ante \hookrightarrow A$

  $\otimes$

  $\forall x, p.\ pro \rightsquigarrow x\ \multimap$
    $(pro \hookrightarrow p \otimes Scope \rightsquigarrow Meaning \otimes Context)]$
  $\multimap$
  $(Scope \rightsquigarrow Quant(A, Meaning) \otimes Updated(Context)$
    $\otimes\ pro \Leftarrow Ante)$

In other words we add a coindexing expression *pro* $\Leftarrow$ *Ante* as an audit
marker that is built up in addition to a meaning assignment and a set of
context assignments. When *Ante* is instantiated in the process of selecting a particular antecedent/contextual premise, the variable occurring
in the audit marker will also be instantiated. By demanding that an
audit marker of the form e.g. *pro* $\Leftarrow$ *subj* be produced as part of the
conclusion of a glue language derivation, we can specify co-indexing
relations between pronouns and antecedents.

To be consistent about doing this, we would need to build up an entire audit trail. That is, in deriving the meaning of any constituent, we
would not only also derive a set of context assignments but also a set of
audit markers. To pass these audit markers around, we would have to
resort to the same sort of higher-order trick as with context assignments
(though since audit markers will not get updated, the technique can be
employed in its most basic form). Thus the skeletal form of a pronoun
that allows the construction and enlargement of an audit trail would
be:

(49) $\forall Scope, Meaning, Context, Audit, Ante, A.$
  $[Ante \hookrightarrow A$

  $\otimes$

  $\forall x, p.\ pro \rightsquigarrow x\ \multimap$
    $(pro \hookrightarrow p \otimes Scope \rightsquigarrow Meaning \otimes Context \otimes Audit)]$
  $\multimap$
  $(Scope \rightsquigarrow Quant(A, Meaning) \otimes Updated(Context)$
    $\otimes\ (pro \Leftarrow Ante \otimes Audit)$

Other meaning constructors would also have to be (relatively trivially) modified to pass around an extra audit trail argument.

In adding an audit trail, it would be wise to impose sortal restrictions on the higher-order variables ranging over audit trails, in the same way that it is possible to do so for variables ranging over collections of context assignments. Thus, anything of the form $node \Leftarrow node$ would be of sort Audit, as would collections of such formulae built up with linear logic connectives.

5.2   Audit markers for scope

Given an audit trail for recording anaphoric co-indexing, it is straightforward to expand it to contain node orderings for recording scope relations. The general form of an NP meaning constructor becomes

(50) $\forall Scope, Meaning, Context, Audit, L.$

$\qquad \forall x, p.\ np \leadsto x \multimap$

$\qquad\quad (np \hookrightarrow p \otimes Scope \leadsto Meaning \otimes Context$

$\qquad\qquad \otimes (LastScoped(L) \otimes Audit))$

$\qquad\quad \multimap$

$\qquad\quad (Scope \leadsto Quant(Restr, Meaning) \otimes Updated(Context)$

$\qquad\qquad \otimes (np \succ L \otimes Scope \succ np \otimes LastScoped(np) \otimes Audit)$

That is, scoping the noun phrase adds various markers to the audit trail, indicating how it is scoped in relation to the other constituents (in particular, in relation to the previously scoped node, L). Although these markers can be given independent justification in terms of the structure of normalized glue language derivations (Section 2), none of this is in fact necessary for the audit markers to reflect scope.

5.3   Audit trails and underspecification

Glue language derivations now proceed from a set of lexical and contextual premises, and derive conclusions consisting of a single meaning assignment to the sentence, an updated set of contextual premises, and an audit trail comprising a conjunction of audit markers. The audit markers reflect certain features of the derivation with regard to (a) the choice of contextual premise (anaphors), and (b) the order of certain steps in the derivation (scope).

6.1.1 Scope parallelism

Consider the sentence

(51)   Every woman hates a man, and so does every girl.

Assuming a wide scope subject reading for the antecedent, the antecedent constraints are (ignoring the creation of context assignments and audit trails, and pre-combining determiners with nouns):

(52)   Antecedent constraints

- **every woman** $\vdash$
  $\forall Scope, S. \ (\forall x. \ subj_a \leadsto x \multimap Scope \leadsto S(x)) \multimap$
  $\qquad Scope \leadsto every(woman, S)$

- **a man** $\vdash$
  $\forall Scope, S. \ (\forall x. \ obj_a \leadsto x \multimap Scope \leadsto S(x)) \multimap$
  $\qquad Scope \leadsto a(man, S)$

- **hates** $\vdash$
  $\forall X, Y. \ (subj_a \leadsto X \otimes obj_a \leadsto Y) \multimap s_a \leadsto hate(X, Y)$

- Scope constraints
  $s_a \succ subj_a \succ obj_a$

Replacing parallel elements (*every woman* by *every girl*), and renaming nodes ($s_a \mapsto s_e$, $obj_a \mapsto obj_e$, $subj_a \mapsto subj_e$) we get

(53)   Ellipsis constraints

- **every girl**
  $\forall Scope, S. \ (\forall x. \ subj_e \leadsto x \multimap Scope \leadsto S(x)) \multimap$
  $\qquad Scope \leadsto every(girl, S)$

- **a man**
  $\forall Scope, S. \ (\forall x. \ obj_e \leadsto x \multimap Scope \leadsto S(x)) \multimap$
  $\qquad Scope \leadsto a(man, S)$

- **hates**
  $\forall X, Y. \ (subj_e \leadsto X \otimes obj_e \leadsto Y) \multimap s_e \leadsto hate(X, Y)$

- Scope constraints
  $s_e \succ subj_e \succ obj_e$

These constraints specify the derivation of an ellipsis meaning

(54) $every(girl,\ \lambda x.\ a(man,\ \lambda y.\ hate(x,y)))$

just as the original constraints specify an antecedent meaning of

(55) $every(woman,\ \lambda x.\ a(man,\ \lambda y.\ hate(x,y)))$

Given an additional lexical premise corresponding to the conjunction combining ellipsis and antecedent,

(56) $\forall X, Y.\ (s_a \rightsquigarrow X \otimes s_e \rightsquigarrow Y) \multimap s \rightsquigarrow X \wedge Y$

we derive

(57) $s \rightsquigarrow every(woman,\ \lambda x.\ a(man,\ \lambda y.\ hate(x,y))) \wedge$
$every(girl,\ \lambda x.\ a(man,\ \lambda y.\ hate(x,y)))$

If the antecedent had instead been given a narrow scope subject, the name substitutions on the scope constraint would have ensured a parallel scoping for the ellipsis.

6.1.2   Sloppy pronouns

If we take the sentence

(58)   John revised a paper of his and so did Bill

there is a sloppy reading where Bill revises one of Bill's papers. This is obtained by making sloppy substitutions. Assuming that *his* in the antecedent is co-indexed with the subject NP *John*, we obtain a co-indexing constraint

$$pro_a \Leftarrow subj_a$$

Substitutions on this constraint for the ellipsis will give rise to

$$pro_e \Leftarrow subj_e$$

That is, in the ellipsis the (implicit) pronoun is co-indexed with the subject of the ellipsis, Bill. As with the scope constraints, this will ensure that in the derivation of the ellipsis meaning that Bill will revise one of his own papers.

6.2   Strict substitutions

There are two other readings for *John revised a paper of his and so did Bill*:

1.   John and Bill both revise the same paper of John's

2.   John and Bill revise (possibly different) papers of John's

These may be obtained by making strict substitutions to the lexical premises for non-parallel noun phrases. A strict substitution enforces identity of reference between the noun phrase in the antecedent and its implicit counterpart in the ellipsis.

For non-parallel noun phrases, we have the option of applying a strict substitution instead of the mere node renamings brought about by sloppy substitutions. A strict substitution on a non-parallel noun phrase may be made by removing all of the (copied) lexical premises that build up the phrase, and replacing them with

$$\forall X.np_a \rightsquigarrow X \multimap (np_a \rightsquigarrow X \otimes np_e \rightsquigarrow X)$$
$$\otimes$$
$$\forall P.np_a \hookrightarrow P \multimap (np_a \hookrightarrow P \otimes np_e \hookrightarrow P)$$

where np_a is the noun phrase node in the antecedent, and np_e is its new name in the ellipsis.

The first conjunct is exactly the meaning constructor presented in Chapter 2 for (bound variable) pronouns. It has the effect of forcing the quantifier associated with the antecedent noun phrase to bind the argument position occupied by the ellipsis noun phrase. The second conjunct is an addition to this necessitated by the introduction of contextual assignments.

6.2.1   Strict pronouns

If we impose a strict substitution on the noun phrase *a paper of his*, this means that it is the same paper that gets revised in both the ellipsis and the antecedent. If we make a strict substitution on the pronoun *his* (while leaving sloppy substitutions on the rest of the noun phrase in which the pronoun is embedded), then it is the same person's papers in both antecedent and ellipsis, though not necessarily the same papers.

To see how strict substitutions operate, let us the consider the case where the entire object noun phrase, *a paper of his*, is given a strict substitution in the ellipsis. Combining the elliptical subject and verb will give us (context assignments shown abbreviated)

(59) **bill, [revised]** $\vdash$

$\forall Y, Q.\ obj_e \rightsquigarrow Y \multimap obj_e \rightsquigarrow Y \otimes\ !(obj_e \hookrightarrow Q)$

$\otimes$

$\forall Y.obj_e \rightsquigarrow Y \multimap$

$\quad (s_e \rightsquigarrow revise(bill, Y)$

$\quad\quad \otimes\ \forall Q'obj_e \hookrightarrow Q' \multimap$

$\quad\quad\quad s_e \hookrightarrow (\ldots Q' \ldots) \otimes subj_e \hookrightarrow (\ldots Q' \ldots))$

Dropping the $!(obj_e \hookrightarrow Q)$ altogether, this can be rewritten to:

(60) **bill, [revised]** $\vdash$

$\forall Y.obj_e \rightsquigarrow Y \multimap$

$\quad (s_e \rightsquigarrow revise(bill, Y)$

$\quad\quad \otimes\ \forall Q'obj_e \hookrightarrow Q' \multimap$

$\quad\quad\quad s_e \hookrightarrow (\ldots Q' \ldots) \otimes subj_e \hookrightarrow (\ldots Q' \ldots))$

Similarly, combining the subject and verb in the antecedent gives

(61) **john, revised** $\vdash$

$\forall Y, Q.\ obj_a \rightsquigarrow Y \multimap obj_a \rightsquigarrow Y \otimes\ !(obj_a \hookrightarrow Q)$

$\otimes$

$\forall Y.obj_a \rightsquigarrow Y \multimap$

$\quad (s_a \rightsquigarrow revise(john, Y)$

$\quad\quad \otimes\ \forall Q'obj_a \hookrightarrow Q' \multimap$

$\quad\quad\quad s_a \hookrightarrow (\ldots Q' \ldots) \otimes subj_a \hookrightarrow (\ldots Q' \ldots))$

The strict substitution for obj_e removes all meaning constructors for obj_e and replaces them by

(62) Strict obj_e: **[revised a paper of his]** $\vdash$

$\forall Y.obj_a \rightsquigarrow Y \multimap (obj_a \rightsquigarrow Y \otimes obj_e \rightsquigarrow Y)$

$\otimes$

$\forall Q.obj_a \hookrightarrow Q \multimap (obj_a \hookrightarrow Q \otimes obj_e \hookrightarrow Q)$

Given the first conjunct of this, we obtain

(63)   **john, revised, bill, [revised a paper of his]** $\vdash$

$$\forall Y, Q.\, obj_a \rightsquigarrow Y \multimap obj_a \rightsquigarrow Y \otimes\, !(obj_a \hookrightarrow Q)$$

$$\otimes$$

$$\forall Y.obj_a \rightsquigarrow Y \multimap$$

$$(s_a \rightsquigarrow revise(john, Y)$$

$$\otimes\, \forall Q'.obj_a \hookrightarrow Q' \multimap$$

$$s_a \hookrightarrow (\ldots Q' \ldots) \otimes subj_a \hookrightarrow (\ldots Q' \ldots))$$

$$\otimes$$

$$(s_e \rightsquigarrow revise(bill, Y)$$

$$\otimes\, \forall Q'.obj_e \hookrightarrow Q' \multimap$$

$$s_e \hookrightarrow (\ldots Q' \ldots) \otimes subj_e \hookrightarrow (\ldots Q' \ldots))$$

Assume a lexical premise for the (elliptical) conjunction

(64)   **and** $\vdash$

$$\forall X, Y, X', Y', \Gamma_x, \Gamma_y, \Delta_x, \Delta_y.$$

$$(s_a \rightsquigarrow X \otimes \Gamma_x \multimap (s_a \hookrightarrow X' \otimes \Delta_x)$$

$$\otimes$$

$$s_e \rightsquigarrow Y \otimes \Gamma_y \multimap (s_e \hookrightarrow Y' \otimes \Delta_y))$$

$$\multimap$$

$$s \rightsquigarrow [X \wedge Y]$$

$$\otimes\, ((\Gamma_x \otimes \Gamma_y) \multimap s \hookrightarrow [X' \wedge Y'] \otimes \Delta_x \otimes \Delta_y)$$

From this we can get

(65)   **john, revised, and, bill, [revised a paper of his]** $\vdash$

$$\forall Y, Q.\, obj_a \rightsquigarrow Y \multimap obj_a \rightsquigarrow Y \otimes\, !(obj_a \hookrightarrow Q)$$

$$\otimes$$

$$\forall Y.obj_a \rightsquigarrow Y \multimap$$

$$(s \rightsquigarrow [revise((john, Y) \wedge revise(bill, Y)]$$

$$\otimes\, \forall Q', Q''.\, (obj_a \hookrightarrow Q' \otimes obj_e \hookrightarrow Q'') \multimap$$

$$s \hookrightarrow \lfloor \ldots Q', Q'' \ldots \rfloor$$

$$\otimes\, subj_a \hookrightarrow [\ldots Q' \ldots]$$

$$\otimes\, subj_e \hookrightarrow [\ldots Q'' \ldots])$$

Using $\forall Q.obj_a \hookrightarrow Q \multimap (obj_a \hookrightarrow Q \otimes obj_e \hookrightarrow Q)$, the second conjunct from the strict substitution, this can be rewritten to give

(66) **john, revised, and, bill, [revised a paper of his]** $\vdash$

$\forall Y, Q.\, obj_a \rightsquigarrow Y \multimap obj_a \rightsquigarrow Y \otimes !(obj_a \hookrightarrow Q)$

$\otimes$

$\forall Y. obj_a \rightsquigarrow Y \multimap$
$\quad (s \rightsquigarrow [revise(john, Y) \wedge revise(bill, Y)]$
$\qquad \otimes \forall Q.\, obj_a \hookrightarrow Q' \multimap$
$\qquad\quad s \hookrightarrow [\ldots Q', Q' \ldots]$
$\qquad\quad \otimes subj_a \hookrightarrow [\ldots Q \ldots]$
$\qquad\quad \otimes subj_e \hookrightarrow [\ldots Q' \ldots])$

Merging the two conjuncts in this, we obtain

(67) **john, revised, and, bill, [revised a paper of his]** $\vdash$

$\forall Y, Q. obj_a \rightsquigarrow Y \multimap$
$\quad (obj_a \hookrightarrow Q \otimes s \rightsquigarrow [revise(john, Y) \wedge revise(bill, Y)]$
$\qquad \otimes \forall Q.\, obj_a \hookrightarrow Q' \multimap$
$\qquad\quad s \hookrightarrow [\ldots Q', Q' \ldots]$
$\qquad\quad \otimes subj_a \hookrightarrow [\ldots Q \ldots]$
$\qquad\quad \otimes subj_e \hookrightarrow [\ldots Q' \ldots])$

This is now in a form where the (antecedent) object noun phrase can be quantified in the standard way, to give a meaning

(68) $s \rightsquigarrow a(\lambda y.\, paper(y) \wedge exists(\lambda x. x = john,\ \lambda x.\, of(y, x),$
$\qquad\qquad \lambda y.\, revise(john, y) \wedge revise(bill, y))$

The reading where just the pronoun receives a strict substitution is similar, except that it is just the pronominal quantifier that receives wide scope over both antecedent and ellipsis.

6.2.2 Wide scope quantifiers

Strict substitutions serve only to force the NPs undergoing the substitution to be given wide scope over both antecedent and ellipsis. Consequently, the same type of substitution accounts for the reading of *Every woman hates a man and so does every girl* where it is the same man that is hated by every woman and by every girl. We merely have to impose a strict substitution on the non-parallel NP *a man*, and it receives wide scope.

6.3 Covariation and comparisons

We have implicitly been treating ellipsis substitutions as though they applied to a fully specified set of constraints determining the form of the antecedent derivation. This might be taken to imply that all decisions resolving scope and anaphoric relations in the antecedent must be taken before deciding how to resolve the ellipsis. This is not so. All that is required is that the audit trail of scope and anaphoric constraints produced by the ellipsis derivation should be identical to the audit trail for the antecedent, subject to the ellipsis substitutions. Even if some of the antecedent constraints are not specified before deciding on strict or sloppy substitutions in the ellipsis, the substitutions will still have the desired effect. That is, whatever constraints hold or turn out to hold for the antecedent, the same constraints modulo substitutions hold for the ellipsis. Thus, even if we have not yet fully resolved scope relations in the antecedent, the scope relations in the ellipsis will always be parallel to them.

In other words, covariation of scope and anaphoric relations between antecedent and ellipsis is ensured regardless of the relative order in which decisions are made about how the antecedent and ellipsis are to be resolved. This order-independence is a valuable computational property (Alshawi and Crouch 1992). It contrasts with the higher-order treatment of ellipsis due to Dalrymple et al. (1991) where the precise order in which decisions are made about scope, anaphora and ellipsis determines the reading obtained. But in other respects, the substitutional glue language treatment of ellipsis gives essentially the same coverage as the higher-order unification account. Moreover, it does so without the need for potentially undecidable forms of unification for dealing with certain types of scope relations (see Crouch (1998) for a more detailed discussion).

The similarities and differences between the higher-order and glue language treatment of ellipsis can perhaps be summed up as follows. The glue language treatment makes minimal changes to derivations of meanings in order to incorporate parallel elliptical material. It can decide on these changes in advance of performing the derivation by expressing certain constraints that the derivations must satisfy. The higher-order account makes minimal changes to the meanings derived, and these decisions are made during the course of the derivation. Since derivations are highly order-dependent (the order in which various steps are performed affects the meaning derived), the order in which decisions are made about ellipsis resolution is significant. By treating semantic derivations as first class objects in semantic theory, one can give a simpler and computationally more attractive account of ellipsis. (The move towards treating semantic derivations as first-class objects in the treatment of ellipsis is also apparent in the Labelled Deduction account of Kempson (1995).)

Finally, we should point out that the substitutional treatment of ellipsis is to some degree independent of the analysis of context update and scope given in preceding sections. All that is required is some way of framing a set of (substitutable) constraints on anaphoric and scope relations that constrains glue language derivations in the appropriate way. If a simpler account of context update than in Section 4 could be found, then so long as it produced some kind of anaphoric audit trail, it would support the same analysis of ellipsis. Similarly with scope.

7   Conclusions

This paper has attempted to do three things. First, it has indicated how the resource sensitive nature of linear logic can be used to model contextual update in the interpretation of natural languages. The treatment of update differs from that in dynamic accounts of semantics, where the meanings of sentences are dynamic, and update contexts when applied to them. Instead, update occurs while deriving meanings, and simpler, static meaning representations are employed. How much of an advantage this confers is not yet clear. Although static meaning representations are in some sense simpler, the complexity of handling context management in the glue language suggests that we have merely transferred difficulties from one place to another. However, it is important to be aware that dynamic meanings are not forced on one by the observation that natural language utterances update context.

Second, we have shown that constraints on glue language derivations can be used to (under)specify scope and anaphoric relations. These constraints can be progressively refined, as required by any practically useful underspecified representation. We have not addressed the issue of underspecified inference, but do not in any case feel that this is the primary motivation for underspecified representations. Nor have we said anything about the mechanisms by which the scope and anaphoric constraints are generated.

Third, we have briefly illustrated how the constraints on derivations can be employed to give a relatively simple account of the relations between scope, anaphora and ellipsis, comparable in coverage to the higher-order unification account of Dalrymple et al. (1991).

We hope that this paper illustrates some of the range and flexibility of a glue language approach to semantics. Much work clearly remains to be done. In particular, our E-type account of anaphora has somewhat rudimentary coverage. But we hope that we have done sufficient groundwork to allow coverage to be extended within the same general framework.

Finally, we should note a background difference in emphasis from some other work on glue languages. Much of this presumes that a linear logic theorem prover is to be employed in using the glue language approach as an actual implementation of natural language interpretation. We have no dispute with this, and regard it as a worthwhile enterprise. However, our initial motivation in starting this work was to take a computationally well worked out approach to natural language interpretation like Quasi Logical Form (Alshawi 1992), and see if there was a more perspicuous, or at any rate alternative, semantics for it. Thus we would see the glue language approach as potentially offering a theoretical underpinning for implementations that do not explicitly employ linear logic. Whether this initial motivation can be satisfied still remains to be seen.

Acknowledgments

We would like to thank Mary Dalrymple, Vineet Gupta, Mark Hepple, Ron Kaplan, Martin Kay, Shalom Lappin, John Lamping, Ruth Kempson, Valeria de Paiva, and three anonymous reviewers for comments on the material covered in this paper. Mistakes are of course our own.

A   Appendix: Derivations for Context Update

This appendix presents glue language derivations dealing with more complex examples of context update. It can be read as a continuation of the material in Section 4.

A.1   They paid them

Consider the mini-discourse

(69)   Every candidate$_c$ appointed a manager$_m$. They$_c$ paid them$_m$.

We will focus on deriving the reading where each candidate pays the manager that he appointed, rather than the reading where there is some non-specific (quasi-collective) payment relation between candidates and managers.

We will assume the set of context assignments for the first sentence to be those given in (35) in Section 4.1. The meaning constructors for the second sentence (with antecedent nodes instantiated to *subj* and *obj*, the nodes for the subject and object NPs in the first sentence) are:

(70)   **paid** $\vdash$

$\forall X, P.\ they \rightsquigarrow X \multimap (they \rightsquigarrow X \otimes\ !(they \hookrightarrow P))$

$\otimes$

$\forall Y, Q.\ them \rightsquigarrow Y \multimap (them \rightsquigarrow Y \otimes\ !(them \hookrightarrow Q))$

$\otimes$

$\forall X, Y.\ (they \rightsquigarrow X \otimes them \rightsquigarrow Y) \multimap$

$\quad (s \rightsquigarrow pay(X, Y) \otimes$

$\quad\quad \forall P, Q.\ (they \hookrightarrow P \otimes them \hookrightarrow Q) \multimap$

$\quad\quad\quad s \hookrightarrow \exists x, y. P(x) \land Q(y) \land pay(x, y))$

(71) **they** $\vdash$

$\forall Scope, S, S', \Gamma, \Delta, A.$

$[subj \hookrightarrow A$

$\quad \otimes \, \forall x, p. \, (they \rightsquigarrow x \otimes !(subj \hookrightarrow A)) \multimap$

$\quad\quad (they \hookrightarrow p \otimes !(subj \hookrightarrow A)$

$\quad\quad\quad \otimes \, Scope \rightsquigarrow S(x, p, A)$

$\quad\quad\quad \otimes \, \forall p'. \, they \hookrightarrow p' \multimap$

$\quad\quad\quad\quad (\Gamma \multimap (Scope \hookrightarrow S'(p', p, A) \otimes \Delta(p', p, A))))]$

$\multimap$

$[Scope \rightsquigarrow forall(A, \; \lambda x. \; S(x, \lambda u.u = x, \lambda u.u = x))$

$\quad \otimes \, \Gamma \multimap$

$\quad\quad (Scope \hookrightarrow forall(A, \; \lambda x. \; S'(\lambda u.u = x, \lambda u.u = x, \lambda u.u = x))$

$\quad\quad\quad \otimes \, they \hookrightarrow \lambda x. \; A(x) \wedge S'(\lambda u.u = x, \lambda u.u = x, \lambda u.u = x)$

$\quad\quad\quad \otimes \, \forall p'. \, they \hookrightarrow p' \multimap (they \hookrightarrow p' \otimes \Delta(p', p', p')))]$

(72) **them** $\vdash$

$\forall Scope, S, S', \Gamma, \Delta, B.$

$[obj \hookrightarrow B$

$\quad \otimes \, \forall y, q. \, (them \rightsquigarrow y \otimes !(obj \hookrightarrow B)) \multimap$

$\quad\quad (them \hookrightarrow q \otimes !(obj \hookrightarrow B)$

$\quad\quad\quad \otimes \, Scope \rightsquigarrow S(y, q, B)$

$\quad\quad\quad \otimes \, \forall q'. \, them \hookrightarrow q' \multimap$

$\quad\quad\quad\quad (\Gamma \multimap (Scope \hookrightarrow S'(q', q, B) \otimes \Delta(q', q, B))))]$

$\multimap$

$[Scope \rightsquigarrow forall(B, \; \lambda y. \; S(y, \lambda u.u = y, \lambda u.u = y))$

$\quad \otimes \, \Gamma \multimap$

$\quad\quad (Scope \hookrightarrow forall(B, \; \lambda y. \; S'(\lambda u.u = y, \lambda u.u = y, \lambda u.u = y))$

$\quad\quad\quad \otimes \, them \hookrightarrow \lambda y. \; B(y) \wedge S'(\lambda u.u = y, \lambda u.u = y, \lambda u.u = y)$

$\quad\quad\quad \otimes \, \forall q'. \, them \hookrightarrow q' \multimap (them \hookrightarrow q' \otimes \Delta(q', q', q')))]$

Here we treat plural pronouns as introducing a universal quantification over the antecedent contextual assignment. It is also important to note a modification to the basic form of pronoun meaning constructors, as exemplified by the constructor for *himself* in Section 4.2.

- The antecedent assignment is added in a repeated form, $!(Ante \hookrightarrow A)$, to the antecedent and consequent of the inner implication. This is needed to account for other (indirect) dependencies on the antecedent.

- The scope meaning and context assignments are dependent on the context assignment to the antecedent as well as on the assignments to the pronoun, again to take account of any further indirect dependencies.

By dropping the repeated antecedent assignments, $!(Ante \hookrightarrow B)$, in the constructor **them**, we obtain

(73)   **them** $\vdash$
$\forall Scope, S, S', \Gamma, \Delta, B.$
$\quad [obj \hookrightarrow B$
$\qquad \otimes \forall y, q.\ them \rightsquigarrow y \multimap$
$\qquad\quad (them \hookrightarrow q$
$\qquad\qquad \otimes Scope \rightsquigarrow S(y, q, B)$
$\qquad\qquad \otimes \forall q'.\ them \hookrightarrow q' \multimap$
$\qquad\qquad\quad (\Gamma \multimap (Scope \hookrightarrow S'(q', q, B) \otimes \Delta(q', q, B)))))]$
$\quad \multimap$
$\quad [Scope \rightsquigarrow forall(B,\ \lambda y.\ S(y, \lambda u.u{=}y, \lambda u.u{=}y))$
$\qquad \otimes \Gamma \multimap$
$\qquad\quad (Scope \hookrightarrow exists(B,\ \lambda y.\ S'(\lambda u.u{=}y, \lambda u.u{=}y, \lambda u.u{=}y))$
$\qquad\qquad \otimes them \hookrightarrow \lambda y.\ B(y) \wedge S'(\lambda u.u{=}y, \lambda u.u{=}y, \lambda u.u{=}y)$
$\qquad\qquad \otimes \forall q'.\ them \hookrightarrow q' \multimap (them \hookrightarrow q' \otimes \Delta(q', q', q')))]$

Under the instantiations

$Scope \mapsto s \quad \Gamma \mapsto they \hookrightarrow p' \quad \Delta \mapsto \lambda_{\text{-}, \text{-}, \text{--}}.\ \top$
$Q \mapsto q \quad Q' \mapsto q'$
$S \mapsto \lambda y, \text{-}, \text{--}.\ s \rightsquigarrow pay(X, y)$
$S \mapsto \lambda Q', \text{-}, \text{--}.\ s \hookrightarrow \exists x, y.\ p'(x) \wedge Q'(y) \wedge pay(x, y)$

we combine **them** with **paid** to get (with simplification of equalities)

(74)   **paid, them** $\vdash$

$\forall X, P.\ they \leadsto X \multimap (they \leadsto X \otimes\ !(they \hookrightarrow P))$

$\otimes$

$\forall X.\ they \leadsto X \multimap$

$\quad \forall B.\ obj \hookrightarrow B \multimap$

$\qquad (s \leadsto forall(B,\ \lambda y.pay(X,y))$

$\qquad\quad \otimes \forall P'.\ they \hookrightarrow P' \multimap$

$\qquad\qquad [s \hookrightarrow forall(B,\ \lambda y.\exists x.P'(x) \wedge pay(x,y))$

$\qquad\qquad\quad \otimes\ them \hookrightarrow \lambda y.B(y) \wedge \exists x.P'(x) \wedge pay(x,y))])$

At this point, there are two ways of bringing in the antecedent assignment $obj \hookrightarrow B$. Given that we have

(75) $subj \hookrightarrow \lambda x.candidate(x) \wedge a(manager, \lambda y.\ \wedge appoint(x,y))$

$\quad \otimes \forall p.\ subj \hookrightarrow p \multimap$

$\qquad subj \hookrightarrow p \otimes obj \hookrightarrow \lambda y.manager(y) \wedge \exists x.p(x) \wedge appoint(x,y)$

we can either construct a non-conditional form of the *obj* assignment:

(76) $obj \hookrightarrow$

$\qquad \lambda y.[manager(y) \wedge \exists x.candidate(x)$

$\qquad\qquad \wedge a(manager, \lambda y.\ \wedge appoint(x,y)) \wedge appoint(x,y)]$

or we can leave it dependent on the assignment to *subj*. We will choose to do the latter. This gives

(77)   **pay, them, obj-assignment** $\vdash$

$\forall X, P.\ they \leadsto X \multimap (they \leadsto X \otimes !(they \hookrightarrow P))$

$\otimes$

$\forall X.\ they \leadsto X \multimap$

$\quad \forall A'.\ subj \hookrightarrow A' \multimap$

$\qquad (subj \hookrightarrow A'$

$\qquad\quad \otimes s \leadsto forall(\lambda y.manager(y) \wedge \exists x.A'(x) \wedge appoint(x,y),$

$\qquad\qquad\qquad\qquad \lambda y.pay(X,y))$

$\qquad\quad \otimes \forall P'.\ they \hookrightarrow P' \multimap$

$\qquad\qquad [s \hookrightarrow forall(\lambda y.manager(y) \wedge \exists x'.A'(x') \wedge appoint(x',y),$

$\qquad\qquad\qquad\qquad \lambda y.\exists x.P'(x) \wedge pay(x,y))$

$\qquad\qquad\quad \otimes\ them \hookrightarrow \lambda y.[manager(y) \wedge \exists x'.A'(x') \wedge appoint(x',y)$

$\qquad\qquad\qquad\qquad\qquad \wedge \exists x.P'(x) \wedge pay(x,y)]])$

That is, although we have discharged the conditional dependence on the assignment B to *obj*, we have introduced a new dependency on the assignment A' to *subj*.

Combining the two top level conjuncts in this, we get

(78)   **pay, them, obj-assignment** $\vdash$

$\forall X, P.\ they \leadsto X\ \multimap$

$(!(they \hookrightarrow P) \otimes$

$\forall A'.\ subj \hookrightarrow A'\ \multimap$

$(subj \hookrightarrow A'$

$\otimes\ s \leadsto forall(\lambda y.manager(y) \wedge \exists x.A'(x) \wedge appoint(x,y),$

$\lambda y.pay(X,y))$

$\otimes\ \forall P'.\ they \hookrightarrow P'\ \multimap$

$[s \hookrightarrow forall(\lambda y.manager(y) \wedge \exists x'.A'(x') \wedge appoint(x',y),$

$\lambda y.\exists x.P'(x) \wedge pay(x,y))$

$\otimes\ them \hookrightarrow \lambda y.[manager(y) \wedge \exists x'.A'(x') \wedge appoint(x',y)$

$\wedge \exists x.P'(x) \wedge pay(x,y)]])$

In order to make this match the inner implication of **they**, we need to add repeated assignments to the antecedent of **they** to both the antecedent and consequent, by means of the following valid inference pattern:

$A \multimap B$

Therefore: $(A \otimes C) \multimap (B \otimes C)$

This gives

(79)   **pay, them, obj-assignment** $\vdash$
$\quad \forall Ante, A.$
$\quad\quad [\forall X, P.\ they \rightsquigarrow X \otimes\ !(Ante \hookrightarrow A)\ \multimap$
$\quad\quad\quad (!(they \hookrightarrow P) \otimes\ !(Ante \hookrightarrow A) \otimes$
$\quad\quad\quad\quad \forall A'.\ subj \hookrightarrow A'\ \multimap$
$\quad\quad\quad\quad\quad (subj \hookrightarrow A' \otimes$
$\quad\quad\quad\quad\quad\quad s \rightsquigarrow forall(\lambda y.manager(y) \wedge \exists x.A'(x) \wedge appoint(x, y),$
$\quad\quad\quad\quad\quad\quad\quad\quad\quad \lambda y.pay(X, y))$
$\quad\quad\quad\quad\quad \otimes$
$\quad\quad\quad\quad\quad \forall P'.\ they \hookrightarrow p\ \multimap$
$\quad\quad\quad\quad\quad\quad [s \hookrightarrow forall(\lambda y.manager(y) \wedge \exists x'.A'(x') \wedge appoint(x', y),$
$\quad\quad\quad\quad\quad\quad\quad\quad \lambda y.\exists x.P'(x) \wedge pay(x, y))$
$\quad\quad\quad\quad\quad\quad \otimes them \hookrightarrow \lambda y.manager(y) \wedge \exists x'.A'(x') \wedge appoint(x', y)$
$\quad\quad\quad\quad\quad\quad\quad\quad \wedge \exists x.P'(x) \wedge pay(x, y)]))]$

Instantiating $Ante \mapsto subj$ and noting that

$$!(subj \hookrightarrow A) \vdash\ !(subj \hookrightarrow A) \otimes (subj \hookrightarrow A)$$

we get

(80)   **pay, them, obj-assignment** $\vdash$
$\quad \forall A.$
$\quad\quad [\forall X, P.\ they \rightsquigarrow X \otimes\ !(subj \hookrightarrow A)\ \multimap$
$\quad\quad\quad (!(they \hookrightarrow P) \otimes\ !(subj \hookrightarrow A) \otimes subj \hookrightarrow A \otimes$
$\quad\quad\quad\quad \forall A'.\ subj \hookrightarrow A'\ \multimap$
$\quad\quad\quad\quad\quad subj \hookrightarrow A' \otimes$
$\quad\quad\quad\quad\quad s \rightsquigarrow forall(\lambda y.manager(y) \wedge \exists x.A'(x) \wedge appoint(x, y),$
$\quad\quad\quad\quad\quad\quad\quad\quad \lambda y.pay(X, y))$
$\quad\quad\quad\quad\quad \otimes \forall P'.\ they \hookrightarrow P'\ \multimap$
$\quad\quad\quad\quad\quad\quad [s \hookrightarrow forall(\lambda y.manager(y) \wedge \exists x'.A'(x') \wedge appoint(x', y),$
$\quad\quad\quad\quad\quad\quad\quad\quad \lambda y.\exists x.P'(x) \wedge pay(x, y))$
$\quad\quad\quad\quad\quad\quad \otimes them \hookrightarrow \lambda y.manager(y) \wedge \exists x'.A'(x') \wedge appoint(x', y)$
$\quad\quad\quad\quad\quad\quad\quad\quad \wedge \exists x.P'(x) \wedge pay(x, y)]]$

Instantiating A' to A and applying modus ponens, we get

(81)   **pay, them, obj-assignment** $\vdash$
$\forall A.$

$[\forall X, P.\ \textit{they} \rightsquigarrow X \otimes\ !(\textit{subj} \hookrightarrow A) \multimap$
$(!(\textit{they} \hookrightarrow P) \otimes\ !(\textit{subj} \hookrightarrow A)$
$\otimes\ \textit{subj} \hookrightarrow A$
$\otimes\ s \rightsquigarrow \textit{forall}(\lambda y.\textit{manager}(y) \wedge \exists x.A(x) \wedge \textit{appoint}(x, y),$
$\lambda y.\textit{pay}(X, y))$
$\otimes\ \forall P'.\ \textit{they} \hookrightarrow P' \multimap$
$[s \hookrightarrow \textit{forall}(\lambda y.\textit{manager}(y) \wedge \exists x'.A(x') \wedge \textit{appoint}(x', y),$
$\lambda y.\exists x.P'(x) \wedge \textit{pay}(x, y))$
$\otimes\ \textit{them} \hookrightarrow \lambda y.\textit{manager}(y) \wedge \exists x'.A(x') \wedge \textit{appoint}(x', y)$
$\wedge \exists x.P'(x) \wedge \textit{pay}(x, y)]]$

By doing this, we have combined two dependencies into a single one:
the indirect dependency of the object pronoun **them** on the subject of
the preceding sentence, and the direct dependency of the subject pronoun **they** on the same constituent. This merging of dependencies is
made possible by allowing the antecedent assignment, $\textit{subj} \hookrightarrow A$, to be
repeated at will via the ! modality. Another way of thinking about this
free repetition is as follows. Until the subject pronoun **they** is scoped
(or indeed any noun phrase), we are allowed to use its initial context assignment any number of times. Since the pronoun is coindexed with its
antecedent, it is natural to take the antecedent assignment to be the pronoun's initial assignment, and so use it repeatedly as well. Moreover,
as we will shortly see, when the pronoun is scoped it is also natural
to continue treating the antecedent assignment in a way parallel to the
pronoun's initial assignment. That is, replace it by a bound variable
property in some places, and by the updated pronoun assignment in
others.

Turning to the meaning constructor for **they** and once again noting
that

$$!(\textit{subj} \hookrightarrow A) \vdash !(\textit{subj} \hookrightarrow A) \otimes (\textit{subj} \hookrightarrow A)$$

we may derive the following

(82)   **they** $\vdash$

$\forall Scope, S, S', \Gamma, \Delta, A.$

$[subj \hookrightarrow A$

$\quad \otimes$

$\quad \forall x, p.\ (they \rightsquigarrow x \otimes !(subj \hookrightarrow A)) \multimap$

$\qquad (they \hookrightarrow p \otimes !(subj \hookrightarrow A)$

$\qquad \otimes subj \hookrightarrow A$

$\qquad \otimes Scope \rightsquigarrow S(x, P, A)$

$\qquad \otimes \forall P'.\ they \hookrightarrow P' \multimap$

$\qquad\qquad (\Gamma \multimap (Scope \hookrightarrow S'(P', P, A)) \otimes \Delta(P', P, A))))]$

$\multimap$

$[Scope \rightsquigarrow forall(A,\ \lambda x.\ S(x, \lambda u.u = x, \lambda u.u = x))$

$\quad \otimes \Gamma \multimap$

$\qquad (Scope \hookrightarrow forall(A,\ \lambda x.\ S'(\lambda u.u = x, \lambda u.u = x, \lambda u.u = x))$

$\qquad \otimes they \hookrightarrow \lambda x.\ A(x) \wedge S'(\lambda u.u = x, \lambda u.u = x, \lambda u.u = x)$

$\qquad \otimes \forall p.\ they \hookrightarrow p \multimap (they \hookrightarrow p \otimes \Delta(p, p, p)))]$

The second conjunct in the antecedent of the implication now matches
(81), under the variable instantiations

$S \mapsto \lambda x, \_, A.$

$\quad s \rightsquigarrow forall(\lambda y.manager(y) \wedge \exists x'.A(x') \wedge appoint(x', y),$

$\qquad\qquad \lambda y.pay(x, y))$

$S' \mapsto \lambda P', \_, A.$

$\quad s \hookrightarrow forall(\lambda y.manager(y) \wedge \exists x'.A(x') \wedge appoint(x', y),$

$\qquad\qquad \lambda y.\exists x'.P'(x') \wedge pay(x', y))$

$\Delta \mapsto \lambda P', \_, A.$

$\quad them \hookrightarrow \lambda y.manager(y) \wedge \exists x'.A(x') \wedge appoint(x', y)$

$\qquad\qquad \wedge \exists x.P'(x) \wedge pay(x, y));$

$Scope \mapsto s; \quad \Gamma \mapsto \top$

Combining them we get

(83)   **they, pay, them, obj-context** $\vdash$
$\forall A.\ subj \hookrightarrow A \multimap$
$\quad s \rightsquigarrow forall(A, \lambda x.forall(\lambda y.manager(y) \wedge \exists x'.x' = x \wedge appoint(x', y),$
$\qquad\qquad\qquad \lambda y.pay(x, y)))$

$\otimes \top \multimap$
$\quad [s \hookrightarrow forall(A,$
$\qquad\qquad\qquad \lambda x.forall(\lambda y.manager(y) \wedge \exists x'.x' = x \wedge appoint(x', y),$
$\qquad\qquad\qquad\quad \lambda y.\exists x'.x' = x \wedge pay(x', y)))$
$\quad \otimes\ they \hookrightarrow \lambda x.A(x)\wedge$
$\qquad\qquad\qquad forall(\lambda y.manager(y) \wedge \exists x'.x' = x \wedge appoint(x', y),$
$\qquad\qquad\qquad\quad \lambda y.\exists x'.x' = x \wedge pay(x', y))$
$\quad \otimes\ \forall p.they \hookrightarrow p \multimap$
$\qquad (they \hookrightarrow p\otimes$
$\qquad\quad them \hookrightarrow \lambda y.manager(y) \wedge \exists x'.p(x') \wedge appoint(x', y)$
$\qquad\qquad\quad \wedge \exists x.p(x) \wedge pay(x, y))]$

Note how this has replaced certain occurrences of the antecedent property A with bound variable properties that are bound by the pronominal quantifier.

Since we have a context assignment

(84) $subj \hookrightarrow \lambda x.candidate(x) \wedge a(manager, \lambda y. \wedge appoint(x, y))$

from the previous sentence, we can apply modus ponens to obtain the following meaning for the sentence (context assignments shown abbreviated and equalities simplified)

(85)   **they, pay, them, obj-context, subj-context** $\vdash$
$\quad s \rightsquigarrow forall(\lambda x.candidate(x) \wedge a(manager, \lambda y. \wedge appoint(x, y))$
$\qquad\qquad\quad \lambda x.forall(\lambda y.manager(y) \wedge appoint(x, y),\ \lambda y.pay(x, y)))$
$\quad \otimes\ s \hookrightarrow \ldots \otimes they \hookrightarrow \ldots$
$\quad \otimes \forall p.they \hookrightarrow p \multimap (they \hookrightarrow p \otimes them \hookrightarrow \ldots)$

That is, the sentence means that "every candidate who appointed a manager paid all the managers that he appointed".

An alternative reading can also be derived, where every candidate that appointed a manager paid every manager appointed by a candidate (a form of collective reading). This may be obtained either by (i) instead using the non-conditional form of the *obj* assignment after step (74), or (ii) by giving the pronoun **them** wide scope, which again forces use of the non-conditional *obj* assignment.

A.2   Every candidate with a manager paid him

A paper like this would be incomplete without at least one example of donkey anaphora. The E-type reading for a sentence like[13]

(86)   Every candidate with a manager paid him.

can be paraphrased as: every candidate with a manager paid one / all of the managers he was with (where the choice of pronominal quantifier gives rise to a strong or weak reading). The way that the pronoun *him* binds a property that is itself dependent on the property assigned to the subject noun phrase is very similar to the way that *them* behaved in the previous section. The additional complexity in this section arises only from the fact that we now have to deal with modified noun phrases, where context assignments may be created in building quantifier restrictions, in addition to those built up in the body of the quantifier. In particular, we need to make sure that the assignments built up in the restriction are available for use in the body. This is achieved by modifying the meaning constructors for determiners.

To see how, suppose that we have derived the following for the modified restriction of a noun phrase:[14]

(87)   **candidate, with, a, manager** $\vdash$

$$\forall x.\, subj.var \rightsquigarrow x \multimap$$
$$(subj.rstr \rightsquigarrow \lambda x.\, candidate(x) \wedge a(manager, \lambda y.with(x,y)) \otimes$$
$$\forall p.subj \hookrightarrow p \multimap$$
$$[subj.rstr \hookrightarrow$$
$$\exists x''.candidate(x'') \wedge$$
$$a(manager, \lambda y.\exists x'.x'' = x' \wedge p(x') \wedge with(x',y))$$
$$\otimes m \hookrightarrow \lambda y.manager(y) \wedge \exists x'.p(x') \wedge with(x',y)]$$

---

[13]Since we do not have a glue language analysis of relative clauses to hand, we illustrate donkey anaphora via a prepositionally modified subject noun phrase. We would expect the same general analysis to hold for relative clauses as well.

[14]We suppress the details of how this is done.

(where m is the node corresponding to *a manager* in f-structure, and *subj.var* and *subj.rstr* are the variable and restriction parts of the *subj* node in the semantic projection from f-structure).

Assume a meaning constructor for the determiner *every* as follows[15]:

(88) **every** $\vdash$
$\forall Scope, S, S', \Gamma, \Delta, \Gamma_1, \Delta_1, R, R'.$
$[\{\forall x.subj.var \leadsto x \multimap$
$(subj.rstr \leadsto R(x) \otimes$
$\forall p.\ subj \hookrightarrow p \multimap (\Gamma_1 \multimap (subj.rstr \hookrightarrow R'(p) \otimes \Delta_1(p)))))\}$

$\otimes$

$\{\forall x, p.[subj \leadsto x \otimes \forall p'.subj \hookrightarrow p' \multimap (\Gamma_1 \multimap \Delta_1(p'))]$
$\multimap$
$(subj \hookrightarrow p \otimes Scope \leadsto S(x, p)$
$\otimes \forall p'.\ subj \hookrightarrow p' \multimap$
$((\Gamma \otimes \Gamma_1) \multimap (Scope \hookrightarrow S'(p', p) \otimes \Delta(p, P)))))\}]$

$\multimap$

$[Scope \leadsto every(R, \lambda x.S(x, \lambda u.u = x))$
$(\Gamma \otimes \Gamma_1) \multimap$
$(Scope \hookrightarrow every(\lambda x.R'(\lambda u.u = x),\ \lambda x.S'(\lambda u.u = x, \lambda u.u = x))$
$\otimes subj \hookrightarrow \lambda x.R'(\lambda u.u = x) \wedge S'(\lambda u.u = x, \lambda u.u = x)$
$\otimes \forall p'.\ subj \hookrightarrow p' \multimap np \hookrightarrow p' \otimes \Delta(p', p'))]$

This has the effect of taking whatever context assignments are built up in the restriction of the noun phrase (minus the assignment to the restriction itself):

$$\forall p.subj \hookrightarrow p \multimap (\Gamma_1 \multimap \Delta_1(p))$$

and passing them on to the scope of the noun phrase. This is achieved by adding the restriction's context assignments to the antecedent of what will form the subject meaning constructor's inner implication.

Combining the determiner with the restriction, we get (instantiating $\Gamma_1 \mapsto \top$, and simplifying equalities):

---

[15]Believe it or not, this meaning constructor is slightly simplified in that it does not allow for the possibility of anaphors in the restriction that are bound by the quantifier. This can be corrected, but we do not do so here.

(89)　**every, candidate, with, a, manager** $\vdash$
$\forall Scope, S, S', \Gamma, \Delta.$

$[\forall x, p.$

$(subj \rightsquigarrow x \otimes$

$\forall p'.subj \hookrightarrow p' \multimap m \hookrightarrow \lambda y.manager(y) \wedge \exists x'.p(x') \wedge with(x', y))$

$\multimap$

$(subj \hookrightarrow p \otimes Scope \rightsquigarrow S(x, p)$

$\otimes \forall p''. \; subj \hookrightarrow p'' \multimap (\Gamma \multimap (Scope \hookrightarrow S'(p'', p) \otimes \Delta(p'', p)))))]$

$\multimap$

$[Scope \rightsquigarrow$

$every(\lambda x. \; candidate(x) \wedge a(manager, \lambda y.with(x, y)),$

$\qquad \lambda x. \; S(x, \lambda u.u = x))$

$\otimes \Gamma \multimap$

$(Scope \hookrightarrow$

$every(\lambda x.candidate(x) \wedge a(manager, \; \lambda y.with(x, y)),$

$\qquad \lambda x. \; S'(\lambda u.u = x, \lambda u.u = x))$

$\otimes subj \hookrightarrow$

$\lambda x.candidate(x) \wedge$

$\qquad a(manager, \lambda y.with(x', y)) \wedge S'(\lambda u.u = x, \lambda u.u = x)$

$\otimes \forall p''.subj \hookrightarrow p'' \multimap subj \hookrightarrow p'' \otimes \Delta(p'', p''))]$

Turning to the scope of the subject NP, the result of combining **him** with **paid**, assuming that m is the antecedent node for the pronoun, is:

(90)　**paid, him** $\vdash$
$\forall X, P. \; subj \rightsquigarrow X \multimap$

$[!(subj \hookrightarrow P) \otimes$

$\forall A. \; m \hookrightarrow A \multimap$

$(s \rightsquigarrow exists(A, \; \lambda y.pay(X, y))$

$\otimes \forall P'. \; subj \hookrightarrow P' \multimap$

$[s \hookrightarrow exists(A, \; \lambda y.\exists x.P'(x) \wedge pay(x, y))$

$\otimes obj \hookrightarrow \lambda y.A(y) \wedge \exists x.P'(x) \wedge pay(x, y))]$

To match the meaning constructor for the subject noun phrase, we need to add the context assignments for its restriction to the antecedent of (90). Noting that

$$A \multimap B \vdash (A \otimes C) \multimap (B \otimes C)$$

adding the restriction assignments to the antecedent passes them on to
the consequent of the implication:

(91)   **paid, him** $\vdash$
$\forall X, P.$
$[subj \rightsquigarrow X \otimes$
$\quad \forall p'.subj \hookrightarrow p' \multimap m \hookrightarrow \lambda y.manager(y) \wedge \exists x'.p'(x') \wedge with(x', y)]$
$\quad \multimap$
$[\forall P'.subj \hookrightarrow P' \multimap m \hookrightarrow \lambda y.manager(y) \wedge \exists x'.P'(x') \wedge with(x', y)$
$\quad \otimes \,!(subj \hookrightarrow P)$
$\quad \otimes \forall A.\, m \hookrightarrow A \multimap$
$\qquad (s \rightsquigarrow exists(A,\ \lambda y.pay(X, y))$
$\qquad\quad \otimes \forall P''.\, subj \hookrightarrow P'' \multimap$
$\qquad\qquad [s \hookrightarrow exists(A,\ \lambda y.\exists x.P''(x) \wedge pay(x, y))$
$\qquad\qquad\quad \otimes obj \hookrightarrow \lambda y.A(y) \wedge \exists x.P''(x) \wedge pay(x, y)])]$

By instantiating P' to P, we can derive from this

(92)   **paid, him** $\vdash$
$\forall X, P.$
$[subj \rightsquigarrow X \otimes$
$\quad \forall p'.subj \hookrightarrow p' \multimap m \hookrightarrow \lambda y.manager(y) \wedge \exists x'.p(x') \wedge with(x', y)]$
$\quad \multimap$
$[!(subj \hookrightarrow P)$
$\quad \otimes m \hookrightarrow \lambda y.manager(y) \wedge \exists x'.P(x') \wedge with(x', y)$
$\quad \otimes \forall A.\, m \hookrightarrow A \multimap$
$\qquad (s \rightsquigarrow exists(A,\ \lambda y.pay(X, y))$
$\qquad\quad \otimes \forall P''.\, subj \hookrightarrow P'' \multimap$
$\qquad\qquad [s \hookrightarrow exists(A,\ \lambda y.\exists x.P''(x) \wedge pay(x, y))$
$\qquad\qquad\quad \otimes obj \hookrightarrow \lambda y.A(y) \wedge \exists x.P''(x) \wedge pay(x, y)])]$

From which we can derive via modus ponens

(93) **paid, him** $\vdash$
$\forall X, P.$

$[subj \rightsquigarrow X \otimes$
$\quad \forall p'.subj \hookrightarrow p' \multimap m \hookrightarrow \lambda y.manager(y) \wedge \exists x'.p(x') \wedge with(x', y)]$
$\quad \multimap$
$[subj \hookrightarrow P$
$\quad \otimes s \rightsquigarrow exists(\lambda y.manager(y) \wedge \exists x'.P(x') \wedge with(x', y),$
$\qquad\qquad\qquad \lambda y.pay(X, y))$
$\quad \otimes \forall P''. subj \hookrightarrow P'' \multimap$
$\qquad [s \hookrightarrow exists(\lambda y.manager(y) \wedge \exists x'.P(x') \wedge with(x', y),$
$\qquad\qquad\qquad \lambda y.\exists x.P''(x) \wedge pay(x, y))$
$\qquad \otimes obj \hookrightarrow \lambda y.manager(y) \wedge \exists x'.P(x') \wedge with(x', y) \wedge$
$\qquad\qquad\qquad \exists x.P''(x) \wedge pay(x, y)]]$

This now matches the antecedent of (92), so that we can derive

(94) **every, candidate, with, a, manager, paid, him** $\vdash$
$s \rightsquigarrow every(\lambda x.candidate(x) \wedge a(manager, \lambda y.with(x, y)),$
$\qquad\qquad \lambda x.exists(\lambda y.manager(y) \wedge \exists x'.x' = x \wedge with(x', y),$
$\qquad\qquad\qquad \lambda y.pay(x, y)))$
$\otimes s \hookrightarrow every(\lambda x.candidate(x) \wedge a(manager, \ with(x, y)),$
$\qquad\qquad \lambda x.exists(\lambda y.manager(y) \wedge \exists x'.x' = x \wedge with(x', y),$
$\qquad\qquad\qquad \lambda y.\exists x''.x'' = x \wedge pay(x'', y)))$
$\otimes subj \hookrightarrow \lambda x.candidate(x) \wedge a(manager, \ with(x, y))$
$\qquad\qquad \wedge exists(\lambda y.manager(y) \wedge \exists x'.x' = x \wedge with(x', y),$
$\qquad\qquad\qquad \lambda y.\exists x''.x'' = x \wedge pay(x'', y)))$
$\otimes \forall p.subj \hookrightarrow p \multimap$
$\quad subj \hookrightarrow p \otimes$
$\quad obj \hookrightarrow \lambda y.manager(y) \wedge \exists x'.p(x') \wedge with(x', y) \wedge$
$\qquad\qquad \exists x''.p(x'') \wedge pay(x'', y))])$

Simplifying equalities in the meaning, we obtain

(95) $s \rightsquigarrow every(\lambda x.candidate(x) \wedge a(manager, \lambda y.with(x, y)),$
$\qquad\qquad \lambda x.exists(\lambda y.manager(y) \wedge with(x, y),$
$\qquad\qquad\qquad \lambda y.pay(x, y)))$

In other words, every candidate with a manager paid a manager he
was with. This weak reading contrasts with the strong reading yielded

by the original DRT approach: every candidate with a manager paid *every* manager he was with. Both the strong and weak readings could be obtained under the glue language treatment if we had some means of choosing between either a universal or an existential quantifier for the pronoun. However, choice of pronominal quantifiers is beyond the scope of this paper.

References

Alshawi, Hiyan, editor. 1992. *The Core Language Engine*. The MIT Press, Cambridge, MA.

Alshawi, Hiyan and Richard Crouch. 1992. Monotonic semantic interpretation. In *Proceedings of the Thirtieth Annual Meeting of the ACL*, Newark, Delaware, pages 32–39. Association for Computational Linguistics.

Bos, Johan, Björn Gambäck, Christian Lieske, Yoshiki Mori, Manfred Pinkal, and Karsten Worm. 1996. Compositional semantics in VERBMOBIL. In *Proceedings of the 16th International Conference on Computational Linguistics (COLING-96)*, Copenhagen, Denmark, pages 131–136.

Cooper, Robin. 1979. The interpretation of pronouns. In Frank Heny, editor, *Syntax and Semantics 10: Selections from the Third Groningen Round Table*, volume 10, pages 61–92. Academic Press, New York.

Crouch, Richard and Josef van Genabith. 1996. Context change and underspecification in glue language semantics. In Miriam Butt and Tracy Holloway King, editors, *On-line Proceedings of the First LFG Conference*, August 26–28, 1996, Rank Xerox, Grenoble. http://www-csli.stanford.edu/publications/LFG/CrouchGenabith.ps.

Crouch, Richard. 1998. Ellipsis and glue languages. In S. Lappin and E. Benmamoun, editors, *Fragments: Studies in Ellipsis and Gapping*. Oxford University Press, Oxford.

Dalrymple, Mary, Stuart M. Shieber, and Fernando C. N. Pereira. 1991. Ellipsis and higher-order unification. *Linguistics and Philosophy*, 14(4):399–452.

Dalrymple, Mary, Angie Hinrichs, John Lamping, and Vijay Saraswat. 1993. The resource logic of complex predicate interpretation. In Keh-jiann Chen and Chu-Ren Huang, editors, *Proceedings of the 1993 Republic of China Computational Linguistics Conference (ROCLING)*, Hsitou National Park, Taiwan. Computational Linguistics Society of R.O.C, Computational Linguistics Society of Republic of China. Also published as Xerox Technical Report ISTL-NLTT-1993-08-03.

Groenendijk, Jeroen and Martin Stokhof. 1991. Dynamic predicate logic. *Linguistics and Philosophy*, 14(1):39–100.

Johnson, Mark and Martin Kay. 1990. Semantic abstraction and anaphora. In Hans Karlgren, editor, *Proceedings of the 13th International Conference on Computational Linguistics (COLING-90)*, Helsinki University, Helsinki, Finland, pages 17–27.

Kamp, Hans. 1981. A theory of truth and semantic representation. In Jeroen Groenendijk, Theo Janssen, and Martin Stokhof, editors, *Formal Methods in the Study of Language*, pages 277–321, Mathematical Centre, Amsterdam.

Kempson, Ruth. 1995. Ellipsis as labelled deduction. *Language and Deduction. Bulletin for Interest Group in Pure and Applied Logics*, 3:189–256.

Lappin, Shalom and Nissim Francez. 1994. E-type pronouns, I-sums and donkey anaphora. *Linguistics and Philosophy*, 17(4):391–428.

Muskens, Reinhard. 1995. Order-independence and underspecification. In *Dyana-2 Deliverable R2.2.C "Ellipsis, Underspecification, Events and More in Dynamic Semantics"*. The DYANA-2 Project Administrator, ILLC, University of Amsterdam.

Nerbonne, John. 1991. Constraint-based semantics. In Paul Dekker and Martin Stokhof, editors, *Proceedings of the 8th Amsterdam Colloquium*, pages 425–444. ILLC, University of Amsterdam.

Pinkal, Manfred. 1996. Radical underspecification. In Paul Dekker and Martin Stokhof, editors, *Proceedings of the Tenth Amsterdam Colloquium*. ILLC, University of Amsterdam.

Poesio, Massimo. 1994. Ambiguity, underspecification and discourse interpretation. In *Proceedings of the First International Workshop on Computational Semantics*, Tilburg, pages 151–160.

Reyle, Uwe. 1993. Dealing with ambiguities by underspecification: Construction, representation and deduction. *Journal of Semantics*, 10:123–179.

Troelstra, A. S. 1992. *Lectures on Linear Logic*. CSLI Lecture Notes, number 29. CSLI Publications, Stanford University.

van der Does, Jaap. 1996. Quantifiers, contexts and anaphora. In P. Dekker and M. Stokhof, editors, *Proceedings of the Tenth Amsterdam Colloquium*. ILLC, Amsterdam.

van Genabith, Josef and Richard Crouch. 1997. How to glue a donkey to an f-structure, or porting a dynamic meaning representation into LFG's linear logic based glue-language semantics. In Harry Bunt, Leen Kievit, Reinhard Muskens, and Margriet Verlinden, editors, *Proceedings of the Second International Workshop on Computational Semantics*, 8–10 January 1997, Tilburg, pages 52–65.

5

Resource Sharing in Glue Language Semantics

Andrew Kehler, Mary Dalrymple, John Lamping, and Vijay Saraswat

1 Introduction

A hallmark of the linear logic approach to glue language semantics is that it ensures that f-structure contributions are utilized exactly once in a derivation, allowing *coherence* and *completeness* conditions on f-structures (Kaplan and Bresnan 1982, pages 211–212) to be maintained. However, there are constructions in natural language in which a single constituent appears to yield more than one contribution to the meaning of an utterance. This is most obvious in, but is not limited to, sentences involving coordination. In example (1a), for instance, *NAFTA* is the object of two different verbs, and thus its meaning fills two roles within the semantic interpretation for the sentence (1b).

(1) a.   Bill supported, and Hillary opposed, NAFTA.

    b.   *and(supported(Bill, NAFTA), opposed(Hillary, NAFTA))*

While such constructions would appear to be problematic for the approach, we argue that resource sharing is afforded a natural treatment by exploiting the structure-sharing in LFG f-structures. We refine the analysis described in Chapter 1 and elsewhere in this volume (henceforth, the 'standard' analysis) to distinguish between a path within an f-structure and the value to which this path leads; this relationship is treated as a resource. As a result, multiple paths to an f-structure from

An earlier version of this paper appeared in the *Proceedings of the 1995 Meeting of the European Chapter of the Association for Computational Linguistics*, Dublin, Ireland. March 1995.

within an enclosing f-structure give rise to multiple resources. This view contrasts with other approaches in which resource sharing is tied specifically to coordination and other surface syntactic constructs.

We review two previous approaches that fall into this latter class in the next section. We describe the revised semantic framework in Section 3, and work through several examples of non-constituent coordination (specifically, right-node raising) in Section 4. We discuss problems introduced by intensional verbs in Section 5.

2   Previous Work

2.1   Combinatory Categorial Grammar

Steedman (1985; 1989; 1990; 1996), working in the framework of Combinatory Categorial Grammar (CCG), presents what is probably the most adequate analysis of non-constituent coordination to date. As noted by Steedman and discussed by Oehrle (1990), the addition of the rule of function composition to the inventory of syntactic rules in Categorial Grammar enables the formation of constituents with right-peripheral gaps, providing a basis for a clean treatment of cases of right node raising (RNR) as exemplified by sentence (1). Such examples are handled by a coordination schema which allows like categories to be conjoined (Steedman 1996).

$$(2)\quad \text{Coordination } (< \Phi^n >)\text{: X:}g \ \text{CONJ:}b \ \text{X:}f \Rightarrow_{\Phi^n} \text{X:}\lambda...b(f...)(g...)$$

This schema gives rise to various actual rules whose semantics depends on the number of arguments that the shared material takes. For the cases of RNR considered here, the rule has the form shown in (3).

$$(3)\quad \text{Coordination: X/Y:}f \ \text{CONJ:}b \ \text{X/Y:}g \Rightarrow \text{X/Y:}\lambda x.b(fx)(gx)$$

The contraction from $\lambda x.(fx)$ and $\lambda x.(gx)$ to $\lambda x.(fx)(gx)$ in the coordination rule allows for the single realization of the argument x to be utilized twice, as demonstrated in the derivation for sentence (1). This derivation also requires the use of a rule for forward composition in CCG,

$$(4)\quad \text{Forward Composition } (> B)\text{: X/Y:}f \ \text{Y/Z:}g \Rightarrow_B \text{X/Z: } \lambda x.f(gx)$$

and also assumes that subjects are type raised; in the following, T is a variable over categories:

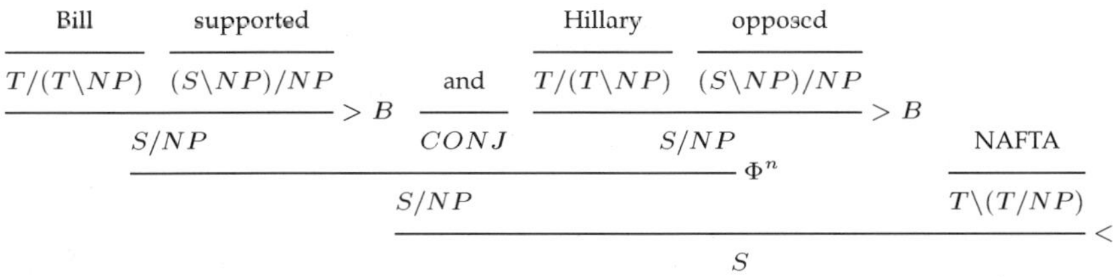

$$
\frac{
\frac{
\dfrac{\text{Bill}}{T/(T\backslash NP)} \quad \dfrac{\text{supported}}{(S\backslash NP)/NP}
}{S/NP} >B
\quad
\frac{\text{and}}{CONJ}
\quad
\frac{
\dfrac{\text{Hillary}}{T/(T\backslash NP)} \quad \dfrac{\text{opposed}}{(S\backslash NP)/NP}
}{S/NP} >B
}{
\dfrac{S/NP}{\ } \quad \Phi^n
\quad\quad
\dfrac{\text{NAFTA}}{T\backslash(T/NP)}
}
$$

$$
\frac{S/NP \quad\quad\quad T\backslash(T/NP)}{S} <
$$

As noted by Hudson (1976), however, not all examples of RNR involve coordinate structures; consider sentence (5).

(5)   Citizens who support, paraded against politicians who oppose, two trade bills.

Obviously, such cases fall outside of the purview of the coordination schema. An analysis for this sentence is available in CCG by using the *forward substitution* combinator as defined in Steedman (1996).

(6)   Forward Substitution ($> S$):
      $(X/Y)/Z\text{:}f \;\; Y/Z\text{:}g \Rightarrow_S X/Z\text{:} \lambda...(f...(g...))$

The use of this combinator assimilates cases of noncoordinate RNR to cases involving parasitic gaps. A partial derivation for example (5) is as follows.

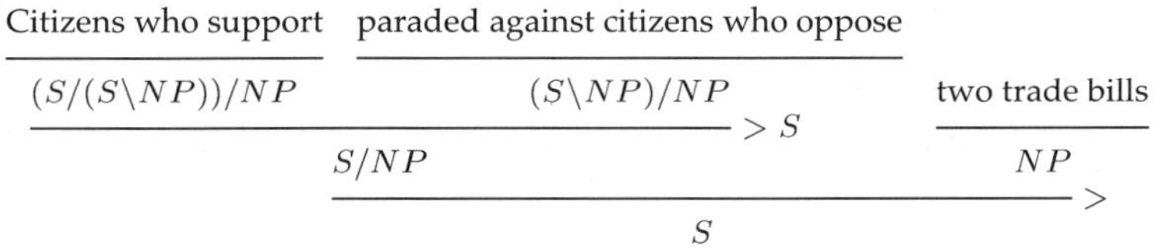

$$
\frac{
\dfrac{\text{Citizens who support}}{(S/(S\backslash NP))/NP}
\quad
\frac{
\dfrac{\text{paraded against citizens who oppose}}{(S\backslash NP)/NP}
}{\ }
}{\dfrac{S/NP}{} \quad >S}
\quad
\frac{\text{two trade bills}}{NP}
$$

$$
\frac{S/NP \quad\quad NP}{S} >
$$

Because of its tight integration between syntax and semantics, the ability to tie resource sharing in the semantics with a rule for a particular syntactic construct is crucial to the CCG framework. In contrast, we seek an analysis of RNR (and of resource sharing in general) that is uniform in the semantics, although we do not offer a competing analysis of the syntax of sentences like (5) here.

2.2 Partee and Rooth

Perhaps the most influential and widely-adopted semantic treatment of coordination is the approach of Partee and Rooth (1983). They propose a generalized conjunction scheme in which conjuncts of the same type can be combined. As is the case with Steedman's operators, contraction inherent in the schema allows for a single shared argument to be distributed as an argument of each conjunct. Type-lifting is allowed to produce like types when necessary; the combination of the coordination scheme and type-lifting can have the effect of 'copying' an argument of higher type, such as a quantifier in the case of coordinated intensional verbs. They propose a 'processing strategy' requiring that expressions are interpreted at the lowest possible type, with type-raising taking place only where necessary.

To illustrate, Partee and Rooth assume that extensional verbs such as *find* are entered in the lexicon with basic type $\langle e, \langle e, t \rangle \rangle$, whereas intensional verbs like *want*, which require a quantifier as an argument, have type $\langle \langle \langle e, t \rangle, t \rangle, \langle e, t \rangle \rangle$ (ignoring intensionality). Two extensional verbs such as *find* and *support* are coordinated at their basic types:

(7) *find and support* (type $\langle e, \langle e, t \rangle \rangle$):
   $\lambda y.\lambda x.[find(x, y) \wedge support(x, y)]$

Two intensional verbs such as *want* and *seek* are also coordinated at their basic (higher) types:

(8) *want and seek* (type $\langle \langle \langle e, t \rangle, t \rangle, \langle e, t \rangle \rangle$):
   $\lambda P.\lambda x.[want(x, P) \wedge seek(x, P)]$

The argument to this expression is a quantified NP. When an intensional and an extensional verb are coordinated, the extensional verb must be type-raised to promote it to the type of the intensional verb:

(9) *want and find* (type $\langle \langle \langle e, t \rangle, t \rangle, \langle e, t \rangle \rangle$):
   $\lambda P.\lambda x.[want(x, P) \wedge P(\lambda y.find(x, y))]$

Again, this leads to the desired result. However, an unwelcome consequence of this approach, which appears to have gone unnoticed in the literature, arises in cases in which more than two verbs are conjoined. In sentence (10), for instance,

(10)   Hillary wanted, found, and supported two candidates.

the desired reading is the one in which *one* quantifier scopes over both extensional verbs (that is, Hillary found and supported the same two candidates), just as in the case where all the verbs are extensional. In the Partee and Rooth analysis, however, if an intensional verb is coordinated with more than one extensional verb, a copy of the quantifier will be distributed to each verb in the coordinate structure. For instance, in (10), two extensional verbs and an intensional verb are coordinated.

(11)   *want, find, and support:*

$$\lambda P.\lambda x.[want(x, P) \wedge \; P(\lambda y.find(x, y)) \wedge \; P(\lambda y.support(x, y))]$$

Application of this expression to a quantifier results in two quantifiers being scoped separately over the extensional verbs. Further, there does not seem to be an obvious way to modify the Partee and Rooth proposal so as to produce the correct result, the problem being that the ability to copy quantifiers inherent in their schema is too unrestricted.

A second problem with the account is that Partee and Rooth's type-raising strategy only applies to coordinate structures. However, the need to type-raise extends to cases not involving coordination, as in sentence (12).

(12)   Citizens who seek, paraded against politicians who have, a decent health insurance policy.

We will present an analysis that preserves the intuition underlying Partee and Rooth's processing strategy, but that predicts and generates the correct reading for cases such as (10). Furthermore, the account applies equally to examples not involving coordination, as is the case in sentence (12).

3   Incorporating Resource Sharing in Glue Language Semantics

Recall that in the standard analysis, as described in Chapter 1, glue language formulas manipulate basic assertions of the form $f_\sigma \leadsto M$, for *f-structures f* and *meaning logic terms M*. Here σ is a mapping, the *semantic projection*, that relates f-structures to semantic structures. For instance, in the f-structure (14) for sentence (13), the function $(f\,\text{SUBJ})$ denotes the f-structure labeled g:

(13)   Bill supported NAFTA.

(14)
$$f: \begin{bmatrix} \text{PRED} & \text{'SUPPORT'} \\ \text{SUBJ} & g: \begin{bmatrix} \text{PRED} & \text{'BILL'} \end{bmatrix} \\ \text{OBJ} & h: \begin{bmatrix} \text{PRED} & \text{'NAFTA'} \end{bmatrix} \end{bmatrix}$$

Each word in this sentence contributes a *meaning constructor*, a premise to be used in the deduction of the meaning of the sentence. Because linear logic does not have any form of logical contraction (as is inherent in the approaches discussed earlier), there is no obvious way to replicate shared resources. Intuitively, however, the need for the multiple use of an f-structure meaning results not from the appearance of a particular lexical item (e.g., a conjunction) or a particular syntactic construction (e.g., a parasitic gap construction), but instead results from multiple paths to it from within the f-structure that contains it, where structure sharing is motivated on syntactic grounds.

To differentiate multiple paths entering an f-structure, we now take σ to map from sets of paths in f-structures to semantic structures. Further, the paths between f-structures are made available in the semantic space as resources. This makes it possible for the semantic formulas to exploit information about the multiple paths into an f-structure in order to account for the multiple uses of the f-structure's semantic contribution.

We revise the standard analysis to model what we will term *occurrences* of f-structures as resources explicitly in the logic. F-structures can mathematically be regarded as (finite) functions from a set of attributes to a set of atomic values, semantic forms and (recursively) other f-structures. We will identify an occurrence of an f-structure with a path (from the root) to that occurrence; sets of occurrences of an f-structure can therefore be identified with path sets in the f-structure. We take, then, the domain of the σ projection to be path sets in the root f-structure. Only those path sets S are considered which satisfy the property that the extensions of each path in S are identical. Therefore the f-structure reached by each of these paths is identical. Hence from a path set S, we can read off an f-structure S_f.

We use the angled bracket notation $\langle f\ p \rangle$ to denote the set of paths f concatenated with the subpath marked by attribute p. The lexical entries for example (13) are thus modified from those used in the standard analysis in accordance with this notation.

$$(15)\quad \text{Bill} \qquad\qquad \text{NP} \quad (\uparrow \text{PRED}) = \text{'BILL'}$$
$$\uparrow_\sigma \leadsto Bill$$

$$\text{supported} \quad\text{V}\quad (\uparrow \text{PRED}) = \text{'SUPPORT'}$$
$$\forall X, Y.\ \langle\uparrow \text{SUBJ}\rangle_\sigma \leadsto X \otimes \langle\uparrow \text{OBJ}\rangle_\sigma \leadsto Y$$
$$\multimap \uparrow_\sigma \leadsto supported(X, Y)$$

$$\text{NAFTA} \qquad \text{NP} \quad (\uparrow \text{PRED}) = \text{'NAFTA'}$$
$$\uparrow_\sigma \leadsto NAFTA$$

Furthermore, the relationship between an attribute and its value is represented explicitly as a resource in the logic by an *R-relation*. R-relations are represented as three-place predicates of the form $R(F,\ P,\ G)$ which indicate that (the path set) G appears at the end of a path P (of length 1) extending (the path set) F. For example, the f-structure given in (14) results in two R-relations:

$$(i)\qquad R(f,\ \text{SUBJ},\ g)$$
$$(ii)\qquad R(f,\ \text{OBJ},\ h)$$

Because f and g represent path sets entering an f-structure that they label, R-relation (i) indicates that the set of paths $\langle f\ \text{SUBJ}\rangle$ is a subset of the set of paths denoted by g. An axiom for interpretation provides the links between meanings of path sets related by R-relations.

$$\textbf{Axiom I:}\quad !(\forall F, G, P, X.\ G_\sigma \leadsto X$$
$$\multimap !(R(F, P, G) \multimap \langle F\ P\rangle_\sigma \leadsto X))$$

According to this axiom, if a set of paths G has meaning X, then a resource $\langle F\ P\rangle_\sigma \leadsto X$ can be produced for each R-relation $R(F, P, G)$ that has been introduced. The linear logic operator '!' allows the conclusion $(R(F, P, G) \multimap \langle F\ P\rangle_\sigma \leadsto X)$ to be used as many times as necessary: once for each R-relation $R(F, P, G)$ introduced by the f-structure.

We show how a deduction can be performed to derive a meaning for example (13) using the meaning constructors in (15), R-relations (i) and (ii), and Axiom I. Instantiating the lexical entries for *Bill*, *NAFTA*, and *supported* according to the labels on the f-structure in (14), we obtain the following premises:

$$\textbf{bill:} \qquad g_\sigma \rightsquigarrow Bill$$

$$\textbf{NAFTA:} \qquad h_\sigma \rightsquigarrow NAFTA$$

$$\textbf{supported:} \quad \forall X, Y.\ \langle f\ \text{SUBJ}\rangle_\sigma \rightsquigarrow X \otimes \langle f\ \text{OBJ}\rangle_\sigma \rightsquigarrow Y \\ \multimap f_\sigma \rightsquigarrow supported(X, Y)$$

At each step of the derivation, universal instantiation and modus ponens are used. First, combining Axiom I with **bill** yields:

$$(16) \quad !\,\forall F, P.\ R(F,\ P,\ g) \multimap \langle F\ P\rangle_\sigma \rightsquigarrow Bill$$

This formula states that if a path set is R-related to the (path set corresponding to the) f-structure for *Bill*, then it receives *Bill* as its meaning. From R-relation (i) and formula (16), we derive (17), giving the meaning of the subject of f.

$$(17) \quad \langle f\ \text{SUBJ}\rangle_\sigma \rightsquigarrow Bill$$

The meaning constructor **supported** combines with (17) to derive the formula for **bill-supported** shown in (18).

$$(18) \quad \forall Y.\ \langle f\ \text{OBJ}\rangle_\sigma \rightsquigarrow Y \multimap f_\sigma \rightsquigarrow supported(Bill, Y)$$

Similarly, using the meaning constructor **NAFTA**, R-relation (ii), and Axiom I, we can derive the meaning shown in (19):

$$(19) \quad \langle f\ \text{OBJ}\rangle_\sigma \rightsquigarrow NAFTA$$

Formula (19) combines with (18) to derive the final interpretation (20):

$$(20) \quad f_\sigma \rightsquigarrow supported(Bill, NAFTA)$$

A second derivation is also possible, in which **supported** and **NAFTA** are combined first and the result combined with **bill**.

In the examples discussed in Chapter 1 and elsewhere in this volume, there is a one-to-one correspondence between the set of path sets S and the set of f-structures S_f picked out by such path sets, so the two methods yield the same predictions for those cases. In the next section, we show how this system applies to several cases in which the correspondence is many-to-one, particularly examples of right-node raising.

4 Examples

4.1 RNR with coordination

First we consider the derivation of the basic case of right-node raising (RNR) illustrated in sentence (1), repeated in (21).

(21) Bill supported, and Hillary opposed, NAFTA.

The f-structure for example (21) is shown in (22).

$$
(22)\quad f: \left\{
\begin{array}{l}
f_1: \begin{bmatrix} \text{PRED} & \text{`SUPPORT'} \\ \text{SUBJ} & g:[\text{PRED}\ \text{`BILL'}] \\ \text{OBJ} & h:[\text{PRED}\ \text{`NAFTA'}] \end{bmatrix} \\[6pt]
f_2: \begin{bmatrix} \text{PRED} & \text{`OPPOSE'} \\ \text{SUBJ} & i:[\text{PRED}\ \text{`HILLARY'}] \\ \text{OBJ} & \end{bmatrix}
\end{array}
\right\}
$$

The meaning constructors contributed by the lexical items are as follows:[1]

bill:	$g_\sigma \rightsquigarrow Bill$
hillary:	$i_\sigma \rightsquigarrow Hillary$
supported:	$\forall X, Y.\ \langle f_1\ \text{SUBJ}\rangle_\sigma \rightsquigarrow X \otimes \langle f_1\ \text{OBJ}\rangle_\sigma \rightsquigarrow Y$
	$\quad\multimap f_{1\sigma} \rightsquigarrow supported(X, Y)$
opposed:	$\forall X, Y.\ \langle f_2\ \text{SUBJ}\rangle_\sigma \rightsquigarrow X \otimes \langle f_2\ \text{OBJ}\rangle_\sigma \rightsquigarrow Y$
	$\quad\multimap f_{2\sigma} \rightsquigarrow opposed(X, Y)$
and:	$\forall X, Y.\ \langle f\ \in\rangle_\sigma \rightsquigarrow X \otimes \langle f\ \in\rangle_\sigma \rightsquigarrow Y$
	$\quad\multimap f_\sigma \rightsquigarrow and(X, Y)$
and2:	$!(\forall X, Y.\ \langle f\ \in\rangle_\sigma \rightsquigarrow X \otimes f_\sigma \rightsquigarrow Y$
	$\quad\multimap f_\sigma \rightsquigarrow and(X, Y))$
NAFTA:	$h_\sigma \rightsquigarrow NAFTA$

Here, we treat *and* as a binary relation. This suffices for this example, but in general we will have to allow for cases in which more than two constituents are conjoined. Therefore, a second meaning constructor

---

[1]The '$\in$' notation picks out a member of the referenced set. For example, the expression $(f\ \in)$ refers to a member of the set f. We treat the elements of the set as unordered.

and2 is also contributed by the appearance of *and*, prefixed with the linear logic operator '!', so that it may be used as many times as necessary (and possibly not at all, as is the case in this example).

The R-relations resulting from the feature-value relationships manifest in the f-structure in (22) are:

(i)	$R(f, \in, f_1)$		(iv)	$R(f_1, \text{OBJ}, h)$
(ii)	$R(f, \in, f_2)$		(v)	$R(f_2, \text{SUBJ}, i)$
(iii)	$R(f_1, \text{SUBJ}, g)$		(vi)	$R(f_2, \text{OBJ}, h)$

There are several equivalent derivation orders; here we step through one. In the previous section, we saw how the meanings for *Bill*, *supported*, R-relation (iii), and Axiom I can be used to generate a meaning for *Bill supported*.

$$(23) \quad \forall Y. \, \langle f_1 \text{ OBJ} \rangle_\sigma \rightsquigarrow Y \multimap f_{1\sigma} \rightsquigarrow supported(Bill, Y)$$

An analogous derivation can be performed for *Hillary opposed* using R-relation (v).

$$(24) \quad \forall Z. \, \langle f_2 \text{ OBJ} \rangle_\sigma \rightsquigarrow Z \multimap f_{2\sigma} \rightsquigarrow opposed(Hillary, Z)$$

The antecedents and consequents of the foregoing formulae can be combined to yield:

$$(25) \quad \forall Y, Z. \, \langle f_1 \text{ OBJ} \rangle_\sigma \rightsquigarrow Y \otimes \langle f_2 \text{ OBJ} \rangle_\sigma \rightsquigarrow Z$$
$$\multimap f_{1\sigma} \rightsquigarrow supported(Bill, Y) \otimes f_{2\sigma} \rightsquigarrow opposed(Hillary, Z)$$

Consuming (25), **and**, and R-relations (i) and (ii), and using Axiom I, we derive:

$$(26) \quad \forall Y, Z. \, \langle f_1 \text{ OBJ} \rangle_\sigma \rightsquigarrow Y \otimes \langle f_2 \text{ OBJ} \rangle_\sigma \rightsquigarrow Z$$
$$\multimap f_\sigma \rightsquigarrow and(supported(Bill, Y), opposed(Hillary, Z))$$

Assuming the meaning constructor $h_\sigma \rightsquigarrow X$ and subsequently discharging it, Axiom I and R-relations (iv) and (vi) can be used to derive the following implication:

$$(27) \quad \forall X. \, h_\sigma \rightsquigarrow X \multimap \langle f_1 \text{ OBJ} \rangle_\sigma \rightsquigarrow X \otimes \langle f_2 \text{ OBJ} \rangle_\sigma \rightsquigarrow X$$

Using these last two formulae, by transitivity we obtain:

(28) $\forall X.\, h_\sigma \leadsto X \multimap f_\sigma \leadsto and(supported(Bill, X), opposed(Hillary, X))$

Finally, consuming the contribution of *NAFTA*, by universal instantiation and modus ponens we obtain a meaning for the whole sentence:

(29) $f_\sigma \leadsto and(supported(Bill, NAFTA), opposed(Hillary, NAFTA))$

At this stage, all accountable resources have been consumed, and the deduction is complete.

4.2   RNR with coordination and quantified NPs

We now consider sentence (30), in which a quantified NP is shared.

(30)   Bill supported, and Hillary opposed, two trade bills.

Partee and Rooth (1983) observe, and we agree, that the quantifier in such cases only scopes once, resulting in the reading in which Bill supported and Hillary opposed the same two bills.[2] Our analysis predicts this fact in the same way as Partee and Rooth's analysis does.

The meanings contributed by the lexical items and f-structure dependencies are the same as in the previous example, except for that of the object NP. Following a variant of the analysis of quantified noun phrases presented in Chapter 2, the meaning derived using the contributions from an f-structure h for *two trade bills* is:

$$\textbf{two-trade-bills:} \quad \forall H, S.\, (\forall x.\, h_\sigma \leadsto x \multimap H \leadsto S(x))$$
$$\multimap H \leadsto two(z, tradebill(z), S(z))$$

The derivation is just as before, up until the final step, at which we have derived formula (28). This formula matches the antecedent of the quantified NP meaning, so by universal instantiation and modus ponens we derive:

(31) $f_\sigma \leadsto two(z, tradebill(z), and(supported(Bill, z),$
$$opposed(Hillary, z)))$$

---

[2] We therefore disagree with Hendricks (1993), who claims that such sentences readily allow a reading involving four trade bills.

With this derivation, there is only one quantifier meaning which scopes over the meaning of the coordinated material. A result in which the quantifier meaning appears twice, scoping over each conjunct separately, is not available with the rules we have given thus far; we return to this point in Section 5.

The analysis readily extends to cases of noncoordinate RNR such as example (5), repeated as example (32).

(32)   Citizens who support, paraded against politicians who oppose, two trade bills.

In our analysis, the f-structure for *two trade bills* is resource-shared as the object of the two verbs, just as it is in the coordinated case. The fact that there is no coordination involved has no bearing on the result, since the semantics of resource-sharing is distinct from that of coordination. Unlike the CCG framework, the syntax/semantics interface in LFG is more loosely coupled, affording the flexibility to handle coordinated and non-coordinated cases of RNR uniformly in the semantics. This also allows for our semantics of coordination not to require schemas or entities of polymorphic type; our meaning of *and* is type $t \times t \to t$.

5   Intensional Verbs

We now return to consider cases involving intensional verbs. The preferred reading for sentence (33), in which only one quantifier scopes over the two extensional predicates, is shown in (34).

(33)   Hillary wanted, found, and supported two candidates.

(34) $and(wanted(Hillary, \hat{}\lambda Q.two(x, candidate(x), [\check{}Q](x))),$
$two(z, candidate(z), and(found(Hillary, z),$
$supported(Hillary, z))))$

The f-structure for example (33) is given in (35).

(35)

$$
f: \left\{
\begin{array}{l}
f_1: \left[
\begin{array}{ll}
\text{PRED} & \text{'WANT'} \\
\text{SUBJ} & g: \left[\,\text{PRED}\quad \text{'HILLARY'}\,\right] \\
\text{OBJ} & h: \left[\begin{array}{ll}\text{PRED} & \text{'CANDIDATE'}\\ \text{SPEC} & \text{'TWO'}\end{array}\right]
\end{array}
\right] \\[2em]
f_2: \left[
\begin{array}{ll}
\text{PRED} & \text{'FIND'} \\
\text{SUBJ} & \\
\text{OBJ} &
\end{array}
\right] \\[2em]
f_3: \left[
\begin{array}{ll}
\text{PRED} & \text{'SUPPORT'} \\
\text{SUBJ} & \\
\text{OBJ} &
\end{array}
\right]
\end{array}
\right.
$$

The meaning constructors for the lexical items are given below. Recall
that a second meaning constructor **and2** is introduced by *and* to handle
cases in which there are more than two conjuncts; this contribution will
be used once in the derivation of the meaning for sentence (33).

hillary: $g_\sigma \rightsquigarrow Hillary$

wanted: $\forall X, Y.\ \langle f_1\ \text{SUBJ}\rangle_\sigma \rightsquigarrow X$
$$\otimes\ (\forall s, p.\ (\forall X.\ \langle f_1\ \text{OBJ}\rangle_\sigma \rightsquigarrow X \multimap s \rightsquigarrow p(X))$$
$$\multimap s \rightsquigarrow Y(\hat{\ }p))$$
$$\multimap f_{1\sigma} \rightsquigarrow wanted(X, \hat{\ }Y)$$

found: $\forall X, Y.\ \langle f_2\ \text{SUBJ}\rangle_\sigma \rightsquigarrow X \otimes \langle f_2\ \text{OBJ}\rangle_\sigma \rightsquigarrow Y$
$$\multimap f_{2\sigma} \rightsquigarrow found(X, Y)$$

supported: $\forall X, Y.\ \langle f_3\ \text{SUBJ}\rangle_\sigma \rightsquigarrow X \otimes \langle f_3\ \text{OBJ}\rangle_\sigma \rightsquigarrow Y$
$$\multimap f_{3\sigma} \rightsquigarrow supported(X, Y)$$

and: $\forall X, Y.\ \langle f\ \in\rangle_\sigma \rightsquigarrow X \otimes \langle f\ \in\rangle_\sigma \rightsquigarrow Y$
$$\multimap f_\sigma \rightsquigarrow and(X, Y)$$

and2: $!(\forall X, Y.\ \langle f\ \in\rangle_\sigma \rightsquigarrow X \otimes f_\sigma \rightsquigarrow Y \multimap f_\sigma \rightsquigarrow and(X, Y))$

two-candidates: $\forall H, S.\ (\forall x.\ h_\sigma \rightsquigarrow X \multimap H \rightsquigarrow S(x))$
$$\multimap H \rightsquigarrow two(z, candidate(z), S(z))$$

The following R-relations result from the f-structural relationships.

(i) $R(f, \in, f_1)$	(iv) $R(f_1, \text{SUBJ}, g)$	(vii) $R(f_1, \text{OBJ}, h)$
(ii) $R(f, \in, f_2)$	(v) $R(f_2, \text{SUBJ}, g)$	(viii) $R(f_2, \text{OBJ}, h)$
(iii) $R(f, \in, f_3)$	(vi) $R(f_3, \text{SUBJ}, g)$	(ix) $R(f_3, \text{OBJ}, h)$

Following the analysis of intensional verbs given in Chapter 2, the lexical entry for *want* requires a quantified NP as an argument. The meaning of example (33) will thus include two quantifier representations, one scoped within the intensional verb, and one scoping over the remaining two predicates. This causes a problem for our framework, because we currently have no mechanism by which to obtain the additional quantifier representation, a fact which up to this point has been a feature. In general, examples containing at least one extensional verb require one quantifier representation for each intensional verb and one more to scope over all remaining extensional verbs, whereas cases in which all verbs are intensional require exactly one quantifier for each verb.

In the spirit of Partee and Rooth, we propose a mechanism for duplicating quantifier resources and a processing strategy governing its use. Specifically, the strategy is to prefer readings which require the least use of a QNP duplication rule:

(36) **QNP Duplication**:

$$!(\forall F, Q.$$
$$[\forall H, S.\ (\forall x.\ F_\sigma \rightsquigarrow x \multimap H \rightsquigarrow S(x))$$
$$\multimap H \rightsquigarrow Q(S)]$$
$$\multimap \quad [\ [\forall H, S.\ (\forall x.\ F_\sigma \rightsquigarrow x \multimap H \rightsquigarrow S(x))$$
$$\multimap H \rightsquigarrow Q(S)]$$
$$\otimes [\forall H, S.\ (\forall x.\ F_\sigma \rightsquigarrow x \multimap H \rightsquigarrow S(x))$$
$$\multimap H \rightsquigarrow Q(S)]\ ])$$

We step through the derivation of example (33). Using the meaning **hillary** with Axiom I, we can produce the following meaning constructors from R-relations (iv), (v), and (vi) respectively:

(37) $\langle f_1\ \text{SUBJ} \rangle_\sigma \rightsquigarrow \textit{Hillary}$

(38) $\langle f_2\ \text{SUBJ} \rangle_\sigma \rightsquigarrow \textit{Hillary}$

(39) $\langle f_3\ \text{SUBJ} \rangle_\sigma \rightsquigarrow \textit{Hillary}$

Combining (38) and **found** yields:

(40) $\forall X.\ \langle f_2\ \text{OBJ} \rangle_\sigma \rightsquigarrow X \multimap f_{2\sigma} \rightsquigarrow \textit{found}(\textit{Hillary}, X)$

Similarly, formula (39) and **supported** can be combined to obtain:

$$(41) \quad \forall Y. \, \langle f_3 \ \mathrm{OBJ} \rangle_\sigma \rightsquigarrow Y \multimap f_{3\sigma} \rightsquigarrow supported(Hillary, Y)$$

By assuming $f_{2\sigma} \rightsquigarrow found(Hillary, X)$ and subsequently discharging this assumption, Axiom I and R-relation (ii) can be used to obtain:

$$(42) \quad \forall X. \, \langle f_2 \ \mathrm{OBJ} \rangle_\sigma \rightsquigarrow X \multimap \langle f_2 \ \in \rangle_\sigma \rightsquigarrow found(Hillary, X)$$

By transitivity with (40) we get:

$$(43) \quad \forall X. \, \langle f_2 \ \mathrm{OBJ} \rangle_\sigma \rightsquigarrow X \multimap \langle f \ \in \rangle_\sigma \rightsquigarrow found(Hillary, X)$$

Axiom I and R-relation (iii) can be used in the same way, combining it with (41) to obtain

$$(44) \quad \forall Y. \, \langle f_3 \ \mathrm{OBJ} \rangle_\sigma \rightsquigarrow Y \multimap \langle f \ \in \rangle_\sigma \rightsquigarrow supported(Hillary, Y)$$

The antecedents and consequents of (43) and (44) can be combined to obtain:

$$(45) \quad \forall X, Y. \, \langle f_2 \ \mathrm{OBJ} \rangle_\sigma \rightsquigarrow X \otimes \langle f_3 \ \mathrm{OBJ} \rangle_\sigma \rightsquigarrow Y \multimap$$
$$\langle f \ \in \rangle_\sigma \rightsquigarrow found(Hillary, X) \otimes \langle f \ \in \rangle_\sigma \rightsquigarrow supported(Hillary, Y)$$

Using (45) with **and**, by transitivity we get:

$$(46) \quad \forall X, Y. \, \langle f_2 \ \mathrm{OBJ} \rangle_\sigma \rightsquigarrow X \otimes \langle f_3 \ \mathrm{OBJ} \rangle_\sigma \rightsquigarrow Y$$
$$\multimap f_\sigma \rightsquigarrow and(found(Hillary, X), supported(Hillary, Y))$$

Assuming the meaning constructor $h_\sigma \rightsquigarrow X$ and subsequently discharging it, Axiom I and R-relations (viii) and (ix) can be used to produce:

$$(47) \quad \forall X. \, h_\sigma \rightsquigarrow X \multimap \langle f_2 \ \mathrm{OBJ} \rangle_\sigma \rightsquigarrow X \otimes \langle f_3 \ \mathrm{OBJ} \rangle_\sigma \rightsquigarrow X$$

Combining (47) with (46) yields:

$$(48) \quad \forall X. \, h_\sigma \rightsquigarrow X \multimap f_\sigma \rightsquigarrow and(found(Hillary, X), supported(Hillary, X))$$

The meaning of *two candidates* is duplicated using QNP Duplication, and one copy combined with (48) to yield:

(49) $f_\sigma \rightsquigarrow two(z, candidate(z), and(found(Hillary, z),$
$$supported(Hillary, z)))$$

We can now combine the meanings (37) and **wanted** to obtain:

(50) $\forall Y. \ (\forall s, p. \ (\forall X. \ \langle f_1 \ \text{OBJ} \rangle_\sigma \rightsquigarrow X \multimap s \rightsquigarrow p(X)) \multimap s \rightsquigarrow Y(\hat{}p))$
$$\multimap f_{1\sigma} \rightsquigarrow wanted(Hillary, \hat{}Y)$$

Once again, by assuming and subsequently discharging the meaning constructor $h_\sigma \rightsquigarrow X$, Axiom I and R-relation (vii) can be used to produce:

(51) $\forall X. \ h_\sigma \rightsquigarrow X \multimap \langle f_1 \ \text{OBJ} \rangle_\sigma \rightsquigarrow X$

It is straightforward to show that combining (51) with (50) yields:

(52) $\forall Y. \ (\forall s, p. \ (\forall X. \ h_\sigma \rightsquigarrow X \multimap s \rightsquigarrow p(X)) \multimap s \rightsquigarrow Y(\hat{}p))$
$$\multimap f_{1\sigma} \rightsquigarrow wanted(Hillary, \hat{}Y)$$

Formula (52) is combined with the remaining instance of **two-candidates** to yield:

(53) $f_{1\sigma} \rightsquigarrow wanted(Hillary, \hat{}\lambda Q.two(x, candidate(x), [\check{}Q](x)))$

Using Axiom I with R-relation (i), along with (53), yields:

(54) $\forall X. \ \langle f \ \in \rangle_\sigma \rightsquigarrow wanted(Hillary, \hat{}\lambda Q.two(z, candidate(z), [\check{}Q](z)))$

Finally, using **and2** with (54) and (49), the desired result is derived:

(55) $and(wanted(Hillary, \hat{}\lambda Q.two(x, candidate(x), [\check{}Q](x))),$
$$two(z, candidate(z), and(found(Hillary, z),$$
$$supported(Hillary, z))))$$

The strategy of preferring the least use of QNP Duplication predicts the desired reading for sentence (33), since that reading requires two quantifiers. While the reading generated by Partee and Rooth is derivable, it requires three quantifiers and thus uses QNP duplication twice. This strategy also predicts the readings generated for the examples in Section 4. Furthermore, stating the rule as a processing strategy allows some flexibility in cases where pragmatics strongly suggests that quantifiers are copied and distributed for multiple extensional verbs; unlike the Partee and Rooth account, this would apply equally to the case where there are also intensional verbs and the case where there are not. Finally, our account readily applies to cases of intensional verbs without coordination as in example (12), since it applies more generally to cases of resource sharing.

6 Conclusions and Future Work

We have given an account of resource sharing in the syntax/semantics interface of LFG. The multiple use of semantic contributions results from viewing dependencies in f-structures as resources; in this way the one-to-one correspondence between f-structure relations and meanings is maintained. The resulting account does not suffer from overgeneration inherent in other approaches, and applies equally to cases of resource sharing that do not involve coordination. Furthermore, it lends itself readily to an extension for the intensional verb case that has advantages over the widely-assumed account of Partee and Rooth (1983).

We have separated the issue of arriving at the appropriate f-structure in the syntax from the issue of deriving the correct semantics from the f-structure. We have argued that this is the correct distinction to make, and have given a treatment of the second issue. A treatment of the first issue is the subject of future work.

Acknowledgments

We would like to thank Sam Bayer, John Maxwell, Fernando Pereira, Dick Oehrle, Stuart Shieber, and especially Ron Kaplan for helpful discussion and comments. The first author was supported in part by National Science Foundation Grant IRI-9009018, National Science Foundation Grant IRI-9350192, and a grant from the Xerox Corporation.

References

Hendriks, Herman. 1993. *Studied Flexibility: Categories and Types in Syntax and Semantics*. ILLC dissertation series 1993-5, University of Amsterdam, Amsterdam.

Hudson, Richard A. 1976. Conjunction reduction, gapping, and right-node raising. *Language*, 52(3):535–562.

Kaplan, Ronald M. and Joan Bresnan. 1982. Lexical-Functional Grammar: A formal system for grammatical representation. In Joan Bresnan, editor, *The Mental Representation of Grammatical Relations*, pages 173–281. The MIT Press, Cambridge, MA. Reprinted in Mary Dalrymple, Ronald M. Kaplan, John Maxwell, and Annie Zaenen, editors, *Formal Issues in Lexical-Functional Grammar*, pages 29–130. CSLI Publications, Stanford University. 1995.

Oehrle, Richard T. 1990. Categorial frameworks, coordination, and extraction. In Aaron Halpern, editor, *Proceedings of the Ninth West Coast Conference on Formal Linguistics*, pages 411–425, 1990.

Partee, Barbara and Mats Rooth. 1983. Generalized conjunction and type ambiguity. In Rainer Bauerle, Christoph Schwarze, and Arnim von Stechow, editors, *Meaning, Use, and Interpretation of Language*, pages 361–383. De Gruyter, Berlin.

Steedman, Mark J. 1985. Dependency and coordination in the grammar of Dutch and English. *Language*, 61:523–568.

Steedman, Mark J. 1989. Constituency and coordination in a combinatory grammar. In Mark Baltin and Anthony Kroch, editors, *Alternative Conceptions of Phrase Structure*, pages 201–231. Chicago University Press, Chicago.

Steedman, Mark J. 1990. Gapping as constituent coordination. *Linguistics and Philosophy*, 13(2):207–263.

Steedman, Mark J. 1996. *Surface Structure and Interpretation*. The MIT Press, Cambridge, MA.

6

Dynamic and Underspecified Semantics for LFG

Josef van Genabith and Richard Crouch

1 Introduction

Lexical Functional Grammar (Kaplan and Bresnan 1982; Dalrymple et al. 1995) has enjoyed a rich variety of semantic interpretation components including Halvorsen (1983); Frey and Reyle (1983); Frey et al. (1983); Reyle (1985); Wada and Asher (1986); Fenstad et al. (1987); Reyle (1988); Halvorsen and Kaplan (1988); Wada and Asher (1988); Wedekind and Kaplan (1993); Muskens (1995); Declerk (1996). The context-dependent nature of natural language interpretation, and the pervasive ambiguity this engenders, motivates the use of semantic analyses that are (a) dynamic, in the broad sense of being able to model interpretation in context and context update, and (b) underspecified, in order to deal with ambiguity in a tractable way. A considerable number of the semantic components for LFG are dynamic in that they provide interpretations for sequences of sentences (witness the DRT inspired Frey and Reyle (1983); Frey et al. (1983); Reyle (1985); Wada and Asher (1986, 1988); Muskens (1995) and the DPL based Declerk (1996)). However, with the exception of Muskens (1995), these approaches concentrate on providing schemas for relating (or translating) f-structures (in)to (sets of) fully specified, disambiguated, semantic representations.

This paper discusses three different approaches to providing LFG with semantic interpretation components that are both underspecified and dynamic. These approaches can be classified as a *mapping*-approach, a *"dynamic" meaning representation language* approach and a *linear logic context management* approach.

The mapping approach (van Genabith and Crouch 1996a,b, 1997b) is based on structural similarities between syntactic LFG f-structure and semantic Quasi-Logical Form (QLF: Alshawi and Crouch 1992) and Underspecified Discourse Representation Structure (UDRS: Reyle 1993, 1995) representations. It establishes one-to-one correspondences between *subsets* of these representation formalisms and interprets an f-structure as its corresponding QLF or UDRS.

The "dynamic" meaning representation language approach (van Genabith and Crouch 1997a) is based on Dalrymple et al. (1996) and imports dynamic meaning representation expressions (Muskens 1996) into the meaning representation slots in the original linear logic based glue language semantics.

The linear logic context management approach (Chapter 4 of this volume) exploits the properties of the linear logic glue language to directly model context update and interpretation in context in glue language derivations, without the need of importing a dynamic meaning representation language.

Both the linear logic context management and the "dynamic" meaning representation language approach can be combined with the fine-grained approach to operator and quantifier scope underspecification developed by Crouch and van Genabith in Chapter 4 of this volume. The set of linear logic premises thus obtained can be given a QLF- or UDRT-style underspecified interpretation (van Genabith and Crouch 1997a). The three approaches are developed independently and discussed at length elsewhere. In the present paper, we give brief presentations of the approaches and compare them against each other and with some of the alternatives discussed in the literature.

The paper is organised as follows. Section 2 discusses earlier approaches to LFG semantics. Section 3 reviews f-structures, QLF and UDRT to prepare the ground for the discussion of the mapping approaches in Section 4. Section 5 presents the compositional DRT (CDRT) and linear logic based "dynamic" meaning representation approach. Section 6 briefly motivates the linear logic based context management approach, which is discussed at greater length in Chapter 4 of this volume. Section 7 compares approaches and concludes.

We have tried to make this paper as self-contained as possible. Because of limits of space, however, we cannot provide comprehensive introductions to LFG, QLF, UDRT, CDRT or linear logic. In each case we supply pointers to the relevant literature.

2   LFG and Semantics

Early proposals for combining LFG and formal semantics can be found in Halvorsen (1983); Frey and Reyle (1983); Frey et al. (1983); Reyle (1985).

Halvorsen (1983) assumes five levels of representation: c-structure, f-structure, s-structure (semantic structure), IL (Montague's intensional logic) and models. F-structures are translated into s-structure by means of translation rules triggered by f-structure templates (in the LFG literature this is referred to as a *description by analysis* approach). The translation assigns quantifier scope. The scope of adjuncts, tense, negation and modal operators is decided by translation rules mapping s-structure to IL. Fully disambiguated IL formulas are then interpreted model theoretically.

Frey and Reyle (1983), Frey et al. (1983) and Reyle (1985) explore a number of ways of combining a DRT-based semantics with LFG grammars in computational settings. Some of these approaches provide algorithms for translating (semantically annotated) f-structures into disambiguated DRSs. Others are early instances of what are now usually referred to as *co-description* based approaches. This line of work has been developed further in Wada and Asher (1986, 1988).

A co-description based approach for relating syntactic and semantic representations is developed in Halvorsen and Kaplan (1988) where quantifier scopes are explicated at s-structure in terms of quantifier scope points (QP features). Scope constraints are formulated lexically in terms of LFG inside-out functional uncertainty equations.[1]

Fenstad et al. (1987) develop a sign based approach (cf. Pollard and Sag 1994) to integrating phonological, syntactic and semantic information. The semantic representations are inspired by Situation Theoretic

---

[1]Functional uncertainty equations allow specification of f-structure paths in terms of regular expressions.

approaches (Barwise and Perry 1983). They underspecify quantifier scope but are not given a direct interpretation. Instead they require disambiguation in terms of externally provided scope (QMODE) specifications resulting in fully disambiguated interpretable representations.

Wedekind and Kaplan (1993) develop type-driven algorithms involving a restriction operator for computing (sets of) disambiguated type-theory based representations from semantically annotated f-structures.

A deductive linear logic based glue language approach to assembly of meaning representation expressions in LFG is developed in a series of papers including those presented in this volume and introduced in Chapter 1.

Despite the many differences in approach and orientation these proposals share two properties. First they require disambiguated semantic representations for the purposes of model-theoretic interpretation (this is even true for Fenstad et al. (1987)). Second, with the exception of Frey and Reyle (1983), Frey et al. (1983), Reyle (1985), and Wada and Asher (1986, 1988), the semantics is sentence based.

Declerk (1996) shows how a disambiguated Dynamic Predicate Logic semantics (Groenendijk and Stokhof 1991) can be integrated into LFG in terms of LFG's projection architecture.

An underspecified and dynamic approach is provided by Muskens (1995). In addition to f-structure annotations, c-structure rules are annotated with what are called l-descriptions and s-descriptions. l-descriptions determine the structure of logical form expressions and allow partial determination of scope possibilities in terms of dominance constraints while s-descriptions determine the composition of semantic representations in the generalised l-trees. f-, l- and s-descriptions are stated as sets of simultaneous constraints (specifications of dominance relations and equality statements) and a good representation is a solution to those constraints.

Ambiguity is all pervasive in natural language, so much so that a simple *generate and test* strategy is plainly infeasible in NLP. Two responses are possible. The first is historically the initial approach. It effectively "ignores" ambiguity and picks a single, fully disambiguated, most likely, default interpretation. If the particular choice turns out to be wrong one has to undo the choice (and everything that depends on it) and consider alternatives, computationally not a very attractive task. The second approach, one that has been developed formally largely in the 1990s, is to underspecify analyses. The basic idea is to represent just as much information as one has evidence for. This is done in such a way that the representations can be enriched (i.e. further specified) monotonically with information yet to be encountered. The representations are capable of covering the whole spectrum of total and partial underspecification to complete specification. Ideally underspecified representations are fully interpreted (i.e. come equipped with a logic with semantic and syntactic consequence relations). Underspecification is computationally attractive because it avoids the generate and test approach by simply accumulating information into a single data-structure. Quasi-Logical Form (QLF) (Alshawi and Crouch 1992) and Underspecified Discourse Representation Theory (UDRT) (Reyle 1993, 1995) are probably the most prominent approaches along these lines developed so far.

Context update and interpretation in context are the hallmarks of dynamic semantics (taken in a general sense of "dynamic", and as opposed to traditional sentence based semantics). UDRT inherits its dynamics from the DRT (Kamp and Reyle 1993) approach. QLF exhibits a looser form of dynamics, based on AI inspired approaches (Alshawi 1990, 1992) to context modeling.

It is interesting to note that several of the developers of earlier LFG semantics have commented on the fact that in a sense f-structures are flat (scopally underspecified) syntactic representations and that this creates tensions with respect to mapping them to fully disambiguated semantic representations. The reason is that traditional syntax/semantics interfaces tend to require strongly hierarchical syntactic structures (e.g., trees) to steer semantic composition. The three approaches presented below turn this apparent disadvantage into an advantage: they relate *underspecified syntactic* to *underspecified semantic* representations. All of this is facilitated by (a) the fact that we can draw on the earlier static and fully disambiguated LFG semantics and (b) the emergence of underspecified and dynamic formal semantics like QLF and UDRT. Part of the aim of the paper is therefore to trace to what extent the "new" approaches are inspired by their predecessors and where they differ.

3   F-Structure, QLF, and UDRS

This section sets the ground for reviewing the mappings between f-structure, QLF and UDRS. We first informally illustrate the nature of the mapping (leaving further details for the next section), and then provide a more detailed specification of the targets of the various mappings.

3.1   Informal mappings

LFG f-structures are abstract flat syntactic representations. Quasi Logical Forms (Alshawi and Crouch 1992) and Underspecified Discourse Representation Structures (Reyle 1993, 1995) are underspecified semantic representations. It is possible to "read" (i.e. interpret) f-structures as either QLFs or UDRSs (van Genabith and Crouch 1996a, 1997b). In both cases the approach is prompted by striking structural similarities between f-structure, QLF and UDRT representations. Consider, for example, (simplified) f-structure, QLF and UDRS representations associated with the sentence *every coach picked a player*:

$$
\left[
\begin{array}{ll}
\text{SUBJ} & \left[\begin{array}{ll} \text{PRED} & \text{'coach'} \\ \text{NUM} & \text{SG} \\ \text{SPEC} & \text{EVERY} \end{array}\right] \boxed{1} \\
\text{PRED} & \text{'pick} \langle \uparrow \text{ SUBJ}, \uparrow \text{ OBJ} \rangle\text{'} \quad \boxed{3} \\
\text{OBJ} & \left[\begin{array}{ll} \text{PRED} & \text{'player'} \\ \text{NUM} & \text{SG} \\ \text{SPEC} & \text{A} \end{array}\right] \boxed{2}
\end{array}
\right]
$$

```
?Scope:pick(+3,term(+1,<num=sg,spec=every>,
                     coach,forall,X^X=X),
             term(+2,<num=sg,spec=a>,
                     player,some,X^X=X))
```

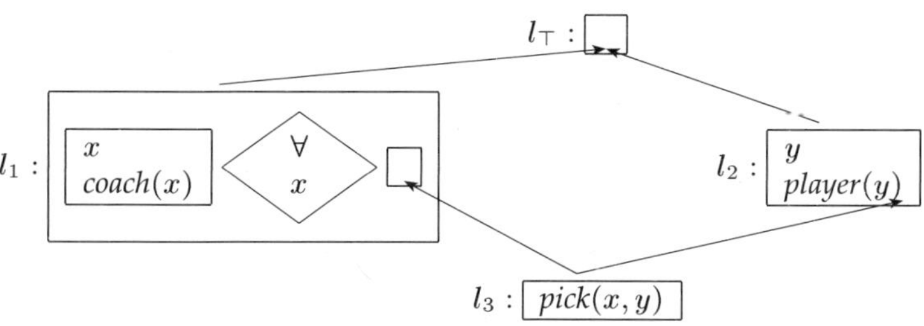

Notice that the syntactic and the two semantic representations under-specify the scope of the quantificational NPs.[2] In the QLF this is man-ifest in the uninstantiated `?Scope` meta-variable, in the UDRS graph in the partial ordering that leaves the scope relations between nodes l_1 and l_2 unspecified and in the flat f-structure representation where the SUBJ and the OBJ functions both occur on the same level of embedding. Notice further that the syntactic representation provides basic seman-tic, predicate-argument information in the form of the values of PRED features as well as quantificational information in terms of the values of SPEC features. While there certainly is a difference in approach and em-phasis, unresolved QLFs, UDRSs and f-structures bear a striking simi-larity and it is easy to see how to get from the syntactic to either of the semantic representations and back.[3] To give an example, the core of a translation τ_q taking us from f-structures to QLFs places the values of subcategorizable grammatical functions into their argument positions in the governing semantic form and recurses on those arguments:[4]

$$\tau_q\left(\begin{bmatrix} \text{SUBJ} & \begin{bmatrix} \text{PRED} & \text{'coach'} \\ \text{NUM} & \text{SG} \\ \text{SPEC} & \text{EVERY} \end{bmatrix} \boxed{1} \\ \text{PRED} & \text{pick}\,\langle\uparrow\ \text{SUBJ},\uparrow\ \text{OBJ}\rangle \quad \boxed{3} \\ \text{OBJ} & \begin{bmatrix} \text{PRED} & \text{'player'} \\ \text{NUM} & \text{SG} \\ \text{SPEC} & \text{A} \end{bmatrix} \boxed{2} \end{bmatrix}\right) =$$

$$\text{?Scope} : \text{pick}(3, \tau_q(\begin{bmatrix} \text{PRED} & \text{'coach'} \\ \text{NUM} & \text{SG} \\ \text{SPEC} & \text{EVERY} \end{bmatrix} \boxed{1}), \tau_q(\begin{bmatrix} \text{PRED} & \text{'player'} \\ \text{NUM} & \text{SG} \\ \text{SPEC} & \text{A} \end{bmatrix} \boxed{2})) =$$

---

[2] Of course, the QLF or UDRT representations need not underspecify scope.

[3] Or, indeed, from any one of the semantic representations to the other.

[4] Both the QLF and the UDRS mappings are simplified to illustrate the basic idea with minimal clutter. For the full definitions see below.

```
?Scope:pick(3,term(1,<num=sg,spec=every>,
                    coach,forall,X^X=X),
            term(2,<num=sg,spec=a>,
                    player,some,X^X=X))
```

Likewise, the basics of a mapping τ_u taking us from f-structures to UDRSs can be illustrated as follows:

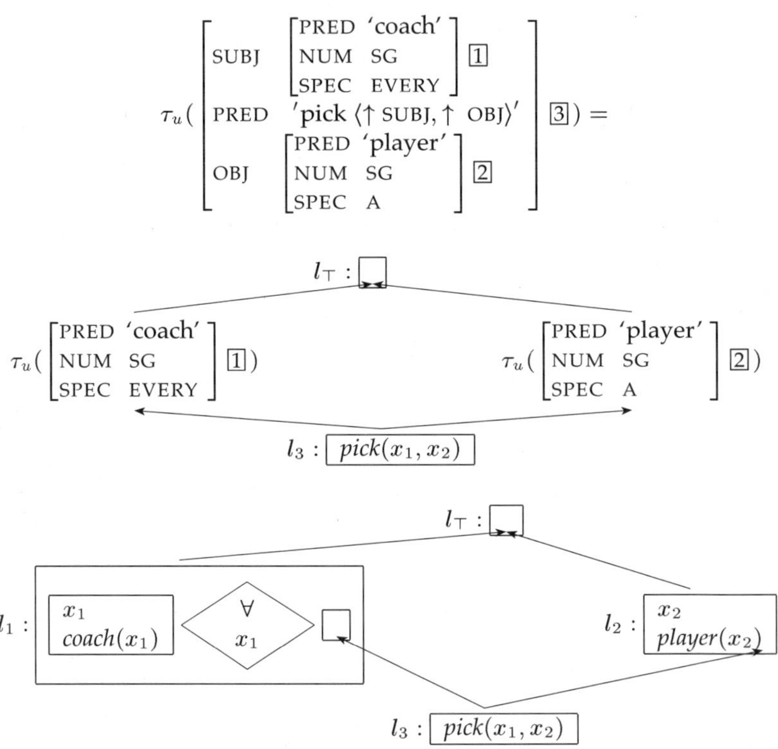

From this general perspective the difference between f-structures and QLF and UDRSs is largely one of information packaging. Abstracting away from some of the details of the representations, all three essentially represent basic predicate-argument structure.

In order to make precise the mappings between f-structures, QLFs and UDRSs we need to give definitions of the formalisms involved. The details of the LFG, QLF and UDRT formalisms are described at length elsewhere: here we briefly present a language of well-formed f-structures $\mathcal{WFS}$ and the very basics of the QLF and UDRS formalisms.

3.2 A language of well-formed f-structures

The language of $\mathcal{WFS}$ (well-formed f-structures) is defined below. The basic vocabulary consists of five disjoint sets: Gf_s (subcategorizable grammatical functions), Gf_n (non-subcategorizable grammatical functions), Sf (semantic forms), Atr (attributes), $Atom$ (atomic values) and Idx (indices):

- $Gf_s = \{\text{SUBJ}, \text{OBJ}, \text{COMP}, \text{XCOMP}, \ldots\}$
- $Gf_n = \{\text{ADJUNCTS}, \text{RELMODS}, \ldots\}$
- $Sf = \{\text{coach}\langle\rangle, \text{pick}\langle\uparrow \text{SUBJ}, \uparrow \text{OBJ}\rangle, \text{promise}\langle\uparrow \text{SUBJ}, \uparrow \text{OBJ}, \uparrow \text{XCOMP}\rangle, \ldots\}$
- $Atr = \{\text{SPEC}, \text{NUM}, \text{PER}, \text{GEN} \ldots\}$
- $Atom = \{\text{A}, \text{SOME}, \text{EVERY}, \text{MOST}, \ldots, \text{SG}, \text{PL}, \ldots\}$
- $Idx = \{\boxed{1}, \boxed{2}, \boxed{3}, \ldots\}$

The formation rules pivot on the semantic form PRED values.

- if $\Pi\langle\rangle \in Sf$ and $\boxed{i} \in Idx$ then $\begin{bmatrix} \text{PRED} & \Pi\langle\rangle \end{bmatrix}\boxed{i} \in \mathcal{WFS}$

- if $\varphi_1\boxed{j}, \ldots, \varphi_n\boxed{k} \in \mathcal{WFS}$, $\Pi\langle\uparrow \Gamma_1, \ldots, \uparrow \Gamma_n\rangle \in Sf$ and $\boxed{i} \in Idx$ then

$$\varphi\boxed{i} \in \mathcal{WFS} \text{ where } \varphi\boxed{i} \equiv \begin{bmatrix} \Gamma_1 & \varphi_1\boxed{j} \\ \ldots & \\ \text{PRED} & \Pi\langle\uparrow \Gamma_1, \ldots, \uparrow \Gamma_n\rangle \\ \ldots & \\ \Gamma_n & \varphi_n\boxed{k} \end{bmatrix}\boxed{i}$$

where for any two substructures $\psi\boxed{l}$ and $\phi\boxed{m}$ occurring in $\varphi\boxed{i}$, $l \neq n$ except possibly where $\psi \equiv \phi$.[5]

- if $\alpha \in Atr$, $v \in Atom$, $\varphi \equiv \begin{bmatrix} \ldots \\ \text{PRED} & \Pi\langle\ldots\rangle \\ \ldots \end{bmatrix}\boxed{i}$, $\varphi \in \mathcal{WFS}$ and $\alpha \notin dom(\varphi)$ then $\begin{bmatrix} \alpha & v \\ \ldots \\ \text{PRED} & \Pi\langle\ldots\rangle \\ \ldots \end{bmatrix}\boxed{i} \in \mathcal{WFS}$

The side condition in the second clause ensures that only identical substructures can have identical tags. Tags are used to represent reentrancies and will often appear vacuously. The definition captures f-structures that are complete, coherent and consistent.[6]

---

[5]Where $\equiv$ denotes syntactic identity modulo permutation of attribute-value pairs.

[6]Proof: simple induction on the formation rules for $\mathcal{WFS}$ using the definitions of completeness, coherence and consistency (Kaplan and Bresnan 1982). Because of lack of space here we can not consider non-subcategorizable grammatical functions. For a treatment of those in a QLF-style interpretation see van Genabith and Crouch (1996a). The notions of *substructure occurring in an f-structure* and $dom(\varphi)$ can easily be spelled out formally. The definition given above uses textual representations of f-structures. It can easily be recast in terms of hierarchical sets, finite functions, directed graphs, etc.

3.3 Quasi Logical Form

QLF (Alshawi 1990, 1992; Alshawi et al. 1992; Alshawi and Crouch 1992; Cooper et al. 1996) is the semantic representation formalism developed for the Core Language Engine (CLE), a large scale natural language processing system developed at SRI, Cambridge. Many of the QLF design decisions are directly informed by computational concerns. QLF provides an underspecified truth conditionally interpreted representation formalism with context modeling, resolution against context and monotonic interpretation. The QLF formalism is monotonic in a number of respects. First, the construction of QLFs does not involve destructive operations but proceeds through cumulative gathering of constraints. Second, the addition of constraints to a QLF reduces its set of readings.[7] Compared to other underspecified semantic representation formalisms it is worth noticing that QLF allows for a great variety of semantic phenomena to be underspecified. The phenomena include (amongst others): quantifier and operator scope, vague relations and predication instances.

We now give a syntax and semantics for a QLF language. The definitions below are mainly from Alshawi and Crouch (1992) and Cooper et al. (1996). A QLF term must be one of the following

- a term variable: x, y, …
- a term index: `+i`, `+j`, …
- a constant term: `7`, `mary1`, …
- an expression of the form: `term(Idx,Cat,Restr,Quant,Reft)`

A term index `Idx` uniquely identifies a term. The `Cat` attribute is a sequence of non-recursive attribute:value pairs encoding relevant syntactic information. `Restr` is a property. For a resolved `term`, `Quant` is a generalised quantifier. `Reft` is a contextual restriction on the range of quantification. For unresolved terms, `Quant` and `Reft` may be QLF meta-variables (`?P`, `?Q`, …).

A QLF formula must be one of the following:

- the application of a predicate to arguments:
  `Pred(Arg_1,...,Arg_n)`

---

[7]It is indeed possible to give a semantics for QLFs based on a subsumption relation where more specific versions of a QLF are subsumed by less specific ones (Cooper et al. 1996).

- an expression of the form: `form(Idx,Cat,Restr,Res)`
- a formula with scoping constraints: `Scope:Formula`

`Pred` is a first or higher-order predicate, including the usual logical operators `and`, `not`, etc. An argument `Arg` may be a term, a formula or predicate. `form`s allow underspecification of predicates. `Restr` is a higher-order predicate, `Res` a meta-variable or a contextually provided predicate. The meaning of the `form` is determined by applying its restriction `Restr` to its resolution `Res`. `Scope` is either a meta-variable when scoping information is underspecified or a (possibly empty) list of term indices, e.g., `[+i,+j]` if term `+i` outscopes `+j`. The degree to which a QLF is unresolved corresponds approximately to the extent to which meta-variables (appearing above in the positions marked by `Quant`, `Reft`, `Scope`, and `Res`) are instantiated to the appropriate kind of object level expressions.

The semantics of a (possibly underspecified) QLF formula ϕ is given in terms of a supervaluation construction over the set of fully specified representations that can be obtained from the underspecified representation. Technically the interpretation function $[\![\cdot]\!]$ is defined in terms of a valuation relation $\mathcal{V}$ which unpacks an underspecified representation into its set of disambiguated representations.

- $[\![\phi]\!]^{M,g} = 1$ iff $\mathcal{V}(\phi, 1)$ but not $\mathcal{V}(\phi, 0)$
- $[\![\phi]\!]^{M,g} = 0$ iff $\mathcal{V}(\phi, 0)$ but not $\mathcal{V}(\phi, 1)$
- $[\![\phi]\!]^{M,g}$ *undefined* iff $\mathcal{V}(\phi, 1)$ and $\mathcal{V}(\phi, 0)$
- $[\![\phi]\!]^{M,g}$ *uninterpretable* iff neither $\mathcal{V}(\phi, 1)$ or $\mathcal{V}(\phi, 0)$

The valuation relation $\mathcal{V}$ may resolve an underspecified representation into a more specific one in terms of a salience relation $\mathcal{S}$ between a context C and (part of) a QLF representation R (cf. the QLF interpretation clauses Q11, Q12 and Q16 below; for detailed accounts of contextual resolution see Alshawi (1990, 1992); Alshawi et al. (1992)). The propositional connectives are interpreted in clauses Q1 to Q8, abstraction and application in Q9 and Q10. Q11 resolves anaphoric elements against contextually provided antecedents. Q12 provides contextual interpretations for unresolved quantificational `terms`. Quantifier scope is treated in Q14 and Q15. In the absence of scope constraints, Q14 scopes non-deterministically; Q15 implements scope constraints. Q16 and Q17 interpret unresolved and resolved `forms`.

Q1: $\mathcal{V}_g(\mathtt{and}(\phi,\psi),1)$ if $\mathcal{V}_g(\phi,1)$ and $\mathcal{V}_g(\psi,1)$

Q2: $\mathcal{V}_g(\mathtt{and}(\phi,\psi),0)$ if $\mathcal{V}_g(\phi,0)$ or $\mathcal{V}_g(\psi,0)$

Q3: $\mathcal{V}_g(\mathtt{or}(\phi,\psi),1)$ if $\mathcal{V}_g(\phi,1)$ or $\mathcal{V}_g(\psi,1)$

Q4: $\mathcal{V}_g(\mathtt{or}(\phi,\psi),0)$ if $\mathcal{V}_g(\phi,0)$ and $\mathcal{V}_g(\psi,0)$

Q5: $\mathcal{V}_g(\mathtt{imply}(\phi,\psi),1)$ if $\mathcal{V}_g(\phi,0)$ or $\mathcal{V}_g(\psi,1)$

Q6: $\mathcal{V}_g(\mathtt{imply}(\phi,\psi),0)$ if $\mathcal{V}_g(\phi,1)$ and $\mathcal{V}_g(\psi,0)$

Q7: $\mathcal{V}_g(\mathtt{not}(\phi),1)$ if $\mathcal{V}_g(\phi,0)$

Q8: $\mathcal{V}_g(\mathtt{not}(\phi),0)$ if $\mathcal{V}_g(\phi,1)$

Q9: $\mathcal{V}_g(x\mathtt{\char`^}\phi,h)$ if for all $k \in type(x)$, $h(k) = v$ and $\mathcal{V}_{g[x/k]}(\phi,v)$

Q10: $\mathcal{V}_g(p(arg_1,\ldots,arg_n), P(Arg_1,\ldots,Arg_n))$ if $\mathcal{V}_g(p,P)$ and $\mathcal{V}_g(arg_1,Arg_1)$ and $\ldots$ and $\mathcal{V}_g(arg_n,Arg_n)$

Q11: if ϕ is a formula containing a term `term(I,C,R,?Q,?R)` and T is a term such that $\mathcal{S}(C,T)$ then $\mathcal{V}_g(\phi,v)$ if $\mathcal{V}_g(\phi[\mathtt{exists}/\mathtt{?Q},T/\mathtt{?R}],v)$ and $\mathcal{V}_g(\mathtt{R}(T),1)$

Q12: if ϕ is a formula containing a term `term(I,C,R,?Q,?R)` and Q is a quantifier such that $\mathcal{S}(C,Q)$ then $\mathcal{V}_g(\phi,v)$ if $\mathcal{V}_g(\phi[Q/\mathtt{?Q},I/\mathtt{?R}],v)$

Q13: $\mathcal{V}_g(\,\mathtt{?Scope{:}}\phi,v)$ if $\mathcal{V}_g(\phi,v)$

Q14: if ϕ is a formula containing a term `T = term(I,C,R,Q,A)` then $\mathcal{V}_g(\phi,v)$ if $\mathcal{V}_g(\mathtt{Q(R',F')},v)$ where `R'` is `X^(and(R(X),X=A))[X/I]`, and `F'` is `X^(and(`ϕ`,X=A))[X/T,X/I]`

Q15: if `[I,J,...]:`ϕ is a formula containing a term `T = term(I,C,R,Q,A)` then $\mathcal{V}_g(\mathtt{[I,J,...]{:}}\phi,v)$ if $\mathcal{V}_g(\mathtt{Q(R',F')},v)$ where `R'` is `X^(and(R(X),X=A))[X/I]`, and `F'` is `X^([J,...]:and(`ϕ`,X=A))[X/T,X/I]`

Q16: $\mathcal{V}_g(\mathtt{form(I,C,R,?R)},v)$ if $\mathcal{V}_g(\mathtt{form(C,R,?R)[R(P)/?R]},v)$ where $\mathcal{S}(\mathtt{C,P})$

Q17: $\mathcal{V}_g(\mathtt{form(I,C,R,}\phi\mathtt{)},v)$ if $\mathcal{V}_g(\mathtt{R}(\phi),v)$ where ϕ is a QLF expression but not a meta-variable

As a simple example consider an underspecified QLF associated with *every coach picked a player*:

```
?Scope:pick(+3,term(+1,<num=sg,spec=every>,
                    coach,?Q,?T),
              term(+2,<num=sg,spec=a>,
                    player,?P,?R))
```

The example QLF is underspecified with respect to quantifier scope `?Scope`, the precise quantificational import `?Q`, `?P` of the `terms` and their contextual restrictions `?T`, `?R`. Scope constraints can be expressed by instantiated `?Scope` meta-variables. A wide scope reading of e.g. *a player* would correspond to instantiating the `?Scope` meta-variable to the scope list `[+2,+1]`. Contextual resolution (Q12) may resolve `?Q` and `?P` to "surface" form[8] and set the contextual restrictions `?T` and `?R` to `X^X=X` (the set of all objects):

```
?Scope:pick(+3,term(+1,<num=sg,spec=every>,
                     coach,forall,X^X=X),
               term(+2,<num=sg,spec=a>,
                     player,some,X^X=X))
```

This QLF is then interpreted in terms of the supervaluation over the two valuations generated by Q14:[9]

```
forall(X^coach(X),X^some(Y^player(Y),Y^pick(X,Y)))
some(Y^player(Y),Y^forall(X^coach(X),X^pick(X,Y)))
```

3.4   Underspecified Discourse Representation Structures

In standard DRT (Kamp and Reyle 1993) scope relations between quantificational structures and operators are unambiguously specified in terms of the structure and nesting of boxes. UDRT (Reyle 1993, 1995) allows partial specifications of scope relations. Textual definitions of UDRS graphs are based on a labeling (indexing) of DRS conditions and a statement of a partial ordering relation between the labels. The language of UDRSs is based on a set L of labels, a set *Ref* of discourse referents and a set *Rel* of relation symbols. It features two types of conditions.[10] Type 1 conditions are sometimes referred to as *content* conditions. They provide the usual predication, quantification and operator information and constitute the nodes in the UDRS graphs. Type 2 conditions are sometimes referred to as *structural* conditions. They specify

---

[8]Alternative resolutions may endow indefinite NPs in certain positions with generic force, etc.

[9]Some clutter removed.

[10]The definition abstracts away from some of the complexities in the full definitions of the UDRS language (Reyle 1993). To give an example, the full language also contains type 1 conditions of the form $l : \sigma(l_1, \ldots, l_n)$ indicating that $(l_1, \ldots, l_n)$ are contributed by a single sentence.

scope relations and provide the scaffolding between the nodes in UDRS graphs:

1.
   - if $l \in L$, $x \in Ref$ then $l : x$ is a condition
   - if $l \in L$, $R \in Rel$ a n-place relation and $x_1, .., x_n \in Ref$ then $l : R(x_1, .., x_n)$ is a condition
   - if $l_i, l_j \in L$ then $l_i : \neg l_j$ is a condition
   - if $l_i, l_j, l_k \in L$ then $l_i : l_j \mathcal{Q} l_k$ is a condition, where $\mathcal{Q}$ is a quantifier
   - if $l_i, l_j, l_k \in L$ then $l_i : l_j \Rightarrow l_k$ is a condition
   - if $l, l_1, \ldots, l_n \in L$ then $l : \vee(l_1, \ldots, l_n)$ is a condition

2.
   - if $l_i, l_j \in L$ then $l_i \leq l_j$ is a condition where $\leq$ is a partial ordering.

UDRSs are pairs of a set of type 2 conditions with a set of type 1 conditions:

- A UDRS $\mathcal{K}$ is a pair $\langle \mathcal{L}, \mathcal{C} \rangle$ where $\mathcal{L} = \langle L, \leq \rangle$ is an upper semi-lattice of labels and $\mathcal{C}$ a set of conditions of type 1 above such that

  - if $l_i : \neg l_j \in \mathcal{C}$ then $l_j \leq l_i \in \mathcal{L}$
  - if $l_i : l_j \left\{ \begin{matrix} \mathcal{Q} \\ \Rightarrow \end{matrix} \right\} l_k \in \mathcal{C}$ then $l_j \leq l_i, l_k \leq l_j \in \mathcal{L}$.[11]

The construction of UDRSs, in particular the specification of the partial ordering between labeled conditions in $\mathcal{L}$, is constrained by a set of meta-level constraints (principles). They ensure, e.g., that verbs are subordinated with respect to their scope inducing arguments, that scope sensitive elements obey the restrictions postulated by whatever syntactic theory is adopted, that potential antecedents are scoped with respect to their anaphoric potential, etc. Below we list some basic cases:

- Clause Boundedness: the scope of genuinely quantificational structures is clause bounded. If l_q and l_{cl} are the labels associated with the quantificational structure and the containing clause, respectively, then the constraint $l_q \leq l_{cl}$ enforces clause boundedness.

- Scope of Indefinites: indefinites labeled l_i may take arbitrarily wide scope in the representation. They cannot exceed the top-level DRS $l_\top$, i.e. $l_i \leq l_\top$.

---

[11]This closes $\mathcal{L}$ under the subordination relations induced by complex conditions.

- Proper Names: proper names, π, always end up in the top-level DRS, $l_\top$. This is specified lexically by $l_\top : \pi$

The semantics of UDRSs is defined in terms of disambiguations δ. δ maps a UDRS $\mathcal{K}$ into one of its disambiguations $\mathcal{K}^\delta$. It does this by monotonically adding structural constraints to the original UDRS. To give an example, the structural scaffolding of the UDRS associated with *every coach picked a player* plus the additional constraint $l_2 \le l_{12}$ results in the narrow scope reading of the indefinite NP

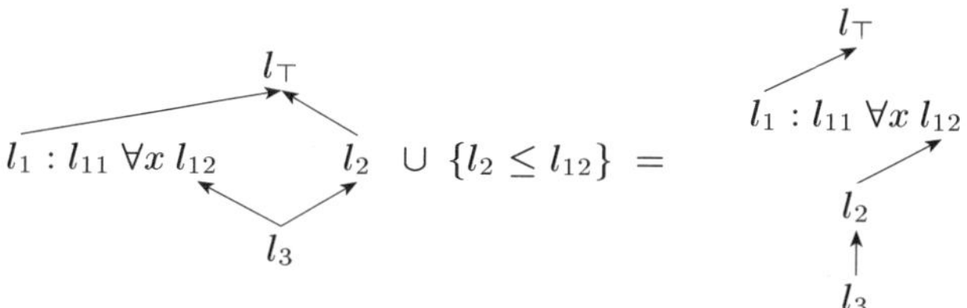

while the constraint $l_1 \le l_2$ forces the wide scope specific reading of the indefinite:

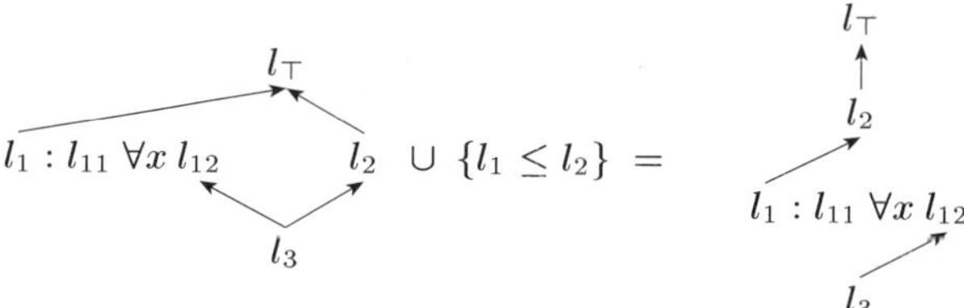

The semantics takes its cue from the definition of the consequence relation, in the most recent version (Reyle 1995) involving correlated disambiguations δ^I. Correlated disambiguations synchronise disambiguations of indexed UDRS components (I is an index set) in premise and goal representations. Wide scope quantification over δ^I ensures that such elements are interpreted alike and that the semantic consequence relation is defined over pairs of corresponding disambiguations:

$$\forall \delta^I (\Gamma^{\delta^I} \models \alpha^{\delta^I})$$

The definition results in a conjunctive interpretation of a goal UDRS against the empty premise set.[12] In this case a UDRS is true iff each of

---

[12] The original semantics in Reyle (1993) took its cue from $\forall \delta_i \exists \delta_j (\Gamma^{\delta_i} \models \alpha^{\delta_j})$ resulting in a disjunctive semantics.

its disambiguations comes out true. Interpreted in context (i.e. against a nonempty premise set), a UDRS follows from premises iff its correlated disambiguations follow from the correlated disambiguations of the premises.

In contrast to other syntactic proof systems the UDRS proof systems (Reyle 1993, 1995; König and Reyle 1996) operate *directly* on underspecified representations avoiding (whenever possible) the need to consider disambiguated cases.[13]

Like QLF, the UDRT formalism is monotonic both with respect to construction, disambiguation and interpretation of semantic representations.

4   Mapping F-structures

4.1   F-structure – QLF maps

We can, in fact, construct a whole family of mappings between f-structures and QLFs. In the forward direction ($\mathcal{WFS} \rightarrow$ QLF), these mappings differ primarily with respect to how much they instantiate the resulting QLF representation. Mappings that underspecify QLF quantifier (`Quant`), referent (`Reft`), restriction (`Restr`) and resolution (`Res`) arguments maximise the effect of QLF contextual resolution. Mappings that hard-wire resolution to "surface form" minimise or switch off QLF contextual resolution. Such mappings are used to show correctness of the translation (see Section 4.3.4).

In this section we first define a simple mapping τ_q from f-structures to QLF, and an inverse τ_q^{-1}. τ_q maximises the effect of QLF contextual resolution. Later we define a mapping τ_{q*} which hard-wires resolution to surface form.

In the forward direction (τ_q), recursive f-structures (i.e. f-structures whose semantic forms feature subcategorizable grammatical functions) are mapped into QLF `form` expressions, and non-recursive f-structures into QLF `terms`. An alternative mapping would relate recursive f-structures to an application of a QLF predicate to arguments (as in the illustrations above): `Predicate(Arg_1, ..., Arg_n)`. The mapping

---

[13]Soundness and completeness results are given for the system in Reyle (1993).

τ_q presented below generalises this approach in that if desired the choice of the `Predicate` can be underspecified and in that syntactic information can be encoded in a `form`'s `Category` attribute.

Definition of τ_q:

- $\tau_q(\Gamma, \begin{bmatrix} \alpha_1 & v_1 \\ \dots & \\ \text{PRED } \Pi\langle\rangle & \\ \dots & \\ \alpha_n & v_n \end{bmatrix} \boxed{\text{I}}) := \begin{array}{l} \texttt{term(I,<gf=}\Gamma\texttt{,}\alpha_1 = v_1,\dots,\alpha_n = v_n\texttt{>,} \\ \Pi\texttt{,\_,\_)} \end{array}$

- $\tau_q(\Gamma, \begin{bmatrix} \Gamma_1 & \varphi_1\boxed{\text{J}} \\ \alpha_1 & v_1 \\ \dots & \\ \text{PRED } \Pi\langle\uparrow\Gamma_1,\dots,\uparrow\Gamma_n\rangle & \\ \dots & \\ \Gamma_n & \varphi_n\boxed{\text{K}} \\ \alpha_m & v_m \end{bmatrix} \boxed{\text{I}}) :=$

$$\texttt{?Scope:form(I,<gf=}\Gamma\texttt{,pred=}\Pi(\Gamma_1,\dots,\Gamma_n)\texttt{), }\alpha_1{=}v_1,\dots,\alpha_m{=}v_m\texttt{>,}$$
$$\texttt{P\^{}P(}\tau_q(\Gamma_1,\varphi_1\boxed{\text{J}})\texttt{),}\dots\texttt{,}\tau_q(\Gamma_n,\varphi_n\boxed{\text{K}})\texttt{),\_)}$$

τ_q takes two arguments: a grammatical function Γ and an f-structure φ. Note that τ_q does not instantiate `Scope`, `Quant`, `Reft` and `Res` variables. The reverse mapping from QLF to f-structure is given by

Definition of τ_q^{-1}:

- $\tau_q^{-1}(\texttt{term(I,<gf=}\Gamma\texttt{,}\alpha_1 = v_1,\dots,\alpha_n = v_n \texttt{ >,}\Pi\texttt{,\_,\_))} :=$

$$\Gamma \begin{bmatrix} \alpha_1 & v_1 \\ \dots & \\ \text{PRED} & \Pi \\ \dots & \\ \alpha_n & v_n \end{bmatrix} \boxed{\text{I}}$$

- $\tau_q^{-1}(\texttt{\_:form(I,<gf=}\Gamma\texttt{,pred=}\Pi(\Gamma_1,\dots,\Gamma_m)\texttt{),}\alpha_1 = v_1,\dots,\alpha_j = v_j\texttt{>,}$
$$\Pi(\varrho_1,\dots,\varrho_m)\texttt{,\_)) :=}$$

$$\Gamma \begin{bmatrix} \alpha_1 & v_1 \\ \dots & \\ \alpha_j & v_j \\ \text{PRED} & \Pi\langle\uparrow\Gamma_1,\dots,\uparrow\Gamma_m\rangle \\ \tau_q^{-1}(\varrho_1) & \\ \dots & \\ \tau_q^{-1}(\varrho_m) & \end{bmatrix} \boxed{\text{I}}$$

Note that the reverse mapping ignores any information the QLF may contain about scope relations, anaphoric relations, and so forth.

4.1.1   A worked example

We illustrate the QLF mappings with the simple control construction *every coach persuaded a player to sign a contract*. In the corresponding f-structure the control relation is encoded in terms of token identical values of the OBJ function of the matrix and the SUBJ function of the subordinate clause. Note that τ_q (and τ_q^{-1}) respects f-structure reentrancies (indicated in terms of identical $\boxed{1}$ annotations) without further stipulation.

$$\tau_q(\text{ SIGMA}, \begin{bmatrix} \text{SUBJ} & \begin{bmatrix} \text{PRED 'coach'} \\ \text{SPEC} \quad \text{EVERY} \end{bmatrix} \boxed{1} \\ \text{PRED} \quad \text{'persuade} \langle \uparrow \text{SUBJ}, \uparrow \text{OBJ}, \uparrow \text{XCOMP} \rangle' \\ \text{OBJ} \quad \begin{bmatrix} \text{PRED 'player'} \\ \text{SPEC} \quad \text{A} \end{bmatrix} \boxed{2} \\ \text{XCOMP} \quad \begin{bmatrix} \text{SUBJ} & \begin{bmatrix} \text{PRED 'player'} \\ \text{SPEC} \quad \text{A} \end{bmatrix} \boxed{2} \\ \text{PRED} & \text{'sign} \langle \uparrow \text{SUBJ}, \uparrow \text{OBJ} \rangle' \ \boxed{5} \\ \text{OBJ} & \begin{bmatrix} \text{PRED 'contract'} \\ \text{SPEC} \quad \text{A} \end{bmatrix} \boxed{3} \end{bmatrix} \end{bmatrix} \boxed{4}) =$$

```
?S1:form(4,<gf=sigma,pred=persuade(subj,obj,xcomp)>,
              P^P(S,O,XC),_)
```

$$S = \tau_q(\text{ SUBJ}, \begin{bmatrix} \text{PRED 'coach'} \\ \text{SPEC} \quad \text{EVERY} \end{bmatrix} \boxed{1}) =$$

```
term(1,<pred=coach,spec=every>,coach,_,_)}
```

$$O = \tau_q(\text{ OBJ}, \begin{bmatrix} \text{PRED 'player'} \\ \text{SPEC} \quad \text{A} \end{bmatrix} \boxed{2}) =$$

```
term(2,<pred=player,spec=a>,player,_,_)
```

$$\mathrm{XC} = \tau_q(\ \mathrm{XCOMP},\ \begin{bmatrix} \mathrm{SUBJ} & \begin{bmatrix} \mathrm{PRED} & \mathrm{'player'} \\ \mathrm{SPEC} & \mathrm{A} \end{bmatrix} \boxed{2} \\ \mathrm{PRED} & \mathrm{'sign}\ \langle\uparrow\ \mathrm{SUBJ},\uparrow\ \mathrm{OBJ}\rangle' \quad \boxed{5} \\ \mathrm{OBJ} & \begin{bmatrix} \mathrm{PRED} & \mathrm{'contract'} \\ \mathrm{SPEC} & \mathrm{A} \end{bmatrix} \boxed{3} \end{bmatrix}\ ) =$$

```
?S2:form(5,<gf=xcomp,pred=sign(subj,obj)>,R^R(Sx,Ox),_)
```

$$\mathrm{Sx} = \tau_q(\ \mathrm{OBJ},\ \begin{bmatrix} \mathrm{PRED} & \mathrm{'player'} \\ \mathrm{SPEC} & \mathrm{A} \end{bmatrix} \boxed{2}\ ) =$$

```
term(2,<pred=player,spec=a>,player,_,_)
```

$$\mathrm{Ox} = \tau_q(\ \mathrm{OBJ},\ \begin{bmatrix} \mathrm{PRED} & \mathrm{'contract'} \\ \mathrm{SPEC} & \mathrm{A} \end{bmatrix} \boxed{3}\ ) =$$

```
term(3,<pred=contract,spec=a>,contract,_,_)
```

Piecing together the various sub-results we get the following QLF as the translation image of the original f-structure:

```
?S1:form(4,<gf=sigma,pred=persuade(subj,obj,xcomp)>,
        P^P(term(1,<pred=coach,spec=every>,coach,_,_),
            term(2,<pred=player,spec=a>,player,_,_),
            ?S2:form(5,<gf=xcomp,pred=sign(subj,obj)>,
                R^R(term(2,<pred=player,spec=a>,
                        player,_,_),
                    term(3,<pred=contract,spec=a>,
                        contract,_,_))
                ,_),
        ,_))
```

where the f-structure reentrancy resurfaces in terms of identical `term` indices as required. This expression may then be further resolved by QLF contextual resolution to:

```
?S1:form(4,<gf=sigma,pred=persuade(subj,obj,xcomp)>,
        P^P(term(1,<pred=coach,spec=every>,
                  coach,forall,X^X=X),
            term(2,<pred=player,spec=a>,
                  player,exists,X^X=X),
            ?S2:form(5,<gf=xcomp,pred=sign(subj,obj)>,
                    Q^Q(term(2,<pred=player,spec=a>,
                             player,exists,X^X=X),
                        term(3,<pred=contract,spec=a>,
                             contract,exists,X^X=X))
                  ,sign),
        ,persuade))
```

The reader may want to check that either of the QLFs if fed into the reverse mapping τ_q^{-1} translates back into the original f-structure. Furthermore, the resolved QLF is equivalent to the more readable

```
?S1:persuade(term(1,<pred=coach,spec=every>,
                 coach,forall,X^X=X),
          term(2,<pred=player,spec=a>,
                player,exists,X^X=X),
          S2:sign(term(2,<pred=player,spec=a>,
                       player,exists,X^X=X),
                  term(3,<pred=contract,spec=a>,
                        contract,exists,X^X=X)))
```

τ_q and τ_q^{-1} relate f-structures to sets of QLFs. The QLFs in a set are partially ordered by a subsumption relation corresponding to the degree and kind of instantiation of QLF meta-variables present in the QLF produced by τ_q prior to contextual resolution.

By contrast, the alternative mapping τ_{q*} presented below establishes one-to-one correspondences between subsets of the QLF and $\mathcal{WFS}$ formalisms. It does this by switching off QLF contextual resolution. Here we give only the forward direction:[14]

---

[14]Formulation of the backward direction τ_{q*}^{-1} is straightforward.

Definition of τ_{q*}:

$$
\bullet\quad \tau_{q*}\!\left(\Gamma,\;
\begin{bmatrix}
\alpha_1 & v_1 \\
\text{SPEC} & Q \\
\ldots & \\
\text{PRED} & \Pi\langle\rangle \\
\ldots & \\
\alpha_n & v_n
\end{bmatrix}\boxed{I}\right).-\quad
\begin{array}{l}
\texttt{term(I,<gf=}\Gamma\texttt{,}\,\alpha_1=v_1,\ldots,\alpha_n=v_n\texttt{>,} \\
\qquad \Pi,Q,\texttt{X\^{}X=X)}
\end{array}
$$

$$
\bullet\quad \tau_{q*}\!\left(\Gamma,\;
\begin{bmatrix}
\Gamma_1 & \varphi_1\boxed{J} \\
\alpha_1 & v_1 \\
\ldots & \\
\text{PRED} & \Pi\langle\uparrow\Gamma_1,\ldots,\uparrow\Gamma_n\rangle \\
\ldots & \\
\Gamma_n & \varphi_n\boxed{K} \\
\alpha_m & v_m
\end{bmatrix}\boxed{I}\right):=
$$

$$
\begin{array}{l}
\texttt{?Scope:form(I,<gf=}\Gamma\texttt{,pred=}\Pi(\Gamma_1,\ldots,\Gamma_n)\texttt{,}\,\alpha_1{=}v_1,\ldots,\alpha_m{=}v_m\texttt{>,} \\
\qquad \texttt{P\^{}P}(\tau_{q*}(\Gamma_1,\varphi_1\boxed{J}),\ldots,\tau_{q*}(\Gamma_n,\varphi_n\boxed{K})),\Pi)
\end{array}
$$

τ_{q*} maps the f-structure corresponding to our example control construction directly to the resolved QLF presented above. It establishes one-to-one correspondences between quantificationally completely underspecified QLFs (using the `form` constructor) and f-structures. τ_{q*} is later used to establish correctness of the mappings (cf. Section 4.3.4).

4.2   F-structure – UDRS maps

We now define translation functions τ_u and τ_u^{-1} between f-structures and UDRSs. The (U)DRT construction principles distinguish between genuinely quantificational NPs, indefinite NPs and proper names. Accordingly we have

Definition of τ_u:

$$
\bullet\quad \tau_u^{\boxed{J}}\!\left(
\begin{bmatrix}
\Gamma_1 & \varphi_1\boxed{I_1} \\
\ldots & \\
\text{PRED} & \Pi\langle\uparrow\Gamma_1,\ldots,\uparrow\Gamma_n\rangle \\
\ldots & \\
\Gamma_n & \varphi_n\boxed{I_n}
\end{bmatrix}\boxed{I}\right):=
\begin{array}{l}
\tau_u^{\boxed{I}}(\varphi_1\boxed{I_1})\cup\ldots\cup\tau_u^{\boxed{I}}(\varphi_n\boxed{I_n}) \\
\cup\{l_{\boxed{I}}:\Pi(\eta_{\boxed{I_1}},\ldots,\eta_{\boxed{I_n}})\}
\end{array}
$$

$$
\text{where}\quad \eta_{\boxed{I_i}}:=
\begin{cases}
x_{\boxed{I_i}} & \text{iff}\quad \Gamma_i\in\{\text{SUBJ},\text{OBJ},\ldots\} \\
l_{\boxed{I_i}} & \text{iff}\quad \Gamma_i\in\{\text{COMP},\text{XCOMP}\}
\end{cases}
$$

$$
\bullet\quad \tau_u^{\boxed{J}}\!\left(
\begin{bmatrix}
\text{SPEC} & \text{EVERY} \\
\text{PRED} & \Pi\langle\rangle
\end{bmatrix}\boxed{I}\right):=
\left\{
\begin{array}{l}
\{l_{\boxed{I}}:l_{\boxed{I}_1}\forall x_{\boxed{I}}\,l_{\boxed{I}_2},\,l_{\boxed{I}_1}:x_{\boxed{I}}, \\
l_{\boxed{I}_1}:\Pi(x_{\boxed{I}}),\,l_{\boxed{I}}\leq l_\top,\,l_{\boxed{J}}\leq l_{\boxed{I}_2}
\end{array}
\right\}
$$

- $\tau_u^{\boxed{J}}\!\left(\begin{bmatrix} \text{SPEC} & \text{A} \\ \text{PRED} & \Pi\langle\rangle \end{bmatrix}\boxed{I}\right) := \{l_{\boxed{I}} : x_{\boxed{I}}, l_{\boxed{I}} : \Pi(x_{\boxed{I}}), l_{\boxed{I}} \leq l_\top, l_{\boxed{J}} \leq l_{\boxed{I}}\}$

- $\tau_u^{\boxed{J}}\!\left(\begin{bmatrix} \text{PRED} & \Pi\langle\rangle \end{bmatrix}\boxed{I}\right) := \{l_\top : x_{\boxed{I}}, l_\top : \Pi(x_{\boxed{I}}), l_{\boxed{J}} \leq l_\top\}$

The first clause defines the recursive part of the translation function and states that the translation of an f-structure is simply the union of the translations of its component parts. The base cases of the definition are provided by the three remaining clauses. They correspond directly to the UDRS construction principles discussed in Section 3.4. The first one deals with genuinely quantificational NPs, the second one with indefinites and the third one with proper names. Note that the definitions allow indefinites to take arbitrary wide scope $\{l_{\boxed{I}} \leq l_\top\}$ and assign proper names to the top level of the resulting UDRS $\{l_\top : x_{\boxed{I}}, l_\top : \Pi(x_{\boxed{I}})\}$ as required. In line with the QLF translations given above, τ_u does not enforce clause boundedness of quantificational NPs. Indices are our book-keeping devices for label and variable management. F-structure reentrancies are handled correctly without further stipulation. Atomic attribute-value pairs can be included as unary definite relations.

For the reverse mapping we require a lexically specified association between subcategorizable grammatical functions in LFG semantic form and argument positions in the corresponding UDRT predicates:

$$\begin{array}{ccccc}
\Pi(& x_1, & x_2, & \ldots, & x_n \quad) \\
& \updownarrow & \updownarrow & \updownarrow & \updownarrow \\
\Pi\langle & \uparrow\Gamma_1, & \uparrow\Gamma_2, & \ldots, & \uparrow\Gamma_n \quad \rangle
\end{array}$$

The scaffolding which allows us to (re)construct a f-structure from a UDRS is provided by UDRS subordination constraints and variables occurring in UDRS conditions. The translation recurses on the semantic contributions of verbs. To translate a UDRS $\mathcal{K} = \langle \mathcal{L}, \mathcal{C} \rangle$ merge the structural with the content constraints into the equivalent $\mathcal{K}' = \mathcal{L} \cup \mathcal{C}$. Define a function ∂ ("dependents") on referents, labels and merged UDRSs as

$$\partial(\eta, \mathcal{K}) := \begin{cases} \{l_\alpha : \eta, l_\alpha : \Pi(\eta)\} \cup Sub(l_\alpha) & \text{if} \quad \eta \in Ref \\ \{l_\alpha : l_{\alpha_1} \forall \eta l_{\alpha_2}, l_{\alpha_1} : \eta, l_{\alpha_1} : \Pi(\eta)\} \cup Sub(l_\alpha) & \text{if} \quad \eta \in Ref \\ \{\eta : \Pi(\gamma_1, \ldots, \gamma_n)\} \cup \partial(\gamma_1, \mathcal{K}) \cup \ldots \cup \partial(\gamma_n, \mathcal{K}) & \text{if} \quad \eta \in L \end{cases}$$

where $\partial(\eta, \mathcal{K}) \subseteq \mathcal{K}$ and $Sub(l_\alpha)$ is the set of subordination constraints a node labeled l_α engages in:

$$Sub(l_\alpha) = \{l_\alpha \leq l | l_\alpha \leq l \in \mathcal{K}\} \cup \{l \leq l_\alpha | l \leq l_\alpha \in \mathcal{K}\} \cup \{l \leq l_{\alpha 2} | l \leq l_\alpha \in \mathcal{K}\}$$

Given a discourse referent x and a UDRS, ∂ picks out components of the UDRS corresponding to proper names, indefinite and genuinely quantificational NPs with x as implicit argument. Given a label l, ∂ picks out the transitive closure over (in our fragment essentially) sentential complements and their dependents. Note that for simple, non-recursive UDRSs $\mathcal{K}$, ∂ defines a partition $\{\{l : \Pi(x_1, \ldots, x_n)\}, \partial(x_i, \mathcal{K}), \ldots, \partial(x_n, \mathcal{K})\}$ of $\mathcal{K}$. Just like the reverse QLF mapping τ_q^{-1}, the definition below ignores subordination constraints. It is straightforward to extend the definition to take account of subordination constraints if that is desired but the translation image (the resulting f-structure) cannot in all cases reflect the constraints (cf. Section 4.3.3 below).

Definition of τ_u^{-1}:

- if $\mathcal{K} = \{l_\alpha : \Pi(\eta_1, \ldots, \eta_n)\} \uplus \mathcal{R}$, then $\tau_u^{-1}(\mathcal{K}) :=$

$$\begin{bmatrix} \Gamma_1 & \tau_u^{-1}(\partial(\eta_1, \mathcal{R})) \\ \ldots & \\ \text{PRED} & \Pi\langle \uparrow \Gamma_1, \ldots, \uparrow \Gamma_n \rangle \\ \ldots & \\ \Gamma_n & \tau_u^{-1}(\partial(\eta_n, \mathcal{R})) \end{bmatrix} \boxed{\alpha} \ \text{where} \quad \begin{array}{c} \partial \text{ covers } \mathcal{R}, \text{ i.e.} \\ \partial(\eta_1, \mathcal{R}) \cup \ldots \cup \partial(\eta_n, \mathcal{R}) = \mathcal{R} \end{array}$$

- $\tau_u^{-1}(\{l_\alpha : l_{\alpha 1} \forall x l_{\alpha 2}, l_{\alpha 1} : x, l_{\alpha 1} : \Pi(x)\} \uplus Sub) := \begin{bmatrix} \text{SPEC} & \text{EVERY} \\ \text{PRED} & \Pi\langle\rangle \end{bmatrix} \boxed{\alpha}$

- $\tau_u^{-1}(\{l_\alpha : x, l_\alpha : \Pi(x)\} \uplus Sub) := \begin{bmatrix} \text{SPEC} & \text{A} \\ \text{PRED} & \Pi\langle\rangle \end{bmatrix} \boxed{\alpha}$

- $\tau_u^{-1}(\{l_\top : x, l_\top : \Pi(x)\} \uplus Sub) := \begin{bmatrix} \text{PRED} & \Pi\langle\rangle \end{bmatrix} \boxed{x}$

$\uplus$ is disjoint union.

4.2.1   A worked example

We illustrate the UDRT mappings with the simple control construction
every coach persuaded a player to sign a contract used to exemplify the QLF
mappings. For the sake of variation here we will show the reverse mapping τ_u^{-1} from UDRSs back to f-structures. The UDRS graph associated
with the control construction is:

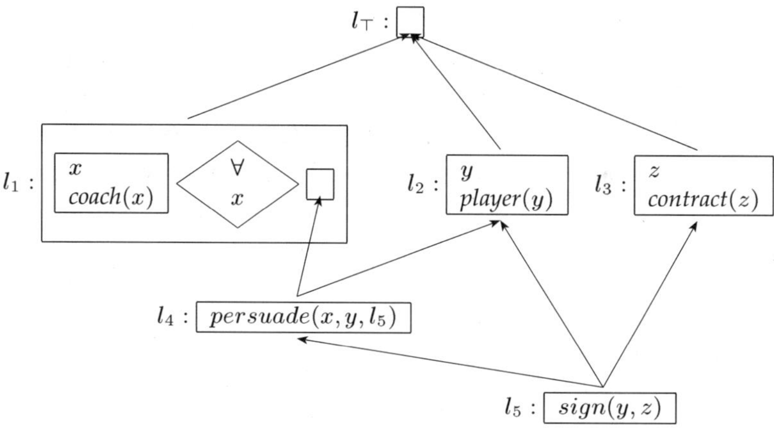

The translation proceeds as follows:

$$\tau_u^{-1}\left(\left\{ \begin{array}{l} l_1 : l_{11}\ \forall x\ l_{12}, l_{11} : x, l_{11} : coach(x), l_1 \leq l_\top, l_4 \leq l_{12}, \\ l_2 : y, l_2 : player(y), l_2 \leq l_\top, l_4 \leq l_2, l_5 \leq l_2, \\ l_3 : z, l_3 : contract(z), l_3 \leq l_\top, l_5 \leq l_3, \\ l_5 : sign(y, z),\ l_4 : persuade(x, y, l_5) \end{array} \right\}\right) =$$

$$\begin{bmatrix} \text{SUBJ} & \tau_u^{-1}(\{l_1 : l_{11}\ \forall x\ l_{12}, l_{11} : x, l_{11} : coach(x), l_1 \leq l_\top, l_4 \leq l_{12}\}) \\ \text{PRED} & \text{'persuade}\ \langle\uparrow\ \text{SUBJ}, \uparrow\ \text{OBJ}, \uparrow\ \text{XCOMP}\rangle\text{'} \\ \text{OBJ} & \tau_u^{-1}(\{l_2 : y, l_2 : player(y), l_2 \leq l_\top, l_4 \leq l_2\}) \\ \text{XCOMP} & \tau_u^{-1}\left(\left\{ \begin{array}{l} l_2 : y, l_2 : player(y), l_2 \leq l_\top, l_5 \leq l_2, \\ l_3 : z, l_3 : contract(z), l_3 \leq l_\top, l_5 \leq l_3, \\ l_5 : sign(y, z)\} \end{array}\right\}\right) \end{bmatrix} \boxed{4} =$$

$$\begin{bmatrix} \text{SUBJ} & \tau^{-1}(\{l_1 : l_{11}\ \forall x\ l_{12}, l_{11} : x, l_{11} : coach(x), l_1 \leq l_\top, l_4 \leq l_{12}\}) \\ \text{PRED} & \text{'persuade}\ \langle\uparrow\ \text{SUBJ}, \uparrow\ \text{OBJ}, \uparrow\ \text{XCOMP}\rangle\text{'} \\ \text{OBJ} & \tau^{-1}(\{l_2 : y, l_2 : player(y), l_2 \leq l_\top, l_4 \leq l_2\}) \\ \text{XCOMP} & \begin{bmatrix} \text{SUBJ} & \tau_u^{-1}(\{l_2 : y, l_2 : player(y), l_2 \leq l_\top, l_5 \leq l_2\}) \\ \text{PRED} & \text{'sign}\ \langle\uparrow\ \text{SUBJ}, \uparrow\ \text{OBJ}\rangle\text{'} \\ \text{OBJ} & \tau_u^{-1}(l_3 : z, l_3 : contract(z), l_3 \leq l_\top, l_5 \leq l_3\}) \end{bmatrix} \boxed{5} \end{bmatrix} \boxed{4} =$$

$$\begin{bmatrix} \text{SUBJ} & \begin{bmatrix} \text{PRED} & \text{'coach'} \\ \text{SPEC} & \text{EVERY} \end{bmatrix} \boxed{1} \\ \text{PRED} & \text{'persuade}\ \langle\uparrow\ \text{SUBJ}, \uparrow\ \text{OBJ}, \uparrow\ \text{XCOMP}\rangle\text{'} \\ \text{OBJ} & \begin{bmatrix} \text{PRED} & \text{'player'} \\ \text{SPEC} & \text{A} \end{bmatrix} \boxed{2} \\ \text{XCOMP} & \begin{bmatrix} \text{SUBJ} & \begin{bmatrix} \text{PRED} & \text{'player'} \\ \text{SPEC} & \text{A} \end{bmatrix} \boxed{2} \\ \text{PRED} & \text{'sign}\ \langle\uparrow\ \text{SUBJ}, \uparrow\ \text{OBJ}\rangle\text{'} \boxed{5} \\ \text{OBJ} & \begin{bmatrix} \text{PRED} & \text{'contract'} \\ \text{SPEC} & \text{A} \end{bmatrix} \boxed{3} \end{bmatrix} \end{bmatrix} \boxed{4}$$

Note that in the resulting f-structure the control relation is encoded in terms of a reentrancy between the object of the matrix verb and the subject of the embedded clause, as required. The reader is invited to verify that the resulting f-structure is mapped back to the source UDRS by τ_u.

4.3 Some applications and properties of the translations

The translation functions τ_q (τ_{q*}) and τ_u enable us to interpret f-structures as their translation images. An f-structure and its component parts inherit the underspecified semantics associated with its translation. In the following sections we will consider some of the consequences of the QLF and UDRS mappings. We will give a direct and underspecified QLF-style interpretation of f-structures; we show how UDRS translation images of f-structures can be used in UDRS deduction systems; we outline how the f-structure - QLF (UDRS) correspondences can be extended by including a QLF-style scope constraint mechanism in f-structure representations and we show that the mappings are correct.

4.3.1   Direct and underspecified interpretation of f-structures

τ_q, τ_{q*} and τ_u are simple mappings. In fact they are homomorphic embeddings. Instead of an f-structure and its component parts indirectly inheriting the semantics of its translation image we can eliminate the mapping and interpret f-structures directly. Van Genabith and Crouch (1996a) do this by adapting a QLF semantics to f-structure representations obtaining a direct and underspecified interpretation for f-structures.

The core of the direct interpretation clauses for $\mathcal{WFS}$ involves a simple variation of the quantifier rule Q14 and the predication rule Q10 of the QLF semantics. As before, the semantics is defined in terms of a supervaluation construction on sets of disambiguated representations. Models, variable assignment functions, generalised quantifier interpretations and the QLF definitions for the connectives, abstraction and application etc. carry over unchanged. The new quantification rule F14 non-deterministically retrieves non-recursive subcategorizable grammatical functions and employs the value of a SPEC feature in a generalised quantifier interpretation:

F14: if $\varphi, \psi \in \mathcal{WFS}$, ψ a sub-f-structure of φ, then

- if $\psi \equiv \begin{bmatrix} \text{SPEC} & Q \\ \cdots & \\ \text{PRED} & \Pi\langle\rangle \\ \cdots & \end{bmatrix} \boxed{\text{I}}$ then

  $\mathcal{V}_g(\varphi, v)$ if $\mathcal{V}_g(Q(\lambda x.\Pi(x), \lambda x.\varphi[x/\psi]), v)$, x new

- if $\psi \equiv \begin{bmatrix} \cdots & \\ \text{PRED} & \Pi\langle\rangle \\ \cdots & \end{bmatrix} \boxed{\text{I}}$ (i.e. SPEC $\notin dom(\psi)$) then

  $\mathcal{V}_g(\varphi, v)$ if $\mathcal{V}_g(\varphi[\Pi/\psi], v)$

The new predication rule F10 is defined in terms of a notion of *nuclear scope* f-structure. Intuitively, a *nuclear scope* f-structure $\varphi \in \mathcal{NFS}$ is an f-structure resulting from exhaustive application of F14. The set $\mathcal{NFS}$ is defined as follows: let $\mathtt{Atom}$ be the set of QLF constants and variables

- if $\gamma_i \in \mathtt{Atom}$ then $\begin{bmatrix} \Gamma_1 & \gamma_1 \\ \dots \\ \textsc{pred} & \Pi\langle\uparrow\Gamma_1,\dots,\uparrow\Gamma_n\rangle \\ \dots \\ \Gamma_n & \gamma_n \end{bmatrix} \in \mathcal{NFS}$

- if $\gamma_i \in \mathcal{NFS} \cup \mathtt{Atom}$ then $\begin{bmatrix} \Gamma_1 & \gamma_1 \\ \dots \\ \textsc{pred} & \Pi\langle\uparrow\Gamma_1,\dots,\uparrow\Gamma_n\rangle \\ \dots \\ \Gamma_n & \gamma_n \end{bmatrix} \in \mathcal{NFS}$

F10:   if $\varphi \equiv \begin{bmatrix} \Gamma_1 & \gamma_1 \\ \dots \\ \textsc{pred}\ \Pi\langle\uparrow\Gamma_1,\dots,\uparrow\Gamma_n\rangle \\ \dots \\ \Gamma_n & \gamma_n \end{bmatrix}\ \boxed{\mathrm{I}}$ and $\varphi \in \mathcal{NFS}$ then $\mathcal{V}_g(\varphi,v)$ if

$\mathcal{V}_g(\Pi(\gamma_1,\dots,\gamma_n),v)$

To give a simple example, under the direct interpretation the f-structure associated with *every coach picked a player* is interpreted as an underspecified semantic representation in terms of the supervaluation over the two generalised quantifier representations

$$forall(coach, \lambda x.exists(player, \lambda y.pick(x,y)))$$

$$exists(player, \lambda y.forall(coach, \lambda x.pick(x,y)))$$

as required.

4.3.2   F-structure translation images and deduction

Unlike other proof systems, UDRS calculi (Reyle 1993, 1995; König and Reyle 1996) are designed to operate *directly* on underspecified representations avoiding (whenever possible) the need to consider disambiguated cases. Here we illustrate how f-structure translation images can be used in such deductions. Consider the following simple argument:

> |1| *Every coach picked a player.*
> |2| *Smith is a coach.*
> ————————————————
> |3| *Smith picked a player.*

Premise |1| is ambiguous between a wide scope and a narrow scope reading of the indefinite NP. From |1| and |2| we can conclude |3| which is not ambiguous. Assume that the following (simplified) f-structures $\varphi|1|, \varphi|2|$ and $\varphi|3|$ are associated with |1|, |2| and |3|, respectively:

$$\left[\begin{array}{ll} \text{SUBJ} & \left[\begin{array}{l}\text{PRED 'coach'}\\ \text{SPEC EVERY}\end{array}\right]_{|4|} \\ \text{PRED} & \text{'pick} \langle \uparrow \text{SUBJ}, \uparrow \text{OBJ}\rangle\text{'} \\ \text{OBJ} & \left[\begin{array}{l}\text{PRED 'player'}\\ \text{SPEC A}\end{array}\right]_{|5|} \end{array}\right]_{|1|}$$

$$\left[\begin{array}{ll} \text{SUBJ} & \left[\text{PRED 'smith'}\right]_{|6|} \\ \text{PRED} & \text{'coach} \langle \uparrow \text{SUBJ}\rangle\text{'} \end{array}\right]_{|2|}$$

$$\left[\begin{array}{ll} \text{SUBJ} & \left[\text{PRED 'smith'}\right]_{|7|} \\ \text{PRED} & \text{'pick} \langle \uparrow \text{SUBJ}, \uparrow \text{OBJ}\rangle\text{'} \\ \text{OBJ} & \left[\begin{array}{l}\text{PRED 'player'}\\ \text{SPEC A}\end{array}\right]_{|8|} \end{array}\right]_{|3|}$$

Given $\varphi|1|, \varphi|2|$ we would like to be able to conclude $\varphi|3|$. Let us translate the premise f-structures $\varphi|1|, \varphi|2|$ into their corresponding UDRS images:

$$\tau_u^\top(\varphi|1|) \;=\; \mathcal{K}_{|1|} \;=$$

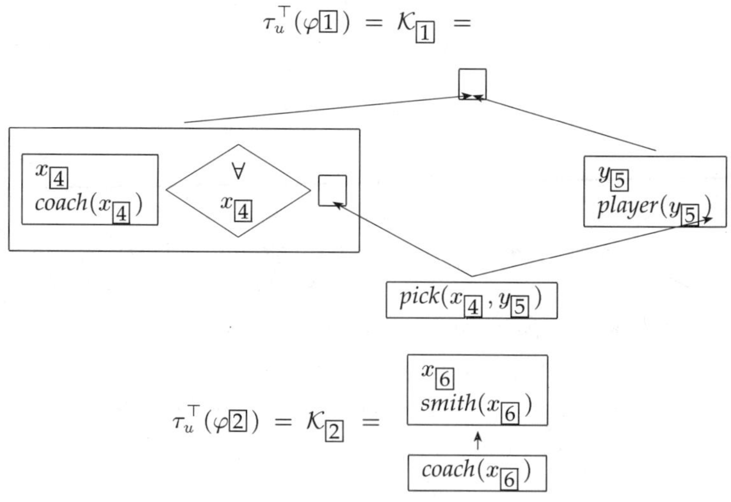

$$\tau_u^\top(\varphi|2|) \;=\; \mathcal{K}_{|2|} \;=$$

In the calculus of Reyle (1995) we obtain the UDRS $\mathcal{K}_{[3]}$ associated with the conclusion in terms of an application of the rule of detachment (DET):

$$
\mathcal{K}_{[1]}, \mathcal{K}_{[2]} \vdash
\left.
\begin{array}{c}
\boxed{\begin{array}{l} x'_{[6]} \\ \hline smith(x'_{[6]}) \end{array}} \\
\uparrow \\
\boxed{\begin{array}{l} x'_{[5]} \\ \hline player(x'_{[5]}) \end{array}} \\
\uparrow \\
\boxed{pick(x'_{[6]}, x'_{[5]})}
\end{array}
\right\}
= \mathcal{K}_{[3]}
$$

and $\mathcal{K}_{[3]}$ turns out to be the translation image $\tau_u^\top(\varphi[3])$ (or conversely $\varphi[3]$ is the translation image of $\tau_u^{-1}(\mathcal{K}_{[3]})$) modulo renaming of variables:[15]

$$
\mathcal{K}_{[3]} = \tau_u^\top \left(
\begin{bmatrix}
\text{SUBJ} & \begin{bmatrix} \text{PRED 'smith'} \end{bmatrix} [7] \\
\text{PRED} & \text{'pick} \langle \uparrow \text{SUBJ}, \uparrow \text{OBJ} \rangle' \\
\text{OBJ} & \begin{bmatrix} \text{PRED 'player'} \\ \text{SPEC A} \end{bmatrix} [8]
\end{bmatrix} [3]
\right)
$$

Summarizing we have that indeed:

$$
\tau^\top(\varphi[1]), \tau^\top(\varphi[2]) \vdash \tau^\top(\varphi[3])
$$

which given that τ_u is correct (see below) does not come as too much of a surprise. The possibility of defining deduction rules directly on f-structures is discussed in König and Reyle (1996).

4.3.3 A QLF-style scope constraint mechanism for f-structures

The translation functions τ_q and τ_u together with the reverse functions τ_q^{-1} and τ_u^{-1} allow us to go back and forth between QLFs, UDRSs and f-structures. It can be shown that for f-structures φ in the set of well-formed f-structures $\mathcal{WFS}$:

$$
\tau_q^{-1}(\tau_q(\varphi)) = \varphi
$$

---

[15]Note that the conclusion UDRS $\mathcal{K}_{[3]}$ can be "collapsed" into the fully specified DRS:

$$
\boxed{\begin{array}{l} x\ y \\ \hline smith(x) \\ player(y) \\ pick(x,y) \end{array}}
$$

$$\tau_u^{-1}(\tau_u(\varphi)) = \varphi$$

Proof is by induction on the structure of φ. The reverse, however, is not true: we cannot expect to translate any arbitrary QLF or UDRS into a corresponding f-structure. The reason is that currently f-structures do not explicitly encode fine-grained scope constraints as available in QLF and UDRT.[16] What the mappings do is establish one-to-one correspondences between *subsets* of the LFG, QLF and UDRS formalisms. It is possible to extend the correspondence by adding a scope constraint mechanism to the original f-structure formalism. Here we outline how a QLF-style scope constraint mechanism can be implemented. Add list valued scope points SCP to f-structure representations as in

$$\begin{bmatrix} \text{SCP} & \begin{bmatrix} \text{FST} & \boxed{2} \\ \text{RST} & \begin{bmatrix} \text{FST} & \boxed{1} \\ \text{RST} & [\,] \end{bmatrix} \end{bmatrix} \\ \text{SUBJ} & \begin{bmatrix} \text{PRED} & \text{'coach'} \\ \text{NUM} & \text{SG} \\ \text{SPEC} & \text{EVERY} \end{bmatrix} \boxed{1} \\ \text{PRED} & \text{'pick} \langle \uparrow \text{ SUBJ}, \uparrow \text{ OBJ} \rangle \text{'} \\ \text{OBJ} & \begin{bmatrix} \text{PRED} & \text{'player'} \\ \text{NUM} & \text{SG} \\ \text{SPEC} & \text{A} \end{bmatrix} \boxed{2} \end{bmatrix}$$

which represents the wide scope reading of the indefinite object NP. Scope constraints are expressed in terms of inside-out functional uncertainty equations (cf. Halvorsen and Kaplan (1988); Dalrymple (1993)) of e.g. the form

$$(\text{GF}^* \uparrow) \text{ SCP RST}^* \text{ FST} = \; \downarrow$$

This constraint is associated with elements that are allowed to take arbitrarily wide scope (as e.g. claimed for indefinites in DRT). It says *go up any number of grammatical functions* GF *until you find a scope point* SCP *and assign scope.* This is a sketch only. A fully worked out theory has to ensure that the constraint does not construct arbitrary scope points and infinite scope lists. In addition, one would need to ensure that during analysis not all possible scopes are constructed—this would defeat the role of f-structures as underspecified representations. An under-

---

[16]Recall that τ_q and τ_u translate a f-structure into fully underspecified QLFs or UDRSs.

specified f-structure is an f-structure plus *satisfiable* (sets of) scope constraints.

4.3.4   Correctness of the translations

Mappings such as τ_q and τ_u are useful only if they are correct. A correctness criterion can be defined as preservation of truth with respect to an independent reference semantics. We will show correctness with respect to the linear logic based glue language semantics presented in Chapters 1 and 2 of this volume. In a sense this reference semantics is going to act as a largest common denominator for both the QLF and the UDRS semantics. Because the semantics of Chapters 1 and 2 is neither underspecified nor dynamic, correctness is with respect to sets of disambiguations and truth. In order to be able to show correctness we have to eliminate the effects of QLF contextual resolution as regards the choice of logical quantifiers replacing `Quant` meta-variables, the choice of predicates replacing `Reft` meta-variables in `form` structures and the choice of properties instantiating `Reft` meta-variables in `term` structures. Note that τ_{q*} instantiates quantifiers and predicates in the QLF to surface form and resolves referent `Reft` arguments in `term` structures to `X^(X=X)` (the set of all objects). This effectively switches off the QLF contextual resolution dynamics for which there is no counterpart in the reference semantics. Note further that τ_u disregards clause boundedness of genuinely quantificational NPs (again, for this there is no counterpart in our reference semantics). In order to show correctness we assume that generalised quantifiers rather than the unselective $\Rightarrow$ DRT conditional are used throughout in the τ_u translations.

Given an f-structure φ, the underspecified semantics of $\tau_{q*}(\varphi)$ and $\tau_u(\varphi)$ are defined in terms of sets of disambiguations.

In the absence of any further scope constraints, given an f-structure φ with n quantificational NP occurrences it can be shown that the QLF disambiguation operation Δ_Q (defined in terms of Q14 above) associates $\tau_{q*}(\varphi)$ with $n!$ disambiguations ϱ^q:

$$\Delta_Q(\tau_{q*}(\varphi)) = \{\varrho_1^q, \ldots, \varrho_{n!}^q\}$$

Similarly, the UDRS disambiguation operation Δ_U (defined in terms of adding subordination constraints) maps $\tau_u(\varphi)$ into $n!$ disambiguations

ϱ^u:[17]

$$\Delta_U(\tau_u(\varphi)) = \{\varrho^u_1, \ldots, \varrho^u_{n!}\}$$

Furthermore, for $\sigma_{ll}(\varphi)$—where $\sigma_{ll}(\varphi)$ is the set of meaning constructors in the linear logic glue language semantics (see Chapter 1) obtained from the σ projection of φ—we get $n!$ disambiguations ϱ^l:

$$\{\varrho^l_i | \sigma_{ll}(\varphi) \vdash_{ll} \varrho^l_i\} = \{\varrho^l_1, \ldots, \varrho^l_{n!}\}$$

where $\vdash_{ll}$ is the linear logic consequence relation. Switching off QLF contextual resolution, disregarding the UDRT dynamics, restricting ourselves to simple truth-conditions and everything else being equal we have a one-to-one correspondence between the elements in the sets of disambiguations obtained from $\sigma_{ll}(\varphi)$, $\tau_{q*}(\varphi)$ and $\tau_u(\varphi)$ defined by

$$\llbracket \varrho^q_i \rrbracket^Q = \llbracket \varrho^u_i \rrbracket^U = \llbracket \varrho^l_i \rrbracket^{TT}$$

where $\llbracket \cdot \rrbracket^Q$, $\llbracket \cdot \rrbracket^U$ and $\llbracket \cdot \rrbracket^{TT}$ are the thus *diluted* QLF, UDRT and the type theory of Chapter 2 (TT) with generalised quantifier interpretations. Notice that this does *not* imply that the *underspecified* semantics (even if restricted as outlined above) associated with $\tau_{q*}(\varphi)$ and $\tau_u(\varphi)$ coincide: $\llbracket \tau_{q*}(\varphi) \rrbracket$ is defined in terms of a supervaluation construction over its disambiguations (Alshawi and Crouch 1992) while $\llbracket \tau_u(\varphi) \rrbracket$ is interpreted conjunctively over its disambiguations if evaluated as a goal UDRS against an empty premise set (Reyle 1995). Interpretation of $\llbracket \tau_u(\varphi) \rrbracket$ in context (i.e. against a nonempty premise set) is defined in terms of wide scope quantification over coindexed (i.e. synchronised) disambiguations in the premise and goal UDRSs. This is discussed further in van Genabith and Crouch (1997b) and in Section 5 below.

5   "Dynamic" Meaning Representation and Glue

As an alternative to the mapping approach we can obtain a dynamic and underspecified semantics for LFG by modifying one of the current LFG semantics. This approach has been explored by van Genabith and Crouch (1997a) which builds on and extends the glue language

---

[17]Note that δ as discussed in Section 3.4 above takes a UDRS to *one* of its disambiguations.

semantics described in Chapter 1 and elsewhere in this volume. The basic idea is twofold: first, replace the static type theoretic meaning representation expressions by *"dynamic"* expressions and second, interpret *sets* of linear logic premises (sets of meaning constructors—thereby the corresponding f-structures) as *underspecified semantic representations*. In order to achieve a fine-grained approach to underspecification as in QLF and UDRT (which allow complete and partial underspecification as well as full disambiguation) sets of linear logic premises need to be complemented with a flexible scope constraint mechanism. It turns out that the mechanism developed in Chapter 4 of this volume and briefly illustrated in Section 6 below carries over unchanged.

The new meaning representation language in the linear logic meaning constructors is Compositional DRT (CDRT) (Muskens 1996). This choice is motivated by the fact that CDRT is expressed in a three-sorted variant TY_3 of standard type theory. In addition to types e for individuals and t for truth values we have a type π for registers and a type s for states (sequences of registers). The basic idea in CDRT is to internalise states and assignments into the language so as to be able to talk *in the language* about updates (i.e. the object of prime concern in dynamic semantics) as transitions between states. Given a suitable axiomatisation of states it can be shown that one does not need to take recourse to special purpose dynamic logics to describe systems like DRT but can stay within the confines of a simple sorted variant of standard type theory. For our purposes this proximity to standard type theory means that transplanting CDRT into the meaning representation slots in Chapter 1 does not cause allergic reactions in the host whose meaning representation slots were occupied by expressions in standard type theory, after all. To be sure, the underlying logic of CDRT is static; the CDRT expressions modeling DRT expressions, however, capture the desired dynamic effects. This is why we quote the *dynamic* as in *"dynamic"* meaning representation language.

The CDRT basics are outlined below. Consider the following relational formulation of the standard DRT semantics:[18]

---

[18]Note that here we assume total rather than partial variable assignment functions as in Kamp and Reyle (1993).

$$\text{(i)} \quad [\![\langle\{x_1 \dots x_n\}|\{\gamma_1, \dots, \gamma_m\}\rangle]\!]$$
$$:= \{\langle i, o\rangle | i[x_1 \dots x_n]o \text{ and } o \in [\![\gamma_1]\!] \cap \dots \cap [\![\gamma_n]\!]\}$$

$$\text{(ii)} \quad [\![x_l = x_k]\!] \quad := \quad \{i|[\![x_l]\!]^i = [\![x_k]\!]^i\}$$

$$\text{(iii)} \quad [\![P(x_1, \dots, x_n)]\!] \quad := \quad \{i|\langle[\![x_1]\!]^i, \dots, [\![x_n]\!]^i\rangle \in \Im(P)\}$$

$$\text{(vi)} \quad [\![\neg K]\!] \quad := \quad \{i|\neg\exists o(\langle i, o\rangle \in [\![K]\!])\}$$

$$\text{(v)} \quad [\![K_1 \vee K_2]\!] \quad := \quad \{i|\exists o(\langle i, o\rangle \in [\![K_1]\!] \text{ or } \langle i, o\rangle \in [\![K_2]\!])\}$$

$$\text{(vi)} \quad [\![K_1 \Rightarrow K_2]\!] \quad := \quad \{i|\forall o(\langle i, o\rangle \in [\![K_1]\!] \rightarrow \exists k(\langle o, k\rangle \in [\![K_2]\!]))\}$$

DRSs (clause (i)) are interpreted as transitions (i.e. relations) between input i and output o assignments (put differently, a DRS updates an input assignment into an output assignment) where o differs from i at most with respect to $x_1 \dots x_n$ and o satisfies the conditions γ_i; DRS conditions (clauses (ii) - (vi)) are interpreted as tests (i.e. sets of assignments). In order to obtain a compositional syntax/semantics interface on the sentential and subsentential level we could introduce lambdas and a sequencing operation ';'. The sequencing operation is interpreted as relational composition:

$$[\![K_1; K_2]\!] := \{\langle i, o\rangle | \exists m(\langle i, m\rangle \in [\![K_1]\!] \text{ and } \langle m, o\rangle \in [\![K_2]\!])\}$$

The lambdas we get via encoding the relational formulation of DRSs in TY_3 where DRSs are unpacked as functions of type $s(st)$, i.e. functions from states into functions from states to truth values (thus shifting from the relational to the functional perspective). The states provide the encoding of assignments. In the same fashion DRS conditions are encoded as functions of type st (i.e. functions from states to truth values). This can be made precise as follows: at a particular state i the value associated with a discourse referent u is the object in the register denoted by u. V is a fixed non-logical constant of type $\pi(se)$ and $V(u)(i)$ denotes the value associated with discourse referent u in state i. The expression

$$i[u_1 \dots u_n]j$$

is short for the term

$$\forall v(((u_1 \neq v) \wedge \dots \wedge (u_n \neq v)) \rightarrow V(v)(i) = V(v)(j))$$

which states that states i and j differ at most with respect to the values associated with the registers denoted by the discourse referents $u_1 \dots u_n$. The following three axioms ensure that we have enough states at our disposal to guarantee that each register can hold each individual object (AX_1); that states are the same if they agree on the values of the registers (AX_2) and that different discourse referents refer to different registers (AX_3):

$$AX_1 \quad \forall i \forall u \forall x \exists j (i[u]j \wedge V(u)(j) = x)$$
$$AX_2 \quad \forall i \forall j (i[\,]j \rightarrow i = j)$$
$$AX_3 \quad u \neq u' \text{ for different discourse referents } u \text{ and } u'$$

With these preparations, DRSs and DRS conditions can be coded in TY_3 as follows:

$$
\begin{array}{lll}
\text{(i)} & (\langle\{x_1 \ldots x_n\} | \{\gamma_1, \ldots, \gamma_m\}\rangle)^{ty} \\
& \qquad := \lambda i \lambda o. i[u_1 \ldots u_n]o \wedge \gamma_1(o) \wedge \ldots \wedge \gamma_m(o) \\
\text{(ii)} & (x_l = x_k)^{ty} & := \quad \lambda i. V(u_l)(i) = V(u_k)(i) \\
\text{(iii)} & (P(x_1, \ldots, x_n))^{ty} & := \quad \lambda i. P(V(u_1)(i), \ldots, V(u_n)(i)) \\
\text{(vi)} & (\neg K)^{ty} & := \quad \lambda i. \neg \exists o\, K^{ty}(i)(o) \\
\text{(v)} & (K_1 \vee K_2)^{ty} & := \quad \lambda i. \exists o (K_1^{ty}(i)(o) \vee K_2^{ty}(i)(o)) \\
\text{(vi)} & (K_1 \Rightarrow K_2)^{ty} & := \quad \lambda i. \forall m (K_1^{ty}(i)(m) \rightarrow \exists o\, K_2^{ty}(m)(o))
\end{array}
$$

Sequencing becomes

$$(K_1; K_2)^{ty} := \lambda i \lambda o \exists m (K_1^{ty}(i)(m) \wedge K_2^{ty}(m)(o))$$

TY_3 expressions are cumbersome to manipulate in full glory. In order to guard against writer's cramp some abbreviations are used in the simulation of the language of DRT in the system outlined above. For some fixed i of type s and for discourse referents u and individual terms t we stipulate:

$$u^\circ = V(u)(i) \text{ and } t^\circ = t$$

Given R of type $\overbrace{e(\ldots(e\,t)\ldots)}^{n}$ and τ a discourse referent or an individual variable, in the case of simple DRS conditions of type st we write

$$
\begin{array}{lll}
R\tau_1 \ldots \tau_n & \text{for} & \lambda i. R\tau_1^\circ \ldots \tau_n^\circ \\
\tau_1 \doteq \tau_2 & \text{for} & \lambda i. \tau_1^\circ = \tau_2^\circ
\end{array}
$$

For complex DRS conditions of type st with K, K' DRSs of type $s(st)$ we write[19]

$$
\begin{array}{lll}
\neg K & \text{for} & \lambda i. \neg \exists j\, K(i)(j) \\
K \Rightarrow K' & \text{for} & \lambda i. \forall j (K(i)(j) \rightarrow \exists k\, K'(j)(k))
\end{array}
$$

---

[19]Strictly speaking, here we should use a new set of logical constants $\hat{\neg}, \hat{\Rightarrow}$, etc. to distinguish the abbreviations from the original DRS connectives $\neg, \Rightarrow$.

DRSs are of type $s(st)$ and we write

$$[u_1 \ldots u_n | \gamma_1 \ldots \gamma_m] \quad \text{for} \quad \lambda i \lambda j.i[u_1 \ldots u_n]j \wedge \gamma_1(j) \wedge \ldots \wedge \gamma_m(j)$$

To give a simple example, $[u|candidate(u)\ smile(u)]$ is short for the term:

$$\lambda i.\lambda j.(\forall v(u \neq v) \to V(v)(i) = V(v)(j)) \wedge candidate(V(u)(j)) \wedge smile(V(u)(j))$$

Sequencing of DRS is represented as ';' and we write

$$K; K' \quad \text{for} \quad \lambda i \lambda j \exists k (K(i)(k) \wedge K'(k)(j))$$

Given these definitions the following (nonsymmetric) merging lemma (ML) allows us to merge certain DRSs:

$$\text{ML:} \quad \text{AX}_{1,2,3} \models [\vec{u}|\vec{\gamma}]; [\vec{u}'|\vec{\gamma}'] = [\vec{u}\ \vec{u}'|\vec{\gamma}\ \vec{\gamma}']$$
$$\text{where } \vec{u}' \text{ does not occur in } \vec{\gamma}$$

The abbreviations have taken us back to a notation close to standard DRT. Have we gained anything along the way? We have: now we have lambdas and sequencing at our disposal. Muskens (1994) presents a compositional categorial grammar based CDRT syntax/semantics interface:

every^n	`(s/(n\s))/cn`	$\lambda R \lambda S.[|([u_n|]; R(u_n)) \Rightarrow S(u_n)]$
	`((s/n)\s))/cn`	
a^n	`(s/(n\s))/cn`	$\lambda R \lambda S.[u_n|]; R(u_n); S(u_n)$
	`((s/n)\s))/cn`	
picked	`(n\s)/n`	$\lambda x \lambda y[|pick(x,y)]$
coach	`cn`	$\lambda x[|coach(x)]$
player	`cn`	$\lambda x[|player(x)]$

Because of the proximity between categorial grammar (a fragment of non-commutative linear logic) and the glue-language approach (which uses a fragment of commutative linear logic; see Chapter 7) it is straightforward to lift the semantic component from the categorial approach into the meaning representation language slots in the glue language meaning constructors: unpack the λ-prefixes in the categorial grammar semantic component as universally quantified variables in antecedents of implicative '$\multimap$' linear logic premises in the glue language meaning constructors. The modified meaning constructors (instantiated to (the σ projection of) the f-structure associated with *every coach picked a player*) are:

$$every^1 \; : \quad \forall Scope, R, S(\forall x.subj.var \rightsquigarrow x \multimap subj.restr \rightsquigarrow R(x))\otimes$$
$$(\forall x.subj \rightsquigarrow x \multimap Scope \rightsquigarrow S(x))$$
$$\multimap Scope \rightsquigarrow [|([u_1|]; R(u_1)) \Rightarrow S(u_1)]$$

$$a^2 \; : \qquad \forall Scope, R, S(\forall x.obj.var \rightsquigarrow x \multimap obj.restr \rightsquigarrow R(x))\otimes$$
$$(\forall x.obj \rightsquigarrow x \multimap Scope \rightsquigarrow S(x))$$
$$\multimap Scope \rightsquigarrow [u_2|]; R(u_2); S(u_2)$$

$$picked \; : \quad \forall X, Y(subj \rightsquigarrow X \otimes obj \rightsquigarrow Y) \multimap s \rightsquigarrow [|pick(X,Y)]$$

$$coach \; : \quad \forall X(subj.var \rightsquigarrow X \multimap subj.restr \rightsquigarrow [|coach(X)])$$

$$player \; : \quad \forall X(obj.var \rightsquigarrow X \multimap obj.restr \rightsquigarrow [|player(X)])$$

The type system in TY_3 is very basic (it is flat and does not have polymorphism). Provided term unification respects type assignment in TY_3, the higher order term matching task reduces to the one described in Chapter 2[20] and both the $\forall\exists$ and the $\exists\forall$ readings are obtained:

$$every^1, coach \vdash_{ll}$$

$$\forall Scope, S(\forall x.subj \rightsquigarrow x \multimap Scope \rightsquigarrow S(x)) \multimap$$

$$Scope \rightsquigarrow [|([u_1|coach(u_1)]) \Rightarrow S(u_1)]$$

with the substitutions $\langle X/x, R/\lambda x.[|coach(x)]\rangle$ and application of ML. Similarly

$$a^2, player \vdash_{ll}$$

$$\forall Scope, S(\forall x.obj \rightsquigarrow x \multimap Scope \rightsquigarrow S(x)) \multimap$$

$$Scope \rightsquigarrow [u_2|player(u_2)]; S(u_2)$$

with $\langle X/x, R/\lambda x.[|player(x)]\rangle$ and ML. The Currying equivalences yield

$$picked_1 \; : \quad \forall X(subj \rightsquigarrow X \multimap \forall Y(obj \rightsquigarrow Y \multimap s \rightsquigarrow [|pick(X,Y)]))$$

$$picked_2 \; : \quad \forall Y(obj \rightsquigarrow Y \multimap \forall X(subj \rightsquigarrow X \multimap s \rightsquigarrow [|pick(X,Y)]))$$

---

[20]In particular matching is still decidable: Fernando Pereira, p.c.

Using transitivity of linear implication we can combine the object NP
with *picked*$_1$:

$$picked_1, a^2, player \vdash_{ll}$$

$$\forall X (subj \rightsquigarrow X \multimap s \rightsquigarrow [u_2 | player(u_2) \, pick(X, u_2)])$$

with $\langle Y/x, Scope/s, S/\lambda x.[|pick(X, x)]\rangle$ and ML. This is combined with
the subject NP to yield the narrow scope reading of the indefinite NP:

$$every^1, coach, picked_1, a^2, player \vdash_{ll}$$

$$s \rightsquigarrow [|([u_1 | coach(u_1)]) \Rightarrow [u_2 | player(u_2) \, pick(u_1, u_2)]]$$

with $\langle S/\lambda x.[u_2 | player(u_2) \, pick(x, u_2)], X/x, Scope/s\rangle$.   The alternative
derivation sequence which first combines the subject NP with *picked*$_2$
and the result with the object NP returns the specific reading of the indefinite NP:

$$every^1, coach, picked_2, a^2, player \vdash_{ll}$$

$$s \rightsquigarrow [u_2 | player(u_2)], [u_1 | coach(u_1)] \Rightarrow [|pick(u_1, u_2)]]$$

Note that, unlike standard DRT, CDRT (as other compositional formulations) assumes anaphorically resolved input (where anaphors are related to their antecedents in terms of some indexing scheme). On this
view anaphora resolution is not part of semantics *proper* but has to be
delivered by syntax, pragmatics or some other component of the grammar. This means that the approach developed here has to be integrated
with, e.g., syntactic approaches to anaphora as in Dalrymple (1993).

The approach described in van Genabith and Crouch (1997a) is of
a general nature and could also be applied to porting what from the
point of view of CDRT look like more special purpose languages such
as λ-DRT (Asher 1993; Bos et al. 1994; Kohlhase et al. 1996), Dynamic
Montague Grammar (Groenendijk and Stokhof 1990), Dynamic Type
Theory (Chierchia 1991) or the compositional version of DRT in van
Eijck and Kamp (1997), see, e.g., Chapter 2 of this volume.

In van Genabith and Crouch (1997a) *sets* of meaning constructors
(plus possible scope constraints) are interpreted as *underspecified* representations. We return to the scope constraint mechanism in Section 6
below. If a set of linear logic premises is regarded as an underspecified
representation then the linear logic deductions mapping this set into

fully specified (i.e., disambiguated) meaning representations do in fact
(part of) the job of the *interpretation* clauses in QLF and the *disambiguation operation* in UDRT. In other words, in this approach linear logic
deductions are instrumental in *defining* the *semantics* of an underspecified representation (construed as a set of linear logic premises—or the
f-structures that give rise to them) rather than being *executed* during the
construction of a disambiguated semantic representation representing
a reading of some phrase as before. Note that this does not yet commit
the resulting semantics to a QLF or a UDRT style semantics. Indeed, a
QLF-style (Alshawi and Crouch 1992) supervaluation semantics for a
set of linear logic premisses Δ is obtained as follows:

$$[\![\Delta]\!] = \begin{cases} 1 & \text{iff for } all \ \alpha \text{ such that } \Delta \vdash_{ll} \alpha, \ [\![\alpha]\!]^c = 1 \\ 0 & \text{iff for } all \ \alpha \text{ such that } \Delta \vdash_{ll} \alpha, \ [\![\alpha]\!]^c = 0 \\ undefined & \text{otherwise} \end{cases}$$

where $\vdash_{ll}$ is the linear logic consequence relation and $[\![\cdot]\!]^c$ (in this case)
the CDRT truth definition. The different UDRT semantics (Reyle 1993,
1995), on the other hand, are defined classically (see Section 3.4) and
take their cue from the definition of the UDRS consequence relations.
The most recent version (Reyle 1995) is[21]

$$\forall \delta^I (\Gamma^{\delta^I} \models_{95} \gamma^{\delta^I})$$

which requires pairwise (in the case of coindexed elements, synchronised) premise (i.e., context) and goal disambiguations. The definition
implies that in the null context (i.e. the empty premise set) a goal UDRS
γ is interpreted conjunctively, i.e. $[\![\gamma]\!] = 1$ iff for all disambiguations δ:
$[\![\gamma^\delta]\!] = 1$, $[\![\gamma]\!] = 0$ otherwise. In the world of sets of linear logic premises
this translates as

$$[\![\Delta]\!] = \begin{cases} 1 & \text{iff for } all \ \alpha \text{ such that } \Delta \vdash_{ll} \alpha, \ [\![\alpha]\!]^c = 1 \\ 0 & \text{otherwise} \end{cases}$$

The original semantics in Reyle (1993) took its cue from

$$\forall \delta \exists \delta' (\Gamma^\delta \models_{93} \gamma^{\delta'})$$

---

[21]We will write $\models_{95}$ for the consequence relation in Reyle (1995) and $\models_{93}$ for the original UDRS consequence relation in Reyle (1993).

which results in a disjunctive interpretation of a goal UDRS. Applying this to a set of linear logic premises Δ, we get

$$[\![\Delta]\!] = \begin{cases} 1 & \text{iff there } \textit{exists} \text{ a } \alpha \text{ such that } \Delta \vdash_{ll} \alpha, \ [\![\alpha]\!]^c = 1 \\ 0 & \text{otherwise} \end{cases}$$

Plugging two different semantics into the same system facilitates comparison. Notice that the original UDRT semantics (Reyle 1993) and the more recent (Reyle 1995) each cover two different corners of the QLF (Alshawi and Crouch 1992) semantics: *definite falsity* (Reyle 1993) or *definite truth* (Reyle 1995).

6   Context Management and Glue

In the "dynamic" meaning representation approach reviewed in the last section, context update is handled at the level of the meaning representation. However, linear logic lends itself well to modelling update. It is therefore natural to explore the extent to which the job of context update and management can instead be handled at the glue language level. This would open the way to having a more "static" meaning level along the lines originally proposed in Chapters 1 and 2, while still accounting for the dynamics of natural language interpretation.

Since the details of this approach are discussed at length in Chapter 4 of this volume, this section will only provide the basic ideas and motivations. Linear logic can model update through the resource sensitive nature of linear implication and multiplicative conjunction. Indeed, in the original formulation of glue language semantics, a form of meaning update is already at work. Suppose some component of (the semantic projection of) an f-structure, σ, has already been associated with a meaning, e.g.,

$$\sigma \leadsto sleep(john)$$

Suppose further that we have a modifier of σ whose meaning constructor is

$$\forall \phi. \ \sigma \leadsto \phi \multimap \sigma \leadsto probably(\phi)$$

The two meaning constructors can be combined through modus ponens to derive an updated meaning assignment for the constituent σ

$$\sigma \rightsquigarrow probably(sleep(john))$$

In classical logic, the inference $A, A \rightarrow B \vdash_c A \wedge B$ holds, but in linear logic it is invalid: $A, A \multimap B \not\vdash_{ll} A \otimes B$. Linear modus ponens consumes the two premises, so that A is no longer available to be conjoined with the conclusion B. This means that from the two meaning constructors above, we cannot conclude that both $\sigma \rightsquigarrow sleep(john)$ and $\sigma \rightsquigarrow probably(sleep(john))$. The original meaning assignment to σ has been wiped out, and replaced by an updated version.

To extend this form of meaning update to context update, we introduce a second uninterpreted binary relation symbol, $\hookrightarrow$, so that $\rightsquigarrow$ represents meaning assignments to parts of f-structure, and $\hookrightarrow$ represents context assignments. In particular, we use $\hookrightarrow$ to assign E-type properties to noun phrases. Context assignments may be created and updated in the same way that meaning assignments can. In general, the meaning and contextual assignments of one constituent will depend on the meaning and/or contextual assignments of other constituents, and may consume or update these assignments by means of linear modus ponens. For example, the meaning of a pronoun is constructed from the E-type property contextually assigned to its antecedent, and also updates the antecedent assignment.

The resource sensitivity of meaning and context assignments are, however, subtly different. In the original glue language semantics we needed to establish conclusions of the form

$$\Gamma \vdash_{ll} s \rightsquigarrow M$$

where Γ was the entire set of lexical premises, and a single meaning assignment occurred on the right hand side. This guarantees that each lexical premise is used *exactly once* and that *all* of the lexically induced premises are consumed and contribute to the final meaning assignment. Context assignments differ from meaning assignments in that some of them may be used repeatedly while others are not used at all. Furthermore, each reuse is liable to update a context contribution.[22]

We therefore modify the form of the desired result of a glue language derivation to allow any number of context assignments to occur on the right hand side of the turnstile, as well as having context assignments derived from previous sentences as premises on the left hand side.

$$\Gamma, \Delta \vdash_{ll} s \rightsquigarrow M \otimes \delta_0 \otimes \ldots \otimes \delta_n$$

where Δ represents the set of input context assignments, and $\delta_0, \ldots, \delta_n$ a possibly updated set of output assignments. Zero usage of a particular context assignment results in it being passed unchanged from input to output. Repeated use depends on setting up the lexical premises so that each use of a context assignment creates an updated version available for further use.

Below we briefly illustrate the basic idea in terms of the mini-discourse

A player entered. He smiled.

where the pronoun will be given a simple E-Type analysis. For the first sentence we have the following meaning constructors:

$$a: \quad \forall Scope, R, S(\forall x.subj1.var \rightsquigarrow x \multimap subj1.restr \rightsquigarrow R(x)) \otimes$$
$$(\forall x.subj \rightsquigarrow x \multimap Scope \rightsquigarrow S(x))$$
$$\multimap (Scope \rightsquigarrow exists(R, S) \otimes subj1 \hookrightarrow \lambda y.R(y) \wedge S(y))$$

$$entered: \quad \forall X \; subj1 \rightsquigarrow X \multimap s1 \rightsquigarrow enter(X)$$

$$player: \quad \forall X \; subj1.var \rightsquigarrow X \multimap subj1.restr \rightsquigarrow player(X)$$

In addition to the usual meaning assignment the constructor for the indefinite *a* features a contextual assignment: the contextual assignment consists of the property derived from the conjunction of restrictor and scope parts of the determiner's meaning assignment. Starting with the empty context we derive

$$a, player, entered \vdash_{ll}$$

$$s1 \rightsquigarrow exists(player, enter) \otimes subj1 \hookrightarrow \lambda y.player(y) \wedge enter(y)$$

---

[22]The need to update assignments makes the use of linear logic's "of course" modality, !, which licenses unlimited use of a resource inappropriate for dealing with zero or repeated use.

where the contextual assignment associated with *subj1* is the property of being a player that enters. For the pronoun in the second sentence we have the constructor

$$he: \quad \forall Scope, Ante, P, S(\forall x.subj2 \rightsquigarrow x \multimap Scope \rightsquigarrow S(x)) \otimes (Ante \hookrightarrow P)$$
$$\multimap Scope \rightsquigarrow exists(P, S) \otimes subj2 \hookrightarrow \lambda y.P(y) \wedge S(y) \otimes$$
$$Ante \hookrightarrow \lambda y.P(y) \wedge S(y)$$

The meaning constructor for *he* features a simple extension to NP-type meaning constructors. Its antecedent contains an additional conjunct $(Ante \hookrightarrow P)$ which picks up the contextual property assigned to some linguistic antecedent. The consequent existentially quantifies this property over the chosen scope (i.e. it interprets the pronoun in the context set up by some antecedent), sets up a context assignment for the pronoun and updates the original context assignment to the antecedent (context update). With the constructor

$$smiled: \quad \forall X \; subj1 \rightsquigarrow X \multimap s1 \rightsquigarrow smile(X)$$

we can interpret the second sentence in the context set up by the first as

$$he, smiled, subj1 \hookrightarrow \lambda y.player(y) \wedge enter(y) \vdash$$
$$s2 \rightsquigarrow exists(\lambda x. \; player(x) \wedge enter(x), smile)$$
$$\otimes subj1 \hookrightarrow \lambda y.player(y) \wedge enter(y) \wedge smile(y)$$
$$\otimes subj2 \hookrightarrow \lambda y.player(y) \wedge enter(y) \wedge smile(y)$$

The meaning for the second sentence entails the meaning of the first and is truth-conditionally equivalent to the DPL formula (Groenendijk and Stokhof 1991) and the DRS (Kamp and Reyle 1993) for the entire discourse

$$\exists x(player(x) \wedge enter(x)) \wedge smile(x)$$

$x\ y$
$player(x)$
$enter(x)$
$smile(y)$
$y = x$

6.1 Underspecification and glue

The context-dependent nature of natural language gives rise to a need both to model context update and to allow underspecification. Having indicated how a linear logic glue language can provide a handle on context update, we turn to the question of how it can support underspecification.

Compositionality holds that the meaning of a sentence depends on (i) the meanings of its constituents, and (ii) the way they are combined. Semantic ambiguity arises because the syntactic structure of a sentence and lexical semantics alone are not always sufficient to fully determine constituent meanings (e.g., pronouns) or their manner of combination (e.g., scope). Context has to fill in the gaps. Underspecification amounts to a way of letting context progressively fill those gaps left by syntax and the lexicon.

Taking glue language derivations to be semantic compositions, we can draw the following parallels:

	Semantic Composition	Glue Language Derivation
Pronouns	Meaning of part	Choice of (contextual) premise
Scope	Mode of combination	Structure of derivation

If we had some way of further specifying premise choice and derivation structure, over and above what is already imposed by the glue language premises and the desired form of the conclusion, we would have a mechanism for underspecification. That is, the premises and form of the conclusion carve out a set of valid derivations producing all possible readings for the sentence; they provide a completely underspecified representation of the sentence meaning. Imposing further constraints on the derivation would allow us to prune out unintended readings, and hence further specify the representation.

Premise choice for pronouns: Meaning constructors for pronouns (universally) quantify over potential antecedent constituents and their contextual assignments. Choosing an antecedent involves instantiating these variables to particular values made available through building up other context assignments, which effectively selects one of the contextual premises. The selection made can be recorded by adding a co-indexation marker ($pro \Leftarrow ante$, where pro and $ante$ are the pronoun and antecedent nodes in f-structure) to the conjunction of context assignments built up. By stipulating that certain co-indexation markers should appear in the conclusion of a glue language derivation, we can specify how pronouns are to be interpreted. Moreover, we can specify this as much or as little as we wish; see Chapter 4 for more discussion.

Derivation structure for scope: Chapter 2 of this volume shows how different quantifier scopings emerge through different derivations starting from the same set of premises. The difference between the derivations lies in their structure, i.e., the order in which certain inference steps are taken. Chapter 4 shows that this structure is reflected by a simple ordering defined over f-structure nodes. By demanding that the derivation respects certain orderings, we can specify scope relations.

In slightly more detail, lexical premises contain channel terms of the form *Node*$\rightsquigarrow$*Meaning*, usually several for each node in the f-structure. Some of the these terms act as producers of meanings and others as consumers. A successful glue language derivation matches all producers on a node with consumers, with the exception of one final meaning producer for the sentence as a whole. In (normal form) sequent-style natural deduction derivations, each matching of a consumer term with a producer term will move the terms out of the right-hand side of the sequent. When all producers on a node have been matched with consumers, channel terms for the node thereafter only occur on the left hand sides of sequents. Scoping a noun phrase involves matching a final remaining consumer-producer pair on the NP's node. By noting the order in which the channel terms for NPs become completely banished to the left hand side of the sequent, we can determine the relative scopes of those NPs.

This treatment of scope specification can be employed independently of any glue language mechanisms for context update. Thus it is available for use in the "dynamic" meaning representation approach in Section 5. Moreover, by making use of the f-structure – QLF – UDRS mappings of Section 4, it is easy to translate the f-structure node orderings into the label orderings of UDRS and index orderings trivially derivable from QLF, both of which are also used to specify scope.

7   Conclusions and Further Work

The mapping approach (Section 4) is probably the most direct approach to associate LFG grammars with an underspecified and dynamic semantics. Its formulation is reminiscent of the translation principle templates in Halvorsen (1983) and an approach by Reyle (1988). In theory at least, interfacing LFG f-structures with QLFs and UDRSs makes available extensive computational work both on contextual resolution in QLF (Alshawi 1990, 1992; Alshawi et al. 1992) and UDRT deduction components (Reyle 1993, 1995; König and Reyle 1996) to LFG grammars. However, it may well turn out to be the case that f-structures do not provide the most suitable representation format for semantic phenomena in all cases. By contrast, the glue language approach presented in Chapter 1 and elsewhere in this volume involves an independent and proper construction of semantic representations which are, however, neither underspecified nor dynamic.

In the "dynamic" meaning glue approach (Section 5) dynamic meaning representation expressions are imported into the meaning representation slots in the glue language premises. Sets of linear logic premises associated with (the semantic projection of) an f-structure can be given QLF- or UDRT-style underspecified interpretations, where the linear logic deductions are instrumental in the interpretation rather than the construction of a semantic representation. In contrast to "standard" DRT (Kamp and Reyle 1993) the "dynamic" approach needs to be integrated with syntactic approaches to anaphora as discussed in Chapter 2. The approach also provides a way of relating deductive approaches to quantifier scope to dynamic semantics. In many respects the approach is reminiscent of a number of recent flat UDRT inspired semantics as in Verbmobil and MRS (Copestake et al. 1995; Bos et al. 1996). In our approach the labels are provided by the nodes in the semantic projections. What is lost in most of these approaches is some of the filtering effect that the "proper" construction of a disambiguated semantic representation may have during a parsing process. Furthermore one cannot *directly* plug in sets of linear logic premises into a "semantic" deduction component (as opposed to the linear logic reasoning component employed for the construction of disambiguated semantic representations) in order to compute consequence relations between underspecified representations (as e.g. in UDRT).

In other respects our "dynamic" meaning and glue approach is reminiscent of Muskens (1995). In the latter, meanings are constrained by both a level of "logical form"-like generalised tree (l-structure) and semantic meaning representation (s-structure) dominance and equality constraints. By contrast, in our approach, as in the original glue language semantics, combination possibilities are determined by the (semantic projection) nodes and the form of glue language premises (plus the additional scope and anaphora selection constraint mechanism in Chapter 4). Declerk (1996) differs from both Muskens' and our approach in that he outlines how a fully specified Dynamic Predicate Logic (Groenendijk and Stokhof 1991) semantics can be integrated into LFG in terms of LFG's projection architecture.

The linear logic context management approach (Section 6) does not involve a dynamic meaning representation language. Instead, context update and interpretation in context are modelled in the glue language derivations. The resulting system provides an E-type treatment of anaphora and thus contrasts with the DRT-style dynamics available in the mapping and the "dynamic" meaning glue based approach. The treatment of scope constraints in terms of constraints on the form of glue language derivations can however be integrated with the original glue approach presented in Chapter 2 and the "dynamic" meaning glue approach (van Genabith and Crouch 1997a).

The treatment of underspecification, as exemplified by the scope constraints, moves towards treating proofs as first class citizens in semantic theory, which has potential applications to the treatment of ellipsis (Crouch (1998); Kempson (1995); Chapter 4 of this volume).

The linear logic context management approach locates the dynamics of interpretation in the construction of meanings, rather than in the meanings thus constructed.[23] But the analysis of linguistic phenomena along these lines (so far, a much simplified E-type treatment of anaphora) is very preliminary, especially compared to the "dynamic" meaning and glue approach, which can help itself to the wider range of

---

[23]In this respect it is reminiscent of the original DRT approach (Kamp and Reyle 1993).

phenomena covered by (compositional) DRT. The relative advantages and disadvantages of locating context dynamics in either meaning construction or the meanings constructed thus remains an entirely open question.[24] Also open is the question of whether it is coherent to employ a mixed strategy, so that some of the dynamics resides in meaning construction and some in the meanings themselves.

There is also scope for further work where the mapping and context management approaches meet. On its own, the mapping approach might incline one towards using QLF or UDRS as independently motivated semantic representations for LFG. Pushing the f-structure–QLF/UDRS maps in the reverse direction opens up the possibility of providing an alternative glue language semantics for QLF and UDRT. The ability to model context update in glue languages provides a necessary first step towards this goal.

Much of what has been discussed in the previous pages is no more than an exploratory exercise in blending results in recent formal and computational semantics (underspecification, interpretation in context and context update) with LFG. Of course, we have exhausted neither the comparison dimensions between the different approaches nor the types of approaches possible. In particular, there is no reason why a considerable number of the original LFG semantics could not be made both dynamic and underspecified. Hopefully this study has provided a contribution to charting such approaches.

Acknowledgments

We would like to thank Mary Dalrymple, Anette Frank, John Fry, Hans Kamp, Carl Vogel, Jürgen Wedekind and our anonymous reviewers for valuable feedback and support. Mistakes and the views expressed are our own.

---

[24]Working on context update in linear logic can have the effect of renewing one's admiration for the elegance of approaches like DRT.

References

Alshawi, Hiyan. 1990. Resolving quasi logical form. *Computational Linguistics*, 16:133–144.

Alshawi, Hiyan, editor. 1992. *The Core Language Engine*. The MIT Press, Cambridge, MA.

Alshawi, Hiyan, David Carter, Richard Crouch, Steve Pulman, Manny Rayner, and Arnold Smith. 1992. CLARE: A contextual reasoning and cooperative response framework for the Core Language Engine. Technical Report CRC-028, SRI International, Cambridge Research Centre. Also available as cmp-lg/9411002.

Alshawi, Hiyan and Richard Crouch. 1992. Monotonic semantic interpretation. In *Proceedings of the Thirtieth Annual Meeting of the ACL*, Newark, Delaware, pages 32–39. Association for Computational Linguistics.

Asher, Nicholas. 1993. *Reference to Abstract Objects in Discourse*. Kluwer, Dordrecht.

Barwise, Jon and John Perry. 1983. *Situations and Attitudes*. The MIT Press, Cambridge, MA.

Bos, Johan, Björn Gambäck, Christian Lieske, Yoshiki Mori, Manfred Pinkal, and Karsten Worm. 1996. Compositional semantics in VERBMOBIL. In *Proceedings of the 16th International Conference on Computational Linguistics (COLING-96)*, Copenhagen, Denmark, pages 131 – 136.

Bos, Johan, Elsbeth Mastenbroek, Scott McGlashan, Sebastian Millies, and Manfred Pinkal. 1994. A compositional DRS-based formalism for NLP applications. In *International Workshop on Computational Semantics*, Tilburg. Also published as *Verbmobil Report 59*, Universität des Saarlandes, Saarbrücken, Germany.

Chierchia, Gennaro. 1991. Anaphora and dynamic binding. *Linguistics and Philosophy*, 15(2):111–183.

Cooper, R., R. Crouch, J. van Eijck, C. Fox, J. van Genabith, J. Jaspars, H. Kamp, M. Pinkal, D. Milward, M. Poesio, and S. Pulman. 1996. Describing the approaches. Technical Report FraCaS deliverable D8, FraCaS: A Framework for Computational Semantics. Also available at ftp://ftp.cogsci.ed.ac.uk/pub/FRACAS/del8.ps.gz.

Copestake, Anne, Dan Flickinger, Rob Malouf, Susanne Riehemann, and Ivan Sag. 1995. Transfer and Minimal Recursion Semantics. In *Proceedings of the 6th International Conference on Theoretical and Methodological Issues in Machine Translation (TMI '95)*, Leuven, Belgium.

Crouch, Richard. 1998. Ellipsis and glue languages. In S. Lappin and E. Benmamoun, editors, *Fragments: Studies in Ellipsis and Gapping*. Oxford University Press, Oxford.

Dalrymple, Mary. 1993. *The Syntax of Anaphoric Binding*. CSLI Lecture Notes, number 36. CSLI Publications, Stanford University.

Dalrymple, Mary, John Lamping, and Vijay Saraswat. 1993. LFG semantics via constraints. In *Proceedings of the Sixth Meeting of the European ACL*, University of Utrecht, pages 97–105. European Chapter of the Association for Computational Linguistics.

Dalrymple, Mary, Ronald M. Kaplan, John T. Maxwell, III, and Annie Zaenen, editors. 1995. *Formal Issues in Lexical-Functional Grammar*. CSLI Publications, Stanford University.

Dalrymple, Mary, John Lamping, Fernando C. N. Pereira, and Vijay Saraswat. 1996. A deductive account of quantification in LFG. In Makoto Kanazawa, Christopher J. Piñón, and Henriette de Swart, editors, *Quantifiers, Deduction, and Context*, pages 33–57. CSLI Publications, Stanford University.

Declerk, Thierry. 1996. Modeling information-passing within the LFG Workbench. In Miriam Butt and Tracy Holloway King, editors, *On-line Proceedings of the First LFG Conference*, Rank Xerox, Grenoble, August 26–28, 1996. http://www-csli.stanford.edu/publications/LFG/declerck.ps.

Fenstad, Jens-Erik, Per-Kristian Halvorsen, Tore Langholm, and Johan van Benthem. 1987. *Situations, Language, and Logic*. D. Reidel, Dordrecht.

Frey, Werner and Uwe Reyle. 1983. A Prolog implementation of Lexical Functional Grammar as a base for a natural language processing system. In *Proceedings of the First Meeting of the European ACL*, Pisa, Italy, pages 52–56. European Chapter of the Association for Computational Linguistics.

Frey, Werner, Uwe Reyle, and Christian Rohrer. 1983. Automatic construction of a knowledge base by analysing texts in natural language. In *Proceedings of the Eighth International Joint Conference on Artificial Intelligence*, Karlsruhe, West Germany, volume 2.

Groenendijk, Jeroen and Martin Stokhof. 1990. Dynamic Montague grammar. In L. Kalman and L. Polos, editors, *Papers from the Second Symposium on Logic and Language*, pages 3–48. Akademiai Kiadoo, Budapest.

Groenendijk, Jeroen and Martin Stokhof. 1991. Dynamic predicate logic. *Linguistics and Philosophy*, 14(1):39–100.

Halvorsen, Per-Kristian. 1983. Semantics for Lexical-Functional Grammar. *Linguistic Inquiry*, 14(4):567–615.

Halvorsen, Per-Kristian and Ronald M. Kaplan. 1988. Projections and semantic description in Lexical-Functional Grammar. In *Proceedings of the International Conference on Fifth Generation Computer Systems (FGCS-88)*, pages 1116–1122, Tokyo, Japan. Reprinted in Mary Dalrymple, Ronald M. Kaplan, John Maxwell, and Annie Zaenen, editors, *Formal Issues in Lexical-Functional Grammar*, pages 279–292. CSLI Publications, Stanford University. 1995.

Kamp, Hans and Uwe Reyle. 1993. *From Discourse to Logic: An Introduction to Modeltheoretic Semantics of Natural Language, Formal Logic and Discourse Representation Theory*. Kluwer Academic Publishers, Dordrecht.

Kaplan, Ronald M. and Joan Bresnan. 1982. Lexical-Functional Grammar: A formal system for grammatical representation. In Joan Bresnan, editor, *The Mental Representation of Grammatical Relations*, pages 173–281. The MIT Press, Cambridge, MA. Reprinted in Mary Dalrymple, Ronald M. Kaplan, John Maxwell, and Annie Zaenen, editors, *Formal Issues in Lexical-Functional Grammar*, pages 29–130. CSLI Publications, Stanford University. 1995.

Kempson, Ruth. 1995. Ellipsis as labelled deduction. *Language and Deduction. Bulletin for Interest Group in Pure and Applied Logics*, 3:189–256.

Kohlhase, M., S. Kuschert, and M. Pinkal. 1996. A type-theoretic semantics for λ-DRT. In P. Dekker and M. Stokhof, editors, *Proceedings of the Tenth Amsterdam Colloquium*. ILLC, University of Amsterdam, 1996.

König, Esther and Uwe Reyle. 1996. A general reasoning scheme for underspecified representations. In Hans-Jürgen Ohlbach and Uwe Reyle, editors, *Logic and its Applications. Festschrift for Dov Gabbay*. Kluwer Academic Publishers, Dordrecht.

Muskens, Reinhard. 1994. Categorial grammar and Discourse Representation Theory. In *Proceedings of the 15th International Conference on Computational Linguistics (COLING-94)*, Kyoto, pages 508–514.

Muskens, Reinhard. 1995. Order-independence and underspecification. In *Dyana-2 Deliverable R2.2.C "Ellipsis, Underspecification, Events and More in Dynamic Semantics"*. The DYANA-2 Project Administrator, ILLC, University of Amsterdam.

Muskens, Reinhard. 1996. Combining Montague Semantics and Discourse Representation Theory. *Linguistics and Philosophy*, 19(2):143–186.

Pollard, Carl and Ivan A. Sag. 1994. *Head-Driven Phrase Structure Grammar*. The University of Chicago Press, Chicago.

Reyle, Uwe. 1985. Grammatical functions, discourse referents and quantification. In *Proceedings of the Ninth International Joint Conference on Artificial Intelligence*, Los Angeles, pages 829–831.

Reyle, Uwe. 1988. Compositional semantics for LFG. In Uwe Reyle and Christian Rohrer, editors, *Natural language parsing and linguistic theories*, pages 448–474. D. Reidel, Dordrecht.

Reyle, Uwe. 1993. Dealing with ambiguities by underspecification: Construction, representation and deduction. *Journal of Semantics*, 10:123–179.

Reyle, Uwe. 1995. On reasoning with ambiguities. In *Proceedings of the Seventh Meeting of the European Association for Computational Linguistics*, Dublin, pages 1–8.

van Eijck, Jan and Hans Kamp. 1997. Representing discourse in context. In Johan van Benthem and Alice ter Meulen, editors, *Handbook of Logic and Language*, pages 179–237. Elsevier / The MIT Press, Amsterdam / Cambridge.

van Genabith, Josef and Richard Crouch. 1996a. Direct and underspecified interpretations of LFG f-structures. In *Proceedings of the 16th International Conference on Computational Linguistics (COLING-96)*, Copenhagen, Denmark, pages 262–267.

van Genabith, Josef and Richard Crouch. 1996b. F-structures, QLFs and UDRSs. In Miriam Butt and Tracy Holloway King, editors, *On-line Proceedings of the First LFG Conference*, Rank Xerox, Grenoble, August 26–28, 1996. http://www-csli.stanford.edu/publications/LFG/genabith.ps.

van Genabith, Josef and Richard Crouch. 1997a. How to glue a donkey to an f-structure, or porting a dynamic meaning representation into LFG's linear logic based glue-language semantics. In Harry Bunt, Leen Kievit, Reinhard Muskens, and Margriet Verlinden, editors, *Proceedings of the Second International Workshop on Computational Semantics*, 8–10 January 1997, Tilburg, pages 52–65.

van Genabith, Josef and Richard Crouch. 1997b. On interpreting f-structures as UDRSs. In *Proceedings of the Thirty-Fifth Annual Meeting of the ACL and Eighth Conference of the EACL*, Madrid, Spain. Association for Computational Linguistics.

Wada, Hajime and Nicholas Asher. 1986. BUILDRS: an implementation of DR theory and LFG. In *Proceedings of the 11th International Conference on Computational Linguistics (COLING-86)*, Bonn, pages 540–545.

Wada, Hajime and Nicholas Asher. 1988. A computational account of syntactic, semantic and discourse principles for anaphora resolution. *Journal of Semantics*, 6(3):309–344.

Wedekind, Jürgen and Ronald M. Kaplan. 1993. Type-driven semantic interpretation of f-structures. In *Proceedings of the Sixth Meeting of the European ACL*, University of Utrecht, pages 404–411. European Chapter of the Association for Computational Linguistics.

7

Relating Resource-based Semantics to Categorial Semantics

Mary Dalrymple, Vineet Gupta, John Lamping, and Vijay Saraswat

We provide a new formulation of the resource-based glue approach to semantics, a formulation that separates the syntactic connections and the meaning. In particular, we show that many applications of the glue approach use a fragment of linear logic which is equivalent to typed linear lambda calculus, where the type captures the syntactic connections and the lambda term captures the meaning.

In addition to presenting a new, possibly cleaner, perspective on the glue approach, this formulation better brings out the essential differences and similarities between the glue style and categorial approaches. For example, the word *yawn* might be encoded in the three approaches as approximately:

$$
\begin{array}{ll}
\text{Categorial} & \lambda x.yawn(x) : \mathrm{N\backslash S} \\
\text{Old Glue} & \forall x.\ s \rightsquigarrow x \multimap r \rightsquigarrow yawn(x) \\
\text{New Glue} & \lambda x.yawn(x) : s \multimap r
\end{array}
$$

An essential difference between the categorial approaches and the glue approach is their relation to syntax. Categorial approaches encode rules for syntactic composition in their type logic. For example, $\mathrm{N\backslash S}$ above, indicates that the subject precedes the verb. The glue approach, on the other hand, does not encode syntactic rules in its logic, but follows the LFG methodology of linking together different formal systems, each charged with handling a different kind of linguistic phenomena. In particular, the glue approach's meaning logic connects to

An earlier version of this paper appeared in the *Proceedings of the Fifth Meeting on Mathematics of Language (MOL5)*, Schloss Dagstuhl, Saarbrücken, Germany. August 1997.

a separate grammar. It specifies how to assemble meanings of sentences that have been analyzed by the grammar. It focuses on mediating differences between the compositional structure of the syntax and the compositional structure of the meaning term, such as those that occur with quantifier scoping.

A historical difference between the categorial approach and the glue approach has stemmed from the categorial approach's use of lambda expressions to manipulate meanings, compared to the glue approach's use of quantification. This has meant that while the composition of meanings in the categorial approach is clearly separated from the syntactic types, the glue approach, as originally formulated, intermixed its syntactic connections and meanings.

This paper shows that a significant fragment of the glue approach can be reformulated to separate out the meaning composition in a way that is very similar to that of the categorial approaches. Specifically, we show the following:

- A core fragment C of linear logic (LL) can be used to define semantic assembly in many cases.

- Every formula in C can be read as an assertion that a particular λ-term has a particular type. These assertions are formulas in System F (Girard 1986).

- The two formulations have equivalent deductive power.

When the glue approach requires only the core fragment, the reformulation allows it to take advantage of one of the primary attractions of the categorial approach: the syntactic well-formedness of a sentence can be reasoned about strictly in terms of types, yet the types can be labeled with lambda terms so that a meaning term for the sentence can be constructed automatically from a proof that the sentence has the appropriate type, following the well-known Curry-Howard connection between the λ-calculus and intuitionistic logic. This is attractive because it captures formally the intuition that the process of meaning construction is sensitive only to the *types* of the terms being assembled, not their actual *values*. This ensures compositionality: no assumptions about the content of the actual meaning are built into the meaning assembly process.

Under the reformulation of the glue approach, the components of the parse resulting from LFG syntactic analysis are reflected in the meaning assembly language as type constants (r and s in the example above). These constants thus capture more information than just the information about individuals (e) and truth-values (t) inherent in the meaning term. Similarly, the propositional structure of the types in the meaning terms reflects the structure of the LFG parse. The *combination* of the meanings is then purely standard.

In the following, we briefly review the categorial approach and the glue approach. We then characterize the fragment, C, of the glue approach that is equivalent to typed lambda calculus and prove the equivalence. Finally, we examine applications of glue semantics that exceed the core fragment C and discuss why this step was necessary.

1   Categorial Grammar

In this section, we provide a brief sketch of the Categorial Grammar approach to facilitate comparison to the revised version of the glue approach that we present here. For a more complete introduction to categorial approaches to syntax, semantics, and the syntax-semantics interface, see Lambek (1958), Oehrle et al. (1988), Morrill (1994), Steedman (1996), and references cited there.

Lexical entries in a typical Categorial Grammar assign syntactic categories such as N to noun phrases like *Bill*, or more complex categories like N\S for intransitive verbs like *yawned*. N\S represents a category that combines with an N to its left to produce an S. Lexical entries are also associated with λ-calculus terms, which are combined via application and abstraction in a manner dictated by the syntactic types to yield a meaning for the entire utterance. For a sentence like *Bill yawned*, the relevant lexical entries are:

$$
\begin{array}{llll}
(1) & \text{Bill} & \textit{Bill} & : \quad \text{N} \\
    & \text{yawned} & \lambda x.\textit{yawn}(x) & : \quad \text{N\S}
\end{array}
$$

Given this lexical information, we can produce the following proof that *Bill yawned* is a sentence:

(2) Derivation:

$$\frac{\textit{Bill} : \mathrm{N} \Rightarrow \textit{Bill} : \mathrm{N} \quad \textit{yawn} : \mathrm{N}\backslash\mathrm{S} \Rightarrow \textit{yawn} : \mathrm{N}\backslash\mathrm{S}}{\textit{Bill} : \mathrm{N}, \textit{yawn} : \mathrm{N}\backslash\mathrm{S} \Rightarrow \textit{yawn}(\textit{Bill}) : \mathrm{S}} \backslash E$$

The derivations are considered to infer types (formulas in intuitionistic logic), and the term corresponding to the meaning can then be built up in a uniform way from the proofs and terms corresponding to the lexical entries.

2 Resource-based Semantics and LFG

In this section we provide a brief overview of the assumptions on which we base this work. For a more detailed presentation, see Chapter 1.

Besides the two syntactic structures of LFG, the constituent structure and the functional structure, we assume a *semantic structure* consisting of *type constants* which will be associated with meanings. In general, there will be a different type constant for every component of the functional structure. They are associated via a *semantic function* σ which maps components of functional structure to type constants. Our use of the term "type constant" as synonymous with "semantic structure" reflects the analogy we intend to draw with categorial grammar. In the following, we generally use names like r, s, and t for type constants, though in this initial discussion, when we emphasize the connection between a type constant and a functional structure, we follow the glue literature and use names like f_σ and g_σ for the type constants corresponding to the functional structures f and g.

We use linear logic (LL) as the "glue" for composing a meaning for an utterance from the meanings of its constituents. A type constant r is associated with a meaning term M (drawn from some pre-specified "meaning language", here Montague's intensional logic (Montague 1974)) via an atomic assertion of the form $r \leadsto_\tau M$, where $\leadsto$ is an otherwise uninterpreted binary predicate symbol and τ is the semantic type of the entry.

Each occurrence of a word in the utterance contributes either an atomic formula involving the type constant corresponding to its syntactic position or a non-atomic LL formula (e.g., $s \leadsto_\alpha M \multimap t \leadsto_\beta N \multimap r \leadsto_\tau P$) that states how a meaning term may be produced by consuming meaning terms associated with syntactically related type constants.

Our LL fragment allows quantification over type constants and over meaning-terms. A meaning M of the type constant r corresponding to the entire utterance is obtained by finding an LL proof of $r \leadsto_\alpha M$ (where α is usually t, the type of propositions) from the contributions of the lexical entries (perhaps in the presence of an underlying LL theory). Each such derivable M provides a meaning for the utterance; for the representation in glue logic to be complete, every meaning for the utterance must be derivable in this way.

Names. The meaning constructor for a particular occurrence of a name such as *Bill*, associated with an f-structure, say g, establishes an association between a type constant g_σ and the constant *Bill* representing its meaning:

(3) $g_\sigma \leadsto_e Bill$

We indicate the type of the meaning term by the subscript e on the "means" relation $\leadsto_e$.

Verbs. As explained in Chapter 1, the meaning constructor for a verb such as *yawned* is a glue language formula that can be thought of as instructions for how to assemble the meaning of a sentence with main verb *yawned* based on the meanings of its arguments: the meaning for the subject is consumed, and the sentential meaning is produced. If *yawned* is the head of an f-structure, f, whose subject is an f-structure, g, this is:

(4) $\forall X.\, g_\sigma \leadsto_e X \multimap f_\sigma \leadsto_t yawn(X)$

Quantifiers.   As discussed in Chapter 2, a generalized quantifier such as *everyone* can be seen as making a semantic contribution like the following:

(5)   **everyone** $\forall R, S. \ (\forall x. \ g_\sigma \rightsquigarrow_e x \multimap R \rightsquigarrow_t S(x))$
$\multimap R \rightsquigarrow_t every(person, S)$

If by giving the arbitrary meaning x to g_σ, the type constant for *everyone*, we can derive the meaning $S(x)$ for the scope of quantification, then S can be the property that the quantifier requires as its scope, yielding the meaning *every(person, S)*. Logically, this means that the semantic constructor for an NP quantifies universally over type constants.

The derivation of the meaning of a sentence like *Everyone yawned* proceeds from the meaning constructors for *everyone* and *yawned*:

(6)   Everyone yawned.

$$f: \begin{bmatrix} \text{PRED} & \text{'YAWN'} \\ \text{SUBJ} & g: \begin{bmatrix} \text{PRED} & \text{'EVERYONE'} \end{bmatrix} \end{bmatrix}$$

everyone: $\forall R, S. \ (\forall x. \ g_\sigma \rightsquigarrow_e x \multimap R \rightsquigarrow_t S(x))$
$\multimap R \rightsquigarrow_t every(person, S)$

yawned: $\forall x. \qquad g_\sigma \rightsquigarrow_e x \multimap f_\sigma \rightsquigarrow_t yawn(x)$

With this, we have the following derivation, where the arrow $\mapsto$ indicates how the variables in the formulas are instantiated:

$$\begin{array}{ll}
\textbf{everyone} \otimes \textbf{yawned} & \text{(Premises)} \\
\vdash \ f_\sigma \rightsquigarrow_t every(person, yawn) & R \mapsto f_\sigma, x \mapsto x, \\
& S \mapsto yawn
\end{array}$$

3   Analysis of $\mathcal{C}$

The examples presented above all lie in the core fragment $\mathcal{C}$. We now turn to an analysis of $\mathcal{C}$ and elucidation of its formal properties.

We make a notational shift to focus on just the meaning assembly process, and use r, s, and t for type constants, rather than f_σ and g_σ. Further, rather than add e or t, as subscript to the $\rightsquigarrow$ relation, we capture that information in a two-sorted logic for our type constants and variables. Thus, when the sort matters, we write $r_e \rightsquigarrow M$ to say that the type constant r_e, which has sort e, is associated with meaning M.

3.1   Informal development

Under this notational shift, the contributions for the sentence *Everyone yawned* can have g_σ renamed as the type constant s and f_σ as r, to yield

$$\textbf{everyone:} \quad \forall R, S.\ (\forall x.\ s \rightsquigarrow x \multimap R \rightsquigarrow S(x)) \multimap R \rightsquigarrow every(person, S)$$

$$\textbf{yawned:} \quad \forall x.\ s \rightsquigarrow x \multimap r \rightsquigarrow yawn(x)$$

We can remove the meaning terms from the atoms and remove quantification over meaning terms, obtaining the "stripped" premises:

$$\textbf{everyone:} \quad \forall R.\ (s \multimap R) \multimap R$$

$$\textbf{yawned:} \quad s \multimap r$$

Notice that quantification over R is left, because R ranges over type constants, not meanings. The stripped premises yield the stripped deduction:

$$(\forall R.\ (s \multimap R) \multimap R) \otimes (s \multimap r)$$
$$\vdash \quad r$$

It is easy to see that stripping meanings from the propositions preserves deductions, since the stripped formulas remove some constraints on what formulas can be combined, and add no new constraints. Thus, if there is a deduction from some original formulas, then there is an equivalent deduction from the stripped formulas.

More interestingly, the implication goes the other way: the meanings do not constrain the deduction. If one starts with the original formulas, strips them, and makes a deduction from the stripped formulas, then there is an analogous deduction from the original formulas. Put another way, the meanings can be added back: a deduction from the stripped formulas can be enriched to become a valid deduction on the original formulas. What is more, there is a unique way to enrich the deduction to work on the original formulas. This claim depends on some properties of $\mathcal{C}$ to be presented shortly.

This result can be strengthened to connect with the λ-calculus: each stripped term can be associated with a λ-expression that records the meaning information, and the meaning of the inferred term can be determined by performing applications and λ-abstractions in correspondence with the proof rules.

Returning to the example, λ-expressions can be added to the stripped meanings for **everyone** and **yawned** to yield:

$$\lambda S.every(person, S) : \forall R.\ (s \multimap R) \multimap R$$
$$yawn : s \multimap r$$

Implication elimination and universal instantiation in the stripped premises now indicates that the corresponding λ-terms should be applied:

$$\lambda S.every(person, S) : \forall R.\ (s \multimap R) \multimap R$$
$$yawn : s \multimap r$$
$$\vdash\ \ \lambda S.every(person, S)(yawn) : r$$

or, equivalently:

$$every(person, yawn) : r$$

This formulation looks very similar to the categorial approach, with the crucial difference that the types involve type constants that connect to the constituents of an independent syntactic analysis.

3.2   Formal development

The core fragment $\mathcal{C}$.   The core fragment has two kinds of terms, those like r that refer to type constants, and those like *Bill* that are in the meaning language. The atoms of the fragment are formulas like $r \rightsquigarrow Bill$ that relate the two kinds of terms.

Larger formulas are built up in only two ways: by quantification over type constants, and by combination of a quantification over a meaning variable and a linear implication (the two together acting as a function definition). An example is $\forall x.\ s \rightsquigarrow x \multimap r \rightsquigarrow yawn(x)$, where the meaning of r is set up as a function of the meaning of s.

Definition 1 (Syntax of C)

$$\langle\text{type}\rangle ::= \langle\text{e-type-const}\rangle \mid \langle\text{t-type-const}\rangle \mid \langle\text{t-type-var}\rangle$$

$$\langle\text{meaning}\rangle ::= \ \langle\text{meaning-const}\rangle$$
$$\mid \langle\text{meaning-var}\rangle$$
$$\mid \langle\text{meaning}\rangle(\langle\text{meaning}\rangle \ldots \langle\text{meaning}\rangle)$$

$$\langle\text{formula}\rangle ::= \ \langle\text{type}\rangle \rightsquigarrow \langle\text{meaning}\rangle$$
$$\mid \forall\langle\text{t-type-var}\rangle.\langle\text{formula}\rangle$$
$$\mid \forall\langle\text{meaning-var}\rangle.\langle\text{formula}\rangle_1 \multimap \langle\text{formula}\rangle_2$$
$$\textit{if generic}(\langle\text{meaning-var}\rangle, \langle\text{formula}\rangle_1)$$

(We will present the definition of the meta-predicate $\textit{generic}(\_,\_)$ shortly.)

Notation: We write r_t or s_t for t-type constants and r_e or s_e for e-type constants. We write r or s for type constants where the sort doesn't matter. We write R or S for t-type variables and M and N for meaning variables. We use italicized words like *Bill* and *yawn* for meaning constants and meaning predicates. When we need meta-variables, we use $\mathcal{M}$ and $\mathcal{N}$ to range over meaning expressions, and P, Q, and R to range over formulas.

We use induction on this syntax to formally define the type projections of formulas, written as $\{P\}$, and the meaning projections of formulas, written as $[\![P]\!]$.

Definition 2 (Type Projections)

$$\{r \rightsquigarrow \mathcal{M}\} = r$$
$$\{\forall R.P\} = \forall R.\{P\}$$
$$\{\forall M.\ P \multimap Q\} = \{P\} \multimap \{Q\}$$

Definition 3 (Meaning Projections)

$$[\![r \rightsquigarrow \mathcal{M}]\!] = \mathcal{M}$$
$$[\![\forall R.P]\!] = [\![P]\!]$$
$$[\![\forall M.\ P \multimap Q]\!] = \lambda M.[\![Q]\!]$$

The motivation behind the *generic*(_,_) meta-predicate is that we want implications to be used only in formulas such as

$$\forall M.\ r \rightsquigarrow M \multimap s \rightsquigarrow yawn(M)$$

that are analogous to a lambda expression. This requires the left hand side of the implication to pick up the argument, via unification, which can then be substituted into the right hand side of the implication. In other words, the meaning of the left hand side of the implication, here $r \rightsquigarrow M$, should be a variable, here M. We do this in this case by requiring *generic*$(M, r \rightsquigarrow M)$, as explained below.

We define *generic*$(\mathcal{M}, P)$ by induction on the syntax. It holds in exactly the following three cases:

Genericity:

1. *generic*$(\mathcal{M}, r \rightsquigarrow \mathcal{M})$.

2. *generic*$(\mathcal{M}, \forall R.P)$ if *generic*$(\mathcal{M}, P)$.

3. *generic*$(\mathcal{M}, \forall N.\ P \multimap Q)$ if *generic*$(\mathcal{M}(N), Q)$.

The last clause in this definition connects with η-conversion. For example *generic*$(M, \forall N.\ s \rightsquigarrow N \multimap r \rightsquigarrow M(N))$, and $[\![\forall N.\ s \rightsquigarrow N \multimap r \rightsquigarrow M(N)]\!]$ is $\lambda N.M(N)$, which η-reduces to M.

The following lemma verifies that the definition of *generic*$(\mathcal{M}, P)$ allows it to hold only when the meaning of P is $\mathcal{M}$.

Lemma 4 (Genericity)   *If generic*$(\mathcal{M}, P)$*, then* $[\![P]\!] = \mathcal{M}$*, up to* α-*,*β-*,*η-*conversion.*

Proof. This is obviously true for the first two cases of Genericity. For the third case $P = \forall N.\ Q_1 \multimap Q_2$, $[\![\forall N.\ Q_1 \multimap Q_2]\!] = \lambda N.[\![Q_2]\!]$. By induction, $[\![Q_1]\!] = N$ and $[\![Q_2]\!] = \mathcal{M}(N)$, so $[\![\forall N.\ Q_1 \multimap Q_2]\!] = \lambda N.[\![Q_2]\!] = \lambda N.\mathcal{M}(N) = \mathcal{M}$. $\qquad\square$

Lemma 5   *If* $[\![P]\!] = [\![Q]\!]$ *and* $\{P\} = \{Q\}$ *then* $P = Q$.

Proof. By induction, and using the Genericity Lemma, since the only information about P in the third case is $\{P\}$. $\qquad\square$

Corollary 6 *If $\mathcal{N}$ is generic in P and $\{P\} = \{Q\}$, then there exists an $\mathcal{M}$ such that $Q = P[\mathcal{M}/\mathcal{N}]$, up to α-,β-,η-conversion.*

Proof. Take $\mathcal{M}$ to be $[\![Q]\!]$. $\qquad\qquad\qquad\qquad\qquad\qquad\qquad\qquad\Box$

Note that the formulas we have are a subset of linear logic with implication and universal quantification. In our formulas, implication always occurs together with a universal quantification. We can combine the Gentzen-style proof rules of linear logic, without any loss of power, to get a simpler proof system for our formulas. This is the proof system $\vdash_C$ that we use in the following theorems. It is formally defined as follows:

$$\frac{}{r \rightsquigarrow \mathcal{M} \vdash_C r \rightsquigarrow \mathcal{M}'} \quad \frac{\Gamma, P, Q, \Delta \vdash_C R}{\Gamma, Q, P, \Delta \vdash_C R}$$
$$\text{where } \mathcal{M} \equiv_{\alpha,\beta,\eta} \mathcal{M}'$$

$$\frac{\Gamma, P[r_t/R] \vdash_C Q}{\Gamma, \forall R.P \vdash_C Q} \quad \frac{\Gamma, P[S/R] \vdash_C Q}{\Gamma, \forall R.P \vdash_C Q} \quad \frac{\Gamma \vdash_C P[R/S]}{\Gamma \vdash_C \forall S.P}(R \text{ new})$$

$$\frac{\Gamma \vdash_C P[\mathcal{M}/M] \quad \Delta, Q[\mathcal{M}/M] \vdash_C R}{\Gamma, \Delta, \forall M.\, P \multimap Q \vdash_C R}$$

$$\frac{\Gamma, P[N/M] \vdash_C Q[N/M]}{\Gamma \vdash_C \forall M.\, P \multimap Q}(N \text{ new})$$

It is straightforward to show that one can prove $\Gamma \vdash_C R$ if and only if one can prove $\Gamma \vdash_{LL} R$, where $\vdash_{LL}$ is the linear logic proof system.

Theorem 7 states that meanings can be stripped off from formulas, with no loss in provability. Theorem 8 states the converse—given a proof with stripped formulas, it is possible to add the meanings to reconstruct the original proof uniquely.

Theorem 7 *If $P_1, \ldots, P_n \vdash_C R$ then $\{P_1\}, \ldots, \{P_n\} \vdash_{LL} \{R\}$*

Proof. Straightforward induction on the proof of $P_1, \ldots, P_n \vdash_C R$. $\qquad\Box$

Theorem 8 *Let $P_1, \ldots, P_n$ be formulas in C, and S be any LL formula such that $\{P_1\}, \ldots, \{P_n\} \vdash_{LL} S$. Let Σ be a proof of $\{P_1\}, \ldots, \{P_n\} \vdash_{LL} S$. Then there is a unique formula R with $S = \{R\}$ and a unique proof Π of $P_1, \ldots, P_n \vdash_C R$, such that $\{\Pi\} = \Sigma$, where $\{\Pi\}$ is obtained by projecting each formula in Π.*

Proof. Given the proof Σ of $\{P_1\}, \ldots, \{P_n\} \vdash_{LL} S$, and the meanings of $P_1, \ldots, P_n$, we can show by induction that there is a unique meaning that can be attached to each formula that occurs in Σ. The only non-trivial case is the implication, but genericity allows us to immediately compute the meaning of the antecedent of an implication. It is also clear that for each proof rule of linear logic, the rule formed by adding the meanings is a proof rule in $\vdash_C$. $\qquad\square$

We now relate proofs in the resource-based semantics to proofs in the categorial semantics. Since we allow universal quantification over t-type constants, we need to extend the typed λ-calculus with type abstraction. Thus, as mentioned earlier, we use a restricted version of System F, a generalization of the typed λ-calculus (Girard 1986). We restrict the power of System F by limiting type abstraction to t-type constant types only.

System F. In the following, Γ is a set of $\mathcal{M} : S$ pairs, where $\mathcal{M}$ is a meaning and S is a type. A well formed Γ has distinct variables (so no variable has more than one type constant)—thus,

$$M : S \in \Gamma, M : S' \in \Gamma \Rightarrow S =_\alpha S'$$

Let S, S' denote type constants; other terms are as before. The proof rules are:

$$\mathcal{M} : S \vdash_F \mathcal{M} : S \qquad \text{(identity)}$$

$$\frac{\Gamma, \mathcal{M} : S \vdash_F \mathcal{N} : S'}{\Gamma \vdash_F \lambda \mathcal{M}.\mathcal{N} : S \multimap S'} \qquad (\lambda\text{-intro})$$

$$\frac{\Gamma \vdash_F \mathcal{M} : S \multimap S' \qquad \Delta \vdash_F \mathcal{N} : S}{\Gamma, \Delta \vdash_F \mathcal{M}(\mathcal{N}) : S'} \qquad (\text{appl})$$

$$\frac{\Gamma \vdash_F \mathcal{M} : S}{\Gamma \vdash_F \mathcal{M} : \forall R.S} \qquad (\Lambda\text{-intro}, R \text{ new in } \Gamma)$$

$$\frac{\Gamma \vdash_F \mathcal{M} : \forall R.S}{\Gamma \vdash_F \mathcal{M} : S[S'/R]} \qquad (\Lambda\text{-elim})$$

Note that we did not need to have $\Lambda R.\mathcal{M}$ in the Λ-intro rule since we know that R cannot occur in $\mathcal{M}$.

Theorem 9   *Let Π be a proof of $P_1, \ldots, P_n \vdash_C R$. Then for any Γ, if each of $\Gamma \vdash_F [\![P_i]\!] : \{P_i\}$ holds in System F, then $\Gamma \vdash_F [\![R]\!] : \{R\}$ holds in System F. The converse is also true.*

Proof. By induction on the proof tree for $P_1, \ldots, P_n \vdash R$.

If the last rule applied is the identity rule, there is nothing to prove.

If the last rule is the left $\forall$ quantification over t-type constants, then we have a proof of $\Gamma \vdash_F \mathcal{M} : \forall R.S$, from our assumption that $\Gamma \vdash_F [\![P_i]\!] : \{P_i\}$. Now we can use the Λ-elimination rule to conclude $\Gamma \vdash_F \mathcal{M} : S[S'/R]$. Thus we have a proof for all the premises of the antecedent, so by induction we can prove $\Gamma \vdash_F [\![R]\!] : \{R\}$.

If the last rule was the right $\forall$ quantification over t-type constants, then we can use the Λ-intro rule to conclude the result.

If the last rule is the left $\forall$ quantification over meaning variables, then we know that

$$\Gamma \vdash_F [\![P_1]\!] : \{P_1\}, \ldots, \Gamma \vdash_F [\![P_n]\!] : \{P_n\}$$

and

$$\Gamma \vdash_F \lambda M.[\![Q_2]\!] : \{Q_1\} \multimap \{Q_2\}$$

Now from the proof of $P_1, \ldots, P_i \vdash Q_1[\mathcal{M}/M]$ and the genericity of $\mathcal{M}$ in Q_1 we have a proof of $\Gamma \vdash_F \mathcal{M} : \{Q_1\}$. Now by the application rule we then have $\Gamma \vdash_F [\![Q_2]\!][\mathcal{M}/M] : \{Q_2\}$. Thus from the induction hypothesis, we can prove $\Gamma \vdash_F [\![R]\!] : \{R\}$.

If the last rule is the right $\forall$ quantification over meaning variables, then $R = \forall N.\ R_1 \multimap R_2$, for some variable N. $\Gamma \vdash_F [\![P_i]\!] : \{P_i\}$ holds in System F for each premise. As N does not occur in Γ, $\Gamma, N : \{R_1\} \vdash_F [\![P_i]\!] : \{P_i\}$ holds in System F, and $\Gamma, N : \{R_1\} \vdash_F N : \{R_1\}$. Thus, by induction $\Gamma, N : \{R_1\} \vdash_F [\![R_2]\!] : \{R_2\}$. Now by λ-intro, we have $\Gamma \vdash_F \lambda N.[\![R_2]\!] : \{R_1\} \multimap \{R_2\}$, which is the required result.

The linearity assures us that each $\Gamma \vdash_F [\![P_i]\!] : \{P_i\}$ is needed exactly once in the proof of $\Gamma \vdash_F [\![R]\!] : \{R\}$.

The converse is true, because if we drop the meaning terms from the System F rules we get rules that are valid in LL. Now we can add the meanings via the previous theorem. $\square$

4   Beyond the Core Fragment

The core fragment is sufficient to cover many linguistic constructs, including proper nouns, quantifiers, extensional verbs, and a variety of other phenomena. As the above results show, it requires only propositional inference. Whenever possible, it seems best to express linguistic phenomena within the core fragment.

Some linguistic constructs, however, appear to require going beyond the core fragment. The glue semantics approach has the advantage that it is possible to move beyond the core fragment when that is appropriate, while staying within the well developed linear logic system. In fact, the extensions to date have stayed within an only slightly larger fragment of linear logic.

In this section we briefly discuss those situations and point out how they affect the above results.

4.1   An alternative formulation of quantifiers

We first give an example of an ill-advised excursion outside the core fragment. A footnote in Dalrymple et al. (1995) considered an alternative formulation of quantifier meaning, under which the meaning constructor for *everyone* looked like

$$(7) \quad \textbf{everyone} \quad \exists x. \ r \rightsquigarrow x \otimes$$
$$(\forall R, M. \ R \rightsquigarrow M(x)$$
$$\multimap R \rightsquigarrow every(person, M))$$

This formulation uses existential quantification in the *meaning language* to assert that there is a new entity, x, which stands for the meaning of the quantified phrase. The derivation of the scope is then expected to consume this information.

Note that the propositional structure of this formula does not require the meaning for r to be consumed by the scope. Rather, it is the existential quantification over the meaning variable x that limits the scope.[1] Because of this dependence on terms in the meaning language, a proof

---

[1] It turns out that this scheme "works" because of our stipulation that we are only interested in proofs of *atomic* formulas, of the form $s \rightsquigarrow M$. Therefore if the $r \rightsquigarrow x$ atom is not consumed in the proof of the antecedent (in the implication), and if there are no "generic consumers" of atoms, e.g. of the form $\forall x. \ r \rightsquigarrow x \multimap 1$, then a formula $(\exists x.(r) \dots)$

that ignores meanings does not guarantee that there is a proof with meanings. Intuitively, the meaning language—and not just the structure provided by the type constants—is being used to represent some control information. There seems to be no point to this shift.

4.2   Intensionality

Intensional verbs require the meaning language to be able to express intensions. To illustrate, one of the readings for *Bill seeks a unicorn* should be

$$seek(Bill, \hat{}\lambda Q.a(\hat{}unicorn, Q))$$

where the meaning language now is the intensional λ-calculus, which we assume the reader is familiar with.[2]

Intensional verbs can be handled by *extending* the core fragment to allow the meaning language to also include intensional expressions:

$$\langle meaning\rangle ::= \quad \lambda\langle meaning\text{-}var\rangle.\langle meaning\rangle$$
$$| \; \hat{}\langle meaning\rangle$$
$$| \; \check{}\langle meaning\rangle$$

This extension allows the above conclusion to be derived from the following contributions of *Bill*, *seek*, and *a unicorn* (labeled **uni**):

$$\textbf{bill:} \quad s \rightsquigarrow \hat{}Bill$$
$$\textbf{uni:} \quad \forall R, N. \, (\forall M. \, t \rightsquigarrow M \multimap R \rightsquigarrow N(M))$$
$$\multimap R \rightsquigarrow \hat{}a(\hat{}unicorn, \hat{}\lambda M.\check{}(N(\hat{}M)))$$
$$\textbf{seek:} \quad \forall M_1, M_2. \, s \rightsquigarrow M_1$$
$$\multimap (\forall R, N_1. \, (\forall N_2. \, t \rightsquigarrow N_2 \multimap R \rightsquigarrow N_1(N_2))$$
$$\multimap R \rightsquigarrow M_2(N_1))$$
$$\multimap r \rightsquigarrow seek(M_1, \hat{}\lambda Q.\check{}(M_2 \lambda x.\hat{}((\check{}Q)(\check{}x))))$$

In order to have intensions available when they might be needed, all meaning variables now refer to intensions, with extensions explicitly taken whenever necessary. This is a departure from the analysis presented in Chapter 2. The equivalent formulation here requires more

---

will always be "left over". In linear logic, this "left over" formula cannot be discarded. Hence there can be no derivation of an atomic formula.

[2]Here we are assuming Montague's treatment of intensionality. Other approaches can be handled similarly.

explicit manipulation of intensions, but stays closest to the core fragment. In particular, we don't need to put intensionality into the type system, because intensionality does not constrain meaning assembly.

Since the only change to the core fragment is to allow a wider meaning language, and since the details of the meaning language do not affect the theorems, the theorems above still apply.

4.3   Non-semantic atoms

In Chapter 3 of this volume, Fry explores the use of additional atoms in the meaning constructors that do not carry meaning terms, but that are, instead, used to limit the number of possible readings that can be derived. These can be used to express restrictions on the appearance of negative polarity items such as *any* or *ever*, for example. Fry proposes that the meaning constructor for an operator like *nobody*, which can license a negative polarity item, is:

$$\textbf{nobody:}\quad \forall R, M.\, (\forall N.\, (r \rightsquigarrow N \otimes \ell) \multimap (R \rightsquigarrow M(N) \otimes \ell))$$
$$\multimap R \rightsquigarrow no(person, M)$$

The non-semantic atom ℓ constitutes a license for negative polarity items that is available only within the scope of the quantifier *nobody*. The meaning constructor for a negative polarity item such as the sentential adverb *ever* is:

$$\textbf{ever:}\quad \forall P.\quad (s \rightsquigarrow P \otimes \ell) \multimap (s \rightsquigarrow ever(P) \otimes \ell)$$

Ever can only be used in the presence of a negative polarity license ℓ, and it reinstates the license so it can be used by other negative polarity items.

The language of the core fragment may be extended to allow these kinds of non-semantic propositions (ns-prop, denoted by ℓ, ℓ') to be interspersed:

$$
\begin{aligned}
\langle\textit{ns-prop}\rangle ::=\ &\langle\textit{non-semantic atom}\rangle \\
&|\ \langle\textit{ns-prop}\rangle \multimap \langle\textit{ns-prop}\rangle \\
&|\ \langle\textit{ns-prop}\rangle \otimes \langle\textit{ns-prop}\rangle \\
\langle\textit{formula}\rangle ::=\ &|\ \langle\textit{ns-prop}\rangle \multimap \langle\textit{formula}\rangle \\
&|\ \langle\textit{ns-prop}\rangle \otimes \langle\textit{formula}\rangle
\end{aligned}
$$

Genericity can be extended to these cases:

1. $generic(\mathcal{M}, \ell \multimap P)$ if $generic(\mathcal{M}, P)$.

2. $generic(\mathcal{M}, \ell \otimes P)$ if $generic(\mathcal{M}, P)$.

These definitions allow a non-semantic atom to be added to any term, either conjoined with the term, or as an antecedent of the term. The idea is that they should play no direct role in determining the meaning, but may constrain what deductions are possible.

Type-constant- and meaning-projections may be defined via:

$$\{l \multimap P\} = l \multimap \{P\}$$
$$\{l \otimes P\} = l \otimes \{P\}$$

$$[\![l \multimap P]\!] = [\![P]\!]$$
$$[\![l \otimes P]\!] = [\![P]\!]$$

Given these definitions, all the results above carry through except the last theorem. Theorem 9 cannot go through because there are no meanings corresponding to the non-semantic atoms.[3]

4.4   Pronoun reference

In Chapter 2, Dalrymple, Lamping, Pereira, and Saraswat propose that the meaning constructors for pronouns such as *he* consume the meaning contribution of the antecedent, then duplicate it, once for the antecedent, and once for the anaphor itself. For example, if *he* occurs at type constant r, and its antecedent is at s, we would have:

he: $\forall M.\ s \rightsquigarrow M \multimap (s \rightsquigarrow M \otimes r \rightsquigarrow M)$

This is not in the core fragment because of the conjunction in $s \rightsquigarrow M \otimes r \rightsquigarrow M$. Extending the results of the core fragment to this richer setting would require extending the meaning language with tuples. We expect this to be the topic of future work.

Alternatively, the conjunction can be avoided by expressing the contribution of *he* differently, in the standard way used to obtain products

---

[3]The meaning projection rule $[\![l \multimap P]\!] = [\![P]\!]$ could be changed to $[\![l \multimap P]\!] = \lambda u.[\![P]\!]$, with vacuous abstraction over u, to allow the last theorem to go through. However, this would violate the spirit of the meaning projection, and still wouldn't handle the $[\![l \otimes P]\!]$ case.

of types in System F (using type-abstraction and functional types: Girard 1989, page 84):

he: $\forall M. \forall R. \forall N. s \rightsquigarrow M$
$$\multimap (s \rightsquigarrow M \multimap r \rightsquigarrow M \multimap R \rightsquigarrow N)$$
$$\multimap R \rightsquigarrow N$$

This statement is implied by the original meaning of *he*, and is strong enough to use in any deduction of a sentence meaning. It stays in the core fragment, at the cost of introducing quantification over R, which can cause multiple proofs of essentially the same result.

5   Discussion

We have presented a reformulation of the glue approach that separates the syntactic connections and the meaning composition, with the former handled by a type system, and the latter handled by lambda terms. This separation is more in line with the LFG methodology of connecting different formal systems, each responsible for a different category of linguistic phenomena. Glue types thus specify how to assemble meanings of sentences that have been analyzed by the grammar. The glue meaning deduction is interesting exactly when the compositional structure of the syntax does not directly align with the compositional structure of meaning.

The reformulation is also more in line with the formal structure of the categorial approaches. Thus for the core fragment, glue logic can be seen as a logic in the categorial framework. Proofs in this fragment of the glue logic can be presented quite simply, merely by consideration of the types. On the other hand, this representation of glue logic (via System F) seems unlike any other categorial logic developed for this purpose.

The similar formal structures more clearly elucidate the essential consequences of the different philosophies of the glue and categorial approaches. One may understand the categorial approach as dealing with the elucidation of a system of logical operators adequate for representing the types of interest in all natural languages. If existing techniques must be extended to deal with hitherto unanalyzed syntactic phenomena, one has to develop new *substructural primitives*, thus altering the underlying logic. In contrast, the glue semantics approach connects to a separate syntactic analysis by objectifying the results of a parse in *type constants*. These are connected with meaning assembly via the standard implication connective of LL ($\multimap$) (combined with the quantification over type constants and meaning terms). The surprise is that such a use of LL as a "meta-logic" has turned out to be quite natural.

The reformulation only applies, however, when the sentences of the glue approach stick to a core fragment of linear logic. Some linguistic constructs appear to call for sentences beyond that fragment, meaning that they have expressive requirements not readily available in a categorial style.

Acknowledgments

We are grateful to John Fry, David Israel, Mark Johnson, Nissim Francez, Dick Oehrle, Fernando Pereira, and Johan van Benthem for helpful discussion of the issues raised here. We also thank the anonymous reviewers for many helpful comments.

References

Dalrymple, Mary, John Lamping, Fernando C. N. Pereira, and Vijay Saraswat. 1995. A deductive account of quantification in LFG. In Makoto Kanazawa, Christopher J. Piñón, and Henriette de Swart, editors, *Quantifiers, Deduction, and Context*. CSLI Publications, Stanford University.

Girard, Jean-Yves. 1986. The system F of variable types, fifteen years later. *Theoretical Computer Science*, 45(2):159–192.

Girard, Jean-Yves. 1989. *Proofs and Types*, volume 7 of *Cambridge Tracts in Theoretical Computer Science*. Cambridge University Press. Translated and with appendices by Y. Lafont and P. Taylor.

Lambek, Joachim. 1958. The mathematics of sentence structure. *American Mathematical Monthly*, 65:154–170.

Montague, Richard. 1974. The proper treatment of quantification in ordinary English. In Richmond Thomason, editor, *Formal Philosophy*. Yale University Press, New Haven.

Morrill, Glyn V. 1994. *Type Logical Grammar: Categorial Logic of Signs*. Kluwer Academic Publishers, Dordrecht.

Oehrle, Richard T., Emmon Bach, and Deirdre Wheeler, editors. 1988. *Categorial Grammars and Natural Language Semantics*. D. Reidel, Dordrecht.

Steedman, Mark J. 1996. *Surface Structure and Interpretation*. The MIT Press, Cambridge, MA.

8

LFG as Concurrent Constraint Programming

Vijay Saraswat

1 Introduction

By now, LFG is a well-established framework for natural language analysis based on the inter-related notions of structure, description and correspondence (Kaplan 1989; Kaplan and Bresnan 1982). The key idea is to analyze an utterance simultaneously along several dimensions—constituent structure, functional structure, semantic structure, with provision for additional dimensions. The analyses on each dimension are not independent, rather they are tied together via *constraints*—pieces of partial information, about some finite aspects of interest. For instance, the *constituent-structure* (c-structure) of the utterance is usually described by means of a (somewhat liberal) context-free grammar. Simultaneously, via the parsing process, constraints are assembled that specify a projection from the c-structure into a *functional structure* (f-structure) that describes the grammatical relations between different constituents (e.g., SUBJ, OBJ), using attribute-value matrices. As Dalrymple et al. (1993) show, it is possible to augment such an architecture by introducing a *semantic* projection (σ-projection) from the f-structure. Inter-relationships between semantic projections are specified by means of formulas in a "glue logic" (taken to be linear logic). Conceptually, deductions with these formulas are performed simultaneously with the elaboration of the c-structure and the f-structure, resulting, on a successful analysis, with the simultaneous synthesis of the c-, f- and σ-structures of the original utterance.

A very attractive and appealing aspect of LFG's architecture is the *separation of concerns.* Different processing techniques and different vocabularies of constraints are appropriate for different aspects of analysis. It is not necessary to dictate the primacy of one dimension of analysis over another, or to use techniques from one dimension to simulate the techniques of another. Nevertheless it is possible for the analyses along these dimensions to be inter-related since each produces constraints that can influence others. This notion of *constraint-based communication* at the heart of its architecture is what crucially supports LFG's elegant compositionality, and makes it a prime exemplar of a general paradigm of *compositional computing* (Saraswat 1997). Constraints enjoy several remarkable properties (van Hentenryck and Saraswat 1996). First, they specify *partial* information—a constraint (e.g., $X + Y \geq Z$) need not uniquely specify the value of its variables, only impose certain restrictions on them. Second, they are additive: the order of imposition of constraints does not matter. Third, they are rarely independent (e.g., from $X + Y \geq Z$ and $X + Y \leq Z$ follows $X + Y = Z$), hence accumulating more constraints can yield much more information than processing them separately. Fourth, they are non-directional: typically a constraint on multiple variables can be used to infer restrictions on each of the variables, given restrictions on the others. Fifth, they are *declarative*: they specify what relationship must hold without necessarily pinning down which *algorithm* to use to actualize that relationship.

Procedural control in LFG. The ideas at the core of LFG are constraint-based, hence declarative. However, LFG originated in an analysis of the very procedural framework of augmented transition networks. A major consequence of this legacy is that several aspects of the LFG architecture are still rather *procedural* in nature. That is to say that they are described in terms of transformations on data-structures representing declarative information, but without any clear analysis of how this declarative information is *preserved* via these transformations, or how these transformations are related to well-known (meaning-preserving) transformations completely familiar from the study of logical systems.[1]

Consider as an example the detailed description of instantiation of schemas when processing a query and description of the algorithms used to solve functional constraints (the *Locate, Merge* and *Include* procedures: Kaplan and Bresnan 1982, pages 41-43, 46-50, Appendix). There is a treatment of designators such as "↑" and "↓" as "meta-variables", which have to be instantiated at run-time with new variables. It may seem that this is just the use of existential quantification in forward deduction: replacing a bound variable with a new variable that does not occur anywhere else in the sequent. However, care must be exercised because the same instantiation mechanism is also used to explain how semantic form representations are indexed during the parsing process so that two occurrences of the same morpheme *girl* are distinguished (Kaplan and Bresnan 1982, page 77). Clearly there are multiple logical notions afoot here which need to be separated for a coherent logical analysis.

Similar considerations apply to the principles of *coherence* and *completeness*. A derivation is considered to be erroneous if it causes an f-structure to possess certain attributes (called the "governable" attributes) which are not referenced in some other related attribute (e.g., PRED), or if it causes an f-structure *not* to possess a referenced attribute. These ideas are very reminiscent of other procedural notions used to describe logical systems in AI, such as closed world assumptions, and negation by failure. The implementation of these principles is described procedurally, in terms of operations that are applied to the syntactic form of the resulting constraints.

Another related procedural notion introduced in LFG is that of "sub-c" and existential constraints. A distinction is made between constraints used for generating solutions (the "normal" equational constraints), and those used for *checking* a property of solutions (the "sub-

---

[1]LFG is by no means the only architecture for reasoning to deal with declarative representations in a procedural manner. For instance, much of the work in qualitative reasoning about physical systems (Weld and de Kleer 1989), especially that of Forbus (1984), falls within this framework. With the tools described below a logical reconstruction of QPE, Forbus' Qualitative Physics Engine, seems quite plausible; naturally such a reconstruction is beyond the scope of this paper.

c″ constraints), such as the existence of a value for a particular attribute of an f-structure (the existential constraint). The "semantics" of the latter kinds of constraints is described in terms of an operation applied to the result of processing the "normal" constraints.

While linguistically motivated, the logical nature of these computational devices remains to be highlighted.

Perhaps this methodological tendency to express "control" mechanisms (in the computer science sense) via procedural means has been most highly developed in the treatment of semantic forms in LFG (Halvorsen 1983). The central question (the "semantics problem for LFG") is: how shall a semantic representation of the utterance be generated, within the LFG framework? Halvorsen proposes to employ an algorithm to "read out" the (possibly many) logical forms of the semantic representation from the f-structure generated for the utterance. There are two primary reasons for considering such a treatment deficient. First, it implies that the semantic analysis must be done *after* the f-structure analysis is complete, rather than being done simultaneously with it, during the parsing phase. This introduces an unusual asymmetry in the LFG architecture, and seems to imply that semantic information cannot simultaneously influence processing along the other dimensions (constituent structure, functional structure). Second, it becomes difficult to grasp the *validity* of the algorithm: what are the properties of the processing involved in computing the f-structure, and the algorithm in reading out the semantic form, that are crucial to establishing soundness? What are the transformations on input f-structures on which the algorithm is invariant?

It seems much more attractive to develop an alternate approach in which there is an additional dimension, along which constraints from the lexicon are composed during the parsing process (exactly as they are accumulated for the f-structure analysis), to yield the resulting semantic form directly via deduction in the "built-in" logic of the constraints.

1.1   Towards a declarative reconstruction of LFG

The desire to develop such a declarative solution for the LFG semantics problem was a prime motivation for Dalrymple et al. (1993). The basic intuition was that developments of the last many years in our understanding of how to express control declaratively could be exploited fruitfully in this setting. Further it seemed that these ideas could be extended to give a logical account of *all* of LFG.

What are these ideas for the logical description of control, and where did they come from? Let me review the history briefly, introducing the technical ideas to be used in the rest of this paper. See Saraswat (1993, Chapter 1.1, Epilog) for a fuller account.

A long tradition in logic and artificial intelligence, going back at least to Hayes (1973), has sought to treat computational systems entirely logically, under the slogan "Computation is Deduction". This means that the knowledge underlying the task domain at hand ("programs") can be specified formally as a theory in a particular logic, and that actually performing the computational task ("executing the program") can be specified as the performing of certain deductions on that theory. Typically, in this framework, one develops execution mechanisms for which soundness *and completeness* guarantees can be given: computation can be regarded as inference (soundness), in a *canonical* way so that any consequent (of a particular logical form) entailed by the theory can be derived by applying the execution mechanism.

The framework articulated in Hayes (1973) was extremely general, however. Significant progress was made with the identification of the definite clause subset (Kowalski 1974), related to work of Colmerauer on natural language processing. Procedurally, it provides *recursive and/or program schemata*: the basic control structures of recursive procedure calls, concurrency with communication, and pattern-matched selection. However, the only "data-structure" natively available within the formalism was that of (non-updatable) trees (so-called Herbrand terms).

The breakthrough with *constraint logic programming* (Jaffar and Lassez 1987; Jaffar and Maher 1994), in 1987, overcame that predicament. It embodies the realization that definite clause logic programs should be thought of as two-level declarative formalisms: the basic idea of programs as recursive and/or schemata can be applied not just over the data-structure of trees, but over any data-structure presented declaratively. In more detail, one can present a different declarative theory, the constraint theory, which captures the data-types in the computation at hand, and then use definite clauses as the program structuring mechanisms to describe computation over these constraints. Examples of constraint systems that have been integrated into this framework include finite domains (for combinatorial applications, such as scheduling), reals (for symbolic/numerical computations), feature-structures, etc.

A drawback of recursive and/or program schemata is that they do not allow *synchronization* between the different concurrently executing procedure calls. The third breakthrough (Maher 1987; Saraswat 1988, 1993), again in 1987, was that the *ad hoc* techniques being used to describe synchronization in the context of "concurrent logic programming" (Shapiro 1983; Ueda 1985) can in fact be looked at as simply checking for entailment at the level of constraints. This corresponds to adding implication to conjunction and disjunction at the level of the program schemata. This is the essential idea behind *concurrent constraint programming*.

The fourth breakthrough (Girard 1987), also in 1987, occurred with the discovery of *linear logic*, arising from a long-standing proof-theoretic research programme in constructive logics.[2] As discussed in Chapter 1, Section 2.4, linear logic highlights the notion of resource conscious manipulation of formulas during the proof-construction process. Fundamentally, this refined analysis now permits the logical treatment of some kinds of state change. By a logical treatment I mean a particular kind of a mathematical system set up within the ontology of "states of affairs" (the "models"), syntactic expressions *describing* the state of affairs, the "formulas", and rules of interpretation of the latter by the former, and rules for allowing the inference of formulas from other formulas which respect the interpretation. The model theory of linear logic is still under active development; an early treatment via "phase-spaces" was provided in Girard (1987). An intriguing treatment involving game-theoretic ideas may be found in Abramsky and Jagadeesan (1994), and in work by Blass.

---

[2]The study of subclassical logics of course has a rich history, now covered in any number of texts, going back to the work of Lambek (1958). The work of Girard has brought this area into sharp relief.

1.2   A logical foundation for LFG

This paper lays out a *logical foundation* for LFG, which allows LFG "programs" (phrase structure rules, lexical entries) to be viewed as *logical theories*. The processing done by LFG in analyzing a query using these programs is viewed merely as deriving a particular kind of formula from these theories. We do this by showing how LFG can be interpreted directly within the separately worked out framework of *(linear) concurrent constraint programming* (linear CCP: Saraswat and Lincoln 1992; Saraswat 1993). No procedural or extra-logical features are required to account for completeness and coherence conditions, or sub-c and existential constraints.

Concretely, we develop lcc(LFG)—a linear CCP language over a particular constraint system developed to express the core constraints of LFG—as an integrated declarative *programming language* for LFG, capable of accounting for the constituent, functional and semantic information. An LFG grammar (lexical entries and phrase structure rules) may be written as a *program* in lcc(LFG). The program is invoked on the presentation of a query (agent) involving the utterance to be analyzed, and on execution will either yield failure (indicating ungrammaticality of the submitted query), or a c-structure together with its associated f- and σ-structures.

There are four major advantages of establishing such a connection between lcc and LFG. First, the ad hoc syntax of LFG rules (the up- and down- arrow meta-variables, combination of context-free productions and constraints) is regularized in a standard logical notation with a well-developed (operational and logical) semantics. In essence, LFG productions and lexical entries can now be read as assertions in logic. Second, a distinction is drawn between the *reading* of a program (its *declarative* semantics) and its *execution* (its *operational* semantics), similar to the competence/performance distinction. The declarative semantics tells us what inferences can be drawn and has to be respected by the operational semantics. However, since execution will involve the search for all proofs of a particular form, various combinatorial techniques may be used to organize these searches (e.g., chart-parsing, delayed splitting (Janson and Haridi 1991), assumptive contexts (Maxwell and Kaplan 1991)). These further *algorithmic* issues can, however, be separated cleanly from the declarative specification, and can be the subject of further detailed study, without affecting *what* is computed.[3] Third, the ongoing work on exploiting the logical reading of lcc to develop complete equational reasoning systems, program transformation and static analysis techniques can now be applied to LFG programs (Saraswat et al. 1991; de Boer et al. 1997; Ruet 1997). Fourth, implemented CCP languages such as Oz (Smolka 1995) and linear Janus (Tse 1992) now become available as alternate implementation vehicles for LFG.

LFG as an exemplar of compositional computing.   On the other side, LFG can be seen as providing a very rich source of programming problems in which both the computational and logical intuitions underlying lcc may be brought into play. In some sense, natural language analysis as practiced within LFG provides a natural setting for the development of ideas related to *compositional computing* (Saraswat 1997). Compositional computing is based on the notion of solving the problem at hand by assembling on-the-fly small, highly modularized, parametric "modules" (which typically capture some declarative information of interest), and processing this assembly using a pre-existing architecture (with built-in algorithms). For instance, one may combine declarative models specifying the behavior of electro-mechanical components such as rollers and inverters to construct a model of a particular reprographics engine (e.g., photocopier); this may then be provided to a standard simulator thus obtaining a simulator for the target engine (Fromherz and Saraswat 1995).

The critical task in compositional computing is (1) designing the language in which the components can be specified, (2) specifying the components, and (3) defining the family of underlying architectures which can use the dynamically constructed assemblies. Clearly, these modules must be designed carefully—the components must be general, and yet must be usable in widely ranging contexts. For this to work, it must be possible for the component to probe the structure of

---

[3]In traditional presentations of LFG (Kaplan and Bresnan 1982), the details of the two are often intermixed, making separate development of the logical and algorithmic ideas complicated.

its environment (in so far as it is relevant to the component) and tune its "behavior" accordingly. One desires modularity, and yet sensitivity to the environment. It is our basic intuition that constraint-based communication is one way of achieving such flexible parameterization (Saraswat 1997).

These intuitions are not unrelated to the intuitions underlying the LFG architecture. The lexicon—a collection of separately specified basic constituents (words), each associated with pieces of declarative information (syntactic category, feature constraints, semantic contributions)—serves as the collection of "modules". Guided by the utterance at hand and the constituent analysis (c-structure), components are pulled together into a composition which is then "run" to yield the desired answer (constituent, feature, semantic structures). The critical task is finding a *language* rich enough to capture the nuances of the declarative information associated with components which allow these components to be used "correctly" in widely differing contexts.

Already such a view of the computational process has helped us in discovering how to represent *quantifiers*, as discussed in Chapter 2 of this volume. As we shall see later, one can think of the semantic contribution of the quantifier as probing its environment (performing an experiment) in a certain way; and then, based on the success of that experiment, offering a contribution to the environment (the meaning of the quantified phrase). It is interesting to note that the representation of quantifiers requires nested implications—and not until this analysis had been completed did I realize the power of such nested implications. It is my belief that in the extraordinarily rich setting of natural language analysis, many more such paradigmatic complex module / environment interactions are to be discovered—and hence, many more insights into the design of the programming languages which can be used to describe the modules.

Rest of this paper.   The rest of this paper is structured as follows. First I introduce the formal notation of constraints and linear CCP. Next I illustrate how LFG "programs" can be expressed in linear CCP, and show how the completeness and coherence conditions of LFG, together with the "sub-c" and "existential" "constraints" can be captured directly within linear CCP. I close with comments about related work.

2   Concurrent Constraint Programming

2.1   Constraint system

Let us start with an infinite set of variables **Var**, and a set D of formulas closed under conjunction and existential quantification. These formulas will be called *tokens* or *primitive constraints*. In general, these formulas will be related via an *entailment* relation ("$\vdash$"), which captures their "semantics". In the following, we wish to present constraint systems in a purely formal way, without any reference to models or interpretations; it may be kept in mind that one way to generate a constraint system is to fix a first-order language (e.g., Schönfinkel-Bernays subset of first-order logic: Johnson 1991) and a class of models with respect to which the language is to be interpreted (e.g., those that interpret "$+$" as real addition). This will automatically give rise to an entailment relation on formulas which satisfies the properties given below. (Note that the general setup makes no commitment to a particular choice of predicate and function symbols; these are determined by the particular application at hand.)

Definition 2.1 (Constraint System, after Saraswat (1992))
A constraint system is a pair $(D, \vdash)$ satisfying the following conditions:

1. D is a set of first-order formulas (called "tokens") closed under conjunction and existential quantification.

2. $\vdash$, a binary relation relating finite sets of tokens to tokens, satisfies the following inference rules. (In the following, a set $\{d_1, \ldots, d_n\}$ shall be written as $d_1, \ldots, d_n$.)

$$\frac{\Gamma, A, B, \Gamma' \vdash D}{\Gamma, B, A, \Gamma' \vdash D} \; (Perm) \qquad \frac{\Gamma, A, A, \Gamma' \vdash D}{\Gamma, A, \Gamma' \vdash D} \; (Dup)$$

$$\frac{\Gamma \vdash D}{\Gamma, A \vdash D} \; (Der)$$

$$\frac{}{D \vdash D} \; (Id) \qquad \frac{\Gamma \vdash A \quad A, \Gamma' \vdash D}{\Gamma, \Gamma' \vdash D} \; (Cut)$$

$$\frac{\Gamma, A, B \vdash D}{\Gamma, A \wedge B \vdash D} \; (\wedge_l) \qquad \frac{\Gamma \vdash A \quad \Gamma \vdash B}{\Gamma \vdash A \wedge B} \; (\wedge_r)$$

$$\frac{\Gamma, A \vdash D}{\Gamma, \exists X.A \vdash D} \; (\exists_l) \qquad \frac{\Gamma \vdash A[t/X]}{\Gamma \vdash \exists X.A} \; (\exists_r)$$

As usual, in $\exists_l$, the variable X must not occur free in the consequent. t is taken from a set of *terms*; the only restriction on this set is that it includes **Var**.

3. $\vdash$ is *uniform*, that is $\Gamma[t/X] \vdash d[t/X]$ whenever $\Gamma \vdash d$, for any term t.

In the following, we will also assume that D contains two constants **0** and **1** which satisfy the rules of inference:

(1)
$$\frac{}{\mathbf{0} \vdash A} \; (\mathbf{0})$$

$$\frac{\Gamma, \mathbf{1} \vdash A}{\Gamma \vdash A} \; (\mathbf{1}_l) \qquad \frac{}{\Gamma \vdash \mathbf{1}} \; (\mathbf{1}_r)$$

We shall also allow the presence of implication ($\supset$) in the constraint language (that is, if c and d are constraints, then $c \supset d$ may be a constraint as well). $\vdash$ must satisfy the additional properties:

(2)
$$\frac{\Gamma \vdash C \quad A, \Gamma' \vdash D}{\Gamma, C \supset A, \Gamma' \vdash D} \; (\supset_l) \qquad \frac{\Gamma, A \vdash D}{\Gamma \vdash A \supset D} \; (\supset_r)$$

The axioms above are the axioms for a Gentzen-style presentation of (a fragment of) intuitionistic logic. The rules (*Perm*), (*Dup*) and (*Der*) are also called *structural rules*, and essentially capture the structure of the underlying logic. They state (respectively) that the order of assumptions does not matter, that an assumption may be used more than once, and that irrelevant assumptions can be added.

From this data, one can identify *constraints* as being (usually infinite) entailed-closed subsets of D, which come naturally endowed with a lattice structure based on set inclusion (Saraswat 1992). Each token naturally generates a constraint by closing under entailment the singleton set containing that token.

A concrete constraint system is thus obtained by specifying the data $(D, \vdash)$. For most purposes it is adequate to provide an algorithmic implementation of the $\vdash$ relation (usually called a *constraint solver*). Such an implementation manages a "store" (pool) of tokens, implementing two operations: a *tell* operation that accepts a new token and integrates it into the store, and an *ask* operation that receives a token and answers whether it is entailed by the information currently known or not. In some cases (e.g., when dealing with the quantifier-free theory of equality), it is possible to build in the notion of *negation* into the constraint system; in such cases the solver may also be able to report that the negation of the query is entailed by the store.

While the *declarative* specification of the language/solver interface given above (in terms of the entailment relation) is essentially definitive, the *algorithmic* specification of the language/solver interface (and the development of constraint satisfaction techniques in particular constraint systems) is a topic of ongoing research. For instance, one looks for *incremental* algorithms for entailment, algorithms that can perform some work when given a store of constraints σ (e.g., "normalizing" the constraints) which can be reused when making inferences from σ, c. In addition, several techniques have been developed to allow the store to contain *several* (disjunctive) pools of constraints which may share some sub-structure, so as to manage the combinatorial explosion that arises with non-deterministic search. The detailed discussion of an implementation architecture that integrates all these ideas is beyond the scope of this paper. The interested reader is referred to work on AKL (Janson and Haridi 1991) and Oz (Smolka 1995), where a full programming framework is developed around these ideas.

2.2 The LFG constraint system

We now briefly sketch out **LFG**, the constraint system of interest to us. Recall that the central idea underlying LFG is that an utterance is to be simultaneously analyzed along multiple dimensions, with cross-influencing constraints. There are four dimensions of interest in this paper: the string structure (operating on the string representation), the constituent structure (operating on the phrasal structure), the functional structure (operating on a level of grammatical relations), and the semantic structure (operating on the level of logical forms). Each of these dimensions has its own vocabulary of constraints, in terms of relationships natural to that dimension.

For simplicity, we shall present the constraints in an untyped setting. That is, variables are not declared with types, and at runtime can take an element of any type as value. In practice, a typed language may be extremely desirable to allow compile-time detection of errors.

In each of these dimensions, alternate constraint systems are possible. In all cases I have tried to present as simple and standard a constraint system as I can.

String structure.   An utterance will be decomposed into a sequence of lexical items, e.g.,

$$\text{a.girl.handed.the.baby.a.toy}$$

It will be desirable to allow such strings to be decomposed via concatenation. Therefore we allow the constraints:

$$
\begin{array}{llll}
(3) & \text{(SeqTerms)} & s \; ::= \; \epsilon & \text{— Empty string} \\
 & & \quad | \quad s \circ s & \text{— String concatenations} \\
 & & \quad | \quad X & \text{— Variables} \\
 & \text{(Terms)} & t \; ::= \; s & \\
 & \text{(Constraints)} & c \; ::= \; s \sqsubseteq s & \text{— Prefixes} \\
 & & \quad | \quad s = s & \text{— Equalities}
\end{array}
$$

(We introduce a separate category of terms, distinguished from SeqTerms, because shortly we will introduce productions that allow other kinds of terms as well. Other productions may refer to terms, not just SeqTerms.)

The interpretation of these operations and relations is standard. (Note that equality can be expressed using prefix.) The processing of these constraints is well known (Jaffar 1990). Basic word unification is undecidable. However, as is standard in constraint programming, we delay the processing of complex constraints until they can be simplified to a tractable form. In this case, we delay processing constraints of the form $X = Y \circ Z$ until either Y and Z are known, or the length of Y is known, and X is known to be at least that length. In reality, these constraints will only be used in processing LFG programs in those situations in which X is known, and Y becomes known at some future time.

Constituent structure.   We need to be able to express parse trees such as:

```
s(np(det(a), n(girl)),
   vp(v(handed), np(det(the), n(baby)),
      np(det(a), n(toy)))))
```

in a simple fashion. This can be accomplished by allowing equalities over Herbrand terms, in the fashion now standard from logic programming:

$$
\begin{array}{llllll}
(4)\text{(Tree Terms)} & z & ::= & k(z_1,\ldots,z_n) & \text{— Tree constructors } (n \geq 0) \\
 & & | & X & \text{— Variables} \\
\text{(Terms)} & t & ::= & z & \\
\text{(Constraints)} & c & ::= & z = z & \text{— Equalities}
\end{array}
$$

Such constraints can be solved efficiently (linear time) via the well-known unification algorithm (Martelli and Montanari 1982). Note that we are choosing an extremely simple representation for parse trees, without concerning ourselves with issues such as ambiguity, etc. Again, we adopt the standard LFG approach along this dimension.

Feature structure.   The presentation of a feature structure constraint system is standard (Johnson 1988; Smolka 1992). Feature structures are finitary partial maps from a domain of attributes to values. The domain of attributes usually contains just constants; the domain of values contains constants as well as feature structures.

(5)   (Attributes) a $::=$ k — Constants

                                         $|$ X — Variables

         (Feature Terms) f $::=$ $f.a$ — Selections

                                         $|$ X — Variables

         (Terms) t $::=$ f — Feature structures

         (Constraints) c $::=$ $f = t$ — Equalities

                                         $|$ $t \in f$ — Set membership

Note that it is possible to state the constraint $F.X = a$, where F and X are variables. Such a constraint is not processed until X itself gets instantiated to a constant, e.g., $X = Z.r.s$, followed by $Z.r.s = b$, leading to the simplified constraint $F.b = a$.

For the purposes of this paper, we do not need a more sophisticated constraint system. Specifically, this paper will not use negation over feature structures or disjunction, even though these ideas can be (and have been) developed quite naturally in this context.

Semantic structure. For the purposes of this paper we shall assume that the semantics of an utterance is supposed to be a term in higher-order logic. As is well-known such terms can be built up simply using the simply-typed lambda calculus (together with constants, e.g., for quantification).

(6)   (Roles) r $::=$ X — Variables

      (Semantic Terms) m $::=$ $\lambda x.m$ — Abstractions

                                     $|$ $m\,m$ — Applications

                                     $|$ j — Constants

                                     $|$ x — Lambda variables

                                     $|$ X — Variables

      (Resources) q $::=$ $r \rightsquigarrow m$ — Primitive Resource

The only "constraint" related to semantic projections is the *primitive resource* $r \rightsquigarrow m$. Unlike constraints discussed above, such an atom is not allowed to be replicated freely; it is a "linear" atom, discussed below. Such an atom entails only itself; that is $r \rightsquigarrow m \vdash a$ iff $a \equiv r \rightsquigarrow m$.[4]

---

[4] Two lambda terms are considered equivalent if they are inter-convertible using α-, β- and η-conversion.

Because of the use of universal quantification (discussed below), unification problems of the form $m = m'$ may arise, requiring *higher-order* unification to be performed. Higher-order unification is undecidable (Huet 1975). However, as in all the previous examples, the use of higher-order unification in **LFG** is extremely limited. In essence, it is used only for "pattern-matching" against linear terms (terms with at most one occurrence of a variable in them). Such unifications can be solved in linear time (Miller 1990).

Projections.   Finally, each of these dimensions is to be brought together via *projections* from some top-level structure. The analysis of an utterance will be represented via projections from a structure representing the analysis.[5] We will have projections corresponding to the string (α), constituent (β), feature (ϕ) and semantic (σ) structure. Conceptually, a projection is to be thought of merely as a function.[6]

(7)   (Constraint) c $::=$ $\pi(t) = t$ — Prefix

This completes the presentation of the **LFG** constraint system. We now have enough machinery in hand to start writing LFG programs.

2.3   A concrete Icc language

We now turn to a programming language that can be used to specify the constraint problems to be solved at runtime. Assume that we have fixed a constraint system $C = (D_C, \vdash_C)$; in the following we let the meta-variable c range over D_C.

The primary syntactic category of interest is that of *agents* (A).[7] To specify that we need the auxiliary category of *guards* which describes

---

[5]Kaplan (1989) states that the domain of the various projections is the constituent structure. For the sake of symmetry, I take the approach here in which the domain of the projections is unspecified, in that it is not of interest for the present level of analysis, and the c-structure is itself regarded as a projection.

[6]In this, there is a close relationship between the computational notion of a projection and that of a feature-structure. For instance, we could express the constraint $\alpha(X) = t$ alternatively as $X.\alpha = t$. Here, as elsewhere, we seek a direct translation of LFG intuitions, rather than an encoding into some "minimal" constraint system. We seek to optimize for the researcher, rather than for the machine. (The converse is not difficult.)

[7]The notation being used here has not actually been implemented. However, all the technical ideas involved in the implementation have been worked out, and several implementations of closely related notations are now available. For someone desirous of

the *tests* on the environment that can be performed by an agent:

$$
\begin{array}{llll}
(8) & \text{(Guard)} \quad G \ ::= & c & \text{— Primitive test} \\
& \mid & q & \text{Primitive Resource} \\
& \mid & G \otimes G & \text{— Simultaneous test} \\
& \mid & \forall \bar{X}.\, G \multimap G & \text{— Recursive test}
\end{array}
$$

A test may check the environment for the presence of a constraint (c) or a primitive resource (a linear atom q). A test may perform two or more tests simultaneously. Finally, a test may be *recursive*: a test $\forall \bar{X}.\, G_1 \multimap G_2$ succeeds if there are values $\bar{t}$ for $\bar{X}$ such that the environment is able to use the resources $G_1[\bar{t}/\bar{X}]$ while passing the test $G_2[\bar{t}/\bar{X}]$.

We may now provide the definition of agents. An agent may either add a constraint or primitive resource to the store, or perform an experiment on it (reducing to another agent on success), or invoke a procedure, or split into two agents, or introduce a new local variable:

$$
\begin{array}{llll}
(9) & \text{(Agents)} \quad A \ ::= & c & \text{— Tell} \\
& \mid & q & \text{— Primitive Resource} \\
& \mid & H & \text{— Procedure Call} \\
& \mid & \forall \bar{X}.\, G \multimap A & \text{— Ask} \\
& \mid & A \ \& \ A & \text{— Choice} \\
& \mid & A \otimes A & \text{— Parallel Composition} \\
& \mid & \exists X.A & \text{— Hiding}
\end{array}
$$

Above, H ranges over the syntactic category of atomic formulas with arguments distinct variables (e.g., $p(X_1, \ldots, X_n)$). We shall identify all alpha-renamed versions of formulas; thus $\exists X.A$ shall be treated as indistinct from $\exists Y.A[Y/X]$, where Y is free for X in A.

A *user program* is a collection of axioms of the form:

$$
H :: A
$$

The free variables of A must be a subset of the free variables of H. As before, we identify alpha-renamed version of axioms. Intuitively, H is defined by A; hence it may be replaced by A.

---

doing an actual implementation of this notation, I would suggest starting with the Oz system.

2.3.1 Execution of CC programs

We can now specify what it means to execute CC programs. Define a *conjunct* to be a multiset of agents; the multiset is to be viewed as the linear (multiplicative) conjunction of its components, and the elements of the multiset will be separated by ",". Let Γ range over such (possibly empty) multisets.

We will now specify the (binary) transition relation $\longrightarrow$ on configurations. $\Gamma \longrightarrow \Gamma'$ is to be read as: "in one step, the configuration Γ evolves into Γ'." As we shall see, the transition relation will be non-deterministic.

The transition rules are as follows, one per program connective. Parallel composition is just rewritten into the conjunctive multiset:

$$(10) \qquad (\Gamma, A \otimes B) \longrightarrow (\Gamma, A, B)$$

The rule can be read as: A configuration containing a conjunct with multiset Γ and agent $A \otimes B$, can evolve into a configuration in which $A \otimes B$ is replaced by A, B.

If X is a variable not free in Γ, then we have:[8]

$$(11) \qquad (\Gamma, \exists X.A) \longrightarrow (\Gamma, A)$$

A conditional can be discharged if the associated test can be performed on the store: By $\sigma(\Gamma)$ we mean the sub-multiset of Γ containing constraint tokens. It is through this rule that the power of constraint-based communication (such as the use of $\supseteq$, Section 2.1) comes into play.

$$(12) \qquad \frac{\sigma(\Gamma), \Delta \vdash G[\bar{t}/\bar{X}]}{(\Gamma, \Delta, \forall \bar{X}.\, G \multimap A) \longrightarrow (\Gamma, A[\bar{t}/\bar{X}])}$$

A choice can be resolved via non-deterministic selection:

$$(13) \qquad (\Gamma, A_1 \,\&\, A_2) \longrightarrow (\Gamma, A_1)$$
$$(\Gamma, A_1 \,\&\, A_2) \longrightarrow (\Gamma, A_2)$$

A procedure call can be replaced by the body:

$$(14) \qquad \frac{H :: A}{(\Gamma, H) \longrightarrow (\Gamma, A)}$$

---

[8]Recall that we identify alpha-renamed versions of formulas; therefore it is always possible to find an alpha-renamed version of $\exists X.A$ such that X does not occur free in Γ.

These specify all the transition rules for programs. On presentation of a query, the transition rules are used to generate a transition sequence. A configuration Γ is said to be *final* if there is no other configuration Γ' such that $\Gamma \longrightarrow \Gamma'$. Of interest to us are *successful* configurations: these are final configurations consisting only of constraints and at most one resource. The purpose of execution is to systematically generate all distinct (non equivalent) successful configurations, given an initial configuration and an input program.

3   LFG in lcc(LFG)

We now see how to write LFG programs in lcc(LFG).

There will be no formal distinction between the translations of phrase structure rules and lexical entries; both will be translated into lcc(LFG) program axioms. Below, we defer to logic programming tradition by using "," instead of $\otimes$, to denote linear multiplicative conjunction when writing agents. We also use "," instead of $\wedge$ when writing conjunctions of constraints; no confusion should result since constraints can be syntactically distinguished from agents, because of their pre-specified vocabulary of predicates and functions.

Phrase structure rules.   Each phase structure rule is translated into a program axiom in lcc(LFG) in a natural way. For instance, the rule:

$$S \quad \longrightarrow \quad \underset{(\uparrow \text{SUBJ})\,=\,\downarrow}{NP} \quad \underset{\uparrow\,=\,\downarrow}{VP}$$

is translated to:

$$
\begin{aligned}
&\text{s}(S) :: \exists \text{NP, VP.} \\
&\quad \text{np(NP), vp(VP),} \\
&\quad \alpha(S) = \alpha(\text{NP}) \circ \alpha(\text{VP}),\ \beta(S) = \text{s}(\beta(\text{NP}),\ \beta(\text{VP})), \\
&\quad \phi(S).\text{subj} = \phi(\text{NP}),\ \phi(S) = \phi(\text{VP}).
\end{aligned}
$$

Intuitively, the rule says that an s can be decomposed into an np and vp, with the string corresponding to s being obtained by concatenating the strings corresponding to np and vp, etc.[9]

---

[9]Note that no constraint is left implicit; even the α-structure is made explicit. Of course, for ease of use a more compact notation such as that of LFG might be prefer-

The rule for NP may be translated similarly:

$$\text{NP} \longrightarrow \quad \underset{\uparrow=\downarrow}{\text{Det}} \quad \underset{\uparrow=\downarrow}{\text{N}}$$

$$\begin{aligned}
&\text{np}(\text{NP}) :: \exists \text{D, N.} \\
&\quad \text{det}(\text{D}), \ \text{n}(\text{N}), \\
&\quad \alpha(\text{NP}) = \alpha(\text{D}) \circ \alpha(\text{N}), \ \beta(\text{NP}) = \text{np}(\beta(\text{D}), \ \beta(\text{N})), \\
&\quad \phi(\text{NP}) = \phi(\text{D}), \ \phi(\text{NP}) = \phi(\text{N}).
\end{aligned}$$

There are many different types of VP rules, corresponding to intransitive VPs, transitive VPs, transitive VPs with an indirect object, etc.:

$$\text{VP} \longrightarrow \quad \underset{\uparrow=\downarrow}{\text{V}}$$

$$\text{VP} \longrightarrow \quad \underset{\uparrow=\downarrow}{\text{V}} \quad \underset{(\uparrow \text{OBJ})=\downarrow}{\text{NP}}$$

$$\text{VP} \longrightarrow \quad \underset{\uparrow=\downarrow}{\text{V}} \quad \underset{(\uparrow \text{OBJ})=\downarrow}{\text{NP}} \quad \underset{(\uparrow \text{OBJ2})=\downarrow}{\text{NP}}$$

Their translations are direct:

$$\begin{aligned}
&\text{vp}(\text{VP}) :: \\
&\quad \text{v}(\text{V}), \\
&\quad \alpha(\text{VP}) = \alpha(\text{V}), \ \beta(\text{VP}) = \text{vp}(\beta(\text{V})), \\
&\quad \phi(\text{VP}) = \phi(\text{V}).
\end{aligned}$$

$$\begin{aligned}
&\text{vp}(\text{VP}) :: \exists \text{V, NP1.} \\
&\quad \text{v}(\text{V}), \ \text{np}(\text{NP1}), \\
&\quad \alpha(\text{VP}) = \alpha(\text{V}) \circ \alpha(\text{NP1}), \ \beta(\text{VP}) = \text{vp}(\beta(\text{V}), \ \beta(\text{NP1})), \\
&\quad \phi(\text{VP}) = \phi(\text{V}), \ \phi(\text{VP}).\text{obj} = \phi(\text{NP1}).
\end{aligned}$$

$$\begin{aligned}
&\text{vp}(\text{VP}) :: \exists \text{V, NP1, NP2.} \\
&\quad \text{v}(\text{V}), \ \text{np}(\text{NP1}), \ \text{np}(\text{NP2}), \\
&\quad \alpha(\text{VP}) = \alpha(\text{V}) \circ \alpha(\text{NP1}) \circ \alpha(\text{NP2}), \ \beta(\text{VP}) = \text{vp}(\beta(\text{V}), \ \beta(\text{NP1}), \ \beta(\text{NP2})), \\
&\quad \phi(\text{VP}) = \phi(\text{V}), \\
&\quad \phi(\text{VP}).\text{obj} = \phi(\text{NP1}), \ \phi(\text{VP}).\text{obj2} = \phi(\text{NP2}).
\end{aligned}$$

---

able; here we focus on a logical notation in which the logical content of the rule is made completely explicit.

Lexical entries. The "lexicon" provides entries for particular words. Consider the LFG specification for an entry for the NP *Terry*:

Terry   NP   ($\uparrow$ PRED) = 'TERRY'

($\uparrow$ NUM) = SG

$\uparrow_\sigma \leadsto$ *Terry*

This would be represented in lcc(LFG) as:

$$np(NP) ::$$
$$\alpha(NP) = \texttt{terry}, \ \beta(NP) = np(\texttt{terry}),$$
$$\phi(NP).\texttt{num} = \texttt{sg}, \ \phi(NP).\texttt{pred} = \texttt{terry}, \ \sigma(\phi(NP)) \leadsto \texttt{terry}.$$

This should be understood as saying: an agent $np(NP)$ can be reduced, adding the constraint that the entire string corresponding to this entry is $\texttt{terry}$ (i.e., $\alpha(NP) = \texttt{terry}$), the c-structure corresponding to this entry is $np(\texttt{terry})$ (i.e., $\beta(NP) = np(\texttt{terry})$), the feature structure has an attribute $\texttt{num}$ with the value $\texttt{sg}$ and an attribute $\texttt{pred}$ with the value $\texttt{terry}$. Assume a similar entry for $\texttt{sam}$.

The lexical entries for verbs are similar.

$$v(V) ::$$
$$\alpha(V) = \texttt{greeted}, \ \beta(V) = v(\texttt{greeted}),$$
$$\phi(V).\texttt{tense} = \texttt{past}, \ \phi(V).\texttt{pred} = \texttt{greet},$$
$$\forall X, \ Y.(\sigma(\phi(V).\texttt{subj}) \leadsto X \otimes \sigma(\phi(V).\texttt{obj}) \leadsto Y$$
$$\multimap \sigma(\phi(V)) \leadsto (\phi(V).\texttt{pred})(X, \ Y)).$$

The semantic entry makes more extensive use of the logical structure available to us (linear implication). Intuitively, the rule requires merely that there be a meaning X for the subject and a meaning Y for the object of the verb phrase, and a predicate for the verb phrase; these can then be combined (with the two meanings being consumed) to produce a meaning for the entire verb phrase. It is not the purpose of this paper to argue for why the particular treatment of the σ projection makes sense here; this is the topic of other papers in this volume. Here we are concerned only with showing that they are expressible within lcc(LFG).

We can now present a derivation for the sentence *Sam greeted Terry*. This will be represented in lcc(LFG) as the initial configuration:

$$s(S), \ \alpha(S) = \texttt{sam.greeted.terry}$$

The goal s(S) may be rewritten in only one way, corresponding to the single production for S. The new configuration has new local variables NP and VP corresponding to the existentially quantified variables in the body of the clause for S, with the goals

$$(15) \qquad\qquad \mathrm{np}(\mathrm{NP}), \mathrm{vp}(\mathrm{VP}),$$

and the store:

$$(16) \quad \alpha(\mathrm{NP}) \circ \alpha(\mathrm{VP}) = \mathtt{sam.greeted.terry},$$
$$\beta(\mathrm{S}) = \mathrm{s}(\beta(\mathrm{NP}), \beta(\mathrm{VP})), \phi(\mathrm{S}).\mathtt{subj} = \phi(\mathrm{NP}), \phi(\mathrm{S}) = \phi(\mathrm{VP})$$

Notice that the store implies that $\alpha(\mathrm{NP})$ starts with the item sam.

Either of the goals may be chosen now to be rewritten; let us say we choose np(NP). All the clauses for NP will eventually yield inconsistent results save those which are consistent with $\alpha(\mathrm{NP})$ starting with sam. Consider therefore the configuration obtained by rewriting the above configuration with the clause corresponding to sam; it will have the goals

$$(17) \qquad\qquad\qquad \mathrm{vp}(\mathrm{VP})$$

and to the store (16) are added the constraints:

$$(18) \quad \alpha(\mathrm{NP}) = \mathtt{sam}, \beta(\mathrm{NP}) = \mathrm{np}(\mathtt{sam}),$$
$$\phi(\mathrm{NP}).\mathtt{num} = \mathtt{sg}, \phi(\mathrm{NP}).\mathtt{pred} = \mathtt{sam}, \sigma(\phi(\mathrm{NP})) \rightsquigarrow \mathtt{sam}$$

Notice again that this store implies that $\alpha(\mathrm{VP})$ starts with the item greeted.

There are three productions available for vp; the production corresponding to the indirect object will yield inconsistency. Again there is only one production for vp which does not lead to inconsistency; firing it yields two new local variables V and NP1. The goals in the new configuration are:

$$(19) \qquad\qquad \mathrm{v}(\mathrm{V}), \mathrm{np}(\mathrm{NP1})$$

and to the store (18) are added the constraints:

$$(20) \qquad \alpha(\text{VP}) = \alpha(\text{V}) \circ \alpha(\text{NP1}),$$
$$\beta(\text{VP}) - \text{vp}(\beta(\text{V}), \beta(\text{NP1})),$$
$$\phi(\text{VP}) = \phi(\text{V}), \phi(\text{VP}).\text{obj} = \text{NP1}$$

Note that in this store $\alpha(\text{V})$ begins with greeted. As with the subject, the v goal may make many transitions (as many as the verbs in the lexicon); the only ones that will yield a consistent result are those that are consistent with this constraint. Choosing the production corresponding to greeted we get:

$$(21) \qquad\qquad \text{np}(\text{NP1})$$

and to the store in (20) are added the constraints:

$$(22) \qquad \alpha(\text{V}) = \text{greeted}, \beta(\text{V}) = \text{v(greeted)},$$
$$\phi(\text{V}).\text{tense} = \text{past}, \phi(\text{V}).\text{pred} = \text{greet},$$
$$\forall \text{X}, \text{Y}.\sigma(\phi(\text{V}).\text{subj}) \rightsquigarrow \text{X} \otimes \sigma(\phi(\text{V}).\text{obj}) \rightsquigarrow \text{Y}$$
$$\multimap \sigma(\phi(\text{V})) \rightsquigarrow (\phi(\text{V}).\text{pred})(\text{X}, \text{Y})$$

The remaining goal may now make a transition, in a manner similar to the earlier np goal, adding to (22) the constraints:

$$(23) \qquad \alpha(\text{NP1}) = \text{terry}, \beta(\text{NP1}) = \text{np(terry)},$$
$$\phi(\text{NP1}).\text{num} = \text{sg}, \phi(\text{NP1}).\text{pred} = \text{terry}, \sigma(\phi(\text{NP1})) \rightsquigarrow \text{terry}$$

S is the only variable appearing in the original query; all others are local variables. Now the formulas:

$$\phi(\text{S}).\text{pred} = \text{greet}, \ \sigma(\phi(\text{S}).\text{subj}) \rightsquigarrow \text{sam}, \ \sigma(\phi(\text{S}).\text{obj}) \rightsquigarrow \text{terry},$$
$$\forall \text{X}, \text{Y}.(\sigma(\phi(\text{S}).\text{subj}) \rightsquigarrow \text{X} \otimes \sigma(\phi(\text{S}).\text{obj}) \rightsquigarrow \text{Y}$$
$$\multimap \sigma(\phi(\text{S})) \rightsquigarrow (\phi(\text{S}).\text{pred})(\text{X}, \text{Y}))$$

can derive:

$$\sigma(\phi(\text{S})) \rightsquigarrow \text{greet(sam, terry)}$$

yielding a configuration with no goals and with a store which contains resources and constraints equivalent to:[10]

$$\alpha(\mathrm{S}) = \mathtt{sam.greeted.terry},$$
$$\beta(\mathrm{S}) = \mathtt{s(np(sam),\ vp(v(greeted),\ np(terry)))},$$
$$\phi(\mathrm{S}).\mathtt{tense} = \mathtt{past},\ \phi(\mathrm{S}).\mathtt{pred} = \mathtt{greet},$$
$$\phi(\mathrm{S}).\mathtt{subj.num} = \mathtt{sg},\ \phi(\mathrm{S}).\mathtt{subj.pred} = \mathtt{sam},$$
$$\phi(\mathrm{S}).\mathtt{obj.num} = \mathtt{sg},\ \phi(\mathrm{S}).\mathtt{obj.pred} = \mathtt{terry},$$
$$\sigma(\phi(\mathrm{S})) \rightsquigarrow \mathtt{greet(sam,\ terry)}$$

Thus given information about the α-structure associated with S and the non-terminal s we have generated the other projections associated with S.

Double NP construction.   Let us now look at how some more sophisticated LFG programs can be represented in lcc(LFG). Consider the analysis of the sentence

(24)   A girl handed the baby a toy.

(We shall defer consideration of quantificational aspects, and the associated σ-structure, till later in this section.)

The relevant phrase structure rules corresponding to

$$\mathrm{VP} \longrightarrow \mathrm{V\ NP\ NP}$$

and

$$\mathrm{NP} \longrightarrow \mathrm{Det\ N}$$

have already been provided above.

Translating the lexical entries from Kaplan and Bresnan (1982, page 40) we get:

$\mathtt{n(N)} :: \alpha(\mathtt{N}) = \mathtt{girl},\ \beta(\mathtt{N}) = \mathtt{n(girl)},\ \phi(\mathtt{N}).\mathtt{num} = \mathtt{sg},\ \phi(\mathtt{N}).\mathtt{pred} = \mathtt{girl}.$

$\mathtt{n(N)} :: \alpha(\mathtt{N}) = \mathtt{baby},\ \beta(\mathtt{N}) = \mathtt{n(baby)},\ \phi(\mathtt{N}).\mathtt{num} = \mathtt{sg},\ \phi(\mathtt{N}).\mathtt{pred} = \mathtt{baby}.$

$\mathtt{det(D)} :: \alpha(\mathtt{D}) = \mathtt{a},\ \beta(\mathtt{D}) = \mathtt{det(a)},\ \phi(\mathtt{D}).\mathtt{num} = \mathtt{sg},\ \phi(\mathtt{D}).\mathtt{spec} = \mathtt{a}.$

$\mathtt{det(D)} :: \alpha(\mathtt{D}) = \mathtt{the},\ \beta(\mathtt{D}) = \mathtt{det(the)},\ \phi(\mathtt{D}).\mathtt{num} = \mathtt{sg},\ \phi(\mathtt{D}).\mathtt{spec} = \mathtt{the}.$

---

[10]Note that consistent constraints on variables all of which are existentially quantified are logically equivalent to the vacuous constraint and can hence be dropped when finding a "canonical" form.

The entry for *handed* is similar to the entry for *greeted*:

v(V) ::
  α(V) = handed, β(V) = v(handed),
  ϕ(V).tense = past, ϕ(V).pred = 'hand$\langle$($\uparrow$ subj), ($\uparrow$ obj), ($\uparrow$ obj2)$\rangle$',
  $\forall$X, Y, Z.(σ(ϕ(V).subj) $\rightsquigarrow$ X $\otimes$ σ(ϕ(V).obj) $\rightsquigarrow$ Y $\otimes$ σ(ϕ(V).obj2) $\rightsquigarrow$ Z
          $\multimap$ σ(ϕ(V)) $\rightsquigarrow$ (ϕ(V).pred)(X, Y, Z)).

With these entries, the systematic expansion of the previous example can be carried through to show that there is only one successful derivation from the initial query:

$$s(S), \ \alpha(S) = \texttt{a.girl.handed.the.baby.a.toy}$$

yielding:

α(S) = a.girl.handed.the.baby.a.toy,
  β(S) = s(np(det(a), n(girl)),
          vp(v(handed), np(det(the), n(baby)),
             np(det(a), n(toy)))),
  ϕ(S).[tense = past, pred = 'hand$\langle$($\uparrow$ subj), ($\uparrow$ obj), ($\uparrow$ obj2)$\rangle$'],
  ϕ(S).subj.[spec = a, num = sg, pred = girl],
  ϕ(S).obj.[spec = the, num = sg, pred = baby],
  ϕ(S).obj2.[spec = a, num = sg, pred = toy]

Here we use an obvious shorthand to summarize a set of equations on nested feature structures.

Double NP, with completeness and coherence. A problem with the above formulation is that ill-formed sentences such as

(25)   *The girl handed.

can also be parsed, via the intransitive VP rule. One gets for the query:

$$s(S), \ \alpha(S) = \texttt{the.girl.handed}$$

the result:

$\alpha(S) = $ `the.girl.handed`,

  $\beta(S) = $ `s(np(det(the), n(girl)), vp(v(handed)))`

  $\phi(S)$`.tense = past, pred = 'hand`$\langle(\uparrow$ `subj`$), (\uparrow$ `obj`$), (\uparrow$ `obj2`$)\rangle$`'`,

  $\phi(S)$`.subj.spec = the, num = sg, pred = girl`

Notice that the `pred` refers to features in the f-structure (e.g., OBJ) which do not exist.

To get around this, LFG introduces the *completeness* and *coherence* "implicit convention" (Kaplan and Bresnan 1982, pages 64-65):

> These conventions are defined in terms of a proper subset of all the features and functions that may be represented in an f-structure ... We refer to these as the *governable grammatical functions*. A given lexical entry mentions only a few of the governable functions, and we say that that entry *governs* the ones it mentions. Our conditions of functional compatibility simply require that an f-structure contain all the governable functions that the lexical entry of its predicate actually governs, and that it contain no other governable function.

Thus sentence (25) would be rejected because the corresponding f-structure does not contain the functions OBJ and OBJ2 governed by the lexical entry for *handed*.

How might this be represented directly in lcc(LFG) without recourse to "implicit conventions" or procedural post-processing? For convenience, let us introduce the shorthand t $\downarrow$ for the constraint $\exists$k.t $=$ k, where t is a feature-term. We would locally modify the rule for *handed* to explicitly express the completeness and coherence condition:

`v(V)` ::

  $\alpha(V) = $ `handed`, $\beta(V) = $ `v(handed)`,

  $\phi(V)$`.tense = past`,

  $(\phi(V)$`.subj` $\downarrow \otimes \phi(V)$`.obj` $\downarrow \otimes \phi(V)$`.obj2` $\downarrow$

        $\multimap \phi(V)$`.pred = 'hand`$\langle(\uparrow$ `subj`$), (\uparrow$ `obj`$), (\uparrow$ `obj2`$)\rangle$`'`$)$,

  $\exists$F. `(phi(V).F` $\downarrow$`, governable(F), F` $\neq$ `subj, F` $\neq$ `obj, F` $\neq$ `obj2` $\supset$ **0**$)$.

The penultimate agent specifies that the PRED contribution to the f-structure cannot be made until and unless the referenced features exist. If any one of the referenced features does not exist, the final configuration will have an undischarged implication (a "suspended" agent), and hence will not yield an answer to the original query. The final agent is a constraint that is added to the store—this constraint ensures that every consistent store is such that there is no other governable function, distinct from the ones referenced, associated with $\phi(V)$. For if there is one, this constraint will ensure that the token $\mathbf{0}$ is added to the store, thereby rendering it inconsistent.[11]

Thus the coherence and completeness conditions can be handled directly within the logic of lcc(LFG), without extra-logical stipulations.

Double NP, with semantics.   We now consider adding in the contributions of each lexical entry along the semantic dimension. We will see that this will obviate the necessity of adding the completeness and coherence conditions explicitly.

The main idea, already introduced, is that the semantic contribution of each lexical entry will be in the form of an agent, possibly involving resources of the form $r \rightsquigarrow t$. All semantic entries except that corresponding to the entire utterance must be consumed, producing a meaning of the form $S \rightsquigarrow t$, for S the variable corresponding to the utterance. The semantic contributions of lexical entries such as those for verbs expect the environment to supply contributions for the grammatical functions of interest to them; these are consumed and then the semantic contribution of the entry is produced. If the parse is such that these grammatical functions to be consumed are not generated, then the derivation will not yield a result of the desired form, and will hence be considered erroneous. If the parse is such that extra semantic contributions are generated, e.g. for the erroneous sentence *A girl greeted the toy the baby*, then extra resources will be left over and again a result of the desired form will not be generated. Thus, a treatment of the semantic dimen-

---

[11] If there isn't, no particularly interesting consequences may be drawn from the presence of this constraint in the store. Crucially, it will still be possible to get a successful configuration, since this formula is just a constraint, and constraints may appear in the final result. This is the crucial reason why $\supset$ is necessary here, and may not be replaced by $\multimap$.

sion takes these semantic dependencies systematically and explicitly into account.

Consider the semantic contributions in more detail. The entries for n are all similar; in particular, a resource capturing the semantic contribution:

$$n(N) ::$$
$$\alpha(N) = \texttt{girl}, \ \beta(N) = n(\texttt{girl}),$$
$$\phi(N).\texttt{num} = \texttt{sg}, \ \phi(N).\texttt{pred} = \texttt{girl},$$
$$\forall X. \ \sigma(\phi(N)).\texttt{var} \rightsquigarrow X \multimap \sigma(\phi(N)).\texttt{restr} \rightsquigarrow \texttt{girl}(X).$$

The entry for *handed* is similarly modified to be:

$$v(V) ::$$
$$\alpha(V) = \texttt{handed}, \ \beta(V) = v(\texttt{handed}),$$
$$\phi(V).\texttt{tense} = \texttt{past}, \ \phi(V).\texttt{pred} = {}'\texttt{hand}\langle(\uparrow \texttt{subj}), (\uparrow \texttt{obj}), (\uparrow \texttt{obj2})\rangle{}',$$
$$\forall X, \ Y, \ Z.(\sigma(\phi(V).\texttt{subj}) \rightsquigarrow X \otimes \sigma(\phi(V).\texttt{obj}) \rightsquigarrow Y \otimes \sigma(\phi(V).\texttt{obj2}) \rightsquigarrow Z$$
$$\multimap \sigma(\phi(V)) \rightsquigarrow (\phi(V).\texttt{pred})(X, \ Y, \ Z)).$$

The translation of the entry for the article *a* is similar, except that the semantic treatment, along the lines of generalized quantifiers, is more sophisticated.

$$det(D) ::$$
$$\alpha(D) = \texttt{a}, \ \beta(D) = det(\texttt{a}),$$
$$\phi(D).\texttt{num} = \texttt{sg}, \ \phi(D).\texttt{spec} = \texttt{a},$$
$$\forall H, \ R, \ S.(\forall x.(\sigma(\phi(D)).\texttt{var} \rightsquigarrow x \multimap (\sigma(\phi(D)).\texttt{restr} \rightsquigarrow Rx)$$
$$\otimes (\forall x.\sigma(\phi(D)) \rightsquigarrow x \multimap H \rightsquigarrow Sx)$$
$$\multimap H \rightsquigarrow (\phi(D).\texttt{spec})(z, \ Rz, \ Sz)).$$

(For simplicity, we treat *the girl* as a generalized quantifier as well; therefore the entry for *the* is identical to the one above, except that "the" is replaced uniformly for "a".)

Intuitively, the semantic entry says that the meaning of some term H is $a(z, Rz, Sz)$, for some values of H, R and S provided that certain conditions are satisfied. Namely, it must be possible to successfully conduct two "experiments" on the environment. The first experiment provides to the environment the resource $\sigma(\phi(D)).\texttt{var} \rightsquigarrow x$ and demands that the environment should be able to consume that resource and produce the resource $(\sigma(\phi(\text{D})).\mathtt{restr} \rightsquigarrow \text{Rx})$ (which intuitively represents the restriction of the generalized quantifier). The second experiment similarly provides to the environment the resource $\sigma(\phi(\text{D})) \rightsquigarrow \text{x}$ (the "hypothesized" individual meaning x for the definite article) and demands that the environment consume it and produce the resource $\text{H} \rightsquigarrow \text{Sx}$ which specifies the meaning of the selected scope. For a more detailed elaboration, see Chapter 2.

The *to* construction. We turn now to the handling of prepositional phrases to show how regular expressions in LFG grammar rules can be handled in lcc(LFG). Consider the analysis of the sentence *The girl handed a toy to the baby.* To analyze this, Kaplan and Bresnan (1982, pages 51–54) introduce the rules:

$$
\begin{array}{lllll}
\text{VP} \longrightarrow & \text{V} & (\text{NP}) & (\text{NP}) & \text{PP}^* \\
 & & ((\uparrow \text{OBJ}) = \downarrow) & ((\uparrow \text{OBJ2}) = \downarrow) & (\uparrow (\downarrow \text{PCASE})) = \downarrow
\end{array}
$$

$$
\begin{array}{lll}
\text{PP} \longrightarrow & \text{P} & \text{NP} \\
 & & (\uparrow \text{OBJ}) = \downarrow
\end{array}
$$

These rules introduce three new features: an optional grammatical category, a Kleene-starred category, and the use of an expression $((\downarrow \text{PCASE}))$ to select an attribute of an f-structure. The first can be handled straightforwardly using &: in the optional branch, the α and β components are null, and there is no contribution to the feature structure. Kleene star can be handled via iteration in the goal structure. The β-contributions of each element in the iterative loop are concatenated together into a list, parallel to the α-contributions. The f-structure contribution has to be specified explicitly by the person providing the phrase-structure rule. In this case, the PCASE attribute of each prepositional phrase is used to determine where the f-structure of the element is to be added to the f-structure of the phrase:

$\text{vp}(\text{VP}) :: \exists \text{V, NP, NP2, PP}.$
$\quad \text{v}(\text{V}), \; ((\text{np}(\text{NP}), \; \phi(\text{VP}).\texttt{obj} = \phi(\text{NP})) \; \& \; \text{null}(\text{NP})),$
$\quad ((\text{np}(\text{NP2}), \; \phi(\text{VP}).\texttt{obj2} = \phi(\text{NP2})) \; \& \; \text{null}(\text{NP2})),$
$\quad \text{pcase}(\text{VP, PP}),$
$\quad \alpha(\text{VP}) = \alpha(\text{V})\text{o}\alpha(\text{NP})\text{o}\alpha(\text{NP2})\text{o}\alpha(\text{PP}), \quad \cdot$
$\quad \beta(\text{VP}) = \text{vp}(\beta(\text{V}), \; \beta(\text{NP}), \; \beta(\text{NP2}), \; \beta(\text{PP})).$
$\text{null}(\text{NP}) :: \alpha(\text{NP}) = \epsilon, \; \beta(\text{NP}) = \epsilon.$
$\text{pcase}(\text{VP, P}) :: \text{null}(\text{P}).$
$\text{pcase}(\text{VP, P}) :: \exists \text{P1, P2}.$
$\quad \text{pp}(\text{P1}), \; \text{pcase}(\text{VP, P2}),$
$\quad \alpha(\text{P}) = \alpha(\text{P1}) \circ \alpha(\text{P2}), \; \beta(\text{P}) = \beta(\text{P1}) \circ \beta(\text{P2}),$
$\quad \phi(\text{VP}).(\phi(\text{P1}).\texttt{pcase}) = \phi(\text{P1}).$
$\text{pp}(\text{PP}) :: \exists \text{P, NP}.$
$\quad \text{p}(\text{P}), \; \text{np}(\text{NP}),$
$\quad \alpha(\text{PP}) = \alpha(\text{P}) \circ \alpha(\text{NP}), \; \beta(\text{PP}) = \text{pp}(\beta(\text{P}), \; \beta(\text{NP})),$
$\quad \sigma(\phi(\text{PP}).\texttt{obj}) = \sigma(\phi(\text{NP})).$

As in LFG, it is not possible for there to be two distinct prepositional phrases with the same PCASE; for the last constraint in `pcase/2` would then introduce an inconsistency.

To the earlier lexical entries for *handed* is now added:

$\text{v}(\text{V}) ::$
$\quad \alpha(\text{V}) = \text{handed}, \; \beta(\text{V}) = \text{v}(\text{handed}),$
$\quad \phi(\text{V}).\texttt{tense} = \text{past}, \; \phi(\text{V}).\texttt{pred} = \text{'hand}\langle(\uparrow \texttt{subj}), \; (\uparrow \texttt{obj}), \; (\uparrow \texttt{to} \; \texttt{obj})\rangle',$
$\quad \forall \text{X, Y, Z}.(\sigma(\phi(\text{V}).\texttt{subj}) \rightsquigarrow \text{X} \otimes \sigma(\phi(\text{V}).\texttt{obj}) \rightsquigarrow \text{Y} \otimes \sigma(\phi(\text{V}).\texttt{to.obj}) \rightsquigarrow \text{Z}$
$\qquad \multimap \sigma(\phi(\text{V})) \rightsquigarrow (\phi(\text{V}).\texttt{pred})(\text{X, Y, Z})).$

And the entry for *to* is:

$\quad \text{p}(\text{P}) ::$
$\qquad \alpha(\text{P}) = \text{to}, \; \beta(\text{P}) = \text{p}(\text{to}), \; \phi(\text{P}).\texttt{pcase} = \text{to}.$

These are adequate to derive the readings of this sentence, as in Kaplan and Bresnan (1982).

'Sub-c' constraint. As discussed in Kaplan and Bresnan (1982, pages 59–62), it is sometimes necessary to specify that a particular constraint must be present. This can be directly stated within lcc(LFG): it corresponds to an agent which performs an experiment on its environment to check that the constraint is present. For instance the entry:

$$
\begin{aligned}
\text{is} \quad\quad \text{V} \quad & (\uparrow \text{TENSE}) = \text{PRES} \\
& (\uparrow \text{SUBJ NUM}) = \text{SG} \\
& (\uparrow \text{PRED}) = \text{'PROG}\langle(\uparrow \text{VCOMP})\rangle\text{'} \\
& (\uparrow \text{VCOMP PARTICIPLE}) =_c \text{PRESENT} \\
& (\uparrow \text{VCOMP SUBJ}) = (\uparrow \text{SUBJ})
\end{aligned}
$$

can be translated to:

$$
\begin{aligned}
&\texttt{v(V)} :: \\
&\quad \alpha(\texttt{V}) = \texttt{is}, \ \beta(\texttt{V}) = \texttt{v(is)}, \\
&\quad \phi(\texttt{V}).\texttt{subj.num} = \texttt{sg}, \ \phi(\texttt{V}).\texttt{pred} = \text{'}\texttt{prog}\langle(\uparrow \texttt{vcomp})\rangle\text{'}, \\
&\quad \phi(\texttt{V}).\texttt{vcomp.participle} = \texttt{present} \multimap 1, \\
&\quad \phi(\texttt{V}).\texttt{vcomp.subj} = \phi(\texttt{V}).\texttt{subj}.
\end{aligned}
$$

The "sub-c" constraint is merely an agent that checks the constraint, and reduces to 1 if it is satisfied; otherwise the agent will not fire, thus preventing any configuration including it from becoming successful.

Existential constraint. Just as one may require that a certain feature have a certain value, it is easy to state merely that a certain feature exists. Consider the phrase structure rule (Kaplan and Bresnan 1982, (71), page 63), where the notation $'(\uparrow \text{TENSE})'$ means that $\phi(\texttt{S}).\texttt{tense}$ is defined:

$$
\begin{array}{ccc}
\text{S} \ \longrightarrow & \text{NP} & \text{VP} \\
& (\uparrow \text{SUBJ}) = \downarrow & \uparrow = \downarrow \\
& (\downarrow \text{CASE}) = \text{NOM} & (\uparrow \text{SUBJ TENSE})
\end{array}
$$

This can be translated into:

$$\text{s}(\text{S}) :: \exists \text{NP, VP}.$$
$$\text{np}(\text{NP}), \text{vp}(\text{VP}),$$
$$\alpha(\text{S}) = \alpha(\text{NP}) \circ \alpha(\text{VP}),\ \beta(\text{S}) = \text{s}(\beta(\text{NP}), \beta(\text{VP})),$$
$$\phi(\text{S}).\text{subj} = \phi(\text{NP}),\ \phi(\text{NP}).\text{case} = \text{nom},$$
$$\phi(\text{S}) = \phi(\text{VP}),\ (\phi(\text{VP}).\text{tense} \downarrow \multimap 1).$$

Thus we can state that it is required that there be a value for $\phi(\text{VP}).\text{tense}$.

Negative existential constraint.   Suppose that it is required to state that a VP after the particle *to* in a VP′ is untensed. In LFG this is stated as (Kaplan and Bresnan 1982, (73), page 64):

$$\text{VP}' \longrightarrow \qquad (to) \qquad \text{VP}$$
$$\neg(\uparrow\text{TENSE}) \qquad \uparrow = \downarrow$$

This is translated in lcc(LFG) to:

$$\text{vp}'(\text{VP}') :: \exists \text{To, VP}.$$
$$((\alpha(\text{To}) = \text{to},\ \beta(\text{To}) = \text{to},\ \phi(\text{VP}').\text{tense} \downarrow \supset \mathbf{0},\ \text{vp}(\text{VP})) \ \&\ \text{null}(\text{To})),$$
$$\alpha(\text{VP}') = \alpha(\text{To}) \circ \alpha(\text{VP}),\ \beta(\text{VP}') = \text{vp}'(\beta(\text{To}), \beta(\text{VP})).$$

The *to* contribution is optional; but if present, it will ensure that the VP′ does not have a TENSE, in any successful derivation.

Adjuncts.   As our last example of the translation of complex LFG phrase structure rules, consider the rule for adjuncts (Kaplan and Bresnan 1982, (89), page 70). (Again we analyze this rule purely for its computational content, not addressing the question of its linguistic validity.)

$$\text{VP} \longrightarrow$$

V	(NP)	(NP)	PP*	(VP)
	$((\uparrow\text{OBJ})=\downarrow)$	$((\uparrow\text{OBJ2})=\downarrow)$	$\{(\uparrow(\downarrow \text{PCASE})) = \downarrow \mid$	$((\uparrow\text{VCOMP}) = \downarrow)$
			$\downarrow \in (\uparrow\text{ADJUNCTS})\}$	

The complexity of this rule arises from the fact that the within the Kleene-star, the f-structure of the contribution of the PP may be chosen arbitrarily. Further, each of the matched PP phrases may contribute to the f-structure for the entire PP* phrase, through set-membership.

It is for situations such as this that set-membership constraints are included in lcc(LFG). The "control-logic" can be specified using the techniques shown earlier. Thus we have the translation:

$$vp(\text{VP}) :: \exists V,\ NP1,\ NP2,\ PP,\ VP'.$$
$$v(V),$$
$$(np(NP1),\ \phi(\text{VP}).\mathtt{obj} = \phi(NP1)\ \&\ \mathtt{null}(NP1)),$$
$$(np(NP2),\ \phi(\text{VP}).\mathtt{obj} = \phi(NP2)\ \&\ \mathtt{null}(NP2)),$$
$$ppmod(PP,\ VP),$$
$$(vp(VP'),\ \phi(\text{VP}).\mathtt{vcomp} = \phi(VP')\ \&\ \mathtt{null}(VP')),$$
$$\alpha(\text{VP}) = \alpha(V) \circ \alpha(NP1) \circ \alpha(NP2) \circ \alpha(PP) \circ \alpha(VP'),$$
$$\beta(\text{VP}) = vp(\beta(V),\ \beta(NP1),\ \beta(NP2),\ \beta(PP),\ \beta(VP')).$$
$$ppmod(PP,\ VP) :: \mathtt{null}(PP).$$
$$ppmod(PP,\ VP) :: \exists PP1.$$
$$pp(PP1),\ ppmod(PP2,\ VP),$$
$$(\phi(\text{VP}).(\phi(VP1).\mathtt{pcase}) = \phi(VP1)\ \&\ \phi(VP1) \in \phi(\text{VP}).\mathtt{adjuncts})$$
$$\alpha(PP) = \alpha(PP1) \circ \alpha(PP2),\ \beta(PP) = \beta(PP1) \circ \beta(PP2).$$

Note that the definition of `null(NP)` has been given earlier.

4   Related Work

There has been considerable work (Johnson 1988) in formalizing the "logic of feature structures" used in LFG; but, to my knowledge, no prior work on expressing logically the control flow of LFG, other than the work on semantics presented in this volume.

Chapter 10 of this volume presents work by Mark Johnson on using a propositional sub-structural logic to account for all aspects of LFG. In my opinion, that paper offers a very interesting and somewhat radical view, attempting to cast LFG entirely within the categorial approach to natural language processing, and seeking to exploit the Curry-Howard isomorphism to carry through some of the formal infrastructure in an elegant way. The work, however, seems to require the development of some approaches to linguistic problems different from the ones traditionally taken by LFG, and seems a very promising area for future work. My tack in this paper has been to not break any new linguistic ground; rather I have attempted to place LFG, as it is commonly understood today, on a firm logical basis, using existing ideas from linear concurrent constraint programming.

Chapter 9 of this volume presents an approach by Dick Oehrle on an alternate logical formulation of LFG, using the framework of labeled deduction. In its current formulation, the approach has difficulty dealing with some of the computational apparatus of LFG, such as "negative" constraints. (We are agnostic about the desirability of such constraints from a linguistic viewpoint.) In the long run, it is not clear whether the specific computational apparatuses introduced in Kaplan and Bresnan (1982) will remain the apparatuses of choice, and clearly there is considerable room for exploration, even while respecting the general architectural framework of LFG. Again, my focus on this paper has been to analyze LFG "as is".

Perhaps the single biggest feature of LFG that remains unanalyzed in this paper is functional uncertainty. I do not expect this to present any conceptual problems; however this must remain the topic of future work.

From the logical point of view, it seems clear that there remains considerable untapped expressiveness in the whole arena of substructural logics. For example, one may consider the extra structure of full linear logic, specifically the multiplicative disjunction, following the work of authors such as Jean-Marc Andreoli, Dale Miller and Joshua Hodas. One may even investigate the development of specialized substructural logics especially designed to allow for a perspicuous treatment of certain linguistic phenomena, as done by authors such as Moortgat. Our philosophy has been to be fairly conservative in our use of logic, and fairly innovative in the "programming" idioms used within the logic to capture linguistic ideas. Again, an analogy with programming languages is useful: one does not change the programming language unless there is strong reason to. Nevertheless, considerable work remains ahead to explore this territory in a principled way.

Acknowledgments

For many reasons, this paper—many many years in discussion and planning—would not have been possible without Mary Dalrymple. To her I owe my heartfelt thanks. I would not have been able to enter and retain my interest in this field without the sustaining collaboration and partnership with Mary Dalrymple and John Lamping. In addition, I particularly want to thank our co-authors on various papers in this area from each of whom I have learnt a lot. Ron Kaplan and John Maxwell have always been generous with their time, ideas and feedback over the years. I am happy to offer this paper to them as the first concrete manifestation of a series of discussions initiated with them when I joined PARC in 1987. I believe this paper is as relevant now as it would have been if it had come out when all the pieces first came together many years ago. I thank Mark Johnson, John Fry, Fernando Pereira and the referees for detailed and useful comments. As usual, whatever errors remain in this paper are entirely due to me. Finally, on a personal note, I want to thank Neeta Saraswat for constructing in the midst of an otherwise very hectic space-time, islands of peace within which to finish this paper.

References

Dalrymple, Mary, John Lamping, and Vijay Saraswat. 1993. LFG semantics via constraints. In *Proceedings of the Sixth Meeting of the European ACL*, University of Utrecht, pages 97–105. European Chapter of the Association for Computational Linguistics.

Abramsky, Samson and Radha Jagadeesan. 1994. Games and full completeness for multiplicative linear logic. *Journal of Symbolic Logic*, 59(2):543–574.

de Boer, Frank S., Maurizio Gabbrielli, Elena Marchiori, and Catuscia Palamidessi. 1997 Proving concurrent constraint programs correct. *ACM Transactions on Programming Languages and Systems (TOPLAS)*, 19(5):685–725.

Forbus, Kenneth D. 1984. *Qualitative process theory*. PhD thesis, MIT.

Fromherz, Markus P.J. and Vijay A. Saraswat. 1995. Model-based computing: Constructing constraint-based software for electro-mechanical systems. In *Proceedings of the Conference on Practical Applications of Constraint Technology*, Paris, pages 63–66.

Girard, Jean-Yves. 1987. Linear logic. *Theoretical Computer Science*, 50(1):1–102.

Halvorsen, Per-Kristian. 1983. Semantics for Lexical-Functional Grammar. *Linguistic Inquiry*, 14(4):567–615.

Hayes, Patrick J. 1973. Computation and deduction. In *Proceedings of the Second Symposium on Mathematical Foundations of Computer Science*. Czechoslovakian Academy of Sciences, Czechoslovakia.

Huet, Gérard. 1975. A unification algorithm for typed $\bar{\lambda}$-calculus. *Theoretical Computer Science*, 1:27–57.

Jaffar, Joxan and Jean-Louis Lassez. 1987. Constraint logic programming. In *Fourteenth Annual ACM Symposium on Principles of Programming Languages*, Munich, Germany, pages 111–119.

Jaffar, Joxan. 1990. Minimal and complete word unification. *Journal of the ACM*, 37(1):47–85.

Jaffar, Joxan and Michael J. Maher. 1994. Constraint logic programming: A survey. *Journal of Logic Programming*, 19/20:503–581.

Janson, Sverker and Seif Haridi. 1991. Programming Paradigms of the Andorra Kernel Language. In Vijay Saraswat and Kazunori Ueda, editors, *Logic Programming: Proceedings of the 1991 International Symposium*. The MIT Press, Cambridge, MA.

Johnson, Mark. 1988. *Attribute-Value Logic and the Theory of Grammar*. PhD thesis, Stanford University. Published in CSLI Lecture Notes, number 16. CSLI Publications, Stanford University.

Johnson, Mark. 1991. Logic and feature structures. In *Proceedings of the Twelfth International Joint Conference on Artificial Intelligence*, pages 992–996, 1991. Reprinted in Mary Dalrymple, Ronald M. Kaplan, John Maxwell, and Annie Zaenen, editors, *Formal Issues in Lexical-Functional Grammar*, pages 369–380. CSLI Publications, Stanford University. 1995.

Kaplan, Ronald M. and Joan Bresnan. 1982. Lexical-Functional Grammar: A formal system for grammatical representation. In Joan Bresnan, editor, *The Mental Representation of Grammatical Relations*, pages 173–281. The MIT Press, Cambridge, MA. Reprinted in Mary Dalrymple, Ronald M. Kaplan, John Maxwell, and Annie Zaenen, editors, *Formal Issues in Lexical-Functional Grammar*, pages 29–130. CSLI Publications, Stanford University. 1995.

Kaplan, Ronald M. 1989. The formal architecture of Lexical-Functional Grammar. In Chu-Ren Huang and Keh-Jiann Chen, editors, *Proceedings of ROCLING II*, pages 3–18, 1989. Reprinted in Mary Dalrymple, Ronald M. Kaplan, John Maxwell, and Annie Zaenen, editors, *Formal Issues in Lexical-Functional Grammar*, pages 7–27. CSLI Publications, Stanford University. 1995.

Kowalski, Robert 1974. Predicate logic as a programming language. In Jack L. Rosenfeld, editor, *Information Processing 74, Proceedings of IFIP Congress 74*, Stockholm, Sweden, pages 569–573. North-Holland, Amsterdam.

Lambek, Joachim. 1958. The mathematics of sentence structure. *American Mathematical Monthly*, 65:154–170.

Maher, Michael. 1987. Logic semantics for a class of committed-choice programs. In Jean-Louis Lassez, editor, *Logic Programming: Proceedings of the Fourth International Conference*, Melbourne, Victoria, Australia, pages 858–876. MIT Press, Cambridge.

Martelli, Alberto and Ugo Montanari. 1982. An efficient unification algorithm. *ACM Transactions on Programming Languages and Systems (TOPLAS)*, 4(2):258–282.

Maxwell, III, John T. and Ronald M. Kaplan. 1991. A method for disjunctive constraint satisfaction. In Masaru Tomita, editor, *Current Issues in Parsing Technology*, pages 173–190, Dordrecht. Kluwer Academic Publishers. Revised version of 'An overview of disjunctive constraint satisfaction', Maxwell and Kaplan, 1989. Proceedings of the International Workshop on Parsing Technologies. Reprinted in Mary Dalrymple, Ronald M. Kaplan, John Maxwell, and Annie Zaenen, editors, *Formal Issues in Lexical-Functional Grammar*, pages 381–401. CSLI Publications, Stanford University. 1995.

Miller, Dale A. 1990. A logic programming language with lambda abstraction, function variables and simple unification. In Peter Schroeder-Heister, editor, *Extensions of Logic Programming*, Lecture Notes in Artificial Intelligence. Springer-Verlag.

Ruet, Paul. 1997. *Logique Linéaire et Programmation Concurrente par Contraintes*. PhD thesis, Ecole Normale Supérieure.

Saraswat, Vijay A. 1988. A somewhat logical formulation of CLP synchronization primitives. In Robert A. Kowalski and Kenneth A. Bowen, editors, *Logic Programming: Proceedings of the Fifth International Conference and Symposium*, Seattle, Washington, pages 1298–1314. The MIT Press, Cambridge.

Saraswat, Vijay A., Martin Rinard, and Prakash Panangaden. 1991. Semantic foundations of concurrent constraint programming. In *Proceedings of the Eighteenth Annual ACM Symposium on Principles of Programming Languages*, Orlando, pages 333–352.

Saraswat, Vijay A. 1992. The Category of Constraint Systems is Cartesian-closed. In *Proceedings of the IEEE Symposium on Logic in Computer Science*, Santa Cruz, pages 341–345.

Saraswat, Vijay A. and Patrick Lincoln. 1992. Higher-order, linear concurrent constraint programming. Technical report, Xerox Palo Alto Research Center.

Saraswat, Vijay A. 1993. *Concurrent Constraint Programming*. The MIT Press, Cambridge.

Saraswat, Vijay A. 1997. Compositional computing. *Constraints: An International Journal*, 2:95–97.

Shapiro, Ehud. 1983. A subset of Concurrent Prolog and its interpreter. Technical Report CS83-06, Weizmann Institute.

Smolka, Gert. 1992. Feature-constraint logics for unification grammars. *Journal of Logic Programming*, 12(1/2):51–87.

Smolka, Gert. 1995. The Oz programming model. In Jan van Leeuwen, editor, *Computer Science Today*, Lecture Notes in Computer Science, vol. 1000, pages 324–343. Springer-Verlag, Berlin.

Tse, Clifford. 1992. Linear Janus: A concurrent programming language. Master's thesis, MIT. Also: Technical Report, Xerox PARC.

Ueda, Kazunori 1985. Guarded horn clauses. Technical Report TR-103, ICOT.

van Hentenryck, Pascal and Vijay A. Saraswat, editors. 1996. *Constraint Programming*. ACM Computing Surveys.

Weld, Daniel and Johan de Kleer. 1989. *Readings in Qualitative Reasoning about Physical Systems*. Morgan Kaufmann, Los Altos.

9

LFG as Labeled Deduction

Dick Oehrle

This paper looks at Lexical Functional Grammar as a form of Labeled Deduction. It has both a general rationale and a specific one. The broad framework of Labeled Deductive Systems (Gabbay 1996) offers a setting in which it is possible to formulate and compare a variety of different grammatical architectures. Attempting to formulate LFG within this setting, then, should allow us to see more clearly how its properties compare with the properties of alternative approaches to grammatical analysis. Just as a general comparison along these lines might make it possible to discern which properties of LFG are shared with alternative approaches and which are really distinctive, it also makes it possible to consider a similar range of questions with regard to specific analyses of grammatical phenomena. The specific analysis of interest here is the treatment of quantification proposed in recent work presented in Chapter 2, which is the focus of this collection.[1]

In Section 1, I sketch the basic properties of Labeled Deduction and give a few pertinent examples, and in Section 2, I present the key fea-

---

[1] After writing the paper, I learned of other work looking at LFG from this general perspective, especially König (1995) and Dörre, König, and Gabbay (1995). The first illustrates how grammars in the LFG style containing subcategorization information, long-distance dependencies (functional uncertainty), and adjunction, can be transformed into a lexicalized form of labeled deduction, with feature-structures labeling categories. The second provides a general logical perspective—proof theory and model theory—on the combination of two logics, illustrated by a combination of product-free Lambek calculus and feature-logic. Although these two papers and the present one all work in the general framework of labeled deduction, the focus in each work is quite different. The primary goal here is to use the framework of labeled deduction to gain insight into quantification, which is not explicitly treated in either of the two papers just mentioned.

tures of LFG, closely following the exposition of Kaplan and Bresnan (1982) and Kaplan (1989). Then in Section 3, I show how we may regard LFG as a system of Labeled Deduction. In Section 4, I extend this system to one which includes labeling by semantic terms and in Section 5 I compare this system with the glue language approach to the structural correspondence between LFG f-structures and semantic terms. The paper concludes in Section 6.

1   Labeled Deduction

1.1   Deductive systems

A standard way to define a deductive system is to specify a formula language, and then define a consequence relation. Consequence relations can take different forms. And they can be defined in various ways, as well—model theoretically or proof theoretically, for example. Here is an illustration in the Gentzen style, starting with a set $\mathcal{A}$ of atoms, building up formulas $\mathcal{F}$, structures $\mathcal{S}$ and then defining a consequence relation proof-theoretically over sequents of the form $\mathcal{S} \Rightarrow \mathcal{F}$:

$$\mathcal{F} := \mathcal{A} \mid \mathcal{F} \rightarrow \mathcal{F}$$
$$\mathcal{S} := \mathcal{F} \mid (\mathcal{S}, \mathcal{S})$$

If $\mathcal{S} \Rightarrow \mathcal{F}$ is a sequent, the structure $\mathcal{S}$ is called the *antecedent* and the formula $\mathcal{F}$ is called the *succedent*.

The postulates below fall into three groups: the *identity* group containing the Identity Axiom and Cut; the *structural* group consisting of Permutation and Associativity; and the *logical* rules governing the behavior of $\rightarrow$.

With $A, B, C, \ldots$ ranging over formulas and $\Gamma, \Delta, \ldots$ ranging over structures (with designated sub-structures enclosed in square brackets), we can state the postulates as follows:

postulates

$$\frac{}{A \Rightarrow A} \; Ax \qquad\qquad \frac{\Gamma \Rightarrow A \quad \Delta[A] \Rightarrow B}{\Delta[\Gamma] \Rightarrow B} \; Cut$$

$$\frac{\Gamma[(A,B)] \Rightarrow C}{\Gamma[(B,A)] \Rightarrow C} \; Permutation$$

$$\frac{\Gamma[(A,(B,C))] \Rightarrow D}{\Gamma[((A,B),C)] \Rightarrow D} \; RAssoc \qquad \frac{\Gamma[((A,B),C)] \Rightarrow D}{\Gamma[(A,(B,C))] \Rightarrow D} \; LAssoc$$

$$\frac{\Theta \Rightarrow A \quad \Gamma[B] \Rightarrow C}{\Gamma[(\Theta, A \to B)] \Rightarrow C} \; \to L \qquad \frac{(A,\Gamma) \Rightarrow B}{\Gamma \Rightarrow A \to B} \; \to R$$

It is conventional to display a proof in deductive systems of this kind as a tree, whose root, identified with the sequent to be proved (called the *endsequent* of the proof), is displayed at the bottom and whose leaves, all instances of the Identity Axiom, are displayed at the top.

As an example, a sequent such as $(A, A \to B) \Rightarrow B$ represents a form of the logical law *Modus Ponens*. This is deducible in the present system, as shown by the following proof, where the endsequent (the Modus Ponens sequent) is derived in one step from two axiom instances:

$$\frac{\dfrac{}{A \Rightarrow A} \; Ax \quad \dfrac{}{B \Rightarrow B} \; Ax}{(A, A \to B) \Rightarrow B} \; \to L$$

As further examples, here are two proofs of the transitivity of the type-constructor $\to$:

$$\frac{\dfrac{}{A \Rightarrow A} \; Ax \quad \dfrac{\dfrac{}{B \Rightarrow B} \; Ax \quad \dfrac{}{C \Rightarrow C} \; Ax}{B, B \to C \Rightarrow C} \; \to L}{\dfrac{\dfrac{((A, A \to B), B \to C) \Rightarrow C}{(A, (A \to B, B \to C)) \Rightarrow C} \; LAssoc}{(A \to B, B \to C) \Rightarrow A \to C} \; \to R} \; \to L$$

$$\frac{\dfrac{\dfrac{}{A \Rightarrow A} \; Ax \quad \dfrac{}{B \Rightarrow B} \; Ax}{(A, A \to B) \Rightarrow B} \; \to L \quad \dfrac{}{C \Rightarrow C} \; Ax}{\dfrac{\dfrac{((A, A \to B), B \to C) \Rightarrow C}{(A, (A \to B, B \to C)) \Rightarrow C} \; LAssoc}{(A \to B, B \to C) \Rightarrow A \to C} \; \to R} \; \to L$$

Note that the two proofs differ, although they have the same endsequent and the same axiom links. The first of these properties is obvious. The second means that if we trace the *atomic sub-formulas* of the endsequent (in these two formulas: the occurrences of the atoms A, B, C) up through the proof, identifying formulas in the conclusion of an inference step with corresponding formulas in the premises in the way stated in the inference rules, then the pairs of atoms linked in the axiom leaves of the two proofs are related to the same pairs of atomic sub-formulas of the endsequent in both proofs. In this particular case, this is not surprising, since any valid proof of this endsequent must pair the two occurrences of A, the two occurrences of B, and the two occurrences of C. But in more complex examples, provability need not enforce a unique axiom-link pairing. Here is an example:

$$
\cfrac{
  \cfrac{
    \cfrac{
      \cfrac{np \Rightarrow np \quad s \Rightarrow s}{(np, np \to s) \Rightarrow s} \to L
    }{np \to s \Rightarrow np \to s} \to R \quad s \Rightarrow s
  }{(np \to s, (np \to s) \to s) \Rightarrow s} \to L
}{
  \cfrac{(np \to s) \to s \Rightarrow (np \to s) \to s \quad s \Rightarrow s}{((np \to s) \to s, ((np \to s) \to s) \to s\,) \Rightarrow s} \to R
} \to L
$$

$$
\cfrac{
  \cfrac{
    \cfrac{
      \cfrac{
        \cfrac{np \Rightarrow np \quad s \Rightarrow s}{(np, np \to s) \Rightarrow s} \to L
      }{(np \to s, np) \Rightarrow s} Perm
    }{np \Rightarrow (np \to s) \to s} \to R \quad s \Rightarrow s
  }{(np, ((np \to s) \to s) \to s\,) \Rightarrow s} \to L
}{
  \cfrac{
    \cfrac{(((np \to s) \to s) \to s) \Rightarrow np \to s \quad s \Rightarrow s}{(((np \to s) \to s) \to s, (np \to s) \to s\,) \Rightarrow s} \to R
  }{((np \to s) \to s, ((np \to s) \to s) \to s\,) \Rightarrow s} Perm
} \to L
$$

In the first proof, the antecedent s of the axiom-leaf in the penultimate line is identifiable with the rightmost s in the right-hand formula of the endsequent antecedent; in the second proof, the antecedent s of the axiom-leaf in the penultimate line is identifiable with the right-most s of the left-hand formula of the endsequent antecedent.

The interest of such examples lies in properties of interpretation. There is a way to associate proofs with λ-terms—the Curry-Howard

Now consider the labeled versions of the proofs of Section 1.1 above. (We suppress overt indications of appropriateness of terms to the formulas they label.)

$$\cfrac{\cfrac{}{u:A \Rightarrow u:A}\ Ax \qquad \cfrac{}{t(u):B \Rightarrow t(u):B}\ Ax}{(u:A, t:A \to B) \Rightarrow t(u):B}\ \to L$$

The endsequent shows that the analog of Modus Ponens in this system is labeled with an application in the term system.

Next is the case involving distinct proofs with the same axiom-link pairing of endsequent atomic sub-formulas—note that the λ-terms associated with the succedent formula are the same:[2]

$$\cfrac{\cfrac{}{v:A \Rightarrow A}\ Ax \quad \cfrac{\cfrac{}{u(v):B \Rightarrow B}\ Ax \quad \cfrac{}{t(u(v)):C \Rightarrow C}\ Ax}{u(v):B, t:B \to C \Rightarrow t(u(v)):C}\ \to L}{\cfrac{\cfrac{((v:A, u:A \to B), t:B \to C) \Rightarrow t(u(v)):C}{(v:A, (u:A \to B, t:B \to C)) \Rightarrow t(u(v)):C}\ LAssoc}{(u:A \to B, t:B \to C) \Rightarrow \lambda v.t(u(v)):A \to C}\ \to R}\ \to L$$

$$\cfrac{\cfrac{\cfrac{}{v:A \Rightarrow A}\ Ax \quad \cfrac{}{u(v):B \Rightarrow B}\ Ax}{(v:A, u:A \to B) \Rightarrow u(v):B}\ \to L \quad \cfrac{}{t(u(v)):C \Rightarrow C}\ Ax}{\cfrac{\cfrac{((v:A, u:A \to B), t:B \to C) \Rightarrow t(u(v)):C}{(v:A, (u:A \to B, t:B \to C)) \Rightarrow t(u(v)):C}\ LAssoc}{(u:A \to B, t:B \to C) \Rightarrow \lambda v.t(u(v)):A \to C}\ \to R}\ \to L$$

We noted earlier that while these two proofs differ, they have the same axiom links and the same endsequent. Under the labeling regime here, if the corresponding axiom links in the two proofs are labeled with the same terms, the endsequents will be as well. (For discussion of this point, see Oehrle (1995).)

In contrast, while the two proofs below share a common endsequent, they differ in their axiom-leaf bindings.

---

[2] To save space, the label on the succedent formula of an axiom leaf is sometimes suppressed; this carries no loss of information, since the suppressed term is in all instances recoverable from the term labeling the single antecedent formula of the axiom leaf.

$$\dfrac{\dfrac{\dfrac{\dfrac{\dfrac{u : np \Rightarrow np \quad t(u) : s \Rightarrow s}{(u : np, t : np \to s) \Rightarrow t(u) : s} \to L}{t : np \to s \Rightarrow \lambda u.t(u) : np \to s} \to R \quad q(\lambda u.t(u)) : s \Rightarrow s}{(t : np \to s, q : (np \to s) \to s) \Rightarrow q(\lambda u.t(u)) : s} \to L}{q : (np \to s) \to s \Rightarrow \lambda t.q(\lambda u.t(u)) : (np \to s) \to s} \to R \quad r(\lambda t.q(\lambda u.t(u))) : s \Rightarrow s}{q : (np \to s) \to s, r : ((np \to s) \to s) \to s\,) \Rightarrow r(\lambda t.q(\lambda u.t(u))) : s} \to L$$

$$\dfrac{\dfrac{\dfrac{\dfrac{\dfrac{u : np \Rightarrow np \quad t(u) : s \Rightarrow s}{\dfrac{\dfrac{(u : np, t : np \to s) \Rightarrow t(u) : s}{(t : np \to s, u : np) \Rightarrow t(u) : s} Perm}{u : np \Rightarrow \lambda t.t(u) : (np \to s) \to s}} \to R \quad r(\lambda t.t(u)) : s \Rightarrow s}{(u : np, r : ((np \to s) \to s) \to s\,) \Rightarrow r(\lambda t.t(u)) : s} \to L}{(r : ((np \to s) \to s) \to s) \Rightarrow \lambda u.r(\lambda t.t(u)) : np \to s} \to R \quad q(\lambda u.r(\lambda t.t(u))) : s \Rightarrow s}{(q : (np \to s) \to s, r : ((np \to s) \to s) \to s\,) \Rightarrow q(\lambda u.r(\lambda t.t(u))) : s} \to L$$

1.3   Deductive power and grammatical discernibility

The system above is the implicational fragment of the Lambek/van Benthem calculus **LP** (van Benthem 1988, 1986, 1995), which differs from the implicational fragment of multiplicative linear logic **MLL** (Girard 1987; Troelstra 1991) only by requiring that sequent antecedents be non-empty. This system has the pleasant property that multiple quantifier scopings arise on the basis of a single lexical quantifier type, simply as a result of proof indeterminacy. Take the basic case involving a two-place predicate with two quantifiers, corresponding to a sentence like *Some bear loves every fish*. The following two proofs assign different terms to the endsequent, as indicated in the last line:

$$\dfrac{\dfrac{\dfrac{\dfrac{\dfrac{\dfrac{\dfrac{\dfrac{np \Rightarrow np \quad s \Rightarrow s}{(np, np \to s) \Rightarrow s}}{np \Rightarrow np \quad (np \to s, np) \Rightarrow s}}{((np, np \to (np \to s)), np) \Rightarrow s}}{(np, (np \to (np \to s), np)) \Rightarrow s}}{(np, (np, np \to (np \to s))) \Rightarrow s}}{(np, np \to (np \to s)) \Rightarrow np \to s \quad s \Rightarrow s}}{\dfrac{\dfrac{((np, np \to (np \to s)), (np \to s) \to s) \Rightarrow s}{(np, (np \to (np \to s), (np \to s) \to s)) \Rightarrow s}}{(np \to (np \to s), (np \to s) \to s) \Rightarrow np \to s \quad s \Rightarrow s}}}{q_1 : ((np \to s) \to s, (r : np \to (np \to s), q_2 : (np \to s) \to s)) \Rightarrow q_1(\lambda u.q_2(\lambda v.(r(v))(u))) : s} \to L$$

$$\cfrac{\cfrac{\cfrac{\cfrac{np \Rightarrow np \quad s \Rightarrow s}{\cfrac{(np, np \rightarrow s) \Rightarrow s}{np \rightarrow s \Rightarrow np \rightarrow s}}}{np \Rightarrow np \quad (np \rightarrow s, (np \rightarrow s) \rightarrow s) \Rightarrow s}}{\cfrac{\cfrac{((np, np \rightarrow (np \rightarrow s)), (np \rightarrow s) \rightarrow s) \Rightarrow s}{(np, (np \rightarrow (np \rightarrow s), (np \rightarrow s) \rightarrow s)) \Rightarrow s \quad s \Rightarrow s}}{\cfrac{\cfrac{(np, ((np \rightarrow s) \rightarrow s, np \rightarrow (np \rightarrow s))) \Rightarrow s}{((np \rightarrow s) \rightarrow s, np \rightarrow (np \rightarrow s)) \Rightarrow np \rightarrow s \quad s \Rightarrow s}}{(((np \rightarrow s) \rightarrow s, np \rightarrow (np \rightarrow s)), (np \rightarrow s) \rightarrow s) \Rightarrow s}}}}{(q_1 : (np \rightarrow s) \rightarrow s, (r : np \rightarrow (np \rightarrow s), q_2 : (np \rightarrow s) \rightarrow s)) \Rightarrow q_2(\lambda v.q_1(\lambda u.(r(v))(u))) : s} \rightarrow L$$

A less pleasant property of the implicational fragment of **LP** is that it delivers further proofs, which do not correspond to available readings for the sentence at hand. Thus, take a sentence with assumptions of the form

$$(q_1 : (np \rightarrow s) \rightarrow s, (r : np \rightarrow (np \rightarrow s), q_2 : (np \rightarrow s) \rightarrow s))$$

We can deduce formula s from these assumptions with any of the following labels:

$$q_1(\lambda u(q_2(\lambda v.ruv)))$$
$$q_2(\lambda u(q_1(\lambda v.ruv)))$$
$$q_1(\lambda v(q_2(\lambda u.ruv)))$$
$$q_2(\lambda v(q_1(\lambda u.ruv)))$$

In fact, the same problem arises even in simpler cases. Thus, consider the set of assumptions corresponding to a sentence with a transitive verb and two simple arguments:

$$(u : np, (r : np \rightarrow (np \rightarrow s), v : np))$$

The succedent s is derivable with two distinct labels:

$$rvu : s$$
$$ruv : s$$

Thus, the implicational fragment of **LP** is too weak to differentiate arguments. This is a severe inadequacy of this system as a model of natural language structure. The problem can be overcome in two ways.

The first is to make the implication operator directionally sensitive, as in the associative and non-commutative system **L**. This allows arguments to be differentiated, but at a cost: we lose the elegance of the type-theoretic account of quantifiers and scope that seems tantalizingly close in **LP**. It is not obvious how to avoid paying this cost, but below we shall consider a solution to this problem due to Moortgat (1996).

The second approach augments the system of labeled deduction based on **LP** with an additional labeling system, involving string terms. In this system (Oehrle 1994, 1995), the string terms ensure a correlation between string position and argument structure. We sketch the essentials of this approach in the next section.

1.4   String labeling

String labels are typed: there is a single atomic string type str and if s_1 and s_2 are string types, then so is $\langle s_1, s_2 \rangle$. Strings of type str are appropriate for atomic formulas. If string type s_1 is appropriate for formula A and string type s_2 is appropriate for formula B, then string type $\langle s_1, s_2 \rangle$ is appropriate for formula $A \to B$. String terms of type str are assumed to form a monoid: they are closed under concatenation with a two-sided concatenative unit ϵ. In addition, string terms are closed under application and abstraction in the obvious way that respects string types. Finally, string terms are associated with inference rules in the same way that our original labeling system is: $\to L$ inferences correspond to applications (in the right-hand premise); $\to R$ inferences correspond to abstraction. If we like, we can enforce the requirement that the terms associated with sequent succedents are in β normal form.

To illustrate this approach, consider the lexicon below, whose elements are listed in the form **String_Term**:*Interpretive_Term*:*Formula*.

> smith : s : np
>
> λ x.x walks : $walk$: $np \to s$
>
> λ x λ y.y loves x : $love$: $np \to (np \to s)$
>
> λ P.P(some bear) : $\lambda P \exists x (bear(x) \wedge Px)$: $(np \to s) \to s$
>
> λ P.P(every fish) : $\lambda P \forall x (fish(x) \supset Px)$: $(np \to s) \to s$

We may take proper names to be associated lexically with string constants. For intransitive and transitive verbs, the position of subject and object arguments is indicated by the first-order string term associated with the verb. The string term associated with a quantifier involves a higher-order string term.

Consider first proofs involving a two-place predicate and two simple arguments. The following examples have the same assumptions, but differ in axiom-leaf bindings and the succedents are labeled with different string terms and with different interpretive terms.

$$\dfrac{\mathsf{u}:u:np\Rightarrow\mathsf{u}:u:np \quad \dfrac{\dfrac{\mathsf{v}:v:np\Rightarrow\mathsf{v}:v:np \quad \mathsf{r(u)(v)}:r(u)(v):s\Rightarrow}{(\mathsf{v}:v:np,\mathsf{r(u)}:r(u):np\to s)\Rightarrow\mathsf{r(u)(v)}:r(u)(v):s}\to L}{(\mathsf{r(u)}:r(u):np\to s,\mathsf{v}:v:np)\Rightarrow\mathsf{r(u)(v)}:r(u)(v):s}\,Perm}{((\mathsf{u}:u:np,\mathsf{r}:r:np\to np\to s),\mathsf{v}:v:np)\Rightarrow\mathsf{r(u)(v)}:r(u)(v):s}\to L}{(\mathsf{u}:u:np,(\mathsf{r}:r:np\to np\to s,\mathsf{v}:v:np))\Rightarrow\mathsf{r(u)(v)}:r(u)(v):s}\,Assoc$$

$$\dfrac{\dfrac{\mathsf{v}:v:np\Rightarrow\mathsf{v}:v:np \quad \dfrac{\dfrac{\mathsf{u}:u:np\Rightarrow\mathsf{u}:u:np \quad \mathsf{r(v)(u)}:r(v)(u):s\Rightarrow\mathsf{r(v)(u)}:r(v)(u):s}{(\mathsf{u}:u:np,\mathsf{r(v)}:r(v):np\to s)\Rightarrow}\to L}{(\mathsf{u}:u:np,(\mathsf{v}:v:np,\mathsf{r}:r:np\to np\to s))\Rightarrow\mathsf{r(v)(u)}:r(v)(u):s}\to L}}{(\mathsf{u}:u:np,(\mathsf{r}:r:np\to np\to s,\mathsf{v}:v:np))\Rightarrow\mathsf{r(v)(u)}:r(v)(u):s}\,Perm$$

The configuration of assumptions in the endsequent does not determine the argument structure of the sentence composed of these assumptions: in the first proof, the argument $\mathsf{u}:u:np$ serves as the first argument to $\mathsf{r}:r:np\to np\to s$; in the second proof, the first argument to the predicate is the argument $\mathsf{v}:v:np$. Depending on whether r is of the form $\lambda x.\lambda y.(xr'y)$ or $\lambda y.\lambda x.(yr'x)$, the first argument will correspond to the preverbal subject position in English or the postverbal object position.

What is important to notice, however, is the correspondence between the two term labeling systems. The first argument to the string function r is also the first argument to the interpretive function r. This holds across both proofs. And unlike the system **LP**, which lacks string labeling, it is impossible to prove in this string-labeled system that the antecedent assumptions common to the two proofs above also yield a succedent $\mathsf{r(u)(v)}:r(v)(u):s$ or $\mathsf{r(v)(u)}:r(u)(v):s$, where the string arguments permute and the corresponding interpretive arguments do not. As a result, the two sentences *Smith admires Jones* and *Jones admires Smith* are assigned distinct interpretations, enforced by the differences in string relations.

Just as string labeling provides a control structure which winnows out unwanted proofs in the case of two-place predicates with simple arguments, it also winnows out, in the same way, unwanted proofs when the simple arguments are replaced by quantifiers (on the lexical assumptions illustrated above). Thus, while scope ambiguity still arises as a form of proof indeterminacy in the presence of string labeling, ambiguity of the argument positions bound to the quantifier disappears, since the argument position of the quantifier is determined by the string position it occurs in. To see this, write **loves**, **some bear**, and **every fish** for the lexical entries given earlier in this section. The sentence *some bear loves every fish* has two non-equivalent proofs (where 'non-equivalent' means that there are two ways in which the atomic subformulas are matched in the axiom leaves, as discussed earlier).

In one of these, the quantifier of **some bear** has wide scope:

$$
\cfrac{
(\textbf{loves, every fish}) \Rightarrow
\begin{array}{l} \lambda\, y.\ y \text{ loves every fish} : \\ \lambda y.\forall z(\mathit{fish}(z) \supset \mathit{love}(z)(y)) : s \end{array}
\qquad \ldots : s \Rightarrow \ldots : s
}{
(\textbf{some bear, (loves, every fish)}) \Rightarrow
\begin{array}{l} \text{some bear loves every fish} : \\ \exists x(\mathit{bear}(x) \wedge \forall z(\mathit{fish}(z) \supset \mathit{love}(z)(x))) : s \end{array}
} \ \to L
$$

In the other proof, the quantifier of **every fish** takes wide scope:

$$
\cfrac{
\cfrac{
(\textbf{some bear, loves}) \Rightarrow
\begin{array}{l} \lambda\, u.\ \text{some bear loves } u : \\ \lambda u.\exists x(\mathit{bear}(x) \wedge \mathit{loves}(u)(x)) : s \end{array}
\quad \to L
\qquad \ldots : s \Rightarrow \ldots : s
}{
(\textbf{(some bear, loves), every fish}) \Rightarrow
\begin{array}{l} \text{some bear loves every fish} : \\ \forall z(\mathit{fish}(z) \supset \exists x(\mathit{bear}(x) \wedge \mathit{love}(z)(x))) : s \end{array}
} \ \to L
}{
(\textbf{some bear, (loves, every fish)}) \Rightarrow
\begin{array}{l} \text{some bear loves every fish} : \\ \forall z(\mathit{fish}(z) \supset \exists x(\mathit{bear}(x) \wedge \mathit{love}(z)(x))) : s \end{array}
} \ Assoc
$$

No further proofs of **some bear loves every fish** are possible. For further details, see Oehrle (1994, 1995).

1.5 Summary

The uses of labeling exemplified above are varied, yet integrated. Each system of terms represents a 'dimension' of linguistic information. Each system of terms is linked to proofs through postulates and appropriateness conditions. These links indirectly constrain the relation between terms in one system and terms in another. Changes in the underlying deductive system or in the term systems themselves can lead directly to different correspondences between the two systems of terms.

The resulting space of possibilities provides a congenial framework for the investigation of problems of composition within and across dimensions.

2   LFG: Structures, Descriptions, Correspondences

Let us now consider the basic properties of Lexical Functional Grammar, which have remained remarkably constant throughout the development of LFG since its inception in the collaborative work of Ron Kaplan and Joan Bresnan in the late 1970's and early 1980's. These basic properties are elegantly described in Kaplan's survey article (Kaplan 1989), whose exposition we follow closely. Kaplan emphasizes the importance of three 'fundamental notions': structures, descriptions, and correspondences. We consider these in turn.

2.1   Structures

Syntactically, LFG associates two independent structures with the analysis of linguistic expressions—c-structure (which assigns a constituent structure tree to the components of the expression and has been regarded as providing the basis for its phonological interpretation) and f-structure (which characterizes the grammatical relations among the components of the expression). In addition, we will assume a form of the theory in which semantic interpretation is represented by λ-terms. Kaplan illustrates these concepts with a running example that exemplifies the analysis of the sentence *I saw the girl*.

2.1.1   Strings

This sentence consists first of all of a string of words—where a string consists of a set W of words together with a relation of immediate precedence whose transitive closure $\prec$ makes $\langle W, \prec \rangle$ a linear ordering.

2.1.2   Trees

In LFG, a well-formed string forms the leaves of a tree which represents constituent structure. In the running example, the tree associated with *I saw the girl* is displayed below.

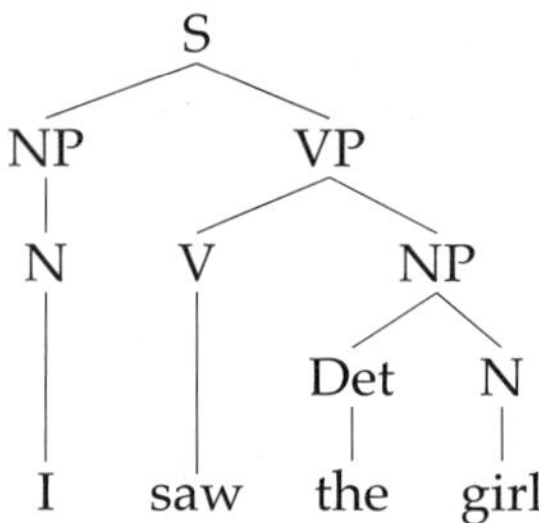

This tree can be described as consisting of a set N of nodes, a set L of labels, and a root node ρ in N, on which a variety of functions and relations are defined:

$M : N \setminus \{\rho\} \to N$ assigns each non-root node to an immediate predecessor (in tree representations, M is simply the edge connecting each non-root node to its parent); regarded as a relation, the transitive, reflexive closure M^* of M is antisymmetric (disallowing cycles);

$< \; \subseteq N \times N$ is a partial ordering relation on N which satisfies an inheritance condition with respect to M:

$$(M^*(n_1, n_i) \wedge M^*(n_2, n_j) \wedge n_i < n_j) \Rightarrow n_1 < n_2;$$

$\lambda : N \to L$ associates with each node a label in L.

2.2 F-structures

LFG also associates with each well-formed expression an f-structure, which displays its grammatical relations and grammatical features. The f-structure for our running example is given below:

$$
\begin{bmatrix}
\text{SUBJ} & \begin{bmatrix} \text{PRED} & \text{'PRO'} \\ \text{PERS} & 1 \\ \text{NUM} & \text{SG} \end{bmatrix} \\[2em]
\text{PRED} & \text{'SEE}\langle(\uparrow \text{SUBJ}), (\uparrow \text{OBJ})\rangle\text{'} \\
\text{TENSE} & \text{PAST} \\[1em]
\text{OBJ} & \begin{bmatrix} \text{PRED} & \text{'GIRL'} \\ \text{DEF} & + \\ \text{PERS} & 1 \\ \text{NUM} & \text{SG} \end{bmatrix}
\end{bmatrix}
$$

Given a set $\mathcal{A}$ of atomic symbols and a set $\mathcal{S}$ of semantic forms, the set $\mathcal{F}$ of f-structures can be defined by the rule:

$$\mathcal{F} := \mathcal{A} \to \mathcal{F} \cup \mathcal{A} \cup \mathcal{S}$$

For example, the first line of the f-structure above indicates that this structure maps the atomic symbol SUBJ to the f-structure displayed to its right, while it maps the atomic symbol PRED to a semantic form, and maps the atomic symbol OBJ to the f-structure which maps the atomic symbol DEF to the atomic symbol $+$.

2.3   Descriptions

A characteristic property of LFG is that structures are treated as models of descriptions, where a description consists of a specification of a structure's defining properties and relations. In the case of a tree, for example, we can name each node and then specify the root, the predecessor relation M, the partial ordering $<$, and the labeling relation λ. Restricting our earlier example to non-terminal nodes, naming yields:

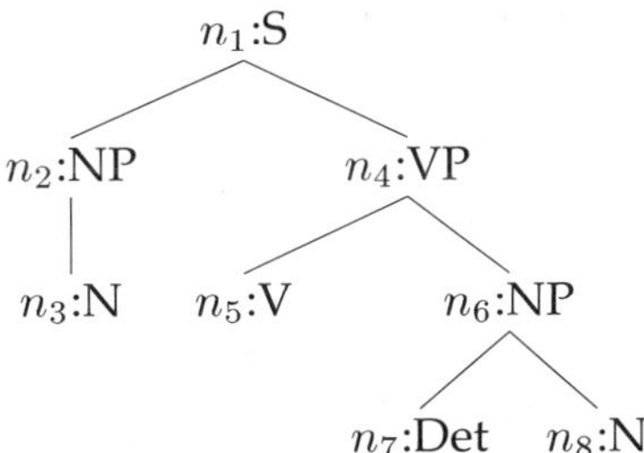

This tree structure can be described as well by the following set of propositions:

$$M(n_2) = n_1 \quad M(n_3) = n_2 \quad M(n_4) = n_1$$
$$M(n_5) = n_4 \quad M(n_6) = n_4 \quad M(n_7) = n_6$$
$$M(n_8) = n_6 \quad \lambda(n_1) = \text{S} \quad \lambda(n_2) = \text{NP}$$
$$\lambda(n_3) = \text{N} \quad \lambda(n_4) = \text{VP} \quad \lambda(n_5) = \text{V}$$
$$\lambda(n_6) = \text{NP} \quad \lambda(n_7) = \text{Det} \quad \lambda(n_8) = \text{N}$$
$$n_2 < n_4 \quad n_5 < n_6 \quad n_7 < n_8$$
$$\rho = n_1$$

Further relations which hold in this tree follow from more general definitions. For example, $n_3 < n_4$ and $n_3 < n_5$ in virtue of the inheritance condition connecting M^* and $<$.

2.3.1 F-structure descriptions

A similar approach allows f-structures to be described in terms of functional application. Take as an example the f-structure associated with *I saw the girl*. Call this structure as a whole f_1. It contains subsidiary f-structures f_2 and f_3. Writing application of a function f to an argument a in its domain as $(f\ a)$, we can describe f_1 as follows:

$$
\begin{array}{ll}
(f_1\ \text{SUBJ}) = f_2 & (f_1\ \text{TENSE}) = \text{PAST} \\
(f_1\ \text{OBJ}) = f_3 & (f_1\ \text{PRED}) = \text{`SEE}\langle(\uparrow \text{SUBJ}), (\uparrow \text{OBJ})\rangle\text{'} \\
(f_2\ \text{PRED}) = \text{`PRO'} & (f_2\ \text{PERS}) = 1 \\
(f_2\ \text{NUM}) = \text{SG} & (f_3\ \text{PRED}) = \text{`GIRL'} \\
(f_3\ \text{DEF}) = {+} & (f_3\ \text{PERS}) = 3 \\
 & (f_3\ \text{NUM}) = \text{SG}
\end{array}
$$

2.3.2 From structures to descriptions and back again

The above examples show how one may trade in structures for descriptions in terms of properties and relations. Kaplan (1989) emphasizes the interest of the converse problem: finding the set of structures which satisfy a given consistent description. This problem is solvable when the description language is relatively simple. For f-structure descriptions involving only equality and functional application, solvability is attainable through unification and other techniques applicable to the quantifier-free theory of equality. When the description language is enriched, the question is more delicate, as Kaplan shows.

2.4 Structural correspondences

If one regards structures of the sort discussed above as models of aspects of natural language, one observes that by fixing structures of one sort, one may constrain in interesting ways structures of other sorts. These constraints are characterized in LFG by structural correspondences, functions from structural descriptions to structural descriptions. For example, consider the description in Section 2.3 of the c-structure for the sentence *I saw the girl.* Let ϕ be the function from the elements of this description—that is, the set $\{n_i\}_{1\leq i\leq 8}$—to the elements of the f-structure description of Section 2.3.1—the set $\{f_j\}_{1\leq j\leq 3}$—with the action described below:

$$\phi(n_1) = \phi(n_4) = \phi(n_5) = f_1$$
$$\phi(n_2) = \phi(n_3) = f_2$$
$$\phi(n_6) = \phi(n_7) = \phi(n_8) = f_3$$

As Kaplan shows, this leads directly to an integrated description of both c-structure and f-structure:

$$
\begin{array}{lll}
M(n_2) = n_1 & M(n_3) = n_2 & M(n_4) = n_1 \\
M(n_5) = n_4 & M(n_6) = n_4 & M(n_7) = n_6 \\
M(n_8) = n_6 & \phi(M(n_4)) = \phi(n_4) & \phi(M(n_5)) = \phi(n_5) \\
\phi(M(n_7)) = \phi(n_7) & \phi(M(n_8)) = \phi(n_8) & (\phi(M(n_2))\text{SUBJ}) = \phi(n_2) \\
(\phi(n_2)\ \text{PRED}) = \text{'PRO'} & (\phi(n_2)\ \text{PERS}) = 1 & (\phi(n_2)\ \text{NUM}) = \text{SG} \\
(\phi(M(n_6))\text{OBJ}) = \phi(n_6) & (\phi(n_3)\ \text{PRED}) = \text{'GIRL'} & (\phi(n_3)\ \text{DEF}) = + \\
(\phi(n_3)\ \text{PERS}) = 3 & (\phi(n_3)\ \text{NUM}) = \text{SG} & (\phi(n_1\text{TENSE}) = \text{PAST} \\
\end{array}
$$
$$\phi(n_1\text{PRED}) = \text{'SEE}\langle(\uparrow\ \text{SUBJ}), (\uparrow\ \text{OBJ})\rangle\text{'}$$

What properties do such structural correspondence functions as ϕ have in general? It is obvious first of all that they need not be injections: in the above case, for example, we have $\phi(n_1) = \phi(n_4) = \phi(n_5)$, and other cases where ϕ takes distinct arguments. Moreover, Kaplan notes that empty argument positions provide evidence that they need not be surjections either. Another question that arises is how structural correspondence functions behave with respect to the structural relations of their domains and co-domains. For example, let M^* be the reflexive, transitive closure of the domination relation of c-structure and $\sqsubseteq$ the least reflexive, transitive relation on any f-structure such that $(f_i\alpha) = f_j \Rightarrow f_i \sqsubseteq f_j$ for any attribute α. In the simplest examples, structural correspondence functions are isotone:

$$M^*(n, n') \Rightarrow \phi(n) \sqsubseteq \phi(n')$$

It is evident that the structural correspondence functions are not simply arbitrary functions from descriptions of c-structures to descriptions of f-structures. But whether they can be required to respect such natural conditions as isotonicity depends on a broader investigation, and, in particular, how quantifiers are to be treated in the LFG framework.

2.5   Notation

In Kaplan and Bresnan (1982), a compact notation is introduced which links phrase structure rules with structural correspondence properties. First, if c-structures are characterized by production rules, the production rules can be annotated to reflect structural correspondence properties. Here is an example from Kaplan (1989).

$$ S \; \to \qquad NP \qquad\qquad VP $$
$$ (\phi(M(n))\mathrm{SUBJ}) = \phi(n) \quad \phi(M(n)) = \phi(n) $$

The annotation indicates that in the f-structure corresponding to any instance of the c-structure justified by this production rule, the f-structure of the NP instance is the value of the SUBJ attribute of the f-structure of the S instance, and the f-structure of the S instance is identical with the f-structure of the VP instance. More succinctly:

$$ S \; \to \qquad NP \qquad VP $$
$$ (\uparrow \mathrm{SUBJ}) = \downarrow \quad \uparrow = \downarrow $$

In Kaplan and Bresnan (1982), where this notation is introduced, this method of annotation is extended in a number of ways. These include the addition of constraint equations, existential constraints, and negative constraints, which result from negating a constraint equation or an existential constraint. A further set of additions, including a notation for bounding nodes and metavariables '⇑' and '⇓', goes beyond the scope of this paper, as do the more recent extensions to the basic methods of indicating correspondence discussed by Kaplan (1989), notably functional uncertainty.

2.6   Models

Descriptions of structures and structural correspondences describe a class of models. The particular models of interest satisfy a number of conditions. Roughly, the f-structure description must have a unique minimal model and must be 'complete' and 'coherent', in a way that has a close affinity with linear resource management. The distinction between an object and its description is a central characteristic of LFG. As Kaplan (1989, page 14) rightly emphasizes, there is often 'no single primitive object that naturally represents the negation or disjunction of some collection of properties, yet it is natural to form descriptions of objects by means of such arbitrary Boolean combinations of defining propositions.' And Kaplan draws a contrast between the 'descriptive, declarative, or model-based methods' of LFG (and other constraint-based grammatical systems) and the 'constructive or procedural methods' which actually specify how the structures in question are to be synthesized or analyzed. In spite of this conceptual distinction, one may wonder to what extent analyses constructed in the LFG framework may be simulated in frameworks based on constructive methods of synthesis or analysis. In the next section, we explore this question from the point of view of labeling.

3   Structural Correspondence as Labeling

If we regard c-structures and f-structures as terms, we may think of structural correspondence as a labeling relation. That is, we may label a formula A with two terms: a c-structure rooted in the category A and the f-structure that corresponds to it.

Informally, one can see that it is possible to define such a system of labeled deduction by extending the term systems with operations of application and λ-abstraction and β-reduction while at the same time extending the type system with residuation.[3] As an example, consider the example below, where a c-structure and an f-structure label a formula s.

---

[3] A referee has made the interesting suggestion that the higher-order f-structures that result be replaced by formulas in an appropriate language for describing f-structures. I have not had the opportunity to pursue this attractive possibility, however.

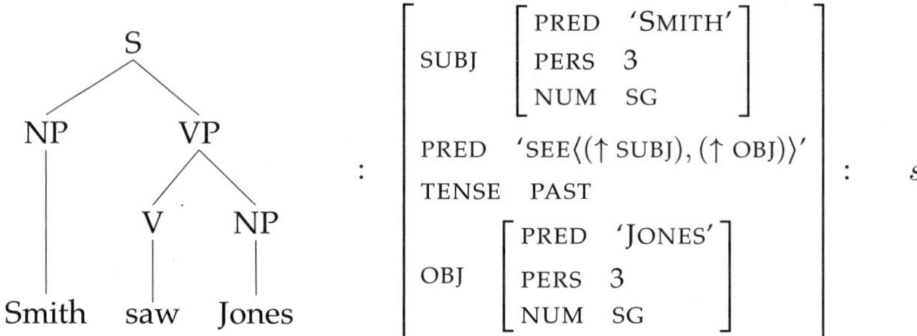

This analysis depends on the following lexical assumptions:

Smith: NP, (↑ PRED) = 'SMITH', (↑ NUM) = SG, (↑ PERS) = 3
Jones: NP, (↑ PRED) = 'JONES', (↑ NUM) = SG, (↑ PERS) = 3
saw: V, (↑ TENSE) = PAST, (↑ PRED) = 'SEE⟨...⟩'

Now, consider the information governing the correspondence found in the annotated (labeled!) phrase structure rules

$$S \; \rightarrow \; \underset{(\uparrow \text{SUBJ}) \,=\downarrow}{\text{NP}} \qquad \underset{\uparrow=\downarrow}{\text{VP}}$$

$$VP \; \rightarrow \; \underset{\uparrow=\downarrow}{\text{V}} \qquad \underset{(\uparrow \text{OBJ}) \,=\downarrow}{\text{NP}}$$

Examination of the phrase structure rules and the lexical entries shows that in this case, all the information associated with the attribute SUBJ comes from the lexical entry for *Smith*; all the information associated with the attribute OBJ comes from the lexical entry for *Jones*; everything else in the f-structure comes from the lexical entry for *saw*. Consequently, we can abstract over the contribution of the subject to form the labeled structure below:

Similarly, we can abstract over the contribution of the object NP *Jones*, yielding the term-labeled type $np \to (np \to s)$:

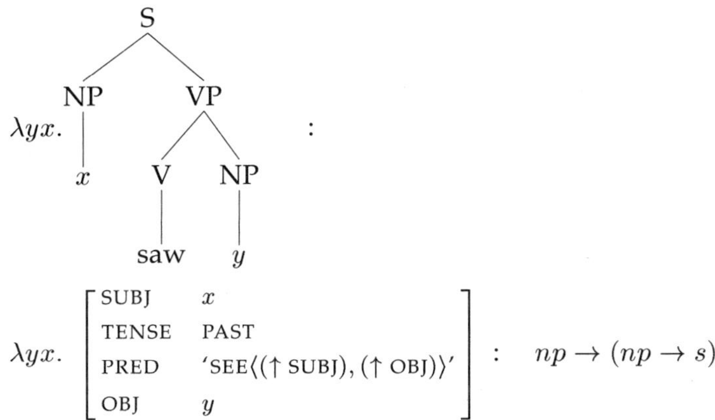

This gives us a lexical entry for *saw*. For the proper names themselves, we can take the entries below:

$$\text{Smith:} \quad \begin{bmatrix} \text{PRED} & \text{'SMITH'} \\ \text{PERS} & 3 \\ \text{NUM} & \text{SG} \end{bmatrix} \quad : \quad np$$

$$\text{Jones:} \quad \begin{bmatrix} \text{PRED} & \text{'JONES'} \\ \text{PERS} & 3 \\ \text{NUM} & \text{SG} \end{bmatrix} \quad : \quad np$$

It is not always the case that f-structure information comes from a single source. As a simple example, the verbal form *sees* carries the information that its subject is third-person singular. Accordingly, the SUBJ attribute of the f-structure that results from combining this verb with an appropriate subject must be associated with the unification of this information and whatever information is derived from the f-structure associated with the subject NP. This can be represented explicitly in the residuated entry for *sees* as follows, where the explicit unification operator $\sqcup$ appears in the f-structure:

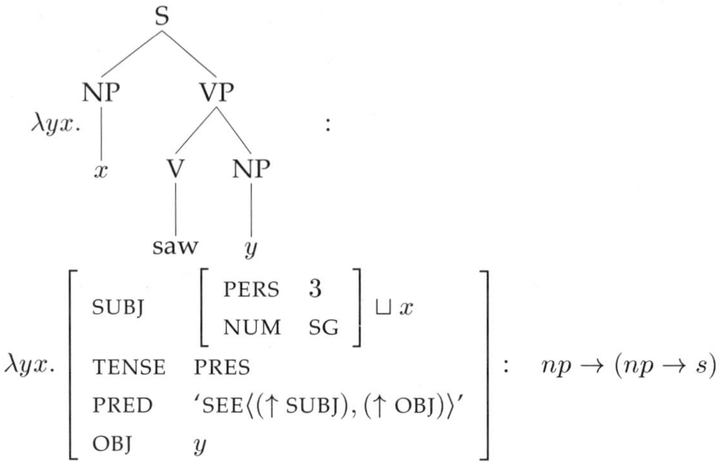

Note that these occurrences of explicit unification operators replace general recourse to unification, rather than forming an additional supplement to it.

Finally, consider the role of constraint equations, and existential and negative constraints in structural correspondences. Kaplan and Bresnan (1982, page 64) note that equational constraints and existential constraints can be avoided 'by introducing ad hoc feature values'—a recourse which they wish to avoid. But on this view equational and (conjunctive) existential constraints can be eliminated. Negative constraints cannot be accommodated this way. The example used to justify negative constraints in Kaplan and Bresnan (1982) involves drawing a distinction between tensed and tenseless VP's. This distinction can be drawn straightforwardly along categorial lines: vp vs. $np \backslash s$ (using Lambek's directional notation). And one can argue that the syntactic distribution of tensed and tenseless VP's supports this distinction. This complicates the phrase structure system: no matter, we will dispense with this in any case. Whether all negative constraints can be reanalyzed in this simple way, I will leave open. This issue represents a situation in which the declarative properties of LFG cannot be simulated in this constructive model. The same conclusion holds when existential or equational constraints are formulated using disjunction in an essential way.

The labeled deductive system that results is virtually identical with the system discussed above in Section 1. Structures are built up from labeled formulas. Sequents consist of an antecedent structure and a succedent labeled formula. The postulates consist of the identity axiom, Cut, structural rules of associativity and permutation, and left- and right-rules governing $\to$. Just as in the earlier system, the rule $\to L$ is associated with functional application in the associated terms; the rule $\to R$ is associated with λ-abstraction. The deductive system itself is the implicational fragment of the Lambek/van Benthem calculus **LP**, closely related to the implicational fragment of **MLL** (multiplicative linear logic). Thus, type deduction in this system is linear. The system of c-structure terms is also linear: each occurrence of the λ-abstraction operator binds exactly one occurrence of a variable inside the body of the term. Whether the system of f-structure terms is to be linear is open: in the example above, the variable y occurs twice; on the other hand, if internal links are used to indicate binding within f-structures, linearity is recovered. We shall leave this issue open.

A less informal account of how to turn an amenable LFG grammar—one without non-eliminable negative or disjunctive constraints—into a weakly-equivalent system of labeled deduction is possible, I believe, using the ideas of the Greibach Normal Form Theorem for context free grammars. I will not pursue this here, however.[4]

4   Semantic Terms

We now add a semantic dimension to this system in a familiar way, using the extensional fragment of Montague's type system *IL* as an illustration. We have a set $\{e, t\}$ of two basic extensional types. The full set of extensional types is obtained by closing the set of basic types under the pairing operator $\langle \cdot, \cdot \rangle$. Each atomic formula of our syntactic system is associated with an appropriate extensional type. In particular, e is appropriate for np and t is appropriate for s. The inductive step is well-known: if α is appropriate for A and β is appropriate for B, then $\langle \alpha, \beta \rangle$

---

[4]A referee points out the relevance to this investigation of Marc Dymetman's thesis and Dymetman (1992), work which I have not seen.

is appropriate for $A \to B$. Each occurrence of a formula is to be labeled with a term of a type which is appropriate for the formula.

To illustrate, suppose we begin with the lexical declarations below, where the semantic term is represented in the third coordinate (and where c-structures are flattened down to strings for ease of exposition):

$$
\textit{Bob} \; : \quad
\begin{bmatrix}
\text{PRED} & \text{'BOB'} \\
\text{PERS} & 3 \\
\text{NUM} & \text{SG}
\end{bmatrix}
\; : \quad b \; : \; np
$$

$$
\textit{Harry} \; : \quad
\begin{bmatrix}
\text{PRED} & \text{'HARRY'} \\
\text{PERS} & 3 \\
\text{NUM} & \text{SG}
\end{bmatrix}
\; : \quad h \; : \; np
$$

$$
\lambda yx.x \; \textit{admired} \; y \; : \quad \lambda yx.
\begin{bmatrix}
\text{PRED} & \text{'ADMIRE'} \\
\text{TENSE} & \text{PAST} \\
\text{SUBJ} & x \\
\text{OBJ} & y
\end{bmatrix}
\; : \; A \; : \; np \to (np \to s)
$$

The semantic terms $b, h,$ and A are assumed to be of types $e, e,$ and $\langle e, \langle e, t \rangle \rangle$, respectively.

Let us use the names **bob**, **harry**, and **admired** for these three lexical assumptions (in the obvious way). Then in our system of labeled deduction, the following two sequents are valid (writing labeling terms vertically on different lines and assuming that normalization of λ-terms is enforced throughout).

$$
\textit{Bob admired Harry} \; :
$$

$$
(\textbf{bob}, (\textbf{admired}, \textbf{harry})) \Rightarrow
\begin{bmatrix}
\text{PRED} & \text{'ADMIRE'} \\
\text{TENSE} & \text{PAST} \\
\text{SUBJ} &
\begin{bmatrix}
\text{PRED} & \text{'BOB'} \\
\text{PERS} & 3 \\
\text{NUM} & \text{SG}
\end{bmatrix} \\
\text{OBJ} &
\begin{bmatrix}
\text{PRED} & \text{'HARRY'} \\
\text{PERS} & 3 \\
\text{NUM} & \text{SG}
\end{bmatrix}
\end{bmatrix}
\; :
$$

$$
A(h)(b) \; :
$$

$$
s
$$

Harry admired Bob :

$$(\textbf{bob}, (\textbf{admired}, \textbf{harry})) \Rightarrow \begin{bmatrix} \text{PRED} & \text{'ADMIRE'} \\ \text{TENSE} & \text{PAST} \\ \text{SUBJ} & \begin{bmatrix} \text{PRED} & \text{'HARRY'} \\ \text{PERS} & 3 \\ \text{NUM} & \text{SG} \end{bmatrix} \\ \text{OBJ} & \begin{bmatrix} \text{PRED} & \text{'BOB'} \\ \text{PERS} & 3 \\ \text{NUM} & \text{SG} \end{bmatrix} \end{bmatrix}$$

$A(b)(h)$:

s

Within this simple deductive system, because of the coordination of λ-abstraction across dimensions and the orchestration across dimensions of functional applications in the term structures, the semantic term labeling the occurrence of the np whose f-structure provides the value of the OBJ attribute of the succedent f-structure corresponding to the f-structure introduced by an antecedent occurrence of **admired** is the first argument of the semantic term A associated with that occurrence. Similarly, the semantic term labeling the occurrence of the np whose f-structure provides the value of the SUBJ attribute of this f-structure is the second argument of this semantic term A.

The examples above involve first-order reasoning. But the types driving deduction in this system are not all first-order. And given the definitions of appropriateness linking formulas and terms, we shall assume that the term structures at our disposal also allow higher-order types. Above, the variables x and y implicitly range over saturated structures. Thus, if $\phi(x)$ is saturated, then $\lambda x.\phi(x)$ represents a function from saturated structures to saturated structures. We will use variables P and Q to range over such first-order functions, regardless of which dimension they belong to. On these assumptions, we can accommodate quantifiers in a way that gives rise to scope ambiguities as an intrinsic form of proof indeterminacy (following Oehrle 1994, 1995).

Take the determiner *every*. Its syntactic type in this system is

$$n \rightarrow ((np \rightarrow s) \rightarrow s).$$

Thus, it combines with a noun to form a quantifier. This is a higher-order type, since its second argument ($np \to s$) is itself a first-order type. The semantic term labeling *every* is also higher-order and familiar from Montague's work:[5]

$$\lambda P \lambda Q.\forall z(P(z) \to Q(z))$$

The string term is first order with respect to the first argument (we assume that formulas of type n are labeled with strings) and second order with respect to the second argument.

$$\lambda x \lambda Q.Q(every \; x)$$

Finally, we follow the LFG tradition (here) in assuming that f-structures do not indicate the scope of quantifiers.[6] This yields the f-structure term for *every* below.

$$\lambda x \lambda Q.Q\left(\begin{bmatrix} \text{SPEC} & \text{'EVERY'} \\ \text{PRED} & x \end{bmatrix}\right)$$

Putting these together yields the labeled formula that we shall denote **every**:

$$\lambda x \lambda Q.Q(every \; x) \; :$$

$$\lambda x \lambda Q.Q\left(\begin{bmatrix} \text{SPEC} & \text{'EVERY'} \\ \text{PRED} & x \end{bmatrix}\right)$$
$$\lambda P \lambda Q.\forall z(P(z) \to Q(z)) \; :$$

$$n \to ((np \to s) \to s)$$

---

[5] In this term, the variables P and Q are of semantic type $\langle e, t \rangle$ and the standard assumption that this type is appropriate for syntactic type n is implicit.

[6] From the present point of view, of course, it is not essential to assume that f-structures are 'scopeless' representations. We could just as well take the f-structure for the determiner *every* to have attributes SCOPE and RESTR(iction), with values filled by variables bound by λ-abstractions:

$$\lambda x \lambda P.\begin{bmatrix} \text{RESTR} & x \\ \text{SCOPE} & P \end{bmatrix}$$

This possibility raises the question of what properties properly belong to which dimension.

If we interpret the indefinite article *a* as the existential quantifier, we have the following labeled formula **a**:

$$\lambda x \lambda Q. Q(a\ x)\ :$$

$$\lambda x \lambda Q. Q(\begin{bmatrix} \text{SPEC} & \text{'A'} \\ \text{PRED} & x \end{bmatrix})$$

$$\lambda P \lambda Q. \exists z (P(z) \wedge Q(z))\ :$$

$$n \rightarrow ((np \rightarrow s) \rightarrow s)$$

It is worth pausing here to note that each occurrence of a formula in a proof is labeled with exactly one string term, one f-structure term, and one semantic term. Moreover, the interaction of labels across dimensions enforces certain regularities. In particular, the semantic term that comes to occupy the position of the variable P in the course of β-reduction must be the semantic term that corresponds to the f-structure value of the attribute PRED that occurs at the same level as the attribute SPEC with the value of the determiner. A similar relation between semantic terms and f-structures is inherent in this labeled formula with respect to the second argument of the determiner, which fixes its scope. What drives this correspondence is a system of linear type deduction: the implicational fragment of the associative, commutative Lambek calculus **LP**.

We now add two nouns to the store of lexical assumptions, **president** and **judge**:

$$president\ :\quad \text{'president'}\ :\quad P\ :\quad n$$

$$judge\ :\quad\quad \text{'judge'}\ :\quad\quad J\ :\quad n$$

A number of labeled formulas are now derivable from the premise structures corresponding to the following multiset of assumptions:

$$[\textbf{a, president, admired, every, judge}]$$

The derivable labeled formulas are enumerated below:

a president admired every judge :

$$\begin{bmatrix} \text{PRED} & \text{'ADMIRE'} \\ \text{TENSE} & \text{PAST} \\ \text{SUBJ} & \begin{bmatrix} \text{SPEC} & \text{'A'} \\ \text{PRED} & \text{'PRESIDENT'} \end{bmatrix} \\ \text{OBJ} & \begin{bmatrix} \text{SPEC} & \text{'EVERY'} \\ \text{PRED} & \text{'JUDGE'} \end{bmatrix} \end{bmatrix}$$:

$\exists x(P(x) \wedge \forall y(J(y) \rightarrow A(y)(x)))$:

s

a president admired every judge :

$$\begin{bmatrix} \text{PRED} & \text{'ADMIRE'} \\ \text{TENSE} & \text{PAST} \\ \text{SUBJ} & \begin{bmatrix} \text{SPEC} & \text{'A'} \\ \text{PRED} & \text{'PRESIDENT'} \end{bmatrix} \\ \text{OBJ} & \begin{bmatrix} \text{SPEC} & \text{'EVERY'} \\ \text{PRED} & \text{'JUDGE'} \end{bmatrix} \end{bmatrix}$$:

$\forall y(J(y) \rightarrow \exists x(P(x) \wedge A(y)(x)))$:

s

a judge admired every president :

$$\begin{bmatrix} \text{PRED} & \text{'ADMIRE'} \\ \text{TENSE} & \text{PAST} \\ \text{SUBJ} & \begin{bmatrix} \text{SPEC} & \text{'A'} \\ \text{PRED} & \text{'JUDGE'} \end{bmatrix} \\ \text{OBJ} & \begin{bmatrix} \text{SPEC} & \text{'EVERY'} \\ \text{PRED} & \text{'PRESIDENT'} \end{bmatrix} \end{bmatrix}$$:

$\exists x(J(x) \wedge \forall z(P(z) \rightarrow A(z)(x)))$:

s

a judge admired every president :

$$
\begin{bmatrix}
\text{PRED} & \text{'ADMIRE'} \\
\text{TENSE} & \text{PAST} \\
\text{SUBJ} & \begin{bmatrix} \text{SPEC} & \text{'A'} \\ \text{PRED} & \text{'JUDGE'} \end{bmatrix} \\
\text{OBJ} & \begin{bmatrix} \text{SPEC} & \text{'EVERY'} \\ \text{PRED} & \text{'PRESIDENT'} \end{bmatrix}
\end{bmatrix} :
$$

$$\forall z(P(z) \to \exists x(J(x) \land A(z)(x))) :$$

s

every president admired a judge :

$$
\begin{bmatrix}
\text{PRED} & \text{'ADMIRE'} \\
\text{TENSE} & \text{PAST} \\
\text{SUBJ} & \begin{bmatrix} \text{SPEC} & \text{'EVERY'} \\ \text{PRED} & \text{'PRESIDENT'} \end{bmatrix} \\
\text{OBJ} & \begin{bmatrix} \text{SPEC} & \text{'A'} \\ \text{PRED} & \text{'JUDGE'} \end{bmatrix}
\end{bmatrix} :
$$

$$\forall z(P(z) \to \exists x(J(x) \land A(x)(z))) :$$

s

every president admired a judge :

$$
\begin{bmatrix}
\text{PRED} & \text{'ADMIRE'} \\
\text{TENSE} & \text{PAST} \\
\text{SUBJ} & \begin{bmatrix} \text{SPEC} & \text{'EVERY'} \\ \text{PRED} & \text{'PRESIDENT'} \end{bmatrix} \\
\text{OBJ} & \begin{bmatrix} \text{SPEC} & \text{'A'} \\ \text{PRED} & \text{'JUDGE'} \end{bmatrix}
\end{bmatrix} :
$$

$$\exists x(J(x) \land \forall z(P(z) \to A(x)(z))) :$$

s

every judge admired a president :

$$\begin{bmatrix} \text{PRED} & \text{'ADMIRE'} \\ \text{TENSE} & \text{PAST} \\ \text{SUBJ} & \begin{bmatrix} \text{SPEC} & \text{'EVERY'} \\ \text{PRED} & \text{'JUDGE'} \end{bmatrix} \\ \text{OBJ} & \begin{bmatrix} \text{SPEC} & \text{'A'} \\ \text{PRED} & \text{'PRESIDENT'} \end{bmatrix} \end{bmatrix}$$:

$$\forall z(J(z) \rightarrow \exists x(P(x) \wedge A(x)(z)))$$:

s

every judge admired a president :

$$\begin{bmatrix} \text{PRED} & \text{'ADMIRE'} \\ \text{TENSE} & \text{PAST} \\ \text{SUBJ} & \begin{bmatrix} \text{SPEC} & \text{'EVERY'} \\ \text{PRED} & \text{'JUDGE'} \end{bmatrix} \\ \text{OBJ} & \begin{bmatrix} \text{SPEC} & \text{'A'} \\ \text{PRED} & \text{'PRESIDENT'} \end{bmatrix} \end{bmatrix}$$:

$$\exists x(P(x) \wedge \forall z(J(z) \rightarrow A(x)(z)))$$:

s

The structure-building operation which puts together sequent antecedents is the direct counterpart of the linear conjunction $\otimes$, governed by the structural rules of associativity and permutation only. Thus, all possible combinations of compatible functors and arguments arise through proof indeterminacy. Term labeling enforces compatibility among string position, f-structure properties, and the binding of semantic argument positions, in exactly the same way as in the system of labeled deduction of Section 1.

5 Glue Language Constraints

In Chapter 2 of this volume, Dalrymple, Lamping, Pereira, and Saraswat propose a theory of quantification in LFG which has interesting affinities with the systems of labeled deduction discussed above.

They propose (following work by Halvorsen and Kaplan, individually and together) to extend the standard set of LFG structures with a semantic structure—σ-structure—whose properties are derived from f-structures in a way that satisfies structural correspondence constraints stated in a fragment of linear logic called the 'glue language'. These constraints are associated directly with individual entries (not phrase-structure rules). For example, the NP *Bob* is associated with the constraint below, where the subscript σ is the correspondence map between an f-structure and the σ-structure associated with it.

$$\text{*Bob*} \quad \text{NP} \quad (\uparrow \text{PRED}) = \text{'BOB'} \quad \uparrow_\sigma \leadsto \text{*Bob*}$$

Thus, the structural correspondence constraint in this sample lexical entry requires that the σ-structure term associated with the f-structure corresponding to an occurrence of the NP *Bob* is the semantic term *Bob*.

Predicates are associated with a universally-quantified linear implication, illustrated by the example of *admired* below:

$$\text{*admired*} \quad \text{V} \quad (\uparrow \text{PRED}) = \text{'ADMIRE'}$$

$$\forall X, Y.((\uparrow \text{SUBJ})_\sigma \leadsto X \otimes (\uparrow \text{OBJ})_\sigma \leadsto Y) \multimap \uparrow_\sigma \leadsto admire(X,Y)$$

Given the standard c-structure for the sentence *Bob admired Harry*, we have the f-structure below (disregarding tense):

$$f: \begin{bmatrix} \text{PRED} & \text{'ADMIRE'} \\ \text{SUBJ} & g: \begin{bmatrix} \text{PRED} & \text{'BOB'} \end{bmatrix} \\ \text{OBJ} & h: \begin{bmatrix} \text{PRED} & \text{'HARRY'} \end{bmatrix} \end{bmatrix}$$

The structural correspondence constraints associated with the lexical entries involved require the following:

$$g_\sigma \leadsto \text{*Bob*}$$
$$h_\sigma \leadsto \text{*Harry*}$$
$$\forall X, Y.(g_\sigma \leadsto X \otimes h_\sigma \leadsto Y) \multimap f_\sigma \leadsto admire(X,Y)$$

If we take these three formulas as the premises of a linear deduction, we may validly infer the conclusion:

$$f_\sigma \leadsto admire(Bob, Harry)$$

The key connection of this setup with the labeled deductive system introduced earlier is that semantic properties arise in a linear setting relative to a set of constraints involving f-structure properties and semantic argument structure. In the labeled deductive system above, they involve, in parallel, both string position (or c-structure position) and f-structure properties. We observed earlier that in the labeled deductive setting, the lexical correspondence constraint associated with the transitive verb *admired* is an intrinsic consequence of the labeling assumptions. This is particularly clear if one reflects on the connections between the λ-operator and universal quantification, as discussed by Pereira (1991, Section 2.2).

The quantificational properties of the two systems also display fundamental affinities. Both depend on the properties of associativity and commutativity for linear conjunction (represented in our labeled deductive system above by the structure-building operator $(\cdot, \cdot)$ and in the glue language directly by $\otimes$).

6 Discussion

6.1 A basic difference?

In the labeled deductive system above, functional application in the semantic dimension corresponds to functional application in two different term systems and indeed to the rule $\to L$ governing the behavior of the operator $\to$ in sequent antecedents. In the glue language account, functional application in σ-structure depends directly only on properties of f-structure—properties of c-structure and syntactic categorization are abstracted away from. This raises the possibility that the grammars of quantification in the two systems compared here might differ in a fundamental way. In particular, one may observe quantificational scoping behavior in a variety of syntactically distinguishable domains: declarative tensed sentences, tenseless sentences, interrogative sentences. If these are syntactically distinct and incompatible, then quantifiers in the labeled deductive system would need to be associated with multiple types, one for each domain. On the other hand, in the 'glue language' approach, it might be found that the distinctions involved are relevant at c-structure, but irrelevant to the constraints on quantification involving f-structure and σ-structure. This distinction between the two systems deserves further exploration.

6.2   Glue constraints vs. labeling

The labeling relation introduced earlier has clear and clearly delimited properties. There is an appropriateness relation between formulas and labels. Residuation (or the analogue of the deduction theorem) in the formula language corresponds to λ-abstraction in each dimension (both at the level of appropriateness and in the course of deduction). The analogue of modus ponens corresponds to application. From these simple properties, interesting constraints on correspondence arise.

The glue language is less constrained. The fragment of linear logic that it contains is limited, to be sure. But it nevertheless allows a much greater range of structural correspondence constraints to be stated than the simple labeling relation just discussed. If it should turn out that this greater range is unnecessary, then this would favor the labeling relation just defined as a more restrictive way to enforce these constraints.

6.3   How many dimensions are necessary?

On the other hand, the multiplicity of dimensions involved in the two systems compared here—string terms (or c-structures), f-structures, σ-structures—raises the issue of whether all these structural characterizations are indeed required for the adequate, insightful, and elegant analysis of natural language phenomena. For example, the occurrence of the PRED attribute in f-structures seems redundant in the presence of σ-structure. And the properties that depend on its values— particularly the classic properties of Coherence and Completeness—are consequences of deeper issues concerning resource-sensitivity and linear reasoning.

6.4   Are cross-dimensional constraints necessary?

The quantificational properties of the two systems compared here depend on constraints linking different dimensions. Is this architectural assumption a necessary one in any system in which scoping arises as a form of proof indeterminacy? The answer to this question, due to work by Michael Moortgat, is 'no'. Moortgat (1996) shows how quantificational behavior can be modeled in a multi-modal type system, where unary modal operators control the relation between the quantifier and the argument position it binds. Unlike earlier attempts to treat discontinuity phenomena within the framework of categorial type deduction (surveyed in Moortgat and Oehrle 1996), Moortgat's system is sound and complete (for relational Kripke models). Moreover, the connection between deduction and interpretation is the standard Curry-Howard correspondence between proofs and terms.

Moortgat's proposal is formulated in the multi-modal setting where a variety of different structural 'modes', of varying arity, are combined. Each structural mode is associated with a product type constructor. Each product comes with residuals that satisfy the 'residuation/adjointness' laws: in particular, just as the binary product has two residuals, left ($\backslash$) and right ($/$), the unary product $\diamond$ has a single residual $\square^{\downarrow}$. (The downarrow decoration on the $\square^{\downarrow}$ is a reminder that these two modal operators are not interdefinable with negation, but rather that one may think of $\diamond$ as existential with respect to a binary accessibility relation R (say, giving access to future times) and that $\square^{\downarrow}$ is universal with respect to the *converse* of the accessibility relation R (say, as past necessity); this satisfies residuation/adjointness.) Each mode is governed by structural rules and modes may be connected by interaction principles.

The key ideas are, first, to introduce a type constant $\mathbf{t}$ to serve as a structural place holder and, second, to add three modal operators $\diamond, \langle l \rangle, \langle r \rangle$ which interact with a 'wrapping mode' $\circ$ and other modes $\bullet_i$ as follows:

$$
\begin{array}{lccr}
(P0) & & \diamond A \longleftrightarrow A \circ \mathbf{t} & (P0') \\
(P1) & (A \circ B) \bullet C & \longleftrightarrow A \circ \langle 0 \rangle (B \bullet C) & (P1') \\
(P2) & A \bullet (B \circ C) & \longleftrightarrow B \circ \langle 1 \rangle (A \bullet C) & (P2')
\end{array}
$$

A connective $q(A, B, C)$ can be defined as $\diamond(C/_w(\square^{\downarrow} A \backslash_w B))$.

The proof below illustrates how such a type behaves (letting $\diamond_r^l \Delta[\mathbf{t}]$ serve as an abbreviation for the result of a sequence of one or more $P1$ or $P2$ inferences that define a path through the structure Δ to the endsequent position of the quantifier):

$$\dfrac{\dfrac{\dfrac{\dfrac{\dfrac{\dfrac{\Delta[A] \Rightarrow B}{\Delta[\Diamond\Box^{\downarrow}A] \Rightarrow B}\;\Box^{\downarrow}L}{\Delta[\Box^{\downarrow}A \circ \mathbf{t}] \Rightarrow B}\;P0'}{\Box^{\downarrow}A \circ \Diamond^{l}_{r}\Delta[\mathbf{t}] \Rightarrow B}\;P1'/P2'}{\Diamond^{l}_{r}\Delta[\mathbf{t}] \Rightarrow \Box^{\downarrow}A\backslash_{w}B}\;\backslash_{w}R \qquad \Gamma[C] \Rightarrow D}{\Gamma[C/_{w}(\Box^{\downarrow}A\backslash_{w}B) \circ \Diamond^{l}_{r}\Delta[\mathbf{t}]] \Rightarrow D}\;/_{w}L}{\Gamma[\Delta[C/_{w}(\Box^{\downarrow}A\backslash_{w}B) \circ \mathbf{t}]] \Rightarrow D}\;P1/P2}{\Gamma[\Delta[\Diamond(C/_{w}(\Box^{\downarrow}A\backslash_{w}B))]] \Rightarrow D}\;P0}{\Gamma[\Delta[q(A,B,C)]] \Rightarrow D}\;(\textit{def})$$

The final step of the proof is merely the definition. Going up, in the penultimate step, the quantifier $\Diamond$ is traded for the constant $\mathbf{t}$. Then the quantifier travels up through the structure using postulates $P1$ and $P2$, until it finds its scope Δ. At this point, the main connective of the quantifier (minus its leading modal $\Diamond$), is removed. This is the point in the proof which corresponds to the application of the quantifier meaning to the meaning of its scope. In the left premise of this rule, the succedent type $\Box^{\downarrow}A\backslash_{w}B$ launches a hypothetical argument $\Box^{\downarrow}A$. Using the trail of switches left behind in the steps below by the moving quantifier, this hypothetical argument $\Box^{\downarrow}A$ finds its way back to the constant $\mathbf{t}$, and trades the constant for a diamond $\Diamond$. Finally, the co-unit rule of the adjointness relation, $\Diamond\Box^{\downarrow}A \rightarrow A$ applies.

In the presence of two quantifiers, scope ambiguities arise, as illustrated by the two proofs displayed below, where Q_1 is a quantifier with the Moortgat type in subject position, $(np\backslash s)/np$ is a transitive verb, and Q_2 is a quantifier with the Moortgat type in object position. The final step of the first proof shows the step in which the abbreviation Q_1 replaces the actual quantifier formula; the final step of the second proof shows the analogous step for the object quantifier Q_2. In the first proof, the subject quantifier takes wide scope; in the second, the object quantifier takes wide scope.

$$\vdots$$

$$np \bullet ((np\backslash s)/np \bullet np) \Rightarrow s$$

$$np \bullet ((np\backslash s)/np \bullet \Diamond\Box^{\downarrow}np) \Rightarrow s$$

$$np \bullet ((np\backslash s)/np \bullet (\Box^{\downarrow}np \circ \mathbf{t})) \Rightarrow s$$

$$np \bullet (\Box^{\downarrow}np \circ \langle 1\rangle((np\backslash s)/np \bullet \mathbf{t})) \Rightarrow s$$

$$\Box^{\downarrow}np \circ (\langle 1\rangle(np \bullet \langle 1\rangle((np\backslash s)/np \bullet \mathbf{t}))) \Rightarrow s$$

$$\langle 1\rangle(np \bullet \langle 1\rangle((np\backslash s)/np \bullet \mathbf{t})) \Rightarrow \Box^{\downarrow}np\backslash_w s \qquad s \Rightarrow s$$

$$s/_w(\Box^{\downarrow}np\backslash_w s) \circ \langle 1\rangle(np \bullet \langle 1\rangle((np\backslash s)/np \bullet \mathbf{t})) \Rightarrow s$$

$$np \bullet (s/_w(\Box^{\downarrow}np\backslash_w s) \circ \langle 1\rangle((np\backslash s)/np \bullet \mathbf{t})) \Rightarrow s$$

$$np \bullet ((np\backslash s)/np \bullet (s/_w(\Box^{\downarrow}np\backslash_w s) \circ \mathbf{t})) \Rightarrow s$$

$$np \bullet ((np\backslash s)/np \bullet \Diamond(s/_w(\Box^{\downarrow}np\backslash_w s))) \Rightarrow s$$

$$\Diamond\Box^{\downarrow}np \bullet (\ldots) \Rightarrow s$$

$$(\Box^{\downarrow}np \circ \mathbf{t}) \bullet (\ldots) \Rightarrow s$$

$$\Box^{\downarrow}np \circ \langle 0\rangle(\mathbf{t} \bullet (\ldots)) \Rightarrow s$$

$$\langle 0\rangle(\mathbf{t} \bullet (\ldots)) \Rightarrow \Box^{\downarrow}np\backslash_w s \qquad s \Rightarrow s$$

$$s/_w(\Box^{\downarrow}np\backslash_w s) \circ \langle 0\rangle(\mathbf{t} \bullet (\ldots)) \Rightarrow s$$

$$(s/_w(\Box^{\downarrow}np\backslash_w s) \circ \mathbf{t}) \bullet (\ldots) \Rightarrow s$$

$$(\Diamond(s/_w(\Box^{\downarrow}np\backslash_w s)) \bullet (\ldots)) \Rightarrow s$$

$$\mathcal{Q}_1 \bullet ((np\backslash s)/np \bullet \mathcal{Q}_2) \Rightarrow s$$

$$\vdots$$

$$np \bullet ((np\backslash s)/np \bullet np) \Rightarrow s$$
$$\Diamond\Box^{\downarrow}np \bullet (\ldots) \Rightarrow s$$
$$(\Box^{\downarrow}np \circ \mathbf{t}) \bullet (\ldots) \Rightarrow s$$
$$\Box^{\downarrow}np \circ \langle 0\rangle(\mathbf{t} \bullet (\ldots)) \Rightarrow s$$
$$\langle 0\rangle(\mathbf{t} \bullet (\ldots)) \Rightarrow \Box^{\downarrow}np\backslash_w s \qquad s \Rightarrow s$$
$$s/_w(\Box^{\downarrow}np\backslash_w s) \circ \langle 0\rangle(\mathbf{t} \bullet (\ldots)) \Rightarrow s$$
$$(s/_w(\Box^{\downarrow}np\backslash_w s) \circ \mathbf{t}) \bullet (\ldots) \Rightarrow s$$
$$(\Diamond(s/_w(\Box^{\downarrow}np\backslash_w s)) \bullet (\ldots)) \Rightarrow s$$
$$\mathcal{Q}_1 \bullet ((np\backslash s)/np \bullet np) \Rightarrow s$$
$$\mathcal{Q}_1 \bullet ((np\backslash s)/np \bullet \Diamond\Box^{\downarrow}np) \Rightarrow s$$
$$\mathcal{Q}_1 \bullet ((np\backslash s)/np \bullet (\Box^{\downarrow}np \circ \mathbf{t})) \Rightarrow s$$
$$\mathcal{Q}_1 \bullet (\Box^{\downarrow}np \circ \langle 1\rangle((np\backslash s)/np \bullet \mathbf{t})) \Rightarrow s$$
$$\Box^{\downarrow}np \circ (\langle 1\rangle(np \bullet \langle 1\rangle((np\backslash s)/np \bullet \mathbf{t}))) \Rightarrow s$$
$$\langle 1\rangle(np \bullet \langle 1\rangle((np\backslash s)/np \bullet \mathbf{t})) \Rightarrow \Box^{\downarrow}np\backslash_w s \qquad s \Rightarrow s$$
$$s/_w(\Box^{\downarrow}np\backslash_w s) \circ \langle 1\rangle(np \bullet \langle 1\rangle((np\backslash s)/np \bullet \mathbf{t})) \Rightarrow s$$
$$\mathcal{Q}_1 \bullet (s/_w(\Box^{\downarrow}np\backslash_w s) \circ \langle 1\rangle((np\backslash s)/np \bullet \mathbf{t})) \Rightarrow s$$
$$\mathcal{Q}_1 \bullet ((np\backslash s)/np \bullet (s/_w(\Box^{\downarrow}np\backslash_w s) \circ \mathbf{t})) \Rightarrow s$$
$$\mathcal{Q}_1 \bullet ((np\backslash s)/np \bullet \Diamond(s/_w(\Box^{\downarrow}np\backslash_w s))) \Rightarrow s$$
$$\mathcal{Q}_1 \bullet ((np\backslash s)/np \bullet \mathcal{Q}_2) \Rightarrow s$$

The characteristic feature of this system is that it is not necessary to add commutativity and associativity as global options of resource management and then constrain them with cross-dimensional labels or other constraints. Instead, the special inference properties of the quantifier type are managed and selectively controlled through modal type constructors which are intrinsic to the deductive system itself. Moreover, this approach to 'discontinuity phenomena' doesn't suffer from the incompleteness of earlier attempts to extend categorial grammars with extraction and infixation operators.

Semantic interpretation obeys the usual canons of the Curry-Howard assignment of terms to proofs. A preliminary study of the interaction of quantification and binding phenomena within this setting can be found in Oehrle (1997).

Acknowledgments

This material is based upon work supported by the National Science Foundation under Grant No. SBR-9510706. Earlier versions were presented at the fourth Mathematics of Language conference at the University of Pennsylvania in October 1995 and at the Rank Xerox Research Centre in spring 1996. I thank the audiences on these occasions for their comments. Wojciech Buszkowski, Mary Dalrymple, Mark Johnson, and Michael Moortgat have been generous with their help. In addition, I have benefited greatly from the comments of two anonymous referees. Errors and oversights are mine.

References

Dörre, Jochen, Esther König, and Dov Gabbay. 1995. Fibred semantics for feature-based grammar logic. *Journal of Logic, Language and Information* 5(3–4): 387–422. Special Issue on Language and Proof Theory.

Dymetman, Marc. 1992. A generalized Greibach Normal Form for definite clause grammars. In *Proceedings of the 15th International Conference on Computational Linguistics (COLING-92)*, Nantes, volume 1, pages 366–372.

Gabbay, Dov M. 1996. *Labelled Deductive Systems*. Clarendon Press, Oxford.

Girard, Jean-Yves. 1987. Linear logic. *Theoretical Computer Science*, 50:1–102.

Kaplan, Ronald M. and Joan Bresnan. 1982. Lexical-Functional Grammar: A formal system for grammatical representation. In Joan Bresnan, editor, *The Mental Representation of Grammatical Relations*, pages 173–281. The MIT Press, Cambridge, MA. Reprinted in Mary Dalrymple, Ronald M. Kaplan, John Maxwell, and Annie Zaenen, editors, *Formal Issues in Lexical-Functional Grammar*, pages 29–130. CSLI Publications, Stanford University. 1995.

Kaplan, Ronald M. 1989. The formal architecture of Lexical-Functional Grammar. In Chu-Ren Huang and Keh-Jiann Chen, editors, *Proceedings of RO-CLING II*, pages 3–18, 1989. Reprinted in Mary Dalrymple, Ronald M. Kaplan, John Maxwell, and Annie Zaenen, editors, *Formal Issues in Lexical-Functional Grammar*, pages 7–27. CSLI Publications, Stanford University. 1995.

König, Esther. 1995. Lexical Functional Grammars and Lexical Grammars. Technical report, Institute for Computational Linguistics, Universität Stuttgart.

Moortgat, Michael. 1996. In situ binding. In *Proceedings of the 10th Amsterdam Colloquium*. ILLC, Amsterdam. Universiteit van Amsterdam.

Moortgat, Michael and Richard T. Oehrle. 1996. Structural abstractions. In V. Michele Abrusci and Claudia Casadio, editors, *Proofs and Linguistic Categories: Application of Logic to the Analysis and Implementation of Natural Language*, Proceedings of the 1996 Roma Workshop, pages 49–64. Società Italiana di Logica e Filosofia della Scienza and Centro Interdipartimentale di Ricerca in Epistemolgia e Storia delle Scienze "F. Enriques", Bologna.

Oehrle, Richard T. 1994. Term-labeled categorial type systems. *Linguistics and Philosophy*, 17:633–678.

Oehrle, Richard T. 1995. Some 3-dimensional systems of labelled deduction. *Bulletin of the Interest Group in Pure and Applied Logics*, 3.2-3.4:29–448.

Oehrle, Richard T. 1997. Binding as deduction. In Geert-Jan Kruijff, Glyn V. Morrill, and Richard T. Oehrle, editors, *Formal Grammar 1997: Linguistic Aspects of Logical and Computational Perspectives on Language*, pages 40–54, Aix en Provence. European Summer School in Logic, Language and Information.

Pereira, Fernando C. N. 1991. Semantic interpretation as higher-order deduction. In Jan van Eijck, editor, *Logics in AI: European Workshop JELIA'90*, pages 78–96. Springer-Verlag, Amsterdam.

Troelstra, A. S. 1991. *Lectures on Linear Logic*. CSLI Lecture Notes, number 29. CSLI Publications, Stanford University.

van Benthem, Johan. 1986. *Essays in Logical Semantics*. D. Reidel, Dordrecht.

van Benthem, Johan. 1988. The Lambek calculus. In Richard T. Oehrle, Emmon Bach, and Deirdre W. Wheeler, editors, *Categorial Grammar and Natural Languages Structures*, pages 35–68. D. Reidel, Dordrecht.

van Benthem, Johan. 1995. *Language in Action: Categories, Lambdas, and Dynamic Logic*. The MIT Press, Cambridge, MA.

10

Type-driven Semantic Interpretation and Feature Dependencies in R-LFG

Mark Johnson

1 Introduction

This paper describes a new formalization of Lexical Functional Grammar called R-LFG (where the "R" stands for "Resource-based"). The formal details of R-LFG are presented in Johnson (1999); the present work concentrates on motivating R-LFG and explaining to linguists how it differs from the "classical" LFG framework presented in Kaplan and Bresnan (1982).

This work is largely a reaction to the linear logic semantics for LFG developed by Dalrymple and colleagues and presented in Chapter 1 and Chapter 2. As explained below, it seems to me that their "glue language" approach bears a partial resemblance to those versions of Categorial Grammar which exploit the Curry-Howard correspondence to obtain semantic interpretation (van Benthem 1995), such as Lambek Categorial Grammar and its descendants. A primary goal of this work is to develop a version of LFG in which this connection is made explicit, and in which semantic interpretation falls out as a by-product of the Curry-Howard correspondence rather than needing to be stipulated via semantic interpretation rules.

Once one has enriched LFG's formal machinery with the linear logic mechanisms needed for semantic interpretation, it is natural to ask whether these make any existing components of LFG redundant. As Dalrymple and her colleagues note, LFG's f-structure completeness and coherence constraints fall out as a by-product of the linear logic machinery they propose for semantic interpretation, thus making those f-structure mechanisms redundant. Given that linear logic machinery or something like it is independently needed for semantic interpretation, it seems reasonable to explore the extent to which it is capable of handling feature structure constraints as well.

R-LFG represents the extreme position that *all* linguistically required feature structure dependencies can be captured by the resource-accounting machinery of a linear or similar logic independently needed for semantic interpretation. The goal is to show that LFG linguistic analyses can be expressed as clearly and perspicuously using the smaller set of mechanisms of R-LFG as they can using the much larger set of mechanisms in LFG: if this is the case then we will have shown that positing these extra f-structure mechanisms is not linguistically warranted. One way to show this would be to present a translation procedure which reduces LFGs to equivalent R-LFGs, but currently no such procedure is known. Thus we proceed on a case by case basis, demonstrating that particular LFG analyses can be expressed at least as well in R-LFG.

R-LFG is also of interest because it proposes a radically different basis for feature structure interaction. In "unification-based" theories of grammar, feature structures are typically viewed as static objects, which are the solutions to systems of feature structure constraints (called *f-descriptions* in LFG) (Kaplan and Bresnan 1982; Shieber 1986; Rounds 1997). However, linguists often talk informally of "feature assignment" and "feature checking", notions which cannot be expressed in a pure unification grammar. As discussed below, LFG does contain formal devices which can express these notions indirectly, viz., the non-monotonic devices of existential constraints and "sub-c" constraint equations. These devices seem to be incompatible with the standard model-theoretic treatments of feature structure constraints, and for this reason formal treatments of feature structures often restrict their attention solely to monotonic constraints. In order to formally account for these non-monotonic devices it seems to be necessary to treat feature structure constraints as objects or resources in their own right, e.g., as in Saraswat's elegant account presented in Chapter 8 of this book. Saraswat's treatment follows LFG closely and incorporates both the constraint-based as well as the resource-based character of feature-structure constraints in LFG, although at the cost of significantly complicating the simple model-theoretic semantics for feature structures. R-LFG presents a simpler response to the incompatibility between non-monotonic constraints and classical model-theoretic feature logics: namely, classical constraint-based feature logic is abandoned, and features are treated simply as resources. This radically simplifies the formal framework while providing a direct and natural formalization of the intuitions behind feature assignment and feature checking.

Because the focus of the work on R-LFG differs from that of the work of Dalrymple and her colleagues, the empirical phenomena treated differ too. As I understand it, the goal of the "glue logic" research is to provide an account of the syntax-semantics interface which is compatible with classical LFG syntactic analyses. The goal of the R-LFG research is to better understand the relationship between "resource accounting" mechanisms and feature structure constraints; specifically, to determine if the work usually done by monotonic feature structure constraints in LFG might not be done as well or better by resource mechanisms. This is a serious empirical question: it is not by any means clear that the resource-oriented mechanisms of R-LFG can support all of the linguistic tasks played by monotonic feature structure constraints. This leads to a different research emphasis: work in the glue language approach focusses on semantic phenomena that classical LFG does not account for, while this paper focusses on syntactic phenomena which classical LFG does already describe.

The rest of this paper is structured as follows. The next section introduces type-driven semantic interpretation from f-structures, and the one after that sketches the architecture of R-LFG and compares it to that of standard LFG. The following section introduces the reader to the idea that features are resources by demonstrating that one method of describing agreement relationships in standard LFG already possesses a resource-oriented character. The section following that describes how very simple agreement relationships can be described in R-LFG, and the final substantive section shows how Andrews' (1982) analysis of Icelandic Quirky Case marking can be re-expressed in R-LFG.

2 Type-driven Interpretation from F-Structures

This section develops type-driven semantic interpretation from graph structured resources used in R-LFG, motivating it by considering type-driven semantic interpretation from linearly ordered structures of categories used in Categorial Grammar.

As has often been observed, the types of semantic objects constrain how they can combine, and hence the interpretations that can be possibly constructed from a bag of semantic objects. For example, suppose the words *Sandy* and *snores* are given the semantic interpretations in (1) and (2) with the types as shown.

(1) $$Sandy : e$$

(2) $$\lambda x.snores(x) : e \multimap t$$

(The symbol '$\multimap$' is the implication symbol of Linear Logic, so the type $e \multimap t$ would be written $e \to t$ in a Montagovian notation for types.) Now, there is only one way of combining these semantic objects to form a saturated proposition of type t, namely by applying the semantic interpretation of the verb *snores* to the interpretation of *Sandy* as its argument, so this is the only possible interpretation of the intransitive clause *Sandy snores*. This combination can be depicted as a proof (shown in natural deduction format here), where the two input semantic forms constitute the assumptions, and the single saturated proposition produced by the combination constitutes the conclusion.[1]

$$\frac{\lambda x.snores(x) : e \multimap t \quad Sandy : e}{snores(Sandy) : t}$$

It is worth reflecting on what is going on here. The types alone determine whether a particular way of combining lexical meanings is possible or not. The λ-terms, which provide the semantic interpretation, are purely decorative labels: they are completely determined (up to reduction and renaming of variables) by the meanings of the lexical inputs and the structure of the combination.

The idea that a logic can be used to describe the possible modes of combination of a collection of objects underlies the Curry-Howard

---

[1] The resulting semantic form has been simplified via β-reduction.

correspondence, and is at the root of much recent work in Categorial Grammar (van Benthem 1995). The formulae of such a logic are the types of the objects being manipulated, and a proof in this logic corresponds to a particular way of combining the objects. The λ-terms are decorative labels adorning subproofs that are images of the structure of the subproof, and play no role in determining whether a combination is possible or not.

Unfortunately, in more complex sentences semantic type constraints alone are not sufficiently restrictive to provide just the actually occurring interpretations. For example, if the semantic interpretations of the three words in the sentence *Sandy likes Kim* are as given in (1), (3) and (4):

(3) $\qquad\qquad\qquad \lambda y\,\lambda x.likes(x,y) : e \multimap e \multimap t$

(4) $\qquad\qquad\qquad\qquad Kim : e$

(where '$\multimap$' associates to the right) then besides permitting a combination corresponding to the available interpretation

$$(5) \quad \frac{\displaystyle Sandy : e \quad \frac{\lambda y\,\lambda x.likes(x,y) : e \multimap e \multimap t \quad Kim : e}{\lambda x.likes(x,Kim) : e \multimap t}}{likes(Sandy,Kim) : t}$$

the semantic type constraints alone also permit an interpretation in which the subject *Kim* and the object *Sandy* are exchanged.

$$(6) \quad \frac{\displaystyle \frac{Sandy : e \quad \lambda y\,\lambda x.likes(x,y) : e \multimap e \multimap t}{\lambda x.likes(x,Sandy) : e \multimap t} \quad Kim : e}{likes(Kim,Sandy) : t}$$

It is obvious why the unintended interpretation was obtained. The semantic types do not reflect any information about the syntactic structure of the sentence: merely requiring semantic type compatibility amounts to treating a sentence as a bag of words, ignoring all other structural relationships between the words. Clearly this is incorrect for a language like English (as this example shows).

Standard categorial grammar deals with this problem by refining the structural sensitivity of the system: the elements manipulated are taken to be a linearly ordered sequence of categories, rather than just a bag. Correspondingly, the types are refined to be sensitive to this additional structural information. The single implication '$\multimap$' used above is specialized into a rightward-looking implication '/' and a leftward-looking implication '\' respectively.

The types associated with intransitive and transitive verbs are refined from (2) and (3) to (7) and (8), which specify the directions in which their arguments are to be found.

$$(7) \qquad\qquad \lambda x.snores(x) : e \setminus t$$

$$(8) \qquad\qquad \lambda y\, \lambda x.likes(x,y) : (e \setminus t)\, /\, e$$

This directional sensitivity rules out the unattested combination (6), only permitting a combination that corresponds to the available interpretation.

$$\frac{\displaystyle Sandy : e \qquad \frac{\lambda y\, \lambda x.likes(x,y) : (e \setminus t)\, /\, e \quad Kim : e}{\lambda x.likes(x,Kim) : e \setminus t}}{likes(Sandy,Kim) : t}$$

Categorial grammarians have developed many insightful linguistic analyses within this framework. The treatment of the syntax-semantics interface within a framework such as Lambek Categorial Grammar and its descendants is especially appealing: once the lexical types and modes of syntactic combination are specified, semantic interpretation comes "for free" via the Curry-Howard correspondence between proofs of type well-formedness and λ-terms.

However, the focus on linear order in categorial grammar goes against one of the central intuitions of Lexical Functional Grammar: that the level of word order and surface syntactic structure is not an appropriate one at which to state many cross-linguistic generalizations. Rather, many interesting cross-linguistic generalizations are more appropriately stated at the level of function-argument or f-structure.

For example, as Bresnan (1982) argues, the relationship between a verb and its direct object NP argument may manifest itself cross-linguistically in many different surface syntactic relationships:

- it may be indicated by an agreement marker on the verb, or by

- a case marker on the direct object NP, or by

- a syntactic configuration, where the object immediately precedes or follows the verb as is appropriate, or by

- any combination of the above.

At the level of function argument structure the cross-linguistic uniformity of grammatical relation changing operations such as Passive becomes apparent. A central assumption underlying LFG is that a description of linguistic processes in terms of function-argument relationships permits simpler and cross-linguistically more uniform accounts of most linguistic phenomena than would corresponding accounts in terms of surface syntactic structures.

Thus from an LFG perspective, the appropriate response to the unattested combination (6) is to make the types sensitive to function-argument structure rather than word order directly. That is, the input to the combinatory process of semantic interpretation should be f-structures, rather than strings of lexical items.

Both R-LFG and the "glue language" framework described in Chapter 1 achieve this to a large extent. In both systems semantic interpretation is obtained by a Curry-Howard correspondence in much the same way as in categorial grammar. They both differ from categorial grammar in that the inputs to the derivational process have the graph structure of an f-structure, rather than the linear structure of a string.

Borrowing the idea that features in feature structures can be described by modal operators in a multi-modal language (Kasper and Rounds 1990; Rounds 1997), grammatical relations in R-LFG are formalized as propositional modal operators. Returning to the earlier example, the NP *Sandy* and the transitive verb *likes* would be associated with the lexical entries (9) and (10).

(9) $\qquad\qquad\qquad\qquad Sandy : e$

(10) $\qquad\qquad\qquad \lambda y\, \lambda x.likes(x, y) : \text{OBJ}\, e \multimap \text{SUBJ}\, e \multimap t$

(The modal operators 'SUBJ', 'OBJ', etc., are semantically vacuous, i.e., always semantically interpreted by identity functions, and bind more tightly than the implication symbol '$\multimap$'.) This entry indicates that the verb *likes* first applies to an object of type e (embedded within the OBJ grammatical relation), yielding a function which in turn applies to a subject of type e to yield a saturated proposition of type t.[2]

Assuming that in a transitive clause such as *Sandy likes Kim* the NP *Sandy* can be identified as subject and *Kim* as object (in English, this occurs by virtue of their c-structure locations), the following derivation yields the one available interpretation for this sentence.

$$\cfrac{\quad Sandy : \text{SUBJ}\, e \quad \cfrac{\lambda y\, \lambda x.likes(x,y) : \text{OBJ}\, e \multimap \text{SUBJ}\, e \multimap t \quad Kim : \text{OBJ}\, e}{\lambda x.likes(x, Kim) : \text{SUBJ}\, e \multimap t}}{likes(Sandy, Kim) : t}$$

Following standard treatments of feature structures, re-entrancies are described by path equations $f_1 \ldots f_m = g_1 \ldots g_n$, which permit a resource structure $f_1 \ldots f_m \alpha$ to be transformed to $g_1 \ldots g_n \alpha$. For example, Subject Raising in LFG is described in terms of a re-entrancy between the matrix subject position and the complement's subject position, licensed by a path equation associated with the Subject Raising verb. The lexical items in the sentence *Sandy seems happy* would be associated with the lexical entries (9), (11) and (12).

(11) $\lambda P.seems(P) : \text{XCOMP}\, t \multimap t, \text{SUBJ} = \text{XCOMP}\,\text{SUBJ}$

(12) $\lambda x.happy(x) : \text{SUBJ}\, e \multimap t$

Again, assuming that *Sandy* and *happy* are identified as filling the SUBJ and XCOMP grammatical functions respectively, the following deduction shows how the available interpretation for *Sandy seems happy* can be obtained.

$$\cfrac{\lambda P.seems(P):\text{XCOMP}\,t \multimap t \quad \cfrac{\cfrac{\lambda x.happy(x):\text{XCOMP}(\text{SUBJ}\, e \multimap t)}{\lambda x.happy(x):\text{XCOMP}\,\text{SUBJ}\, e \multimap \text{XCOMP}\, t} \quad * \quad \cfrac{Sandy:\text{SUBJ}\, e \quad \text{SUBJ} = \text{XCOMP}\,\text{SUBJ}}{Sandy:\text{XCOMP}\,\text{SUBJ}\, e}}{happy(Sandy):\text{XCOMP}\, t}}{seems(happy(Sandy)) : t}$$

---

[2]The terms SUBJ e and OBJ e correspond to distinct constants of type e in the "glue language" approach of Chapter 1. The use of modal operators in R-LFG permits these modal formulae to play the role of a feature structure, so extra mechanisms for computing the glue language formulae from f-structures are not required in R-LFG.

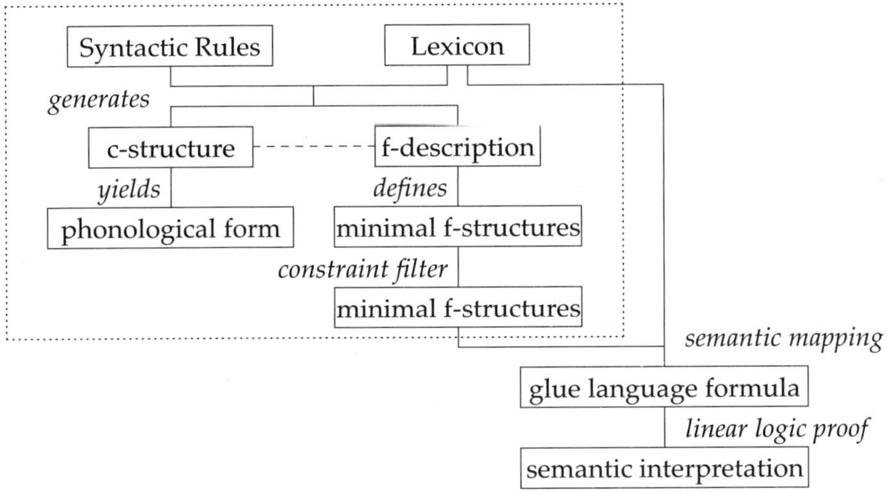

Figure 10.1: The architecture of standard LFG. The linear logic semantics component is shown outside the dotted box.

The inference labelled '∗' requires the grammatical relation XCOMP to distribute over the implication operator '−∘'.

3　R-LFG: A Simplification of LFG

The architectural simplification of R-LFG is best appreciated when compared with that of standard LFG together with the linear logic semantics augmentation of Dalrymple and colleagues. This section starts by sketching the architecture of standard LFG, and then presents the revised architecture of R-LFG.

3.1　The architecture of standard LFG

Figure 10.1 shows the architecture of "standard" LFG. The components of LFG as presented by Kaplan and Bresnan (1982) are shown inside the dotted box in this figure, and the linear logic machinery for semantic interpretation posited by Dalrymple and colleagues is depicted outside this box.

In LFG, a syntactic description of an utterance is taken to be a pair consisting of a c-structure and an f-structure.[3] The yield of the c-structure tree determines the phonological form of the sentence it describes.

The c-structure/f-structure pairs generated by an LFG are determined by the following procedure. The syntactic rules and lexical entries of an LFG together generate a set of c-structure trees, each of which is paired with a formula called an f-description which identifies which (if any) f-structures this c-structure can be paired with. The f-descriptions are boolean combinations of equations. These equations come in two kinds: *defining* and *constraining* equations.

The relationship between f-descriptions and the f-structures as outlined by Kaplan and Bresnan (1982) has a distinctly procedural flavour. First, the f-description is expanded into Disjunctive Normal Form (DNF) and the f-structure solution to each conjunct is determined as follows. The constraining equations are temporarily ignored (i.e., replaced with *true*) and if the resulting formula is satisfiable and has a unique minimal satisfying f-structure, that f-structure is a candidate solution to the conjunct. This candidate solution is a (true) solution to the conjunct just in case it also satisfies the formula obtained by replacing each constraining equation in the conjunct with corresponding defining equations. The set of solutions to an f-description is the union of the set of solutions to each conjunct of its DNF, so the f-description determines a finite number of f-structures.[4]

---

[3] There are proposals for additional structures, which for simplicity are ignored here.

[4] To appreciate some of the difficulties in giving a declarative treatment of LFG's constraint equations, consider a treatment of Case marking in which subject NPs are optionally assigned a nominative Case feature NOM, such as the Andrews (1982) analysis of Icelandic quirky case marking discussed in section 5.2, using the following LFG syntactic rule.

$$S \rightarrow \quad \begin{array}{c} \text{NP} \\ (\uparrow \text{ SUBJ}) = \downarrow \\ ((\uparrow \text{ SUBJ CASE}) = \text{NOM}) \end{array} \quad \begin{array}{c} \text{VP} \\ \uparrow = \downarrow \end{array}$$

The parentheses surrounding the lower equation annotating the NP indicates that this defining equation is optional, reflecting the fact that the subject NP is only optionally assigned nominative case (as it may be assigned a 'quirky' non-nominative case by the verb, as explained below). This annotation presumably abbreviates the following disjunction:

$$(\uparrow \text{ SUBJ CASE}) = \text{NOM} \ \lor \ \textit{true}$$

Clearly replacing this disjunction with *true* does not change the set of minimal models for any f-description which contains it, so the equation itself has no effect on the minimal

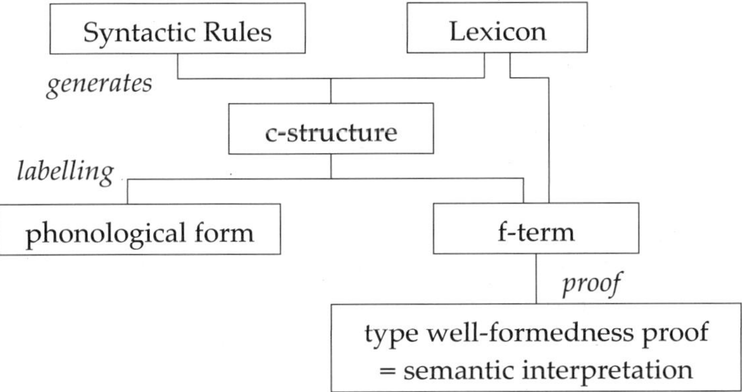

Figure 10.2: The architecture of R-LFG.

Dalrymple et al. use these f-structures as the input to their semantic interpretation procedure. Certain elements in an f-structure are associated with formulae in a *glue language*, which is an amalgam of linear logic and classical first-order logic, in effect mapping each f-structure into a formula of the glue language. For semantic interpretation to succeed this glue language formula must derive a term with the type of a saturated proposition: the argument of this term is the semantic interpretation of the sentence.

3.2 The architecture of R-LFG

The architecture of R-LFG is depicted in Figure 10.2. The most striking difference between LFG and R-LFG is that R-LFG does not contain an independent level of f-structure representation, since the same mechanisms used for semantic interpretation are also used to account for syntactic feature dependencies. Given that it is a simpler architecture, it should be preferred on grounds of parsimony.

---

models, and hence cannot result in the satisfaction of any constraint equations. Clearly this is not the intended interpretation: the "purpose" of this equation is to provide a Case feature to satisfy the requirements of the subject NP.

Saraswat's account in Chapter 8 avoids this difficulty by using linear disjunction '&', but at the expense of losing the original model-theoretic feature structure semantics, as discussed above.

The lexical entries and syntactic rules of R-LFG generate c-structure/f-term pairs in the same way that they generate c-structure/f-description pairs in LFG. In LFG several steps are required to obtain the f-structures that serve as the input to semantic interpretation from the f-descriptions. However, in R-LFG the f-term serves as the input to semantic interpretation directly. Thus in R-LFG the linguistic effects of f-structure constraints must be obtained by other means, viz., the same logical mechanisms used for semantic interpretation.

As explained below, these logical mechanisms enforce a *resource accounting* which ensures that every predicate combines with an appropriate number of arguments and that every non-root semantic unit appears as the argument of some predicate. The semantic interpretation itself is determined by the pattern of predicate-argument combination via a Curry-Howard correspondence, as explained in more detail in Johnson (1999).

This same resource accounting mechanism is also used to describe feature dependencies. Purely syntactic features with no semantic content differ from semantically interpreted elements only in that they are semantically vacuous, i.e., given trivial interpretations which are systematically ignored by any functors which take them as arguments.

The resource logic used here differs considerably from the glue language used by Dalrymple et al. That language includes first-order terms with equality, which can be used to encode feature structure unification in the manner of e.g., Definite Clause Grammars, and hence directly simulate f-structure attribute-value constraints (see Shieber (1986) for a description of the relationship between the first-order terms of Definite Clause Grammars and attribute-value "unification" grammars). While this would provide a straightforward way to encode f-structure constraints in the glue language, it is not clear that such an approach would constitute a real simplification of LFG, rather than just a reshuffling of its complexity.

For this reason, R-LFG uses a much simpler resource logic than the glue language of Dalrymple et al. Inspired by recent work in Categorial Grammar such as Morrill (1994), the resource logic is based on a propositional modal logic, which encodes the types of the semantic objects being manipulated, and the semantic interpretation itself is provided by a Curry-Howard correspondence between proofs and λ-terms (Girard et al. 1989). As van Benthem (1995) demonstrates, a wide variety of substructural logics possess a Curry-Howard correspondence, so the requirement that semantic interpretation is obtained in this way does not identify a particular logic. Rather, the precise logic used should be chosen to best fit the linguistic phenomena described by the theory. Moortgat (1997) develops the theory of propositional multimodal logics used here.

4   Describing Agreement Relationships with LFG

This section argues that Lexical Functional grammarians typically use the formal devices of LFG to manipulate features as resources that are assigned and checked. It introduces two methods often used for describing agreement relationships in LFGs. It turns out that one method, which crucially relies on "constraining equations", can be viewed as describing agreement in terms of resource dependencies. Thus resource-based accounts of agreement are not a new innovation of R-LFG, but are already a familiar part of LFG. The principal claim behind R-LFG is that *all* linguistic dependencies can be expressed in this manner, and that the explicit resource-orientation of R-LFG simplifies and clarifies the nature of the linguistic dependencies concerned.

As explained in more detail in Kaplan and Bresnan (1982), LFG's f-descriptions contain two different kinds of equations. A defining equation instantiates the value of an attribute, while a constraining equation checks that a value is instantiated by a defining equation elsewhere in the f-description. The linguistic dependencies involved in simple agreement can be described using defining equations alone, or by using a mixture of defining and constraining equations. This latter method has a natural resource interpretation.

To keep things clear, the two methods for describing agreement relationships are explained using the same examples (13).

(13) a.   Sandy snores.

      b.   Professors snore.

Both methods of describing agreement relationships require that the agreeing items (in (13a), *Sandy* and *snores*) are capable of constraining the value of the same f-structure element; this is usually achieved by defining equations associated with syntactic rules. The agreeing items both impose constraints on the value of that shared f-structure element, thus ensuring that only compatible items can appear simultaneously in a syntactic structure.

4.1   Agreement using defining equations alone

In this method, both agreeing items constrain the shared f-structure element using defining equations. For example, the grammar fragment in (14–18) generates exactly the two sentences in (13). The c-structure and f-structure generated by this fragment for (13a) is depicted in Figure 10.3.

(14)   *Sandy*   NP $(\uparrow$ PRED$) = $ 'Sandy'
    $(\uparrow$ NUM$) = $ SG

(15)   *Professors*   NP $(\uparrow$ PRED$) = $ 'professor'
    $(\uparrow$ NUM$) = $ PL

(16)   *snores*   VP $(\uparrow$ PRED$) = $ 'snore$\langle(\uparrow$ SUBJ$)\rangle$'
    $\underline{(\uparrow$ SUBJ NUM$) = $ SG}

(17)   *snore*   VP $(\uparrow$ PRED$) = $ 'snore$\langle(\uparrow$ SUBJ$)\rangle$'
    $\underline{(\uparrow$ SUBJ NUM$) = $ PL}

(18)   S $\longrightarrow$ NP   VP
    $(\uparrow$ SUBJ$) = \downarrow$ $\uparrow = \downarrow$

The lexical entries for subject NPs require that the value of their NUM attribute is SG or PL as appropriate. In addition, the underlined equation in each verb's lexical entry also requires that this value is appropriate for the verb's inflection. If the subject and the verb require different values for this f-structure element (as in the ungrammatical **Professors snores*), the corresponding f-description will require this element to be equal to two different values (e.g., SG and PL). However, the well-formedness conditions on f-structures do not permit this (Kaplan and

$$
\begin{array}{c}
\text{S} \\
\diagup \diagdown \\
\text{NP} \quad \text{VP} \\
| \qquad | \\
\text{Sandy} \quad \text{V} \\
| \\
\text{snores}
\end{array}
\qquad
\begin{bmatrix}
\text{SUBJ} & \begin{bmatrix} \text{NUM} & \text{SG} \\ \text{PRED} & \text{'Sandy'} \end{bmatrix} \\
\text{PRED} & \text{'snore}\langle(\uparrow\ \text{SUBJ})\rangle\text{'}
\end{bmatrix}
$$

Figure 10.3: The c-structure and f-structure for *Sandy snores* generated by the fragment (14–18).

Bresnan 1982; Johnson 1995) so the f-descriptions associated with such sentences are inconsistent, and the sentences themselves are correctly predicted to be ungrammatical.

Thus this method functions by arranging for ungrammatical sentences to be associated with an inconsistent f-description. This observation is in fact quite general: if all grammatical relationships are described using defining equations (i.e., if we restrict attention to the monotonic constraints) then the only way such an equation can have a grammatical "effect" is by being inconsistent with other equations, i.e., by "causing" ungrammaticality.

More precisely, suppose we identify a subset of the elements of an f-structure as follows. The *semantically interpreted elements* are those which serve as the input to the semantic interpretation procedure (in the framework of Dalrymple et al. these elements are associated with glue language formulae at some stage during the interpretation process). The idea is that the semantically uninterpreted elements can be deleted from an f-structure without changing its semantic interpretation. In a typical LFG, the values of attributes such as PRED, SUBJ, OBJ, etc., are semantically interpreted, while the values of CASE and GENDER (in a grammatical gender language) are not semantically interpreted.

Now consider a "pure unification" grammar without non-monotonic devices such as "constraining equations", e.g., in which all equations are defining equations, such as the PATR grammars of Shieber (1986). These are grammars in which all linguistic relationships are expressed with defining equations. It is possible to show that in such a grammar, if an equation which equates only non-semantic values is not inconsistent with other equations on some input, then deleting it from the grammar does not affect the language generated or the interpretations assigned. (A similar observation holds in monotonic grammars such as HSPG.)

This means that if all grammatical relationships are described using defining equations, a nonsemantic feature defining equation only has an effect on the language generated if somewhere else in the grammar there are defining equations that are inconsistent with this one. For example, there is no point in adding a defining equation that introduces an attribute that does not appear elsewhere in the grammar, such as

(19) $(\uparrow$ HISTORICAL-ORIGIN$) =$ ROMANCE

unless other defining equations that can possibly be inconsistent with it are also introduced. But in order to be inconsistent with (19) these other equations must require the attribute's value to be *different* to the value specified in the former equation, e.g.,

$(\uparrow$ HISTORICAL-ORIGIN$) =$ GERMANIC.

Thus with defining equations alone, different grammatical properties are based on feature *oppositions* or contrasts. The formal machinery of these monotonic "pure unification" grammars does not completely support non-contrastive or "privative" feature values.

Indeed, f-structures seem to have been specifically designed to enable systems of defining equations to be inconsistent. For example, if we removed either the "functionality" axiom (which requires attributes to be single-valued) or the "constant-constant" clash axiom (which specifies that distinct constants denote distinct f-structure elements) from the formal definition of f-structures, then f-descriptions such as

$(f$ CASE$) =$ ACC$, (f$ CASE$) =$ DAT

would not be inconsistent. R-LFG does not possess either the functionality axiom or the constant-constant clash axiom, and hence it does permit a single constituent to bear two such distinct features, so long as both are checked or consumed as described below.

4.2   Agreement using defining and constraining equations

Writers of LFGs typically employ constraining equations in order to describe asymmetric linguistic relationships. The subject-verb agreement examples (13) would be described using this method by replacing the lexical entries (16–17) with the following.

(20)   *snores*   VP $(\uparrow$ PRED$) =$ 'snore$\langle(\uparrow$ SUBJ$)\rangle$'
                                   $(\uparrow$ SUBJ NUM$) =_c$ SG

(21)   *snore*   VP $(\uparrow$ PRED$) =$ 'snore$\langle(\uparrow$ SUBJ$)\rangle$'
                                   $(\uparrow$ SUBJ NUM$) =_c$ PL

These entries differ from the previous ones in that the underlined defining equations have been replaced with constraining equations.

While these two fragments both generate the same language in this case, in general the two methods for describing agreement behave quite differently. For example, if an NP's f-description contains the constraint equation

(22) $(\uparrow$ CASE$) =_c$ ACC

then this NP must be independently "assigned" a value for the Case feature in order for the f-structure to be well-formed.

This method behaves quite differently to the method that only uses defining equations. It does not rely on feature oppositions in the same way that the defining equation method does. For example, the constraint equation (22) requiring that the NP receive an ACC case value does not rely on the existence of other Case values besides ACC; it functions just as well if ACC is the only Case value used in the grammar. That is, while a defining equation ensures that an attribute has one value rather than another, a constraining equation ensures in addition that the feature has in fact been given a value independently. Thus this method more fully supports privative features than the defining equation method does.

Further, the constraining equation method does not rely on the functionality axiom or the constant-constant clash axioms in the same way that the defining equation method does. For example, even if the functionality requirement on f-structures were relaxed so that the defining equations in the f-description for (13a) could have the second minimal

$$
\left[
\begin{array}{ll}
\text{SUBJ} & \left[\begin{array}{ll} \text{PRED} & \text{'Sandy'} \\ \text{NUM} & \text{SG} \end{array}\right] \\
\text{SUBJ} & \left[\begin{array}{ll} \text{NUM} & =_c \text{SG} \end{array}\right] \\
\text{PRED} & \text{'snore}\langle(\uparrow\ \text{SUBJ})\rangle\text{'}
\end{array}
\right]
$$

Figure 10.4: A alternative minimal f-structure solution to the f-description for (13a) obtained by relaxing the functionality requirements on f-structures. Note that this f-structure nevertheless does not satisfy the constraining equations expressing subject-verb agreement because the constraint equation embedded in the lower SUBJ is not satisfied.

f-structure solution depicted in Figure 10.4 besides the one depicted in Figure 10.3, that f-structure would fail to satisfy the constraining equation expressing subject-verb agreement, and so would be ill-formed for independent reasons.

In fact, feature structures in R-LFG behave very much in this way. While attributes are permitted to be single-valued, no feature structure axiom forces them to be so. But since grammatical relationships are described in a way very similar to the constraining equation method, in general the grammatical requirements of predicates will require that attributes are single-valued. However, 'single-valuedness' is not built into the R-LFG formalism the way it is in standard LFG, opening the possibility of analyses which require multiple instantiations of the same grammatical relation within a single clause.

4.3 Resource management in LFG

The constraining equation method of describing agreement relationships can be described in terms of *resources*, where the resource is the feature value of the shared f-structure entity. Each such feature value is *produced* by *one or more* defining equations, and is *consumed* by *zero or more* constraining equations. This pattern of resource management is formalized by Intuitionistic Logic.

Interestingly, the special properties LFG endows the values of PRED attributes with provides them with special resource management properties also. The values of PRED attributes must be *produced* by *exactly one* argument, and must be *consumed* by *one or more* predicates. The logic LPC developed by van Benthem (1995) formalizes this resource management.

Thus LFG already incorporates a number of mechanisms which can be seen as performing resource management. R-LFG attempts to describe all syntactic relationships in terms of such resource management. Identifying the appropriate resource management mode for a particular grammatical relationship is a key step in developing its R-LFG description.

It is interesting that Multiplicative Linear Logic (MLL) enforces a different resource management regime than either Intuitionistic Logic or LPC (MLL requires each resource to be produced exactly once and consumed exactly once), although it can simulate other modes by means of its exponential operators (Girard 1995). For more discussion of appropriate resource management in LFG, particularly controlled applications of Contraction, see Johnson (1999).

5   Resource Accounting in R-LFG

Johnson (1999) formally defines R-LFG's f-terms and presents a Gentzen sequent calculus that describes the resource management relationships between features. It also presents labelled deduction systems for describing the mappings from c-structures to f-terms, and semantic interpretation from f-terms. That paper should be consulted for the technical details of R-LFG; this section presents that material in an informal and hopefully more accessible manner.

An f-formula is an expression that indicates the type of a constituent, or more generally, a single resource. The semantic type of a constituent can be determined from its f-formula, but just as in the categorial grammar example above, f-formulae also specify additional syntactic constraints.

Following Morrill (1994), we distinguish semantically contentful types from semantically impotent types. The basic semantically contentful types e, t, etc., are f-formulae (these are the types of individuals and truth values respectively), as are the basic semantically impotent types NOM, ACC, etc., (which are interpreted by constants, and whose value is systematically ignored by any function that takes them as an argument). The full set of f-formulae used here are obtained by closing these under the following operations.

> If φ is an f-formula then $f\,\varphi$ is also an f-formula, where f is an attribute; it denotes the result of embedding φ under the attribute f.

> If φ_1, φ_2 are f-formulae then $\varphi_1 \multimap \varphi_2$ is also an f-formula; it is a linear implication which consumes φ_1 to produce φ_2.

To formulate larger grammars it would be worthwhile introducing additional Linear Logic connectives. For example, the additive connective '&' provides disjunction of features, while the additive connective '$\oplus$' can be used to express the "overspecified" features required by the Bayer and Johnson (1995) analysis of feature distributivity in coordination. Indeed, it is straightforward to translate these analyses into R-LFG. Johnson (1999) shows how optionality can be expressed using the additive connective '&' and the additive identity '1'.

The relationship between f-formulae and the more usual types of model-theoretic semantics is given by the mapping $(\cdot)^\natural$, which maps f-formulae to standard model-theoretic types. In this mapping $\emptyset$ is a new type constant interpreted by a single element domain that is used to interpret semantically impotent f-formulae.

$(\varphi)^\natural = \varphi$ if φ is a semantically contentful basic type,

$(\varphi)^\natural = \emptyset$ if φ is a semantically impotent basic type,

$(f\,\varphi)^\natural = (\varphi)^\natural$ where f is an attribute, and

$(\varphi_1 \multimap \varphi_2)^\natural = (\varphi_2)^\natural$ if $(\varphi_1)^\natural = \emptyset$, and $(\varphi_1)^\natural \to (\varphi_2)^\natural$ otherwise.

For example, the natural type of an f-formula for an NP requiring a nominative case marking is $(\text{NOM} \multimap e)^\natural = e$. In general, it is required that any λ-term labelling an f-formulae φ (i.e., giving the constituent's semantic interpretation) be of type $(\varphi)^\natural$. (Semantically impotent f-formulae are not labelled with λ-terms, as they have no natural semantic interpretation.)

F-formulae are the building blocks of f-terms. Informally, an f-term is a graph-structured configuration of one or more constituents, or more generally, resources. F-formulae are f-terms, and if $\alpha, \alpha_1, \ldots, \alpha_n$ are f-terms then:

$\alpha_1, \ldots, \alpha_n$ is the *multiset* of resource structures $\{\alpha_1, \ldots, \alpha_n\}$ (order is unimportant in a multiset, but the number of times an element appears is important),

$f\,\alpha$ is the result of *embedding* the structure α under the attribute f,[5]

$f_1 \ldots f_m = g_1 \ldots g_n$ is a path equation which *restructures* an f-term by moving a resource structure embedded under the sequence of attributes $f_1 \ldots f_m$ so that it is located under the sequence of attributes $g_1 \ldots g_n$, and

(α) is an *optional* occurrence of the structure α.

An f-term describes a graph structure of constituents, or more generally, resources. The f-term associated with a sentence is required to simplify to a single resource of type t in order for the sentence to be grammatical. (This single requirement subsumes both the requirement that the f-description be satisfiable and the requirement that the Linear Logic glue formula simplify to an expression of type t in standard LFG.) An f-term simplifies by applying linear implications, restructuring using path equations, distributing attributes over multisets and implications, and either deleting optional elements or replacing them with their non-optional counterpart.

Attributes are permitted, but not required, to distribute and factor over multisets. That is, the following bi-implication holds, where f is an attribute and α_1 and α_2 are f-terms:

$$f(\alpha_1, \alpha_2) \iff (f\,\alpha_1), (f\,\alpha_2).$$

---

[5]Johnson (1999) follows Moortgat (1997) in introducing a separate punctuation symbol to distinguish modal structures in f-terms from modal operators in f-formulae, but here we rely on context to distinguish these two usages.

Unlike LFG, R-LFG does not require that attributes are single-valued, nor does it enforce a constant-constant clash. Every f-term is "satisfiable" in that it represents some configuration of resources; grammaticality is determined by whether those resources can combine to produce a single element of type t (the type of a saturated proposition).

5.1   Nominative case marking in English

A simple R-LFG fragment which describes structural nominative case assignment to subject NPs is presented below. The lexical entry for the nominative Case marked subject NP *Sandy* in (23) requires it to consume a NOM case resource in order to produce a resource of type e, and the lexical entry for the verb *snores* in (24) requires it to consume a resource of type e embedded within a SUBJ attribute in order to produce a resource of type t.

The syntactic rule (25) specifies how the f-terms associated with the NP and VP (referred to by the meta-variable '↓' just as in LFG) are to be combined to produce the f-term for the S. In this case, a multiset consisting of the NP's f-term and a NOM case resource is embedded within a SUBJ attribute, which together with the f-term associated with the VP yields the multiset f-term associated with the S. (The interface between c-structure and f-terms is formalized in Johnson (1999) as a labelled deductive system.)

(23)   *Sandy*   NP $Sandy : \text{NOM} \multimap e$

(24)   *snores*   VP $\lambda x.snores(x) : \text{SUBJ}\ e \multimap t$

(25)   S $\longrightarrow$ NP   VP

$\qquad\qquad\qquad\qquad$ SUBJ(NOM, ↓)   ↓

This fragment generates the c-structure and f-term depicted in Figure 10.5. The f-term simplifies to type t in the following steps:

$$\dfrac{\dfrac{\dfrac{Sandy : \text{SUBJ}(\text{NOM} \multimap e)}{Sandy : \text{SUBJ}\,\text{NOM} \multimap \text{SUBJ}\,e \quad \text{SUBJ}\,\text{NOM}}}{Sandy : \text{SUBJ}\,e} \qquad \lambda x.snores(x) : \text{SUBJ}\,e \multimap t}{snores(Sandy) : t}$$

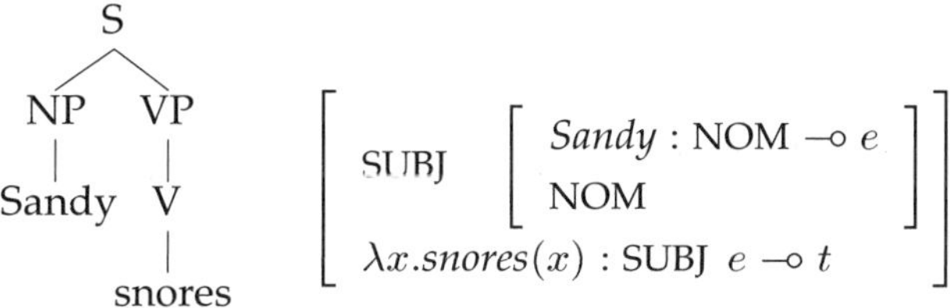

Figure 10.5: The c-structure and f-term for *She snores* generated by the fragment (23–25). The f-term simplifies straightforwardly to type t, yielding the semantic labelling *snores(Sandy)*.

5.2 Icelandic quirky case marking

Quirky Case marking in Icelandic presents a more complex array of linguistic data which exercises a wider range of f-term machinery. This construction has proven difficult to encode in unification-based grammars, and has motivated several non-monotonic extensions to the basic unification grammar machinery, such as LFG's constraint equations and a complex inheritance system in HPSG (Sag 1995).[6] The analysis presented here demonstrates how the resource sensitivity of R-LFG provides a simple way to encode the LFG analysis of Andrews (1982) without requiring recourse to complex extensions to the basic machinery of R-LFG.

In Icelandic, subject NPs are usually case marked nominative, as in (26a). However, a few verbs, such as *vantar* 'lacks', exceptionally case mark their subject NPs with accusative or some other non-nominative "quirky" case (26b). The subjects of subject raising verbs, such as *virðist* 'seems', usually appear in nominative case (26c), but if the embedded verb is a quirky case assigning verb then the matrix subject is assigned the quirky case, rather than nominative (26d).

---

[6]As far as I am aware, the only feature structure account of Icelandic quirky case marking that does not make use of non-monotonic devices was given by Sag et al. (1992). That account requires each NP to be associated with *two* case features, which are threaded as a difference list through the tree. It would be interesting to investigate whether other examples which motivate non-monotonic devices can be expressed using purely monotonic constraints in this manner.

(26) a. *drengurinn   kyssti   stúlkuna*
     the-boy.nom kissed the-girl.acc
     'The boy kissed the girl'

   b. *drengina   vantar mat*
     the-boys.acc lacks   food.acc
     'The boys lack food'

   c. *hann   virðist elska hana*
     he.nom seems love her.acc
     'He seems to love her'

   d. *hana   virðist vanta peninga*
     her.acc seems lack   money.acc
     'She seems to lack money'

This pattern of data receives a straightforward informal account in terms of case assignment if we make the following assumptions:

- All NPs must receive exactly one case,

- Quirky case marking verbs always assign a quirky case,

- Case is preserved in Raising and other grammatical operations, and

- Structural nominative case is only optionally assigned.

Thus if a subject NP receives a quirky case, then that must be the case that it appears in. On the other hand, if the subject NP is not assigned a quirky case, then the only case available is structural nominative case.

This account can be formalized in R-LFG as follows. The phrase structure rules for this Icelandic fragment are the following.

$$(27) \qquad S \longrightarrow \begin{array}{cc} NP & VP \\ SUBJ((NOM),\downarrow) & \downarrow \end{array}$$

$$(28) \quad VP \longrightarrow \begin{array}{c} V \\ \downarrow \end{array} \left(\begin{array}{c} NP \\ OBJ((ACC),\downarrow) \end{array} \right) \left(\begin{array}{c} VP \\ XCOMP \downarrow \end{array} \right)$$

The phrase structure rule (27) differs from the corresponding English rule (25) in that it optionally embeds a NOM case under the SUBJ attribute. The phrase structure rule (28) introduces a verb, an optional

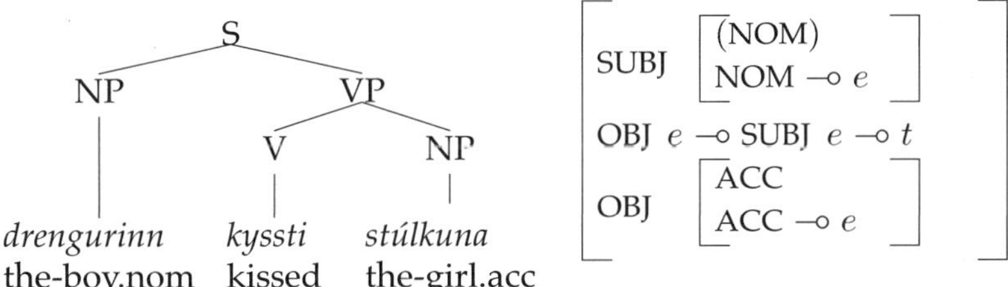

Figure 10.6: The c-structure and f-term for the single clause non-quirky Icelandic example (26a) generated by (27–31).

direct object NP with optional accusative case marking, and an optional VP. It embeds the direct object NP's f-term under the OBJ attribute and the VP's f-term under the XCOMP attribute, as is standard in LFG.

The lexical entries (29–31) are required to generate the non-quirky single clause example (26a). The c-structure and f-term associated with this example are shown in Figure 10.6. It is straightforward to check that this f-term reduces to t, labelled with *kissed*(*boy*, *girl*).

(29) *drengurinn* NP *boy* : NOM $\multimap$ e

(30) *stúlkuna* NP *girl* : ACC $\multimap$ e

(31) *kyssti* V $\lambda y\, \lambda x. kissed(x, y)$: OBJ e $\multimap$ SUBJ e $\multimap$ t

The single clause quirky case marked example is only slightly more complex. It can be described with the three additional lexical entries (32–34).

(32) *drengina* NP *boys* : ACC $\multimap$ e

(33) *mat* NP *food* : ACC $\multimap$ e

(34) *vantar* V $\lambda y\, \lambda x. lacks(x, y)$: OBJ e $\multimap$ SUBJ e $\multimap$ t,
OBJ ACC, SUBJ ACC

The lexical entry for the quirky case marking verb *vantar* 'lacks' in (34) differs from that for the non-quirky verb *kyssti* 'kissed' in that it assigns an accusative case to its subject (in the underlined part of the

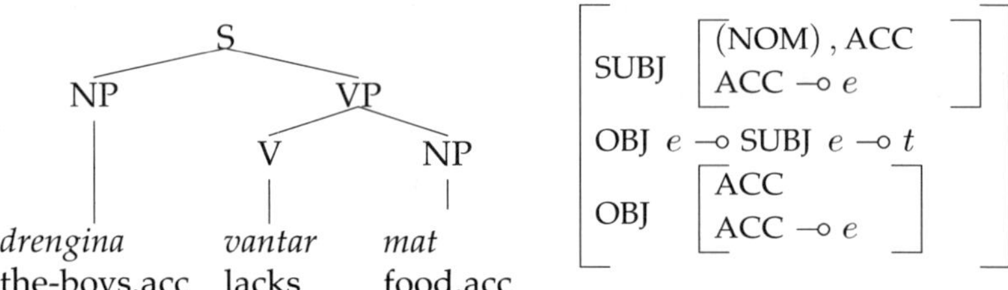

Figure 10.7: The c-structure and f-term for the single clause quirky case example (26b) generated by (27–34).

f-term) as well as to its object. The c-structure and f-term for (26b) are depicted in Figure 10.7. Again, it is straightforward to check that the f-term reduces to t, and is labelled with the λ-term *lacks(boys, food)*. Note that if the subject were replaced with a nominative NP the f-term would no longer reduce to t, since the ACC case feature embedded under the SUBJ attribute could not be consumed.

The formalization of the non-quirky case Subject Raising example (26c) is very similar to the standard LFG account of Subject Raising (Bresnan 1982). The lexical entry (35) for the Raising verb *virðist* 'seems' contains the path equation SUBJ = XCOMP SUBJ which permits resources embedded under the SUBJ attribute to be restructured under the XCOMP SUBJ attributes. In this example, a resource of type e is lowered into the embedded clause. The f-term associated with this example is depicted in Figure 10.8. Here we ignore the complexities of pronominal binding, and treat the pronouns simply as NPs that consume a nominative or accusative case resource. It is straightforward to check that this reduces to t, and is labelled with the λ-term *seems(loves(he, her))*.

(35)   *virðist*   V $\lambda P.seems(P)$: XCOMP $t \multimap t$,
SUBJ = XCOMP SUBJ

(36)   *elska*   V $\lambda y\,\lambda x.love(x, y)$: OBJ $e \multimap$ SUBJ $e \multimap t$,
OBJ ACC

The syntactic rules and lexical entries introduced above that are independently needed to account for quirky case marking in single clause

$$
\begin{bmatrix}
\text{SUBJ} & \begin{bmatrix} \text{NOM} \multimap e \\ (\text{NOM}) \end{bmatrix} \\
\text{XCOMP } t \multimap t \\
\text{XCOMP} & \begin{bmatrix} \text{SUBJ} & [\ ] \\ \text{OBJ } e \multimap \text{SUBJ } e \multimap t \\ \text{OBJ} & \begin{bmatrix} \text{ACC} \multimap e \\ \text{ACC} \end{bmatrix} \end{bmatrix}
\end{bmatrix}
$$

Figure 10.8: The f-term for the non-quirky Subject Raising example (26c) generated by (27–36).

$$
\begin{bmatrix}
\text{SUBJ} & \begin{bmatrix} \text{ACC} \multimap e \\ (\text{NOM}) , \underline{\text{ACC}} \end{bmatrix} \\
\text{XCOMP } t \multimap t \\
\text{XCOMP} & \begin{bmatrix} \text{SUBJ} & [\ ] \\ \text{OBJ } e \multimap \text{SUBJ } e \multimap t \\ \text{OBJ} & \begin{bmatrix} \text{ACC} \multimap e \\ \text{ACC} \end{bmatrix} \end{bmatrix}
\end{bmatrix}
$$

Figure 10.9: The f-term for the quirky case marked Subject Raising example (26d) generated by (27–36).

constructions and for Subject Raising without quirky case also correctly account for the interaction of those two constructions, which was presented in (26d) on page 382. The f-term for this example is shown in Figure 10.9.

Just as in the single clause quirky case marking example (26b), the subject NP is assigned both an accusative case and an optional nominative case, so only an accusative subject NP can appear. If a nominative subject were inserted in matrix subject position it could consume the optional nominative case resource, but the accusative case resource assigned by the quirky verb to the subject would not be consumed, and so an f-term of type t could not be derived. It is straightforward to check that the f-term depicted in Figure 10.9 simplifies to t, and that it is labelled with the λ-term *seems(lack(she, money))*, correctly providing the required semantic interpretation.

6 Conclusion

The glue language approach to semantic interpretation in LFG augments the basic feature structure constraints of LFG with resource-sensitive mechanisms. Accepting these extensions, this paper explored the idea that appropriate resource-sensitive mechanisms are capable of completely expressing linguistic analyses usually expressed by f-structure constraints in LFG. We introduced a simplified version of LFG called R-LFG in which a single representation called an f-term plays the role of both f-description and f-structure. This unification dramatically simplifies the architecture of R-LFG, as compared to LFG augmented with the glue language interpretation machinery presented in the other chapters of this volume.

Semantic interpretation in R-LFG follows directly from a Curry-Howard correspondence, so semantic interpretation is obtained as a by-product of the syntactic type well-formedness checking process, and does not need to be described in terms of stipulative, independently specified semantic rules.

LFG's f-structure well-formedness constraints are re-expressed in terms of feature resource dependencies, which permits them to be checked by the same mechanism that performs semantic interpretation. It is not implausible that this can be done for many, if not most, LFG analyses, as many standard LFG analyses already have a resource oriented character, and it seems that the "core" LFG analyses of Raising, Control, etc., can be straightforwardly re-expressed in R-LFG. Treatments of phenomena such as quantifier scoping, which motivate much of the glue logic work described in this volume, still remain to be developed, but there seems to be no principled problem here.

Acknowledgements

I would like to thank Mary Dalrymple, Ron Kaplan, Dick Oehrle and the anonymous reviewers for this volume, all of whom were generous with their detailed, insightful suggestions.

References

Andrews, Avery D. 1982. The representation of Case in modern Icelandic. In Joan Bresnan, editor, *The Mental Representation of Grammatical Relations*, pages 427–502. The MIT Press, Cambridge, MA.

Bayer, Samuel and Mark Johnson. 1995. Features and agreement. In *Proceedings of the 33rd Annual Meeting of the ACL*, San Francisco, pages 70–76. Association for Computational Linguistics.

Bresnan, Joan. 1982. Control and complementation. In Joan Bresnan, editor, *The Mental Representation of Grammatical Relations*, pages 282–390. The MIT Press, Cambridge, MA.

Girard, Jean-Yves, Yves Lafont, and Paul Taylor. 1989. *Proofs and Types*, volume 7 of *Cambridge Tracts in Theoretical Computer Science*. Cambridge University Press, Cambridge, England.

Girard, Jean-Yves. 1995. Linear Logic: Its syntax and semantics. In Jean-Yves Girard, Yves Lafont, and Laurent Regnier, editors, *Advances in Linear Logic*, pages 1–42. Cambridge University Press, Cambridge, England.

Johnson, Mark. 1995. Logic and feature structures. In Mary Dalrymple, Ronald M. Kaplan, John Maxwell, and Annie Zaenen, editors, *Formal Issues in Lexical-Functional Grammar*, pages 369–380. CSLI Publications, Stanford University.

Johnson, Mark. 1999. A resource sensitive reinterpretation of Lexical Functional Grammar. *Journal of Logic, Language and Information*, 8(1).

Kaplan, Ronald M. and Joan Bresnan. 1982. Lexical-Functional Grammar: A formal system for grammatical representation. In Joan Bresnan, editor, *The Mental Representation of Grammatical Relations*, pages 173–281. The MIT Press, Cambridge, MA. Reprinted in Mary Dalrymple, Ronald M. Kaplan, John Maxwell, and Annie Zaenen, editors, *Formal Issues in Lexical-Functional Grammar*, pages 29–130. CSLI Publications, Stanford University. 1995.

Kasper, Robert T. and William C. Rounds. 1990. The logic of unification in grammar. *Linguistics and Philosophy*, 13(1):35–58.

Moortgat, Michael. 1997. Categorial type logics. In Johan van Benthem and Alice ter Meulen, editors, *Handbook of Logic and Language*, pages 93–178. Elsevier/The MIT Press, Amsterdam/Cambridge.

Morrill, Glyn V. 1994. *Type-logical Grammar: Categorial Logic of Signs*. Kluwer Academic Publishers, Dordrecht.

Park, Jong C. 1992. Quantifier scope and constituency. In *Proceedings of the 30th Annual Meeting of the Association for Computational Linguistics*, San Francisco, pages 209–215. Association for Computational Linguistics.

Pereira, Fernando C.N. and Stuart M. Shieber. 1987. *Prolog and Natural Language Analysis*. CSLI Lecture Notes, number 10. CSLI Publications, Stanford University.

Pereira, Fernando C. N. 1991. Semantic interpretation as higher-order deduction. In Jan van Eijck, editor, *Logics in AI: European Workshop JELIA '90*, pages 78–96. Springer Verlag.

Rounds, William C. 1997. Feature logics. In Johan van Benthem and Alice ter Meulen, editors, *Handbook of Logic and Language*, pages 475–533. Elsevier / The MIT Press, Amsterdam / Cambridge.

Sag, Ivan, Lauri Karttunen, and Jeffrey Goldberg. 1992. A lexical analysis of Icelandic case. In Ivan Sag and Anna Szabolcsi, editors, *Lexical Matters*, CSLI Lecture Notes Series, chapter 11, pages 301–318. CSLI Publications, Stanford University.

Sag, Ivan A. 1995. HPSG problem set 4: Icelandic case. Technical report, CSLI Publications, Stanford University. Available as http://hpsg.stanford.edu/hpsg/lecture-materials/pset4-icelandic.ps.

Shieber, Stuart M. 1986. *An Introduction to Unification-based Approaches to Grammar*. CSLI Lecture Notes, number 4. CSLI Publications, Stanford University.

van Benthem, Johan. 1995. *Language in Action: Categories, Lambdas and Dynamic Logic*. The MIT Press, Cambridge, MA.

Author Index

Subject Index